PREPARE!

An Ecumenical
Music and Worship Planner

2023–2024, NRSVue Edition

David L. Bone
and
Mary Scifres

Abingdon Press
Nashville

Do you have the planner you need?

We want you to have the best planner, designed to meet your specific needs.
How do you know if you have the right resource? Simply complete this one-question quiz:

Do you lead worship in a United Methodist congregation?

Yes?
Use *The United Methodist Music and Worship Planner 2023–2024*
(CEB Edition—ISBN: 9781791015565; eBook– ISBN: 9781791015572)
(NRSVue Edition—ISBN: 9781791015589; eBook– ISBN: 9781791015596)

No?
Use *Prepare! An Ecumenical Music and Worship Planner 2023–2024*
(CEB Edition—ISBN: 9781791015688; eBook– ISBN: 9781791015701)
(NRSVue Edition—ISBN: 9781791015701; eBook– ISBN: 9781791015718)

**TO ORDER THESE RESOURCES, CALL COKESBURY
TOLL FREE AT 800-672-1789 OR SHOP ONLINE AT WWW.COKESBURY.COM.**

**Do you find yourself rushing at the last minute to order your new planner?
Subscribe today and receive your new *The United Methodist Music and Worship
Planner* or *Prepare!* automatically next year and every year.
Call toll free 800-672-1789 to request a subscription.**

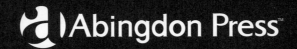

Using *Prepare!*

How We Organize the Resource Lists

Prepare! is designed to give you as many ideas as possible about a given worship service. Use it along with a worship plan notebook that you create, a copy of your church's hymnal, and other supplements you use such as *The Faith We Sing or Worship & Song*. Features of *Prepare!* include:

- **NEW THIS YEAR!** The lectionary verses found on left-hand pages of *Prepare!* come from the New Revised Standard Version **Updated Edition** of the Bible. (For more information on the new edition of this translation, see https://bit.ly/3NJcYj2.) Where available, we have added psalter numbers from standard hymnals, which are noted in the Resource Key on p. 7. *Prepare!* is also available with lectionary texts from the Common English Bible, the CEB (ISBN: 9781791015688).
- **NEW HYMNALS LISTED! Two hymnals were added to the resource list recently (p. 7).** *Celebrating Grace Hymnal*, along with *Santo, Santo, Santo*, a truly bilingual hymnal. This hymnal will be especially useful to those serving in Spanish-speaking and bilingual contexts.
- **AGAIN THIS YEAR! The Contemporary and Modern Suggestions** now include the CCLI number from https://songselect.ccli.com. These numbers are used universally by musicians working in these worship styles.
- **AGAIN THIS YEAR! Themes** for the day are listed in the Other Suggestions and found in the **Theme Index** on p. 136. These tools will help with thematic planning when a community is following a thematic/sermon series rather than the Lectionary.
- **ALSO THIS YEAR!** Most **Anthem** suggestions include a link to the publisher's online version of the anthem, which often includes recordings. Simply enter the http://bit.ly/... link in your browser to reach the appropriate page.
- Each week **Primary Hymns and Songs for the Day** are suggested first. These suggestions include various helps for singing the hymns. These hymns and songs have the closest relationship to the scriptures and are widely known. The lengthier lists of **Additional Hymn Suggestions** and **Additional Contemporary and Modern Suggestions** will add variety to your musical selections.
- The musical suggestions are chosen to suggest a wide variety of styles.
- Each item is referenced to scripture and/or occasion.
- **Opening (O)** and **Closing (C)** hymns are suggested for each worship service.
- At least one **Communion (Comm.)** hymn is recommended for the first Sunday of each month and liturgical season. When appropriate, Communion hymns related to the scriptures are noted on other days as well.

- **Additional Contemporary and Modern Suggestions** include not only praise choruses but also global and ethnic music, folk music, and meditative music from traditions such as Taizé. Please note that contemporary songs may also be listed under **Additional Hymn Suggestions, Vocal Solos,** or **Other Suggestions.**
- **One word of advice:** Be sure to consult all the music suggestions regardless of the type of service you are planning. In the changing world of worship, no one style defines a song or a worship service. Many items appropriate for contemporary and emergent styles are listed under the **Additional Hymn Suggestions,** and many resources for traditional and blended services can be found in the **Additional Contemporary and Modern Suggestions** list. **Vocal Solos, Anthems,** and **Other Suggestions** may be appropriate for congregational use as well. Don't let the "category" here deter you from using any item that will enhance your worship service. Planners should consult all lists when choosing congregational music.
- **Vocal Solos** and **Anthems** provide ideas for vocal music "performance" offerings, and may also inspire ideas for additional congregational selections.
- The recommended **Vocal Solos** are taken from a group of ten collections that range from contemporary settings of hymn texts and praise choruses to spirituals to well-known classics (see p. 7). Augment these suggestions from your own library.
- The **Anthem** suggestions include new works as well as generally known works that are already in many church choral libraries. Your study of the scripture and hymn texts will lead you to anthems in your church library that are appropriate.
- **Other Suggestions** also include words for worship, suggestions for choral introits and sung benedictions, and ideas for musical responses related to the spoken liturgy.
- Suggestions for **Visuals** are offered for each service. See the article "Visuals in Worship" (p. 4) for discussion on these suggestions. Visual ideas are found in **Other Suggestions.** They have been compiled by Ashley M. Calhoun and supplemented by our authors. Ashley is known for his inventive use of "found" items in creating visual worship settings. Worship committees, visual artists, dancers, and altar guilds can use these ideas to create their own unique worship centers, altarpieces, banners, and dance images. Screen visual artists can use these themes to select appropriate background and theme screens for worship.
- A two-year, at-a-glance **2023–2024 Calendar** follows the **Worship Planning Sheets** (see p. 144). It includes a note on the lectionary years covered in this edition of *Prepare!*

- *Prepare!* uses the *Revised Common Lectionary*. From the Second Sunday after Pentecost to Christ the King Sunday, the lectionary includes two patterns of readings. One pattern includes semi-continuous readings from the Hebrew Scriptures, Epistles, and Gospels. These readings are not necessarily related but allow for a sequential experience of the biblical narrative. **This is the pattern used to determine the scripture texts included in** *Prepare!* It is the pattern followed by most users of the hymnals referenced. In the second pattern, the Hebrew scripture is chosen to relate to the Gospel passage. This pattern is used primarily in traditions where Communion is celebrated at every service of worship. These **Alternate Lections** may be found in *The Revised Common Lectionary* (Abingdon Press, 1992) or online at http://lectionary.library.vanderbilt.edu/. Worship planners may certainly choose to follow the pattern that best serves the needs and traditions of your church. Neither pattern is necessarily better than the other; they are simply different ways of offering scripture in the worship setting over a three-year cycle in the church.

Planning Worship with These Resources

When planning any worship service, we recommend starting with the primary scripture to let it guide your thoughts and plans. If your church is not using the *Revised Common Lectionary* but you do know what the scripture text will be for a service, look up that text in the **Scripture Index** on page 137 or consult the **Theme Index** on page 136.

As you read and study the scripture passages, read all of the suggested hymn texts. The hymns may remind you of anthems, solos, or keyboard selections. It is wise to mark your hymnal with the dates individual hymns are sung to avoid singing some too frequently. The **Hymn Resources** (see p. 7) can enhance congregational singing but should be used sparingly.

Use a three-ring binder to organize your plans. For each service of worship, include a copy of one of the **Worship Planning Sheets** found on pages 140–42 (or design your own!) along with blank paper for listing further ideas. Do not simply "fill in the blanks" for each service, but use the Planning Sheet to guide your work.

Use the suggestions in *Prepare!* along with your own page of ideas to begin making decisions about worship. Will the choir sing a "Call to Worship"? Can a hymn verse serve as a prayer response? Can a particular anthem or vocal solo give direction to the sermon? What prayers will be used?

Once your decisions are made, complete the **Worship Planning Sheet**. Make a separate list of tasks related to that service. Planning worship is an awesome responsibility that can be accomplished with an organized effort along with spiritual guidance.

VISUALS IN WORSHIP
Ashley M. Calhoun

The suggestions for visuals in this planner are meant to help worship leaders use objects and images to increase the impact of the gospel on a people who are increasingly visually oriented. These suggestions can be incorporated into many visual elements: hanging and processional banners, worship settings (whether on the altar or in the chancel or narthex), worship folder covers, and bulletin boards. The ideas can also be used to suggest ways to use classical and contemporary works of art, sculpture, needlework, and photography in worship services.

With more churches incorporating screens and video walls into their worship spaces, there is tremendous potential for the use of still or moving imagery. Also, interpretive movement and drama can be very strong in visual impact.

The visual suggestions in this *Planner* have several characteristics:

- The suggestions are not meant to give detailed plans but to spark your imagination and creativity.
- Some are drawn literally from the lessons; others are thematic.
- The suggestions are organized by reference to the lectionary passages:

O	Old Testament or Easter season, Acts reading
P	Psalm reading or Canticle
E	Epistle or New Testament reading
G	Gospel reading

- Chapter and verse numbers are sometimes given to indicate actual phrases in the scripture passage that can serve as visual elements.
- Themes such as forgiveness, love, or rejoicing are offered to encourage creative use of video and photographic images of people engaged in demonstrating those themes.

So much about worship is visual and intended to strengthen the proclamation of the gospel. The worship space is filled with visual elements that send a message. The church year is a treasure trove of color, texture, symbolism, and visual imagery. Special Sundays and special days in the cultural and denominational calendars also offer opportunities for visual expression. Evaluate the visual aspects of your worship services and find ways to enhance the worship experience with thoughtful, intentional use of visual elements and images.

TIME FOR TEAMWORK
A TEAM-BASED PLAN FOR DESIGNING HYBRID WORSHIP IN A DIGITAL AGE
Mary Scifres

Wow, have we been through it! "It" being a global pandemic, the addition of digital worship platforms to our already harried schedules, the increased demand for technological ways of connecting and worshiping together, and the increased challenge of creating strong teams when so many demands pull us in different directions. Yet, teamwork has never been needed more.

Many of us were forced to go it alone when the pandemic first struck back in early 2020. We cobbled digital worship together with many of our musicians and pastors, learning the technological demands almost single-handedly. But three years in, the lone-wolf approach is wearing thin. Many have retired, resigned. Others are burnt out but still trying to serve and create. The best creative spark we can give ourselves is to find partners and develop a method to work as a team.

This Planner was designed to help you do just that. You've picked up this book, so you already have Mary Scifres and David Bone on your team. If you add *The Abingdon Worship Annual* to your resource library, you'll add B. J. Beu and a dozen other writers too. If you visit www.creativeworship madeeasy.com and add *Creative Worship Made Easy* to your resource library, you'll add a creative cornucopia of sermon starters and worship words from Mary and B. J., images and film clip suggestions from Michael Beu, along with nontraditional song ideas and other worship ideas to help people put their faith into action, all corresponding to a seasonal worship theme and specific scriptures.

Even with all those great resources at your fingertips, people who sit down with you in person to help make Sunday's service more meaningful can ramp up your energy and enthusiasm. This is why it's particularly life-giving to move beyond the lone-wolf approach for a team-based approach. It allows you to integrate and represent *your* worshiping community into the worship planning process. We offer these resources in hopes that pastors, musicians, and worship leaders find encouragement and assistance for worship planning in cooperation with one another.

A Team-based Approach for Today's Digital Age

Even if putting a team together seems like more work than planning alone, we encourage you to try it out and see how it can spark your creativity and support your worship ministry. Even a monthly meeting between musicians and the preacher can expand insights and ideas while offering both parties much-needed support. If monthly meetings feel daunting, try planning special services like Christmas Eve or Easter. Afterward, assess who "fit" into your worship style, who was inspired or inspiring, or who just liked the work and was dependable implementing the service. When you're ready for more, gather a team for a season or a monthly series. Here are some basic suggestions to get you started.

Finding Team Members

Review the talents of your church for artists, musicians, visionaries, tech experts, leaders, organizers, and workers. Choose team members, balancing gifts and talents, as well as time and commitment levels. School musicians and drama teachers can add different perspectives than church musicians and preachers, and they can deepen their spiritual walk and scriptural knowledge while helping plan worship. Your team may be as few as two or as many as twelve. Don't have those folks in your church? How about reaching out to a colleague serving in a nearby church? Again, preachers often find musicians a huge help, even if the musician is serving in a different church. And vice versa! Tech experts can help with the planning, particularly as they educate us on what is possible, what is manageable, and what might be too cumbersome.

Team Meetings

Set a meeting time and location, whether in person or via video conference, that maximizes participation. Some teams find video meeting helpful because people have their resources at their fingertips. Other teams find the synergy of being together in person the most valuable aspect of the meetings. Try different formats with your team, and figure out how you are best inspired and most efficient. Designate start and end times, stick to your agenda, and be respectful of one another's time.

While many models exist for team worship planning, we offer the following model to maximize your use of this *Planner,* particularly for coordinating scripture readings and hymn lists. Provide a copy of the *Planner* for each team member and invite members to bring extra resources to the meeting—like Bibles, hymnals, your denominational Book of Worship, and resources like Mary's sermon starters and liturgy planning documents from *Creative Worship Made Easy.* Musicians find it helpful to have copies of the music collections suggested in this planner as well as a list of the anthem and praise song repertoire of your church.

Distribute copies of the **Worship Planning Sheets** from pages 140–42 to each team member for each service being discussed. Then follow these twelve steps.

1. If possible, distribute sermon titles and scriptures from your preacher before the meeting.
2. Prepare an agenda with estimated time frames so that people can plan to begin and end on time.
3. Open meetings with prayer. On your first meeting together, designate a little extra time to talk about the worship planning approach and even the worship theology and ecclesiology that you hope to undergird your planning process. As your team strengthens and works together over time, strive to develop a shared approach.
4. At every meeting, review the sermon themes or titles and chosen scriptures. If time permits, read through the scriptures aloud. Otherwise, invite the preacher or worship planning leader to summarize the weekly scriptures and briefly discuss the theme. (Preachers, this is just a summary, not the whole sermon!)
5. Discuss and outline seasonal needs, particularly if planning seasons like Advent or Lent. Introduce and discuss special ideas or plans for specific worship services (e.g., Palm Sunday cantata, Christmas Eve candlelight service, children's Sunday, etc.).
6. Brainstorm congregational song and musician anthems and offerings that correspond with the theme and scripture. If your congregation has a limited repertoire, it's okay to choose familiar songs—particularly if you don't have a strong team of paid musical leaders. If you have strong musical leadership, make use of their gifts to expand the musical and spiritual awareness of your congregation.
7. For many teams, this is all they get to. And that's okay!
8. But if you want to do more, discuss visual ideas and images to enhance the worship experience.
9. Get even more cohesive by adding the words for congregational prayers from your favorite resources or invite team members to find words from their favorite resources. Invite members to write prayers and responsive readings themselves. Experiment and allow for the inevitable imperfections and foibles that are part of the journey.
10. Review services for integration, unity, and diversity.
11. Address or delegate specific service logistics (like purchase of communion elements or finding a decorating team).
12. Close with prayer.

Members of the planning team may have valuable input on any number of these steps. A preacher may have an idea for a choral anthem to enhance a sermon idea; a musician may have an insight into a sermon topic as it relates to the congregation. Regardless, all members of the team will find helpful suggestions in this *Planner*.

Team Meeting Frequency

While members of ongoing worship planning teams meet at least biannually, most find monthly or seasonal planning meetings helpful to stay connected. Remember, meetings don't have to be in the sanctuary, on the church campus, or even in person. Meetings can be on video conference, telephone, or at a favorite retreat center.

Some teams meet weekly, but those meetings tend to be logistical in nature. Some teams form for just one specific service. If so, they meet once to brainstorm creatively, meet again to plan logistics, then have a follow-up meeting to assess and give feedback for future teams. Remember, creative team members don't need to be involved in every implementation step. People who like to do the work often don't have an interest in attending meetings or talking about creative design. The workers meet when there's a task to complete, or they show up, do their part, and move along. Tech experts often fall into this category, those who prefer to "work more, talk less." Try to assess those who benefit from team meetings and those who just need information so they can do their work. Some teams find implementation more easily managed with an online communication stream like Google Docs or services like planningcenter.com. Even those not involved in the team meetings can receive the needed information online.

Team planning can eventually ease your work load. But it always holds the promise of enhancing the synergy of Spirit-led worship. Unity among the worship leadership team ends up strengthening the entire worshiping community. Good team worship planning invites the Holy Spirit to bring a unity and freedom into the worship process that draws the entire body of Christ closer together.

Hire a Worship Consultant

A consultant-run worship planning retreat will inspire your team and alleviate extra work for your staff. We know lots of people who offer these services, so contact Mary or David if you need a referral.

Convocations and Training Events

Organizations like The Fellowship of United Methodists in Music and Worship Arts (UMFellowship.org) and Mary Scifres Ministries (www.maryscifres.com) provide webinars and training events (both online and in-person) to assist worship leaders and teams develop skills to plan worship. Both resources will help you learn to think outside the box.

FREE GIFTS!
We want to thank you with a **free book of Communion Resources**. Sign up today for your free download:
https://maryscifres.simplero.com/communionbook

Enjoy a free trial of creative worship ideas to help you with focused worship themes, film clip and pop song suggestions, and ideas for putting "faith into action." Sign up for your free trial:
www.creativeworshipmadeeasy.com

RESOURCE KEY

AH   *The Africana Hymnal*. Nashville: Abingdon Press, 2015. ISBN #9781426776441.

C   *Chalice Hymnal*. St. Louis: Chalice Press, 1996. ISBN: 9780827280359.

CG   *Celebrating Grace Hymnal*. Macon: Celebrating Grace, 2010. ISBN: 9781936151103.

E   *The Hymnal 1982*. New York: The Church Hymnal Corporation, 1985. ISBN: 9780898691214.

EL   *Evangelical Lutheran Worship*. Minneapolis: Augsburg Fortress, 2006. ISBN: 9780806656182.

G   *Glory to God: The Presbyterian Hymnal*. Louisville: Presbyterian Publishing Corporation, 2013. ISBN: 9780664238971.

N   *The New Century Hymnal*. Cleveland, OH: The Pilgrim Press, 1995. ISBN: 9780829810509.

P   *The Presbyterian Hymnal*. Louisville: Westminster/John Knox Press, 1990. ISBN: 9780664100971.

S   *The Faith We Sing*. Nashville: Abingdon Press, 2000. ISBN: 9780687090549 (Pew edition).

SA   *The Song Book of the Salvation Army*. London: The Salvation Army, 2015. ISBN: 9780854129447.

SH   *Santo, Santo, Santo*. Chicago: GIA Publications, Inc., 2019. ISBN: 9781622773961.

UM   *The United Methodist Hymnal*. Nashville: The United Methodist Publishing House, 1989. ISBN: 9780687431328.

VU   *Voice United*. Etobicoke, Ontario, Canada: The United Church Publishing House, 1996. ISBN: 9781551340173.

WS   *Worship & Song*. Nashville: Abingdon Press, 2011. Accompaniment, singer, guitar, and planning editions available. ISBN: 9781426709937 (Pew edition).

WSL   *Worship & Song Leader's Edition*. Nashville: Abingdon Press, 2011. ISBN: 9781426709944 (Leader's edition). NOTE: The resources WSL1–WSL222 refer to the written words for worship (prayers, litanies, benedictions) available in worship resource editions of *Worship & Song*.

HYMN RESOURCES

S-1   Smith, Gary Alan, ed. *The United Methodist Hymnal: Music Supplement*. Nashville: Abingdon Press, 1991. ISBN: 9780687431472.

S-2   Bennett, Robert C., ed. *The United Methodist Hymnal: Music Supplement II*. Nashville: Abingdon Press, 1993. ISBN: 9780687430130.

H-3   Hopson, Hal H. *The Creative Church Musician Series*. Carol Stream, IL: Hope Publishing Co.
     Hbl Vol. 1. *The Creative Use of Handbells in Worship*. *1997*. Hope Publishing #1956.
     Chr Vol. 2. *The Creative Use of Choirs in Worship*. *1999*. Hope Publishing #8013.
     Desc *The Creative Use of Descants in Worship*. *1999*. Hope Publishing #8018.
     Org *The Creative Use of the Organ in Worship*. *1997*. Hope Publishing #8070.

CONTEMPORARY RESOURCES

The Contemporary and Modern Suggestions now include the CCLI number from https://songselect.ccli.com. These numbers are used universally by musicians working in these worship styles.

See also Vocal Solo suggestions from V-3, V-5, and V-9.

VOCAL SUGGESTION RESOURCES

V-1   Pote, Allen. *A Song of Joy*. Carol Stream, IL: Hope Publishing, 2003. Cokesbury Ord. #505068.

V-2   Handel, George Frederick. *Messiah*. Various editions available.

V-3   Hayes, Mark. *The Mark Hayes Vocal Solo Collection*
     V-3 (1) *Ten Spirituals for Solo Voice*. Van Nuys, CA: Alfred Music Publishing, 2007. ISBN: 9780882848808.
     V-3 (2) *Seven Praise and Worship Songs for Solo Voice*. Van Nuys, CA: Alfred Music Publishing, 2010. ISBN: 9780739037249.
     V-3 (3) *Ten Hymns and Gospel Songs for Solo Voice*. ISBN: 9780739006979.

V-4   Scott, K. Lee. *Sing a Song of Joy*. Minneapolis, MN: Augsburg Fortress, 1989. ISBN: 9780800647889, (*Medium High Voice*) ISBN: 9780800647889, (*Medium Low Voice*) ISBN: 9780800652821.

V-5   Various Editors. *With All My Heart: Contemporary Vocal Solos*. Minneapolis, MN: Augsburg Fortress, 2004.
     V-5 (1) *Volume 1: Autumn and Winter*. ISBN: 9780800676841.
     V-5 (2) *Volume 2: Spring and Summer*. ISBN: 9780800676858.
     V-5 (3) *Volume 3: Baptisms, Weddings, Funerals*. ISBN: 9780800679460.

V-6   Walters, Richard, Arr. *Hymn Classics: Concert Arrangements of Traditional Hymns for Voice and Piano*. Milwaukee, WI: Hal Leonard Publishing, 1993. ISBN: 9780793560080. *High Voice*. Cokesbury Ord. #811290. *Low Voice*. Cokesbury Ord. #811233.

NEW
V-7   Duncan IV, Norah, Arr. *Give Me Jesus: Sacred Spirituals*. Chicago: GIA Publications, Inc., 2021.

V-8   Wilson, John F., Don Doig, and Jack Schrader, eds. *Everything for the Church Soloist*. Carol Stream, IL: Hope Publishing Company, 1980. Cokesbury Ord. #810103.

NEW
V-9   Various Artists. *Top Christian Hits of 2020-2021: 21 Powerful Songs Arranged for Piano/Vocal/Guitar*. Milwaukee, WI: Hal Leonard Publishing, 2021. ISBN: 9781705133460.

V-10   Hayes, Mark et al. *From the Manger to the Cross—Seasonal Solos for Medium Voice*. Dayton, OH: The Lorenz Corporation, 2006. Cokesbury Ord. #526369.

Exodus 3:1-15

Moses was keeping the flock of his father-in-law Jethro, the priest of Midian; he led his flock beyond the wilderness and came to Mount Horeb, the mountain of God. ²There the angel of the LORD appeared to him in a flame of fire out of a bush; he looked, and the bush was blazing, yet it was not consumed. ³Then Moses said, "I must turn aside and look at this great sight and see why the bush is not burned up." ⁴When the LORD saw that he had turned aside to see, God called to him out of the bush, "Moses, Moses!" And he said, "Here I am." ⁵Then he said, "Come no closer! Remove the sandals from your feet, for the place on which you are standing is holy ground." ⁶He said further, "I am the God of your father, the God of Abraham, the God of Isaac, and the God of Jacob." And Moses hid his face, for he was afraid to look at God.

⁷Then the LORD said, "I have observed the misery of my people who are in Egypt; I have heard their cry on account of their taskmasters. Indeed, I know their sufferings, ⁸and I have come down to deliver them from the Egyptians and to bring them up out of that land to a good and spacious land, to a land flowing with milk and honey, to the country of the Canaanites, the Hittites, the Amorites, the Perizzites, the Hivites, and the Jebusites. ⁹The cry of the Israelites has now come to me; I have also seen how the Egyptians oppress them. ¹⁰Now go, I am sending you to Pharaoh to bring my people, the Israelites, out of Egypt." ¹¹But Moses said to God, "Who am I that I should go to Pharaoh and bring the Israelites out of Egypt?" ¹²He said, "I will be with you, and this shall be the sign for you that it is I who sent you: when you have brought the people out of Egypt, you shall serve God on this mountain."

¹³But Moses said to God, "If I come to the Israelites and say to them, 'The God of your ancestors has sent me to you,' and they ask me, 'What is his name?' what shall I say to them?" ¹⁴God said to Moses, "I AM WHO I AM." He said further, "Thus you shall say to the Israelites, 'I AM has sent me to you.' " ¹⁵God also said to Moses, "Thus you shall say to the Israelites, 'The LORD, the God of your ancestors, the God of Abraham, the God of Isaac, and the God of Jacob, has sent me to you':

This is my name forever,
and this my title for all generations.

Psalm 105:1-6, 23-26, 45c (G59, N691, UM828)

O give thanks to the LORD; call on his name;
    make known his deeds among the peoples.
²Sing to him, sing praises to him;
    tell of all his wonderful works.
³Glory in his holy name;
    let the hearts of those who seek the LORD rejoice.
⁴Seek the LORD and his strength;
    seek his presence continually.
⁵Remember the wonderful works he has done,
    his miracles and the judgments he has uttered,
⁶O offspring of his servant Abraham,
    children of Jacob, his chosen ones.

. . . .

²³Then Israel came to Egypt;
    Jacob lived as an alien in the land of Ham.
²⁴And the LORD made his people very fruitful
    and made them stronger than their foes,
²⁵whose hearts he then turned to hate his people,
    to deal craftily with his servants.
²⁶He sent his servant Moses
    and Aaron, whom he had chosen.

. . . .

⁴⁵ᶜPraise the LORD!

Romans 12:9-21

⁹Let love be genuine; hate what is evil; hold fast to what is good; ¹⁰love one another with mutual affection; outdo one another in showing honor. ¹¹Do not lag in zeal; be ardent in spirit; serve the Lord. ¹²Rejoice in hope; be patient in affliction; persevere in prayer. ¹³Contribute to the needs of the saints; pursue hospitality to strangers.

¹⁴Bless those who persecute you; bless and do not curse them. ¹⁵Rejoice with those who rejoice; weep with those who weep. ¹⁶Live in harmony with one another; do not be arrogant, but associate with the lowly; do not claim to be wiser than you are. ¹⁷Do not repay anyone evil for evil, but take thought for what is noble in the sight of all. ¹⁸If it is possible, so far as it depends on you, live peaceably with all. ¹⁹Beloved, never avenge yourselves, but leave room for the wrath of God, for it is written, "Vengeance is mine; I will repay, says the Lord." ²⁰Instead, "if your enemies are hungry, feed them; if they are thirsty, give them something to drink, for by doing this you will heap burning coals on their heads." ²¹Do not be overcome by evil, but overcome evil with good.

Matthew 16:21-28

²¹From that time on, Jesus began to show his disciples that he must go to Jerusalem and undergo great suffering at the hands of the elders and chief priests and scribes and be killed and on the third day be raised. ²²And Peter took him aside and began to rebuke him, saying, "God forbid it, Lord! This must never happen to you." ²³But he turned and said to Peter, "Get behind me, Satan! You are a hindrance to me, for you are setting your mind not on divine things but on human things."

²⁴Then Jesus told his disciples, "If any wish to come after me, let them deny themselves and take up their cross and follow me. ²⁵For those who want to save their life will lose it, and those who lose their life for my sake will find it. ²⁶For what will it profit them if they gain the whole world but forfeit their life? Or what will they give in return for their life?

²⁷"For the Son of Man is to come with his angels in the glory of his Father, and then he will repay everyone for what has been done. ²⁸Truly I tell you, there are some standing here who will not taste death before they see the Son of Man coming in his kingdom."

Primary Hymns and Songs for the Day

"The God of Abraham Praise" (Exod) (O)
    C24, CG45, E401, EL831, G49, N24, P488, SH50, UM116
    (PD), VU255
            H-3   Hbl-62, 95; Chr-59; Org-77
            S-1   #211. Harm.

"Go Down, Moses" (Exod)
    AH4052, C663, E648, G52, N572, P334, SH28, UM448
            H-3   Chr-215; Org-46

"Praise God for This Holy Ground" (Exod)
    G405, WS3009

"The Servant Song" 72673 (Rom)
    C490, CG289, EL659, G727, N539, S2222, SA1005, SH264,
    VU595

"I Have Decided to Follow Jesus" (Matt)
    C344, CG497, S2129 (PD), SH610

"Walk with Me" (Exod, Matt)
    S2242, VU649

"Take Up Thy Cross" (Matt) (C)
    E675, EL667, G718, P393
            H-3   Chr-178
    N204
            H-3   Chr-178; Org-27
            S-2   #48-49. Desc. and harm.
    UM415 (PD)
            H-3   Chr-178, 180; Org-44
            S-1   #141-143 Various treatments
    SH605, VU561

Additional Hymn Suggestions

"Source and Sovereign, Rock and Cloud" (Exod)
    C12, G11, UM113

"Come, Ye Faithful, Raise the Strain" (Exod)
    E215, CG218, E199, EL363, G234, N230, P115, UM315 (PD),
    VU165

"God of Grace and God of Glory" (Exod)
    C464, CG285, E594/595, EL705, G307, N436, P420, SA814,
    SH250, UM577 (PD), VU686

"God the Sculptor of the Mountains" (Exod)
    EL736, G5, S2060

"Why Stand So Far Away, My God" (Exod)
    C671, G786, S2180

"Deep in the Shadows of the Past" (Exod)
    G50, N320, P330, S2246

"In the Desert, on God's Mountain" (Exod)
    WS3029

"Forgive Our Sins as We Forgive" (Rom)
    CG694 E674, EL605, G444, P347, SH504, UM390, VU364

"Cuando el Pobre" ("When the Poor Ones") (Rom)
    C662, EL725, G762, P407, SH240, UM434, VU702

"Where Charity and Love Prevail" (Rom)
    CG264, E581, EL359, G316, N396, SH271, UM549

"Like the Murmur of the Dove's Song" (Rom)
    C245, CG233, E513, EL403, G285, N270, P314, SH407,
    UM544, VU205

"The Church of Christ, in Every Age" (Rom)
    C475, EL729, G320, N306, P421, UM589, VU601

"God, How Can We Forgive" (Rom)
    G445, S2169

"Healer of Our Every Ill" (Rom)
    C506, EL612, G795, S2213, SH339, VU619

"In Remembrance of Me" (Rom, Comm.)
    C403, CG462, G521, S2254, SH667

"Lord, I Want to Be a Christian" (Rom, Matt)
    C589, CG507, G729, N454, P372 (PD), SH621, UM402

"Be Still, My Soul" (Rom, Matt)
    C566, CG57, G819, N488, SH330, UM534, VU652

"Lord, Whose Love Through Humble Service" (Rom, Matt)
    C461, CG650, E610, EL712, P427, SH239, UM581

"Beneath the Cross of Jesus" (Matt)
    C197, CG184, E498, EL338, G216, N190, P92, SA161, SH166,
    UM297 (PD), VU135

"Take My Life, and Let It Be" (Matt)
    C609, CG490, E707, EL583/EL685, G697, P391, N448,
    SA623, SH627/628, UM399 (PD), VU506

"More Love to Thee, O Christ" (Matt)
    C527, CG365, G828, N456, P359, UM453 (PD)

"Nearer, My God, to Thee" (Matt)
    C577, N606, SA611, UM528 (PD), VU497 (Fr.)

"The Summons" (Matt)
    CG473, EL798, G726, S2130, SA695, SH598, VU567

Additional Contemporary and Modern Suggestions

"We Will Glorify the King of Kings" 19038 (Exod)

"Holy Ground" 21198 (Exod)
    C112, G406, S2272, SA400

"Awesome in This Place" 847554 (Exod)

"Nobody" 7121827 (Exod)

"Thank You, Lord" 865000 (Pss)

"How Great Is Our God" 4348399 (Pss)

"Make Me a Channel of Your Peace" (Rom)
    G753, S2171, SA608, SH616 VU684

"Make Me a Channel of Your Peace" 6399315 (Rom)

"Make Us One" 695737 (Rom)

"They'll Know We Are Christians" 26997 (Rom)
    AH4074, C494, CG272, G300, S2223, SH232

"Bind Us Together" 1228 (Rom)

"Ubi Caritas" ("Live in Charity") (Rom)
    C523, EL642, G205, S2179

"Feed Us, Lord" 4636207 (Rom, Comm)
    G501, WS3167

"Somlandela" ("We Will Follow") (Matt)
    WS3160

"Let It Be Said of Us" 1855882 (Matt)

"Every Move I Make" 1595726 (Matt)

"Everyday" 2798154 (Matt)

"Take Up Our Cross" 5358955 (Matt)

Vocal Solos

"May the Mind of Christ" (Rom)
    V-8   p. 114

"Nothing . . . Everything" (Matt)
    V-8   p. 162

Anthems

"Lord, I Want to Be a Christian" (Rom, Matt)
Arr. Brazeal W. Dennard; Alliance AMP0029
SATB *divisi, a cappella* (https://bit.ly/AMP0029)

"Jesus, My All, To Heaven Is Gone" (Matt)
arr. Howard Helvey; Beckenhorst BP1562
2-part mixed, piano (http://bit.ly/BP1562)

Other Suggestions

Visuals:
    O   Sandals, burning bush, mountain, milk/honey, 3:14
    P   Musical notes, singing
    E   Images of love overcoming hate, service to others
    G   Wooden cross on its side, self-denial, sandals
Canticle: UM646. "Canticle of Love" (Rom)
Prayer: WSL57. "Days pass and the years vanish" (Exod)
Offertory Prayer: WSL103. "Blessed God" (Rom)
Blessing: WSL165. "Go out into the world" (Rom)
Sung Benediction: WS3159. "Let Our Earth Be Peaceful" (Rom)
Theme Ideas: Compassion, Cross, Discipleship / Following God,
    God: Call of God / Listening, Love / Great Commandment

Exodus 12:1-14

The LORD said to Moses and Aaron in the land of Egypt, 2"This month shall mark for you the beginning of months; it shall be the first month of the year for you. 3Tell the whole congregation of Israel that on the tenth of this month they are to take a lamb for each family, a lamb for each household. 4If a household is too small for a whole lamb, it shall join its closest neighbor in obtaining one; the lamb shall be divided in proportion to the number of people who eat of it. 5Your lamb shall be without blemish, a year-old male; you may take it from the sheep or from the goats. 6You shall keep it until the fourteenth day of this month; then the whole assembled congregation of Israel shall slaughter it at twilight. 7They shall take some of the blood and put it on the two doorposts and the lintel of the houses in which they eat it. 8They shall eat the lamb that same night; they shall eat it roasted over the fire with unleavened bread and bitter herbs. 9Do not eat any of it raw or boiled in water but roasted over the fire, with its head, legs, and inner organs. 10You shall let none of it remain until the morning; anything that remains until the morning you shall burn with fire. 11This is how you shall eat it: your loins girded, your sandals on your feet, and your staff in your hand, and you shall eat it hurriedly. It is the Passover of the LORD. 12I will pass through the land of Egypt that night, and I will strike down every firstborn in the land of Egypt, from human to animal, and on all the gods of Egypt I will execute judgments: I am the LORD. 13The blood shall be a sign for you on the houses where you live: when I see the blood, I will pass over you, and no plague shall destroy you when I strike the land of Egypt.

14"This day shall be a day of remembrance for you. You shall celebrate it as a festival to the LORD; throughout your generations you shall observe it as a perpetual ordinance.

Psalm 149 (G550, N722, P257)

Praise the LORD!
Sing to the LORD a new song,
    his praise in the assembly of the faithful.
2Let Israel be glad in its Maker;
    let the children of Zion rejoice in their King.
3Let them praise his name with dancing,
    making melody to him with tambourine and lyre.
4For the LORD takes pleasure in his people;
    he adorns the humble with victory.
5Let the faithful exult in glory;
    let them sing for joy on their couches.
6Let the high praises of God be in their throats
    and two-edged swords in their hands,
7to execute vengeance on the nations
    and punishment on the peoples,
8to bind their kings with fetters
    and their nobles with chains of iron,
9to execute on them the judgment decreed.
    This is glory for all his faithful ones.
Praise the LORD!

Romans 13:8-14

8Owe no one anything, except to love one another, for the one who loves another has fulfilled the law. 9The commandments, "You shall not commit adultery; you shall not murder; you shall not steal; you shall not covet," and any other commandment, are summed up in this word, "You shall love your neighbor as yourself." 10Love does no wrong to a neighbor; therefore, love is the fulfilling of the law.

11Besides this, you know what time it is, how it is already the moment for you to wake from sleep. For salvation is nearer to us now than when we became believers; 12the night is far gone; the day is near. Let us then throw off the works of darkness and put on the armor of light; 13let us walk decently as in the day, not in reveling and drunkenness, not in illicit sex and licentiousness, not in quarreling and jealousy. 14Instead, put on the Lord Jesus Christ, and make no provision for the flesh, to gratify its desires.

Matthew 18:15-20

15"If your brother or sister sins against you, go and point out the fault when the two of you are alone. If you are listened to, you have regained that one. 16But if you are not listened to, take one or two others along with you, so that every word may be confirmed by the evidence of two or three witnesses. 17If that person refuses to listen to them, tell it to the church, and if the offender refuses to listen even to the church, let such a one be to you as a gentile and a tax collector. 18Truly I tell you, whatever you bind on earth will be bound in heaven, and whatever you loose on earth will be loosed in heaven. 19Again, truly I tell you, if two of you agree on earth about anything you ask, it will be done for you by my Father in heaven. 20For where two or three are gathered in my name, I am there among them."

Primary Hymns and Songs for the Day

"Christ Is Made the Sure Foundation" (Matt) (O)
    C275, CG248, E518, EL645, G394, N400, P416/417, SA246,
    SH225, UM559 (PD), VU325

"Brethren, We Have Met to Worship" (Exod, Rom, Matt)
    C277, CG296, G396
        H-3   Chr-80; Desc-52
        S-1   #160-162. Various treatments
        S-2   #87-88. Brass and timpani intro. and arr.

"Just as I Am, Without One Plea" (Exod, Matt)
    C339, CG500, E693, EL592, G442, N207, P370, SA503,
    SH500, UM357 (PD), VU508
        H-3   Chr-120; Org-186

"Arise, Your Light Is Come" (Rom)
    CG87, EL314, G744, N164, P411, VU79

"Jesu, Jesu" (Rom, Matt)
    C600, CG656, E602, EL708, G203, N498, P367, SH155,
    UM432, VU593; S-1 #63 Vocal part

"Draw Us in the Spirit's Tether" (Rom, Matt, Comm.)
    C392, EL470, G529, N337, P504, UM632, VU479
        H-3   Chr-62
        S-1   #337. Performance Note

"Kum Ba Yah" (Matt)
    C590, G472, P338, UM494

"I Want to Walk as a Child of the Light" (Rom) (C)
    CG96, E490, EL815, G377, SH352, UM206
        S-2   #91. Descant

Additional Hymn Suggestions

"Go Down, Moses" (Exod)
    C663, E648, G52, N572, P334, SH28, UM448

"God the Sculptor of the Mountains" (Exod)
    EL736, G5, S2060

"Deep in the Shadows of the Past" (Exod)
    G50, N320, P330, S2246

"Cantad al Señor" ("O Sing to the Lord") (Pss)
    CG328, EL822, G637, P472, SH429, VU241

"Wake, Awake, for Night Is Flying" (Rom)
    E61, EL436, G349, P17, UM720 (PD), VU711

"Healer of Our Every Ill" (Rom)
    C506, EL612, G795, S2213, SH339, VU619

"In Remembrance of Me" (Rom, Comm.)
    C403, CG462, G521, S2254, SH667

"Love Divine, All Loves Excelling" (Rom, Matt)
    C517, CG281, E657, EL631, G366, N43, P376, SA262,
    SH353/354, UM384 (PD), VU333

"Lord, I Want to Be a Christian" (Rom, Matt)
    C589, CG507, G729, N454, P372 (PD), SH621, UM402

"Where Charity and Love Prevail" (Rom, Matt)
    CG264, E581, EL359, G316, N396, SH271, UM549

"Help Us Accept Each Other" (Rom, Matt)
    C487, G754, N388, P358, UM560

"I Come with Joy" (Rom, Matt, Comm.)
    C420, CG456, E304, EL482, G515, N349, P507, SH682,
    UM617, VU477

"Joyful, Joyful, We Adore Thee" (Matt)
    C2, CG310, E376, EL836, G611, N4, P464, SA39, SH390,
    UM89 (PD), VU232

"Forgive Our Sins as We Forgive" (Matt)
    CG694 E674, EL605, G444, P347, SH504, UM390, VU364

"Father, We Thank You" (Matt)
    E302/303, EL478, SH686, UM563/565

"Blessed Jesus, at Thy Word" (Matt)
    E440, EL520, G395, N74, P454, UM596 (PD), VU500

"God, How Can We Forgive" (Matt)
    G445, S2169

"O-So-So" ("Come Now, O Prince of Peace") (Matt)
    EL247, G103, S2232, SH235

"We All Are One in Mission" (Matt)
    CG269, EL576, G733, P435, S2243

"Built on a Rock" (Matt)
    C273, EL652, WS3147

Additional Contemporary and Modern Suggestions

"El-Shaddai" 26856 (Exod)
    UM123, S-2 #54 Verses for Vocal Solo

"Mighty to Save" 4591782 (Exod)

"I Will Enter His Gates" 1493 (Exod, Pss)

"We Bring the Sacrifice of Praise" 9990 (Exod, Pss)

"Sing unto the Lord a New Song" 571215 (Pss)

"I Will Celebrate" 21239 (Pss)

"Let Everything That Has Breath" 2430979 (Pss)

"As It Is in Heaven" 4669748 (Pss, Lord's Prayer)

"I Could Sing of Your Love Forever" 1043199 (Pss, Rom)

"Awaken" 5491647 (Rom)

"Salvation Is Here" 4451327 (Rom)

"Make Us One" 695737 (Rom)

"Freedom Is Coming" 4194244 (Rom)
    G359, S2192, SA29

"Blessed Be Your Name" 3798438 (Rom)

"They'll Know We Are Christians" 26997 (Rom, Matt)
    AH4074, C494, CG272, G300, S2223, SH232

"Bind Us Together" 1228 (Rom, Matt) (C)

"Make Me a Channel of Your Peace" (Rom, Matt)
    G753, S2171, SA608, SH616 VU684

"Freedom in the Spirit" 7127886 (Rom, Matt)

"As We Gather" 35469 (Matt)

"Dwell" 4085652 (Matt)

"Better Than A Hallelujah" 5622564 (Matt)

"Restored" 5894615 (Matt)

Vocal Solos

"I Will Sing of Thy Great Mercies" (Exod, Pss)
    V-4   p. 43

"Make Me a Channel of Your Peace" (Rom, Matt)
    V-3 (2)   p. 25
    V-3 (3)   p. 28

"Truth Be Told" (Rom, Matt)
    V-9   p. 118

Anthems

"Just as I Am" (Exod, Matt)
Arr. Emily Lund; Hope C5682
SATB, piano (https://bit.ly/C-5682)

"Draw Us in the Spirit's Tether" (Rom, Matt, Comm.)
Freidell/Curry; HW Gray 00-32234
SAB, organ (https://bit.ly/HL-32234)

Other Suggestions

Visuals:
    O   Sin/salvation (black/gold), darkness/light, lamp,
            candles, Passover meal, lamb, blood, wine/bread
    P   Dancing figures, tambourine, lyre
    E   Paschal Lamb, portrait of Christ
    E/G   Reconciliation, bridges, alarm clock
    G   Worship, reconciliation, joined hands, four hands
            folded in prayer

Introit: C273, CG247, EL652, WS3147, stanza 3. "Built on a
    Rock" (Matt)

Greeting: C279. Reach Out and Worship (Matt)

Response: C523, EL642, G205, S2179. "Ubi Caritas" (Rom, Matt)

Alternate Lessons: Eze 33:7-11; Ps 119:33-40 (See p. 3.)

Theme Ideas: Light, Love / Great Commandment, Passover,
    Reconciliation, Remembrance, Repentance

Exodus 14:19-31

[19]The angel of God who was going before the Israelite army moved and went behind them, and the pillar of cloud moved from in front of them and took its place behind them. [20]It came between the army of Egypt and the army of Israel. And so the cloud was there with the darkness, and it lit up the night; one did not come near the other all night.

[21]Then Moses stretched out his hand over the sea. The LORD drove the sea back by a strong east wind all night and turned the sea into dry land, and the waters were divided. [22]The Israelites went into the sea on dry ground, the waters forming a wall for them on their right and on their left. [23]The Egyptians pursued and went into the sea after them, all of Pharaoh's horses, chariots, and chariot drivers. [24]At the morning watch the LORD, in the pillar of fire and cloud, looked down on the Egyptian army and threw the Egyptian army into a panic. [25]He clogged their chariot wheels so that they turned with difficulty. The Egyptians said, "Let us flee from the Israelites, for the LORD is fighting for them against Egypt."

[26]Then the LORD said to Moses, "Stretch out your hand over the sea, so that the water may come back upon the Egyptians, upon their chariots and chariot drivers." [27]So Moses stretched out his hand over the sea, and at dawn the sea returned to its normal depth. As the Egyptians fled before it, the LORD tossed the Egyptians into the sea. [28]The waters returned and covered the chariots and the chariot drivers, the entire army of Pharaoh that had followed them into the sea; not one of them remained. [29]But the Israelites walked on dry ground through the sea, the waters forming a wall for them on their right and on their left.

[30]Thus the LORD saved Israel that day from the Egyptians, and Israel saw the Egyptians dead on the seashore. [31]Israel saw the great work that the LORD did against the Egyptians. So the people feared the LORD and believed in the LORD and in his servant Moses.

Exodus 15:1b-11, 20-21

"I will sing to the LORD, for he has triumphed gloriously;
    horse and rider he has thrown into the sea.
[2]The LORD is my strength and my might,
    and he has become my salvation;
    this is my God, and I will praise him;
    my father's God, and I will exalt him.
[3]The LORD is a warrior;
    the LORD is his name.
[4]Pharaoh's chariots and his army he cast into the sea;
    his elite officers were sunk in the Red Sea.
[5]The floods covered them;
    they went down into the depths like a stone.
[6]Your right hand, O LORD, glorious in power—
    your right hand, O LORD, shattered the enemy.
[7]In the greatness of your majesty you overthrew your adversaries;
    you sent out your fury; it consumed them like stubble.
[8]At the blast of your nostrils the waters piled up;
    the floods stood up in a heap;
    the deeps congealed in the heart of the sea.
[9]The enemy said, 'I will pursue; I will overtake;
    I will divide the spoil; my desire shall have its fill of them.
    I will draw my sword; my hand shall destroy them.'
[10]You blew with your wind; the sea covered them;
    they sank like lead in the mighty waters.
[11]Who is like you, O LORD, among the gods?
    Who is like you, majestic in holiness,
    awesome in splendor, doing wonders?
. . . .
[20]Then the prophet Miriam, Aaron's sister, took a tambourine in her hand, and all the women went out after her with tambourines and with dancing. [21]And Miriam sang to them:
    "Sing to the LORD, for he has triumphed gloriously;
    horse and rider he has thrown into the sea."

Romans 14:1-12

Welcome those who are weak in faith but not for the purpose of quarreling over opinions. [2]Some believe in eating anything, while the weak eat only vegetables. [3]Those who eat must not despise those who abstain, and those who abstain must not pass judgment on those who eat, for God has welcomed them. [4]Who are you to pass judgment on slaves of another? It is before their own lord that they stand or fall. And they will be upheld, for the Lord is able to make them stand.

[5]Some judge one day to be better than another, while others judge all days to be alike. Let all be fully convinced in their own minds. [6]Those who observe the day, observe it for the Lord. Also those who eat, eat for the Lord, since they give thanks to God, while those who abstain, abstain for the Lord and give thanks to God.

[7]For we do not live to ourselves, and we do not die to ourselves. [8]If we live, we live to the Lord, and if we die, we die to the Lord; so then, whether we live or whether we die, we are the Lord's. [9]For to this end Christ died and lived again, so that he might be Lord of both the dead and the living.

[10]Why do you pass judgment on your brother or sister? Or you, why do you despise your brother or sister? For we will all stand before the judgment seat of God. [11]For it is written,
    "As I live, says the Lord, every knee shall bow to me,
    and every tongue shall give praise to God."
[12]So then, each one of us will be held accountable.

Matthew 18:21-35

[21]Then Peter came and said to him, "Lord, if my brother or sister sins against me, how often should I forgive? As many as seven times?" [22]Jesus said to him, "Not seven times, but, I tell you, seventy-seven times.

[23]"For this reason the kingdom of heaven may be compared to a king who wished to settle accounts with his slaves. [24]When he began the reckoning, one who owed him ten thousand talents was brought to him, [25]and, as he could not pay, the lord ordered him to be sold, together with his wife and children and all his possessions and payment to be made. [26]So the slave fell on his knees before him, saying, 'Have patience with me, and I will pay you everything.' [27]And out of pity for him, the lord of that slave released him and forgave him the debt. [28]But that same slave, as he went out, came upon one of his fellow slaves who owed him a hundred denarii, and seizing him by the throat he said, 'Pay what you owe.' [29]Then his fellow slave fell down and pleaded with him, 'Have patience with me, and I will pay you.' [30]But he refused; then he went and threw him into prison until he would pay the debt. [31]When his fellow slaves saw what had happened, they were greatly distressed, and they went and reported to their lord all that had taken place. [32]Then his lord summoned him and said to him, 'You wicked slave! I forgave you all that debt because you pleaded with me. [33]Should you not have had mercy on your fellow slave, as I had mercy on you?' [34]And in anger his lord handed him over to be tortured until he would pay his entire debt. [35]So my heavenly Father will also do to every one of you, if you do not forgive your brother or sister from your heart."

Primary Hymns and Songs for the Day

"Come, Ye Faithful, Raise the Strain" (Exod 15) (O)
　C215, CG218, E199, EL363, G234, N230, P115, UM315 (PD),
　VU165
　　　　H-3　　Hbl-53; Chr-57; Desc-94; Org-141
　　　　S-2　　#161. Descant
"Guide Me, O Thou Great Jehovah" (Exod) (O)
　C622, CG33, E690, EL618, G65, N18/19, P281, SA27, SH51,
　UM127 (PD), VU651 (Fr.)
　　　　H-3　　Hbl-25, 51; Chr-89; Desc-26; Org-23
　　　　S-1　　#76-77. Descant and harmonization
"Crashing Waters at Creation" (Exod 14)
　EL455, G476, N326, VU449
"Out of Deep, Unordered Water" (Exod 14)
　G484, P494, VU453
"Awesome God" 41099 (Exod 15)
　G616, S2040
"There's a Wideness in God's Mercy" (Rom, Matt)
　C73, CG41, E470, EL587/88G435, N23, P298, SH526,
　UM121, VU271
　　　　H-3　　Chr-195; Desc-102; Org-179
"Forgive Our Sins as We Forgive" (Matt)
　CG694 E674, EL605, G444, P347, SH504, UM390, VU364
　　　　H-3　　Chr-68; Desc-28; Org-27
　　　　S-1　　#85. Choral harmonization
"Pues Si Vivimos" ("When We Are Living") (Rom) (C)
　C536, CG265, EL639, G822, N499, P400, SH299, UM356,
　VU581
　　　　S-1　　#320. Orff instrument arrangement
　　　　H-3　　Chr-218; Org-155

Additional Hymn Suggestions

"Go Down, Moses" (Exod)
　C663, E648, G52, N572, P334, SH28, UM448
"In the Midst of New Dimensions" (Exod)
　G315, N391, S2238
"Deep in the Shadows of the Past" (Exod)
　G50, N320, P330, S2246
"Cantad al Señor" ("O Sing to the Lord") (Pss)
　CG328, EL822, G637, P472, SH429, VU241
"At the Name of Jesus" (Rom)
　CG424, E435, EL416, G264, SA74, SH657, UM168, VU335
"Crown Him with Many Crowns" (Rom)
　C234, CG223. E494, EL855, G268, N301, P151, SA358,
　SH208, UM327 (PD), VU211
"Lord, Speak to Me" (Rom)
　CG503, EL676, G722, N531, SA773, SH557, UM463, VU589
"Creator of the Stars of Night" (Rom)
　C127, E60, EL245, G84, N111, P4, SH74, UM692 (PD)
"O How I Love Jesus" (Rom, Matt)
　AH4020, C99, CG601, N52, SA94, UM170 (PD)
"Joyful, Joyful, We Adore Thee" (Matt)
　C2, CG310, E376, EL836, G611, N4, P464, SA39, SH390,
　UM89 (PD), VU232
"Lord, I Want to Be a Christian" (Matt)
　C589, CG507, G729, N454, P372 (PD), SH621, UM402
"Where Charity and Love Prevail" (Matt)
　CG264, E581, EL359, G316, N396, SH271, UM549
"Help Us Accept Each Other" (Matt)
　C487, G754, N388, P358, UM560
"O-So-So" ("Come Now, O Prince of Peace") (Matt)
　EL247, G103, S2232, SH235
"Come, Share the Lord" (Matt, Comm.)
　C408, CG459, G510, S2269, VU469

Additional Contemporary and Modern Suggestions

"El-Shaddai" 26856 (Exod)
　UM123, S-2 #54 Verses for Vocal Solo
"How Majestic Is Your Name" 26007 (Exod)
　C63, CG326, G613, S2023, SA90

"Mighty to Save" 4591782 (Exod)
"Shout to the North" 1562261 (Exod, Pss)
　G319, SA1009, WS3042
"Promises" 6454250 (Exod, Pss)
"Nobody" 7121827 (Exod, Pss)
"Ancient of Days" 798108 (Exod, Rom)
"Majesty" 1527 (Exod, Rom)
　CG346, SA382, SH212, UM176
"My Life Is in You, Lord" 17315 (Exod, Rom)
"I Exalt You" 17803 (Exod, Rom)
"We Will Dance" 1034438 (Exod, Rom)
"The Highest and the Greatest" 4769758 (Exod, Rom)
"Sing unto the Lord a New Song" 571215 (Pss)
"I Will Celebrate" 21239 (Pss)
"He Is Exalted" 17827 (Pss, Rom)
"Jesus, Name above All Names" 21291 (Rom)
"Sanctuary" 24140 (Rom)
　G701, S2164, SH265
"He Is Lord" 1515225 (Rom)
　C117, CG208, SA222, SH657, UM177
"What A Beautiful Name" 7068424 (Rom)
"No Sweeter Name" 4447984 (Rom)
"The Heavens Shall Declare" 904033 (Rom)
"You are the Light" 6238098 (Rom)
"Grace Alone" 2335524 (Matt)
"Make Me a Channel of Your Peace" (Matt)
　G753, S2171, SA608, SH616 VU684
"Make Me a Channel of Your Peace" 6399315 (Matt)

Vocal Solos

"God Will Make a Way" (with "He Leadeth Me") (Exod)
　V-3 (2)　　p. 9
"Great Things" (Exod, Pss)
　V-9　　　　p. 36
"In Jesus' Name" (Rom)
　V-8　　　　p. 188

Anthems

"Guide Me, O Thou Great Jehovah" (Exod)
Arr. Lloyd Larson; Lorenz 10/5215L
SATB, piano, opt. 4-hand and handbells (https://bit.ly/L-5215)

"I Then Shall Live" (Matt)
Gaither, arr. Fettke; Lorenz 10/5136L
SATB, piano (https://bit.ly/L-5136L)

Other Suggestions

Visuals:
　O　　Symbols of hope: cloud, pillar of fire, rainbow, star
　P　　Musical notes, sea, tambourine, dancing, Exod 15:21b
　E　　Reconciliation, unity, clasped hands, Christ, scales of
　　　　justice
　G　　Reconciliation, forgiveness, embrace, no. 77, 70x7,
　　　　scales of justice
Call to Worship: C60, EL555, N39, SH432, UM149, stanza 1.
　"Cantemos al Señor" ("Let's Sing Unto the Lord") (Exod)
Responsive Reading: SH30. "Psalm/Salmo 114" (Exod)
Canticle: UM135. "Canticle of Moses and Miriam" (Exod)
Prayer: C332. God of Wondrous Darkness (Exod)
Scripture Response: C589, CG507, G729, N454, P372 (PD),
　SH621, UM402, st. 2. "Lord I Want to Be a Christian" (Matt)
Alternate Lessons: Gen 50:15-21; Ps 103: (1-7) 8-13 (See p. 3.)
Theme Ideas: Compassion, God: Providence / God our
　Help, Inclusion, Jesus: Mind of Christ, Journey, Passover,
　Reconciliation

Exodus 16:2-15

²The whole congregation of the Israelites complained against Moses and Aaron in the wilderness. ³The Israelites said to them, "If only we had died by the hand of the LORD in the land of Egypt, when we sat by the pots of meat and ate our fill of bread, for you have brought us out into this wilderness to kill this whole assembly with hunger."

⁴Then the LORD said to Moses, "I am going to rain bread from heaven for you, and each day the people shall go out and gather enough for that day. In that way I will test them, whether they will follow my instruction or not. ⁵On the sixth day, when they prepare what they bring in, it will be twice as much as they gather on other days." ⁶So Moses and Aaron said to all the Israelites, "In the evening you shall know that it was the LORD who brought you out of the land of Egypt, ⁷and in the morning you shall see the glory of the LORD, because he has heard your complaining against the LORD. For what are we, that you complain against us?" ⁸And Moses said, "When the LORD gives you meat to eat in the evening and your fill of bread in the morning, because the LORD has heard the complaining that you utter against him—what are we? Your complaining is not against us but against the LORD."

⁹Then Moses said to Aaron, "Say to the whole congregation of the Israelites: 'Draw near to the LORD, for he has heard your complaining.'" ¹⁰And as Aaron spoke to the whole congregation of the Israelites, they looked toward the wilderness, and the glory of the LORD appeared in the cloud. ¹¹The LORD spoke to Moses, ¹²"I have heard the complaining of the Israelites; say to them, 'At twilight you shall eat meat, and in the morning you shall have your fill of bread; then you shall know that I am the LORD your God.'"

¹³In the evening quails came up and covered the camp, and in the morning there was a layer of dew around the camp. ¹⁴When the layer of dew lifted, there on the surface of the wilderness was a fine flaky substance, as fine as frost on the ground. ¹⁵When the Israelites saw it, they said to one another, "What is it?" For they did not know what it was. Moses said to them, "It is the bread that the LORD has given you to eat.

Psalm 105:1-6, 37-45 (G59, N691, UM828)

O give thanks to the LORD; call on his name;
 make known his deeds among the peoples.
²Sing to him, sing praises to him;
 tell of all his wonderful works.
³Glory in his holy name;
 let the hearts of those who seek the LORD rejoice.
⁴Seek the LORD and his strength;
 seek his presence continually.
⁵Remember the wonderful works he has done,
 his miracles and the judgments he has uttered,
⁶O offspring of his servant Abraham,
 children of Jacob, his chosen ones.
. . . .
³⁷Then he brought Israel out with silver and gold,
 and there was no one among their tribes who stumbled.
³⁸Egypt was glad when they departed,
 for dread of them had fallen upon it.
³⁹He spread a cloud for a covering
 and fire to give light by night.
⁴⁰They asked, and he brought quails
 and gave them food from heaven in abundance.
⁴¹He opened the rock, and water gushed out;
 it flowed through the desert like a river.
⁴²For he remembered his holy promise
 and Abraham, his servant.
⁴³So he brought his people out with joy,
 his chosen ones with singing.

⁴⁴He gave them the lands of the nations,
 and they took possession of the wealth of the peoples,
⁴⁵that they might keep his statutes
 and observe his laws.
Praise the LORD!

Philippians 1:21-30

²¹For to me, living is Christ and dying is gain. ²²If I am to live in the flesh, that means fruitful labor for me, yet I cannot say which I will choose. ²³I am hard pressed between the two: my desire is to depart and be with Christ, for that is far better, ²⁴but to remain in the flesh is more necessary for you. ²⁵Since I am convinced of this, I know that I will remain and continue with all of you for your progress and joy in faith, ²⁶so that, by my presence again with you, your boast might abound in Christ Jesus because of me.

²⁷Only, live your life in a manner worthy of the gospel of Christ, so that, whether I come and see you or am absent and hear about you, I will know that you are standing firm in one spirit, striving side by side with one mind for the faith of the gospel ²⁸and in no way frightened by those opposing you. For them, this is evidence of their destruction but of your salvation. And this is God's doing. ²⁹For he has graciously granted you the privilege not only of believing in Christ but of suffering for him as well, ³⁰since you are having the same struggle that you saw I had and now hear that I still have.

Matthew 20:1-16

"For the kingdom of heaven is like a landowner who went out early in the morning to hire laborers for his vineyard. ²After agreeing with the laborers for a denarius for the day, he sent them into his vineyard. ³When he went out about nine o'clock, he saw others standing idle in the marketplace, ⁴and he said to them, 'You also go into the vineyard, and I will pay you whatever is right.' So they went. ⁵When he went out again about noon and about three o'clock, he did the same. ⁶And about five o'clock he went out and found others standing around, and he said to them, 'Why are you standing here idle all day?' ⁷They said to him, 'Because no one has hired us.' He said to them, 'You also go into the vineyard.' ⁸When evening came, the owner of the vineyard said to his manager, 'Call the laborers and give them their pay, beginning with the last and then going to the first.' ⁹When those hired about five o'clock came, each of them received a denarius. ¹⁰Now when the first came, they thought they would receive more; but each of them also received a denarius. ¹¹And when they received it, they grumbled against the landowner, ¹²saying, 'These last worked only one hour, and you have made them equal to us who have borne the burden of the day and the scorching heat.' ¹³But he replied to one of them, 'Friend, I am doing you no wrong; did you not agree with me for a denarius? ¹⁴Take what belongs to you and go; I choose to give to this last the same as I give to you. ¹⁵Am I not allowed to do what I choose with what belongs to me? Or are you envious because I am generous?' ¹⁶So the last will be first, and the first will be last."

Primary Hymns and Songs for the Day

"Guide Me, O Thou Great Jehovah" (Exod, Pss) (O)
   C622, CG33, E690, EL618, G65, N18/19, P281, SA27, SH51,
   UM127 (PD), VU651 (Fr.)
        H-3   Hbl-25, 51, 58; Chr-89; Desc-26; Org-23
        S-1   #76-77. Descant and harmonization

"Morning Has Broken" (Exod) (O)
   C53, CG27, E8, EL556, G664, SH465, UM145, VU409

"Glorious Things of Thee Are Spoken" (Exod, Matt)
   C709, CG282, E522/523, EL647, G81, N307, P446, SA535,
   UM731 (PD)
        H-3   Hbl-61; Chr-72; Desc-17; Org-11
        S-1   #27. Descant
                #28. Harmonization in F major

"Lift Every Voice and Sing" (Exod, Pss)
   AH4055, C631, CG638, E599, EL841, G339, N593, P563,
   SH36, UM519
        H-3   Chr-128

"Jesus, the Very Thought of Thee" (Phil)
   C102, CG386, E642, EL754, G629, N507, P310, UM175
        H-3   Hbl-66, 73; Chr-90; Desc-92; Org-131
        S-1   #291-292. Descant and harmonization

"Pues Si Vivimos" ("When We Are Living") (Phil)
   C536, CG265, EL639, G822, N499, P400, SH299, UM356,
   VU581
        S-1   #320. Orff instrument arrangement
        H-3   Chr-218; Org-155

"Take Up Thy Cross" (Phil)
   E675, EL667, G718, N204, SH605, UM415, VU561

"Christ Beside Me" (Phil)
   G702, S2166
        H-3   Hbl-77; Chr-136; Desc-21; Org-16
        S-1   #50-51. Flute and vocal descants

"Fight the Good Fight" (Phil)
   E552, G846, P307 (PD), SA952, VU674
        H-3   Hbl-29, 57; Chr-117; Desc-31; Org-31
        S-1   #100-103. Various treatments.

"Come, Labor On" (Matt)
   E541, G719, N532, P415
        H-3   Org-109
        H-5   #91. Harmonization

"O Jesus, I Have Promised" (Matt) (C)
   C612, E655, EL810, G724/725, N493, P388/389, SA613,
   SH623, UM396 (PD), VU120
        S-2   #9. Descant

Additional Hymn Suggestions

"Lord, Dismiss Us with Thy Blessing" (Exod) (C)
   C439, E344, EL545, G546, N77, UM671 (PD), VU425

"In the Midst of New Dimensions" (Exod)
   G315, N391, S2238

"God Will Take Care of You" (Exod, Pss)
   N460, SA5, SH289, UM130 (PD)

"I'm Gonna Live So God Can Use Me" (Phil)
   C614, G700, P369, S2153, SH632, VU575

Ubi Caritas ("Live in Charity") (Phil)
   C523, EL642, G205, S2179

"We All Are One in Mission" (Phil)
   CG269, EL576, G733, P435, S2243

"O Master, Let Me Walk with Thee" (Matt)
   C602, CG660, E659/E660, EL818, G738, N503, P357, SA667,
   SH612, UM430 (PD), VU560

"O God of Every Nation" (Matt)
   C680, CG46, E607, EL713, G756, P289, UM435, VU677

"Lord, Whose Love Through Humble Service" (Matt)
   C461, CG650, E610, EL712, P427, SH239, UM581

"Lord of All Hopefulness" (Matt)
   CG678, E482, EL765, G683, S2197, SA772, SH464

"As We Gather at Your Table" (Matt, Comm.)
   EL522, N332, S2268, SH411, VU457

Additional Contemporary and Modern Suggestions

"Hungry" ("Falling on My Knees") 2650364 (Exod)

"Gentle Shepherd" 15609 (Exod)

"Feed Us, Lord" 4636207 (Exod, Comm.)
   G501, WS3167

"O Come To The Altar" 7051511 (Exod, Comm.)

"Let It Rise" 2240585 (Exod)

"All Who Are Thirsty" 2489542 (Exod)

"Enough" 3599479 (Exod)

"There Will Be Bread" 4512352 (Exod)

"Came to My Rescue" 4705190 (Exod, Pss)

"You Who Are Thirsty" 814453 (Exod, Comm.)

"Someone Asked the Question" 1640279 (Pss)
   N523, S2144

"How Great Is Our God" 4348399 (Pss)

"My Life Is in You, Lord" 17315 (Phil)

"Sanctuary" 24140 (Phil)
   G701, S2164, SH265

"Make Us One" 695737 (Phil)

"Ain't Gonna Let Nobody Turn Me 'Round" (Phil)
   AH4051

"All of Me" 6290160 (Phil)

"Today" 5775617 (Phil)

"Humble Thyself in the Sight of the Lord" 26564 (Matt)

"Make Me a Servant" 33131 (Matt)

Vocal Solos

"Who You Are to Me" (Exod)
   V-9   p. 124

"If My People Will Pray" (Exod, Pss)
   V-8   p. 66

Anthems

"A Prayer of Compassion" (Phil)
Gwyneth Walker; ECSchirmer 8730
SATB divisi a cappella (https://bit.ly/MS-8730

"The Apple Tree" (Phil)
K. Lee Scott; Hinshaw HMC-646
SATB, keyboard (https://bit.ly/HMC-646)

Other Suggestions

Visuals:
  O   Bread, quails, hungry being fed
  P   Singing, praising, cloud, fire, bread, quails, rock/
         water
  E   People at work, service to God with people (bowl/
         pitcher/towel)
  G   Grapes, leaves, tools for work, clocks set at 6:00 a.m.,
         9:00 a.m., noon, 3:00 p.m., 6:00 p.m.

Call to Worship: C622, CG33, E690, EL618, G65, N18/19, P281,
   SA27, SH51, UM127 (PD), VU651 (Fr.). "Guide Me, O Thou
   Great Jehovah." *A selected stanza may be used each Sunday
   from today until Nov. 5, when the Hebrew scripture tells of Israel's
   crossing the Jordan.*

Prayer: UM409 (Matt) or C597 (Phil)

Song of Preparation: E303/E302, EL478, SH686, UM563/565,
   stanza 1. "Father, We Thank You" (Pss)

Scripture Response: C709, CG282, E522/523, EL647, G81,
   N307, P446, SA535, UM731 (PD), stanza 3. "Glorious Things
   of Thee Are Spoken" (Exod)

Alternate Lessons: Jonah 3:10–4:11; Ps 145:1-8 (See p. 3.)

Theme Ideas: Faithfulness, God: Kingdom of God, God:
   Providence / God our Help, Journey, Lament, Service /
   Servanthood, Thanksgiving / Gratitude

Exodus 17:1-7

From the wilderness of Sin the whole congregation of the Israelites journeyed by stages, as the LORD commanded. They camped at Rephidim, but there was no water for the people to drink. ²The people quarreled with Moses and said, "Give us water to drink." Moses said to them, "Why do you quarrel with me? Why do you test the LORD?" ³But the people thirsted there for water, and the people complained against Moses and said, "Why did you bring us out of Egypt, to kill us and our children and livestock with thirst?" ⁴So Moses cried out to the LORD, "What shall I do for this people? They are almost ready to stone me." ⁵The LORD said to Moses, "Go on ahead of the people and take some of the elders of Israel with you; take in your hand the staff with which you struck the Nile and go. ⁶I will be standing there in front of you on the rock at Horeb. Strike the rock, and water will come out of it, so that the people may drink." Moses did so, in the sight of the elders of Israel. ⁷He called the place Massah and Meribah, because the Israelites quarreled and tested the LORD, saying, "Is the LORD among us or not?"

Psalm 78:1-4, 12-16 (G632, N669, UM799)

Give ear, O my people, to my teaching;
　　incline your ears to the words of my mouth.
²I will open my mouth in a parable;
　　I will utter dark sayings from of old,
³things that we have heard and known,
　　that our ancestors have told us.
⁴We will not hide them from their children;
　　we will tell to the coming generation
　　the glorious deeds of the LORD and his might
　　and the wonders that he has done.
. . . .
¹²In the sight of their ancestors he worked marvels
　　in the land of Egypt, in the fields of Zoan.
¹³He divided the sea and let them pass through it
　　and made the waters stand like a heap.
¹⁴In the daytime he led them with a cloud
　　and all night long with a fiery light.
¹⁵He split rocks open in the wilderness
　　and gave them drink abundantly as from the deep.
¹⁶He made streams come out of the rock
　　and caused waters to flow down like rivers.

Philippians 2:1-13

If, then, there is any comfort in Christ, any consolation from love, any partnership in the Spirit, any tender affection and sympathy, ²make my joy complete: be of the same mind, having the same love, being in full accord and of one mind. ³Do nothing from selfish ambition or empty conceit, but in humility regard others as better than yourselves. ⁴Let each of you look not to your own interests but to the interests of others. ⁵Let the same mind be in you that was in Christ Jesus,
　　⁶who, though he existed in the form of God,
　　　　did not regard equality with God
　　　　as something to be grasped,
　　⁷but emptied himself,
　　　　taking the form of a slave,
　　　　assuming human likeness.
And being found in appearance as a human,
　　⁸he humbled himself
　　　　and became obedient to the point of death—
　　　　even death on a cross.
　　⁹Therefore God exalted him even more highly
　　　　and gave him the name
　　　　that is above every other name,
　　¹⁰so that at the name given to Jesus
　　　　every knee should bend,
　　　　in heaven and on earth and under the earth,

¹¹and every tongue should confess
　　that Jesus Christ is Lord,
　　to the glory of God the Father.
¹²Therefore, my beloved, just as you have always obeyed me, not only in my presence but much more now in my absence, work on your own salvation with fear and trembling, ¹³for it is God who is at work in you, enabling you both to will and to work for his good pleasure.

Matthew 21:23-32

²³When he entered the temple, the chief priests and the elders of the people came to him as he was teaching and said, "By what authority are you doing these things, and who gave you this authority?" ²⁴Jesus said to them, "I will also ask you one question; if you tell me the answer, then I will also tell you by what authority I do these things. ²⁵Did the baptism of John come from heaven, or was it of human origin?" And they argued with one another, "If we say, 'From heaven,' he will say to us, 'Why, then, did you not believe him?' ²⁶But if we say, 'Of human origin,' we are afraid of the crowd, for all regard John as a prophet." ²⁷So they answered Jesus, "We do not know." And he said to them, "Neither will I tell you by what authority I am doing these things. ²⁸"What do you think? A man had two sons; he went to the first and said, 'Son, go and work in the vineyard today.' ²⁹He answered, 'I will not,' but later he changed his mind and went. ³⁰The father went to the second and said the same, and he answered, 'I go, sir,' but he did not go. ³¹Which of the two did the will of his father?" They said, "The first." Jesus said to them, "Truly I tell you, the tax collectors and the prostitutes are going into the kingdom of God ahead of you. ³²For John came to you in the way of righteousness, and you did not believe him, but the tax collectors and the prostitutes believed him, and even after you saw it you did not change your minds and believe him.

Primary Hymns and Songs for the Day

"Guide Me, O Thou Great Jehovah" (Exod, Pss, Matt) (O)
　　C622, CG33, E690, EL618, G65, N18/19, P281, SA27, SH51,
　　UM127 (PD), VU651 (Fr.)
　　　　H-3　　Hbl-25, 51, 58; Chr-89; Desc-26; Org-23
　　　　S-1　　#76-77. Desc. and harm.
"Come, Thou Fount of Every Blessing" (Exod)
　　AH4086, C16, CG295/559, E686, EL807, G475, N459, P356,
　　SA830, SH394, UM400 (PD), VU559
　　　　H-3　　Chr-57; Desc-79; Org-96
　　　　S-1　　#244. Descant
"Jesus Shall Reign" (Phil)
　　C95, CG158, E544, EL434, G265, N300, P423, SA258, SH209,
　　UM157 (PD), VU330
　　　　C95　　Descant
　　　　H-3　　Hbl-29; Chr-117; Desc-31; Org-31
　　　　S-1　　#100-103. Various treatments.
"Fairest Lord Jesus" (Phil, Matt)
　　C97, CG159, E383, EL838, G630, N44, P306, SA77, SH7,
　　UM189 (PD), VU341
　　　　H-3　　Hbl-57; Chr-63; Desc-25, 94; Org-22, 135
　　　　S-1　　#301. Descant
　　　　S-2　　#158. Choral harmonization
"O For a World" (Phil)
　　C683, G372, N575, P386, VU697
"All Hail the Power of Jesus' Name" (Phil, Matt)
　　C91/92, CG339/340, E450/451, EL634, G263, N304,
　　P142/143, SA73, SH207, UM154/155, VU334
"Jesus, the Light of the World" (Matt)
　　WS3056 (See also AH4038, CG129, G127, N160, SH103)
"Trust and Obey" (Phil, Matt) (C)
　　C556, CG509, SA690, SH636, UM467 (PD)
　　　　H-3　　Chr-202
　　　　S-1　　#336. Harmonization

Additional Hymn Suggestions

"O God, Our Help in Ages Past" (Exod, Pss) (O)
　　C67, CG566, E680, EL632, G687, N25, P210, SA47, SH41,
　　UM117 (PD), VU806
"Glorious Things of Thee Are Spoken" (Exod, Matt)
　　C709, CG282, E522/523, EL647, G81, N307, P446, SA535,
　　UM731 (PD)
"At the Name of Jesus" (Phil)
　　CG424, E435, EL416, G264, SA74, SH657, UM168, VU335
"What Wondrous Love Is This" (Phil)
　　C200, CG171, E439, EL666, G215, N223, P85, SA207, SH177,
　　UM292, VU147 (Fr.)
Canto de Esperanza ("Song of Hope") (Phil) (C)
　　G765, P432, S2186, SH721, VU424
"Forth in Thy Name, O Lord" (Matt) (O)
　　SA642, UM438 (PD), VU416
"Lord, Dismiss Us with Thy Blessing" (Matt) (C)
　　C439, E344, EL545, G546, N77, P538, UM671 (PD), VU425
"All Who Hunger" (World Comm.)
　　C419, CG303, EL461, G509, S2126, VU460
"God Made from One Blood" (World Comm.)
　　C500, CG686, N427, S2170, VU554
"One Bread, One Body" (World Comm.)
　　C393, EL496, G530, SH678, UM620, VU467

Additional Contemporary and Modern Suggestions

"Fill My Cup, Lord" 15946 (Exod, Comm.)
　　C351, UM641 (refrain only), WS3093
"Hungry" ("Falling on My Knees") 2650364 (Exod)
"Feed Us, Lord" 4636207 (Exod, Comm.)
　　G501, WS3167
"O Come To The Altar" 7051511 (Exod, Comm.)
"All Who Are Thirsty" 2489542 (Exod)

"Enough" 3599479 (Exod)
"Came to My Rescue" 4705190 (Exod, Pss)
"You Who Are Thirsty" 814453 (Exod, Comm.)
"Ancient of Days" 798108 (Exod, Pss, Phil)
"Shout to the North" 1562261 (Phil)
　　G319, SA1009, WS3042
"He Is Exalted" 17827 (Phil)
　　AH4082, CG342, S2070, SH423
"Majesty" 1527 (Phil)
"He Is Lord" 1515225 (Phil)
　　C117, CG208, SA222, SH657, UM177
"How Majestic Is Your Name" 26007 (Phil)
　　C63, CG326, G613, S2023, SA90
"Jesus, Name above All Names" 21291 (Phil)
"Humble Thyself in the Sight of the Lord" 26564 (Phil)
"Make Us One" 695737 (Phil)
"You are the Light" 6238098 (Phil)
"No Sweeter Name" 4447984 (Phil)
"I Exalt You" 17803 (Phil)
"What A Beautiful Name" 7068424 (Phil)
"Knowing You" 1045238 (Phil, Matt)
"We Will Dance" 1034438 (Phil)
"Majestic" 4573308 (Phil)
"Jesus Messiah" 5183443 (Phil)
"Let It Be Said of Us" 1855882 (Phil, Matt)
"Take My Life" 1617154 (Phil, Matt)
"Glory To God Forever" 5384338 (Phil, Matt)
"To Know You More" 1767420 (Phil, Matt)
"More Like You" 2145051 (Phil, Matt)
"Seek Ye First" 1352 (Matt)
　　C354, CG436, E711, G175, P333, SA675, SH126, UM405,
　　VU356
"Make Us One" 695737 (World Comm.)

Vocal Solos

"Come, Thou Fount of Every Blessing" (Exod)
　　V-3 (3)　　p. 22
"The Blessing" (Phil)
　　V-9　　　　p. 10

Anthems

"Beautiful Savior" (Phil, Matt)
Michael Burkhardt: MorningStar 60-9033
SATB, organ, opt. congregation (https://bit.ly/MSM-9033)

"Let This Mind Be In You" (Phil)
Austin C. Lovelace; Alfred Music 00-FEC08458
SATB, organ (https://bit.ly/A-8458)

Other Suggestions

Visuals:
O/P/G　　Rock, flowing water, sand, staff, images of baptism
E　　　　Reminders of Crucifixion, Resurrection, Birth of
　　　　　　Christ
G　　　　Vineyard, grapes, vine, leaves, "Reconsider Your Call"
Canticle: C96 or UM167 (See S-1, p. 381) (Phil)
Scripture Response: C709, CG282, E522/523, EL647, G81,
　　N307, P446, SA535, UM731 (PD), stanza 2. "Glorious Things
　　of Thee Are Spoken" (Exod)
Prayer: WSL19. "God of the wilderness" (Exod)
Prayer: WSL204. "God of compassion" (Matt)
World Communion Resources Include: C394, C481, UM556,
　　UM564, N786, N853, WSL68 and WSL67.
Alternate Lessons: Eze 18:1-4, 25-32; Ps 25:1-9 (See p. 3.)
Theme Ideas: Communion, Faithfulness, God: Providence /
　　God our Help, Jesus: Mind of Christ, Journey, Lament, Unity

Exodus 20:1-4, 7-9, 12-20

Then God spoke all these words,

²"I am the LORD your God, who brought you out of the land of Egypt, out of the house of slavery; ³you shall have no other gods before me.

⁴"You shall not make for yourself an idol, whether in the form of anything that is in heaven above or that is on the earth beneath or that is in the water under the earth. . . .

⁷"You shall not make wrongful use of the name of the LORD your God, for the LORD will not acquit anyone who misuses his name.

⁸"Remember the Sabbath day and keep it holy. ⁹Six days you shall labor and do all your work. . . .

¹²"Honor your father and your mother, so that your days may be long in the land that the LORD your God is giving you.

¹³"You shall not murder.

¹⁴"You shall not commit adultery.

¹⁵"You shall not steal.

¹⁶"You shall not bear false witness against your neighbor.

¹⁷"You shall not covet your neighbor's house; you shall not covet your neighbor's wife, male or female slave, ox, donkey, or anything that belongs to your neighbor."

¹⁸When all the people witnessed the thunder and lightning, the sound of the trumpet, and the mountain smoking, they were afraid and trembled and stood at a distance ¹⁹and said to Moses, "You speak to us, and we will listen, but do not let God speak to us, lest we die." ²⁰Moses said to the people, "Do not be afraid, for God has come only to test you and to put the fear of him upon you so that you do not sin."

Psalm 19 (G61/690, N630, P166/167, SH559, UM750)

The heavens are telling the glory of God,
    and the firmament proclaims his handiwork.
²Day to day pours forth speech,
    and night to night declares knowledge.
³There is no speech, nor are there words;
    their voice is not heard;
⁴yet their voice goes out through all the earth
    and their words to the end of the world.
In the heavens he has set a tent for the sun,
⁵which comes out like a bridegroom from his wedding canopy,
    and like a strong man runs its course with joy.
⁶Its rising is from the end of the heavens
    and its circuit to the end of them,
    and nothing is hid from its heat.
⁷The law of the LORD is perfect,
    reviving the soul;
the decrees of the LORD are sure,
    making wise the simple;
⁸the precepts of the LORD are right,
    rejoicing the heart;
the commandment of the LORD is clear,
    enlightening the eyes;
⁹the fear of the LORD is pure,
    enduring forever;
the ordinances of the LORD are true
    and righteous altogether.
¹⁰More to be desired are they than gold,
    even much fine gold;
sweeter also than honey
    and drippings of the honeycomb.
¹¹Moreover, by them is your servant warned;
    in keeping them there is great reward.
¹²But who can detect one's own errors?
    Clear me from hidden faults.
¹³Keep back your servant also from the insolent;
    do not let them have dominion over me.

Then I shall be blameless
    and innocent of great transgression.
¹⁴Let the words of my mouth and the meditation of my heart
    be acceptable to you,
    O LORD, my rock and my redeemer.

Philippians 3:4b-14

⁴ᵇIf anyone else has reason to be confident in the flesh, I have more: ⁵circumcised on the eighth day, a member of the people of Israel, of the tribe of Benjamin, a Hebrew born of Hebrews; as to the law, a Pharisee; ⁶as to zeal, a persecutor of the church; as to righteousness under the law, blameless.

⁷Yet whatever gains I had, these I have come to regard as loss because of Christ. ⁸More than that, I regard everything as loss because of the surpassing value of knowing Christ Jesus my Lord. For his sake I have suffered the loss of all things, and I regard them as rubbish, in order that I may gain Christ ⁹and be found in him, not having a righteousness of my own that comes from the law but one that comes through faith in Christ, the righteousness from God based on faith. ¹⁰I want to know Christ and the power of his resurrection and the sharing of his sufferings by becoming like him in his death, ¹¹if somehow I may attain the resurrection from the dead.

¹²Not that I have already obtained this or have already reached the goal, but I press on to lay hold of that for which Christ has laid hold of me. ¹³Brothers and sisters, I do not consider that I have laid hold of it, but one thing I have laid hold of: forgetting what lies behind and straining forward to what lies ahead, ¹⁴I press on toward the goal, toward the prize of the heavenly call of God in Christ Jesus.

Matthew 21:33-46

³³"Listen to another parable. There was a landowner who planted a vineyard, put a fence around it, dug a winepress in it, and built a watchtower. Then he leased it to tenants and went away. ³⁴When the harvest time had come, he sent his slaves to the tenants to collect his produce. ³⁵But the tenants seized his slaves and beat one, killed another, and stoned another. ³⁶Again he sent other slaves, more than the first, and they treated them in the same way. ³⁷Then he sent his son to them, saying, 'They will respect my son.' ³⁸But when the tenants saw the son, they said to themselves, 'This is the heir; come, let us kill him and get his inheritance.' ³⁹So they seized him, threw him out of the vineyard, and killed him. ⁴⁰Now when the owner of the vineyard comes, what will he do to those tenants?" ⁴¹They said to him, "He will put those wretches to a miserable death and lease the vineyard to other tenants who will give him the produce at the harvest time."

⁴²Jesus said to them, "Have you never read in the scriptures:
'The stone that the builders rejected
    has become the cornerstone;
    this was the Lord's doing,
    and it is amazing in our eyes'?

⁴³"Therefore I tell you, the kingdom of God will be taken away from you and given to a people that produces its fruits. ⁴⁴The one who falls on this stone will be broken to pieces, and it will crush anyone on whom it falls."

⁴⁵When the chief priests and the Pharisees heard his parables, they realized that he was speaking about them. ⁴⁶They wanted to arrest him, but they feared the crowds, because they regarded him as a prophet.

Primary Hymns and Songs for the Day

"Jesus Shall Reign" (Pss, Phil) (O)
   C95, CG158, E544, EL434, G265, N300, P423, SA258, SH209, UM157 (PD), VU330
          C95   Descant
          H-3   Hbl-29; Chr-117; Desc-31; Org-31
          S-1   #100-103. Various treatments.
"The Church's One Foundation" (Phil, Matt) (O)
   C272, CG246, E525, EL654, G321, N386, P442, SH233, UM545/546, VU332 (Fr.)
          H-3   Hbl-94; Chr-180; Desc-16; Org-9
          S-1   #25-26. Descant and harmonization
"Spirit, Spirit of Gentleness" (Exod)
   C249, EL396, G291, N286, P319, S2120, VU375
"How Great Thou Art" (Pss)
   AH4015, C33, CG323, EL856, G625, N35, P467, SA49, SH14, UM77, VU238 (Fr.)
          H-3   Chr-103; Org-105
          S-1   #163. Harmonization
"Pues Si Vivimos" ("When We Are Living") (Phil)
   C536, CG265, EL639, G822, N499, P400, SH299, UM356, VU581
"O God, We Bear the Imprint of Your Face" (Phil)
   C681, G759, N585, P385
"Fight the Good Fight" (Phil)
   E552, G846, P307 (PD), SA952, VU674
"My Hope Is Built" (Phil, Matt)
   AH4105, C537, CG590, EL596/597, G353, N403, P379, SA662, SH324, UM368 (PD)
          H-3   Chr-191
          S-2   #171-172. Trumpet and vocal descants
"I Come with Joy" (Matt, Comm.)
   C420, CG456, E304, EL482, G515, N349, P507, SH682, UM617, VU477
"My Song Is Love Unknown" (Matt)
   E458, EL343, G209, N222, P76, S2083, SA149, VU143
"Christ Is Made the Sure Foundation" (Matt) (C)
   C275, E518, EL645, G394, P416, SA246, SH225, UM559, VU325
          H-3   Chr-49; Desc-103; Org-180
          S-1   #346. Descant
   CG248, N400, P417

Additional Hymn Suggestions

"Every Time I Feel the Spirit" (Exod)
   C592, G66, N282, P315, UM404
"Jesus Calls Us" (Exod, Phil)
   C337, CG486, E549/550, EL696, G720, N171/172, SA653, SH604, UM398, VU562
"How Firm a Foundation" (Exod, Matt)
   C618, CG425, E636/637, EL796, G463, N407, P361, SA804, SH291, UM529 (PD), VU660
"Cantemos al Señor" ("Let's Sing unto the Lord") (Pss)
   C60, EL555, G669, N39, SH432, UM149
"Jesus, the Very Thought of Thee" (Phil)
   C102, CG386, E642, EL754, G629, N507, P310, SA85, UM175
"When I Survey the Wondrous Cross" (Phil)
   C195, CG186, E474, EL803, G223/224, N224, P100/101, SA208, SH163/164, UM298/299, VU149 (Fr.)
"Canto de Esperanza" ("Song of Hope") (Phil) (C)
   G765, P432, S2186, SH721, VU424
"Healer of Our Every Ill" (Phil)
   C506, EL612, G795, S2213, SH339, VU619
"O Love, How Deep" (Matt)
   E448/449, EL322, G618, N209, P83, SH115, UM267, VU348
"All Who Love and Serve Your City" (Matt)
   C670, E570/571, EL724, G351, P413, UM433
"We Are God's People" (Matt)
   CG255, S2220
"Built on a Rock" (Matt)
   C273, CG247, EL652, WS3147

Additional Contemporary and Modern Suggestions

"Honor and Praise" 1867485 (Exod)
"I Will Call upon the Lord" 11263 (Pss)
   G621, S2002
"Awesome God" 41099 (Pss)
   G616, S2040
"God of Wonders" 3118757 (Pss)
   SH9, WS3034
"Praise Him" 684779 (Pss)
"All Heaven Declares" 120556 (Pss)
"The Heavens Shall Declare" 904033 (Pss)
"Knowing You" 1045238 (Phil)
"In the Secret" 1810119 (Phil)
"The Wonderful Cross" 3148435 (Phil)
"Something Beautiful" 18060 (Phil)
"He Who Began a Good Work in You" 15238 (Phil)
"Sanctuary" 24140 (Phil)
   G701, S2164, SH265
"Guide My Feet" (Phil)
   CG637, G741, N497, P354, S2208, SH54
"Come to the Table" 675056 (Phil, Comm.)
   EL481, S2264
"Cornerstone" 6158927 (Phil, Matt)
"We Believe" 6367165 (Matt)
"Grace Alone" 2335524 (Phil, Matt)
   CG43, S2162, SA699.
"Praise the Name of Jesus" 12712 (Matt)

Vocal Solos

"The Heavens Declare His Glory" (Pss)
   V-8   p. 248a
"Into My Heart" (Phil)
   V-8   p. 121
"How Firm a Foundation" (Phil, Mark)
   V-6   p. 31

Anthems

"Teach Me, O Lord" (Exod)
Thomas Attwood; ECS Publishing 50-3425
SATB, keyboard (https://bit.ly/ECS-50-3425)

"The Meditations of My Heart" (Pss)
Elaine Hagenberg; Beckenhorst BP2134
SATB, piano (https://bit.ly/BP2134)

Other Suggestions

Visuals: flags, artifacts of nations, breads of the world, globe
   O   Clay tablets, Ten Commandments, lightning, trumpet, mountain
   P   Tent, wedding canopy, planets/stars/space, gold, rock, honey/comb
   E   "Yet," rubbish, portrait of Christ, resurrection, crown of laurel leaves, trophy
   G   Vineyard, wine press, building cornerstone, fruit
Call to Worship: C119, CG79, E56, EL257, G88, N116, P9, SA117, SH73, UM211, VU1(Fr.), stanza 3. "O Come, O Come, Emmanuel" (Exod)
Sung Creed: "We Believe" 6367165 (Matt)
Offering Prayer: WSL156. "Almighty God, you gave." (Exod)
Alternate Lessons: Isa 5:1-7; Ps 80:7-15 (See p. 3.)
Theme Ideas: Covenant, Creation, Discipleship / Following God, Faithfulness, God: Faithfulness, God: Kingdom of God, God: Word of God, Jesus: Cornerstone, Praise, Sin and Forgiveness

Exodus 32:1-14

When the people saw that Moses delayed to come down from the mountain, the people gathered around Aaron and said to him, "Come, make gods for us, who shall go before us; as for this Moses, the man who brought us up out of the land of Egypt, we do not know what has become of him." ²Aaron said to them, "Take off the gold rings that are on the ears of your wives, your sons, and your daughters and bring them to me." ³So all the people took off the gold rings from their ears and brought them to Aaron. ⁴He took these from them, formed them in a mold, and cast an image of a calf, and they said, "These are your gods, O Israel, who brought you up out of the land of Egypt!" ⁵When Aaron saw this, he built an altar before it, and Aaron made a proclamation and said, "Tomorrow shall be a festival to the Lord." ⁶They rose early the next day and offered burnt offerings and brought sacrifices of well-being, and the people sat down to eat and drink and rose up to revel.

⁷The Lord said to Moses, "Go down at once! Your people, whom you brought up out of the land of Egypt, have acted perversely; ⁸they have been quick to turn aside from the way that I commanded them; they have cast for themselves an image of a calf and have worshiped it and sacrificed to it and said, 'These are your gods, O Israel, who brought you up out of the land of Egypt!'" ⁹The Lord said to Moses, "I have seen this people, how stiff-necked they are. ¹⁰Now let me alone so that my wrath may burn hot against them and I may consume them, and of you I will make a great nation."

¹¹But Moses implored the Lord his God and said, "O Lord, why does your wrath burn hot against your people, whom you brought out of the land of Egypt with great power and with a mighty hand? ¹²Why should the Egyptians say, 'It was with evil intent that he brought them out to kill them in the mountains and to consume them from the face of the earth'? Turn from your fierce wrath; change your mind and do not bring disaster on your people. ¹³Remember Abraham, Isaac, and Israel, your servants, how you swore to them by your own self, saying to them, 'I will multiply your descendants like the stars of heaven, and all this land that I have promised I will give to your descendants, and they shall inherit it forever.'" ¹⁴And the Lord changed his mind about the disaster that he planned to bring on his people.

Psalm 106:1-6, 19-23 (G60, N692, UM829)

Praise the Lord!
   O give thanks to the Lord, for he is good,
   for his steadfast love endures forever.
²Who can utter the mighty doings of the Lord
   or declare all his praise?
³Happy are those who observe justice,
   who do righteousness at all times.
⁴Remember us, O Lord, when you show favor to your people;
   help us when you deliver them,
⁵that we may see the prosperity of your chosen ones,
   that we may rejoice in the gladness of your nation,
   that we may glory in your heritage.
⁶Both we and our ancestors have sinned;
   we have committed iniquity, have done wickedly.
. . . .
¹⁹They made a calf at Horeb
   and worshiped a cast image.
²⁰They exchanged the glory of God
   for the image of an ox that eats grass.
²¹They forgot God, their Savior,
   who had done great things in Egypt,
²²wondrous works in the land of Ham,
   and awesome deeds by the Red Sea.
²³Therefore he said he would destroy them—
   had not Moses, his chosen one,
stood in the breach before him,
   to turn away his wrath from destroying them.

Philippians 4:1-9

Therefore, my brothers and sisters, whom I love and long for, my joy and crown, stand firm in the Lord in this way, my beloved.

²I urge Euodia and I urge Syntyche to be of the same mind in the Lord. ³Yes, and I ask you also, my loyal companion, help these women, for they have struggled beside me in the work of the gospel, together with Clement and the rest of my coworkers, whose names are in the book of life.

⁴Rejoice in the Lord always; again I will say, Rejoice. ⁵Let your gentleness be known to everyone. The Lord is near. ⁶Do not be anxious about anything, but in everything by prayer and supplication with thanksgiving let your requests be made known to God. ⁷And the peace of God, which surpasses all understanding, will guard your hearts and your minds in Christ Jesus.

⁸Finally, brothers and sisters, whatever is true, whatever is honorable, whatever is just, whatever is pure, whatever is pleasing, whatever is commendable, if there is any excellence and if there is anything worthy of praise, think about these things. ⁹As for the things that you have learned and received and heard and noticed in me, do them, and the God of peace will be with you.

Matthew 22:1-14

Once more Jesus spoke to them in parables, saying: ²"The kingdom of heaven may be compared to a king who gave a wedding banquet for his son. ³He sent his slaves to call those who had been invited to the wedding banquet, but they would not come. ⁴Again he sent other slaves, saying, 'Tell those who have been invited: Look, I have prepared my dinner, my oxen and my fat calves have been slaughtered, and everything is ready; come to the wedding banquet.' ⁵But they made light of it and went away, one to his farm, another to his business, ⁶while the rest seized his slaves, mistreated them, and killed them. ⁷The king was enraged. He sent his troops, destroyed those murderers, and burned their city. ⁸Then he said to his slaves, 'The wedding is ready, but those invited were not worthy. ⁹Go therefore into the main streets, and invite everyone you find to the wedding banquet.' ¹⁰Those slaves went out into the streets and gathered all whom they found, both good and bad, so the wedding hall was filled with guests.

¹¹"But when the king came in to see the guests, he noticed a man there who was not wearing a wedding robe, ¹²and he said to him, 'Friend, how did you get in here without a wedding robe?' And he was speechless. ¹³Then the king said to the attendants, 'Bind him hand and foot, and throw him into the outer darkness, where there will be weeping and gnashing of teeth.' ¹⁴For many are called, but few are chosen."

Primary Hymns and Songs for the Day

"Rejoice, Ye Pure in Heart" (Phil) (O)
  C15, CG312, E556, EL873, G804, N55, P145, UM160
      H-3   Hbl-17, 90; Chr-166; Desc-73; Org-85
      S-1   #228. Descant
  E557, EL874, N71, P146, UM161
      H-3   Chr-166; Desc-102
"Great Is Thy Faithfulness" (Exod)
  AH4011, C86, CG48, EL733, G39, N423, P276, SA26, SH48,
  UM140, VU288
      H-3   Chr-87; Desc-39; Org-39
      S-2   #59. Piano arrangement
"I Want Jesus to Walk with Me" (Phil)
  C627, CG635, EL325, G775, N490, P363, SH135, UM521
      H-3   Chr-108
"Sanctuary" 24140 (Phil)
  G701, S2164, SH265
"O for a Closer Walk with God" (Phil)
  CG679, E684, G739, N450, P396, SA612
"Come, Ye Sinners, Poor and Needy" (Matt)
  CG471, G415, UM340
      S-1   #283. Choral harmonization
"I'm Gonna Eat at the Welcome Table" (Matt)
  C424, G770
"Where Cross the Crowded Ways of Life" (Matt) (C)
  C665, CG657, E609, EL719, G343, N543, UM427, VU681
      H-3   Chr-178, 180; Org-44
      S-1   #141-143 Various treatments

Additional Hymn Suggestions

"Sing Praise to God Who Reigns Above" (Exod)
  C6, CG315, EL871, G645, N6, P483, UM126 (PD), VU216
"There's a Wideness in God's Mercy" (Exod, Matt)
  C73, CG41, E470, EL587/88G435, N23, P298, SH526,
  UM121, VU271
"Jesus Calls Us" (Exod, Matt)
  C337, CG486, E549/550, EL696, G720, N171/172, SA653,
  SH604, UM398, VU562
"Christ, Whose Glory Fills the Skies" (Phil)
  EL553, G662, P462/463, SA249, UM173, VU336
"Take Time to Be Holy" (Phil)
  C572, SA790, UM395 (PD), VU672
"What a Friend We Have in Jesus" (Phil)
  C585, CG409, EL742, G465, N506, P403, SA795, SH585/586,
  UM526 (PD), VU661
"Rejoice, the Lord Is King" (Phil) (C)
  C699, CG215, E481, EL430, G363, N303, P155, SA271,
  SH213, UM715/716, VU213
"My Life Flows On" (Phil)
  C619, CG592, EL763, G821, N476, S2212, SA663, VU716
"Lord of All Hopefulness" (Phil, Matt)
  CG678, E482, EL765, G683, S2197, SA772, SH464
"Come, My Way, My Truth, My Life" (Matt)
  E487, EL816, N331, UM164 (PD), VU628
"O Jesus, I Have Promised" (Matt)
  C612, E655, EL810, G724/725, N493, P388/389, SA613,
  SH623, UM396 (PD), VU120
"Softly and Tenderly Jesus Is Calling" (Matt)
  C340, CG474, EL608 (PD), G418, N449, SA435, SH601, UM348
"Trust and Obey" (Matt)
  C556, CG509, SA690, SH636, UM467 (PD)
"Together We Serve" (Matt)
  G767, S2175
"Gather Us In" (Matt)
  C284, EL532, G401, S2236, SH393
"Jesus, Thou Joy of Loving Hearts" (Matt)
  C101, CG394, E649, G494, N329, P510, SA340, SH6688,
  VU472
"As We Gather at Your Table" (Matt, Comm.)
  EL522, N332, S2268, SH411, VU457

Additional Contemporary and Modern Suggestions

"Perdón, Señor" ("Forgive Us, Lord") 3409466 (Exod)
  G431, S2134, SH505
"God Is So Good" 4956994 (Pss)
  G658, S2056, SH461
"Give Thanks" (Pss)
  C528, CG373, G647, S2036, SA364, SH489
"God Is Good All the Time" 1729073 (Pss)
"Hallelujah" ("Your Love Is Amazing") 3091812 (Pss)
"You Are Good" 3383788 (Pss)
  AH4018, SH455, WS3014
"Your Love, Oh Lord" 1894255 (Pss)
"I Will Enter His Gates" 1493 (Phil)
"I've Got Peace Like a River" (Phil)
  C530, G623, N478, P368, S2145, SH276, VU577
"Lord, Listen to Your Children Praying" 22829 (Phil)
  C305, CG389, G469, S2193, SH577, VU400
"Wait for the Lord" (Phil)
  CG644, EL262, G90, SH580, VU22, WS3049
"You Never Let Go" 4674166 (Phil)
"I Will Rise" 5183450 (Phil)
"I Will Give Thanks" 6266091 (Phil)
"Let the Peace of God Reign" 1839987 (Phil)
"Give Us Your Peace" 5767807 (Phil)
"Surrender" 3033179 (Matt)
"Come to the Table" 675056 (Matt, Comm.)
"Come to the Table of Grace" 7034746 (Matt, Comm.)
  G507, WS3168

Vocal Solos

"A Song of Trust" (Phil)
  V-4   p. 20
"Chosen of the Lord" (Matt)
  V-8   p. 34

Anthems

"As We Gather At Your Table" (Matt, Comm.)
K. Lee Scott; Augsburg 9780800678081
SAB, organ (https://bit.ly/7808-7)

"I Want Jesus to Walk with Me" (Phil)
Arr. Christopher Aspaas; Augsburg 9781506465371
SATB *divisi, a cappella* (https://bit.ly/AF-65371)

Other Suggestions

Visuals:
  O/P   Gold, jewelry, golden calf, hands folded/lifted in
            prayer
  E   Praying hands, "Rejoice in the Lord always," "Again I
            say, Rejoice"
  G   Wedding garments, other wedding items (invitations,
            rings, flowers)
Introit or Sung Blessing: WS3125. "Peace for the Children" (Phil)
Call to Prayer: EL538, G466, S2157. "Come and Fill Our Hearts"
  (Phil)
Prayer: C547, UM329, UM392, or UM459 (Phil)
Response: G654, S2195, SH316. "In the Lord I'll Be Ever
  Thankful" (Pss)
Blessing: Phil 4:8-9
Response: C444, UM668. "Let Us Now Depart in Your Peace" (Phil)
Alternate Lessons: Isa 25:1-9; Ps 23 (See p. 3.)
Theme Ideas: God: Kingdom of God, God: Peace of God, Jesus:
  Mind of Christ, Preparation, Priorities, Sin and Forgiveness,
  Thanksgiving / Gratitude

Exodus 33:12-23

[12]Moses said to the Lord, "See, you have said to me, 'Bring up this people,' but you have not let me know whom you will send with me. Yet you have said, 'I know you by name, and you have also found favor in my sight.' [13]Now if I have found favor in your sight, please show me your ways, so that I may know you and find favor in your sight. Consider, too, that this nation is your people." [14]He said, "My presence will go with you, and I will give you rest." [15]And he said to him, "If your presence will not go, do not bring us up from here. [16]For how shall it be known that I have found favor in your sight, I and your people, unless you go with us? In this way, we shall be distinct, I and your people, from every people on the face of the earth."

[17]The Lord said to Moses, "I will also do this thing that you have asked, for you have found favor in my sight, and I know you by name." [18]Moses said, "Please show me your glory." [19]And he said, "I will make all my goodness pass before you and will proclaim before you the name, 'The Lord,' and I will be gracious to whom I will be gracious and will show mercy on whom I will show mercy." [20]But," he said, "you cannot see my face, for no one shall see me and live." [21]And the Lord continued, "See, there is a place by me where you shall stand on the rock, [22]and while my glory passes by I will put you in a cleft of the rock, and I will cover you with my hand until I have passed by; [23]then I will take away my hand, and you shall see my back, but my face shall not be seen."

Psalm 99 (G57, N687, UM819)

The Lord is king; let the peoples tremble!
    He sits enthroned upon the cherubim; let the earth quake!
[2]The Lord is great in Zion;
    he is exalted over all the peoples.
[3]Let them praise your great and awesome name.
    Holy is he!
[4]Mighty King, lover of justice,
    you have established equity;
you have executed justice
    and righteousness in Jacob.
[5]Extol the Lord our God;
    worship at his footstool.
    Holy is he!
[6]Moses and Aaron were among his priests,
    Samuel also was among those who called on his name.
    They cried to the Lord, and he answered them.
[7]He spoke to them in the pillar of cloud;
    they kept his decrees
    and the statutes that he gave them.
[8]O Lord our God, you answered them;
    you were a forgiving God to them
    but an avenger of their wrongdoings.
[9]Extol the Lord our God,
    and worship at his holy mountain,
    for the Lord our God is holy.

1 Thessalonians 1:1-10

Paul, Silvanus, and Timothy,
    To the church of the Thessalonians in God the Father and the Lord Jesus Christ:
    Grace to you and peace.
[2]We always give thanks to God for all of you and mention you in our prayers, constantly [3]remembering before our God and Father your work of faith and labor of love and steadfastness of hope in our Lord Jesus Christ. [4]For we know, brothers and sisters beloved by God, that he has chosen you, [5]because our message of the gospel came to you not in word only but also in power and in the Holy Spirit and with full conviction; just as you know what kind of persons we proved to be among you for your sake. [6]And you became imitators of us and of the Lord, for in spite of persecution you received the word with joy from the Holy Spirit, [7]so that you became an example to all the believers in Macedonia and in Achaia. [8]For the word of the Lord has sounded forth from you not only in Macedonia and Achaia but in every place your faith in God has become known, so that we have no need to speak about it. [9]For they report about us what kind of welcome we had among you and how you turned to God from idols to serve a living and true God [10]and to wait for his Son from heaven, whom he raised from the dead—Jesus, who rescues us from the coming wrath.

Matthew 22:15-22

[15]Then the Pharisees went and plotted to entrap him in what he said. [16]So they sent their disciples to him, along with the Herodians, saying, "Teacher, we know that you are sincere, and teach the way of God in accordance with truth, and show deference to no one, for you do not regard people with partiality. [17]Tell us, then, what you think. Is it lawful to pay taxes to Caesar or not?" [18]But Jesus, aware of their malice, said, "Why are you putting me to the test, you hypocrites? [19]Show me the coin used for the tax." And they brought him a denarius. [20]Then he said to them, "Whose head is this and whose title?" [21]They answered, "Caesar's." Then he said to them, "Give therefore to Caesar the things that are Caesar's and to God the things that are God's." [22]When they heard this, they were amazed, and they left him and went away.

Primary Hymns and Songs for the Day

"Immortal, Invisible, God Only Wise" (Exod, 1 Thess) (O)
C66, CG58, E423, EL834, G12, N1, P263, SA37, UM103 (PD), VU264
- H-3   Hbl-15, 71; Chr-65; Desc-93; Org-135
- S-1   #300. Harmonization

"Rock of Ages, Cleft for Me" (Exod)
C214, E685, EL623, G438, N596, SA671, SH301, UM361
- H-3   Chr-167; Org-164
- S-2   #179. Harmonization

"Come, Thou Fount of Every Blessing" (Exod)
AH4086, C16, CG295/559, E686, EL807, G475, N459, P356, SA830, SH394, UM400 (PD), VU559
- H-3   Chr-57; Desc-79; Org-96
- S-1   #244. Descant

"Near to the Heart of God" (Exod)
C581, CG383, G824, P527, UM472 (PD)

"Glorious Things of Thee Are Spoken" (Exod, Pss)
C709, CG282, E522/523, EL647, G81, N307, P446, SA535, UM731 (PD)
- H-3   Hbl-61; Chr-72; Desc-17; Org-11
- S-1   #27. Descant
-        #28. Harmonization in F major

"Holy, Holy, Holy! Lord God Almighty" (1 Thess)
C4, CG1, E362, EL413, G1, N277, P138, SA31, SH450, UM64/65, VU315
- N277   Descant
- C4   Descant
- H-3   Hbl-68; Chr-99; Desc-80; Org-97
- S-1   #245-248. Various treatments.

"Where Cross the Crowded Ways of Life" (Matt)
C665, CG657, E609, EL719, G343, N543, UM427, VU681
- H-3   Chr-178, 180; Org-44
- S-1   #141-143 Various treatments

"God of Grace and God of Glory" (Matt)
C464, CG285, E594/595, EL705, G307, N436, P420, SA814, SH250, UM577, VU686
- H-3   Hbl-25, 51; Chr-89; Desc-26; Org-23
- S-1   #76-77. Descant and harmonization

"God, Whose Giving Knows No Ending" (Matt)
C606, CG671, G716, N565, P422
- H-3   Hbl-14, 64; Chr-132, 203
- S-2   #22. Descant

"Lord, Dismiss Us with Thy Blessing" (Exod) (C)
C439, E344, EL545, G546, N77, P538, UM671 (PD), VU425
- H-3   Chr-75, 116, 130; Desc-98; Org-151

"God Be with You Till We Meet Again" (Exod, Matt) (C)
C434, CG523, EL536, G541/G542, N81, P540, SA1027, UM672/UM673, VU422/VU423
- H-3   Chr-74
- S-2   #149. Descant

Additional Hymn Suggestions

"The God of Abraham Praise" (Exod)
C24, CG45, E401, EL831, G49, N24, P488, SH50, UM116 (PD), VU255

"Sing Praise to God Who Reigns Above" (Exod)
C6, CG315, EL871, G645, N6, P483, UM126 (PD), VU216

"Pass Me Not, O Gentle Savior" (Exod)
AH4107, N551, SA782, UM351 (PD), VU665

"Abide with Me" (Exod)
C636, CG543, E662, EL629, G836, N99, P543, SA529, SH475, UM700 (PD), VU436

"How Firm a Foundation" (Exod, 1 Thess) (C)
C618, CG425, E636/637, EL796, G463, N407, P361, SA804, SH291, UM529 (PD), VU660

"Rejoice in God's Saints" (1 Thess)
C476, EL418, G732, UM708

"O, How I Love Jesus" (1 Thess, Matt)
AH4020, C99, CG601, N52, SA94, UM170 (PD)

"Jesus Shall Reign" (Matt)
C95, CG158, E544, EL434, G265, N300, P423, SA258, SH209, UM157 (PD), VU330

"Lord of the Dance" (Matt)
G157, P302, SA141, UM261, VU352

"All Who Love and Serve Your City" (Matt)
C670, E570/571, EL724, G351, P413, UM433

"What Does the Lord Require" (Matt)
C659, E605, P405, UM441

Additional Contemporary and Modern Suggestions

"I Love You, Lord" 25266 (Exod)
CG362, G627, S2068, SA369, SH417

"El-Shaddai" 26856 (Exod, Pss)

"Psalm 62" 5040902 (Exod, Pss)

"Awesome God" 41099 (Exod, Pss)
G616, S2040

"Step by Step" 696994 (Exod, Matt)
CG495, G743, WS3004

"I Exalt You" 17803 (Pss)

"I Extol You" 18307 (Pss)

"Awesome Is the Lord Most High" 4674159 (Pss)

"He Is Exalted" 17827 (Pss, Matt)
AH4082, CG342, S2070, SH423

"Lord, Be Glorified" 26368 (Pss, Matt)
EL744, G468, S2150, SA593, SH420

"Came to My Rescue" 4705190 (1 Thess)

"Santo, Santo, Santo" ("Holy, Holy, Holy") (1 Thess)
C111, CG3, EL473, G595, N793, S2007, SH452

"More Precious than Silver" 11335 (Matt)

"What Does the Lord Require of You" 456859 (Matt)
C661, CG690, G70, S2174, VU701

"Make Me a Servant" 33131 (Matt)
CG651, S2176

"Take This Life" 2563365 (Matt, Stewardship)

"Glory To God Forever" 5384338 (Matt)

Vocal Solos

"God, Our Ever Faithful Shepherd" (Exod, Pss)
- V-4   p. 15

"Man of Your Word" (Phil, Matt)
- V-9   p. 71

Anthems

"Rock of Ages" (Exod)
Arr. Lloyd Larson; Hope C6223
SATB, piano (https://bit.ly/H-C6223)

"Rejoice, the Lord Is King!" (Pss)
Arr. Dan Forrest; Beckenhorst BP2179
SATB, piano, opt. string quartet (https://bit.ly/BP-2179)

Other Suggestions

Visuals:
- **O**   Rock, cleft rock, hand
- **P**   Earthquake, cloud, footstool
- **E**   Symbols of the Holy Spirit, Trinity
- **G**   Array of coins around an empty offering plate, cross

Call to Worship: EL819, G388, S2274, SH405. *"Uyai Mose"* ("Come, All You People") (Pss)

Prayer: C31, C52, or UM152 (Exod)

Response: C380, UM588. "All Things Come of Thee" (Matt)

Alternate Lessons: Isa 45:1-7; Ps 96:1-9, (10-13) (See p. 3.)

Theme Ideas: Faithfulness, God: Glory of God, God: Presence, Priorities, Stewardship

Deuteronomy 34:1-12

The Lord said to Moses, "Cut two tablets of stone like the former ones, and I will write on the tablets the words that were on the former tablets, which you broke. [2]Be ready in the morning and come up in the morning to Mount Sinai and present yourself there to me on the top of the mountain. [3]No one shall come up with you, and do not let anyone be seen throughout all the mountain, and do not let flocks or herds graze in front of that mountain." [4]So Moses cut two tablets of stone like the former ones, and he rose early in the morning and went up on Mount Sinai, as the Lord had commanded him, and took in his hand the two tablets of stone. [5]The Lord descended in the cloud and stood with him there and proclaimed the name, "The Lord." [6]The Lord passed before him and proclaimed,

"The Lord, the Lord,
a God merciful and gracious,
slow to anger,
and abounding in steadfast love and faithfulness,
[7]keeping steadfast love for the thousandth generation,
forgiving iniquity and transgression and sin,
yet by no means clearing the guilty,
but visiting the iniquity of the parents
upon the children
and the children's children
to the third and the fourth generation."

[8]And Moses quickly bowed down to the ground and worshiped. [9]He said, "If now I have found favor in your sight, my Lord, I pray, let my Lord go with us. Although this is a stiff-necked people, pardon our iniquity and our sin, and take us for your inheritance."

[10]He said, "I hereby make a covenant. Before all your people I will perform marvels, such as have not been done in all the earth or in any nation, and all the people among whom you live shall see the work of the Lord, for it is an awesome thing that I will do with you.

[11]"Observe what I command you today. See, I will drive out before you the Amorites, the Canaanites, the Hittites, the Perizzites, the Hivites, and the Jebusites. [12]Take care not to make a covenant with the inhabitants of the land to which you are going, or it will become a snare among you.

Psalm 90:1-6, 13-17 (N680, P211, UM809)

Lord, you have been our dwelling place
   in all generations.
[2]Before the mountains were brought forth
   or ever you had formed the earth and the world,
   from everlasting to everlasting you are God.
[3]You turn us back to dust
   and say, "Turn back, you mortals."
[4]For a thousand years in your sight
   are like yesterday when it is past
   or like a watch in the night.
[5]You sweep them away; they are like a dream,
   like grass that is renewed in the morning;
[6]in the morning it flourishes and is renewed;
   in the evening it fades and withers.

. . . .

[13]Turn, O Lord! How long?
   Have compassion on your servants!
[14]Satisfy us in the morning with your steadfast love,
   so that we may rejoice and be glad all our days.
[15]Make us glad as many days as you have afflicted us
   and as many years as we have seen evil.
[16]Let your work be manifest to your servants
   and your glorious power to their children.
[17]Let the favor of the Lord our God be upon us
   and prosper for us the work of our hands—
   O prosper the work of our hands!

1 Thessalonians 2:1-8

You yourselves know, brothers and sisters, that our coming to you was not in vain, [2]but though we had already suffered and been shamefully mistreated at Philippi, as you know, we had courage in our God to declare to you the gospel of God in spite of great opposition. [3]For our appeal does not spring from deceit or impure motives or trickery, [4]but, just as we have been approved by God to be entrusted with the message of the gospel, even so we speak, not to please mortals but to please God, who tests our hearts. [5]As you know and as God is our witness, we never came with words of flattery or with a pretext for greed, [6]nor did we seek praise from mortals, whether from you or from others, [7]though we might have made demands as apostles of Christ. But we were gentle among you, like a nurse tenderly caring for her own children. [8]So deeply do we care for you that we are determined to share with you not only the gospel of God but also our own selves, because you have become very dear to us.

Matthew 22:34-46

[34]When the Pharisees heard that he had silenced the Sadducees, they gathered together, [35]and one of them, an expert in the law, asked him a question to test him. [36]"Teacher, which commandment in the law is the greatest?" [37]He said to him, " 'You shall love the Lord your God with all your heart and with all your soul and with all your mind.' [38]This is the greatest and first commandment. [39]And a second is like it: 'You shall love your neighbor as yourself.' [40]On these two commandments hang all the Law and the Prophets."

[41]Now while the Pharisees were gathered together, Jesus asked them this question: [42]"What do you think of the Messiah? Whose son is he?" They said to him, "The son of David." [43]He said to them, "How is it then that David by the Spirit calls him Lord, saying,

[44]'The Lord said to my Lord,
"Sit at my right hand,
   until I put your enemies under your feet" '?

[45]"If David thus calls him Lord, how can he be his son?" [46]No one was able to give him an answer, nor from that day did anyone dare to ask him any more questions.

Primary Hymns and Songs for the Day

"The God of Abraham Praise" (Deut) (O)
  C24, CG45, E401, EL831, G49, N24, P488, SH50, UM116
  (PD), VU255

"O God, Our Help in Ages Past" (Pss)
  C67, CG566, E680, EL632, G687, N25, P210, SA47, SH41,
  UM117 (PD), VU806
          H-3   Hbl-87; Chr-60, 143; Desc-93; Org-132
          S-1   #293-296. Various treatments

"Take My Life, and Let It Be" (1 Thess)
  C609, G697, P391
          H-3   Chr-34, 177; Desc-51; Org-53
          S-2   #78-80. Various treatments
  CG490, E707, EL583/EL685, N448, SA623, SH627/628,
  UM399 (PD), VU506

"Lord, Speak to Me" (1 Thess)
  CG503, EL676, G722, N531, SA773, SH557, UM463, VU589
          H-3   Hbl-75; Chr-131; Desc-22; Org-18
          S-1   #52. Descant

"God the Spirit, Guide and Guardian" (1 Thess)
  C450, G303, N355, P523, UM648, VU514

Jesu, Jesu 3049039 (Matt)
          S-1   #63 Vocal part
  C600, CG656, E602, EL708, G203, N498, P367, SH155,
  UM432, VU593

"More Love to Thee, O Christ" (Matt) (C)
  C527, CG365, G828, N456, P359, UM453 (PD)
          H-3   Org-94

"Lord, I Want to Be a Christian" (Matt) (C)
  C589, CG507, G729, N454, P372 (PD), SH621, UM402
          H-3   Chr-130

Additional Hymn Suggestions

"I'll Praise My Maker While I've Breath" (Deut)
  C20, CG336, E429 (PD), G806, P253, UM60, VU867

"Go Down, Moses" (Deut)
  C663, E648, G52, N572, P334, SH28, UM448

"Swing Low, Sweet Chariot" (Deut)
  C643, G825, UM703

"Praise, My Soul, the King of Heaven" (Pss, 1 Thess)
  C23, CG337, E410, EL864/865, G619/620, P478/479, SA55,
  SH418, UM66 (PD), VU240

"The Care the Eagle Gives Her Young" (1 Thess)
  C76, N468, UVU269

"Blest Be the Tie That Binds" (1 Thess) (C)
  C433, CG267, EL656, G306, N393, P438, SA812, SH701,
  UM557 (PD), VU602

"God Be with You Till We Meet Again" (1 Thess) (C)
  C434, CG523, EL536, G541/542, N81, P540, SA1027,
  UM672/673, VU422/423

"O Master, Let Me Walk with Thee" (1 Thess, Matt) (C)
  C602, CG660, E659/E660, EL818, G738, N503, P357, SA667,
  SH612, UM430 (PD), VU560

"All Hail the Power of Jesus' Name" (Matt)
  C91/92, CG339/340, E450/451, EL634, G263, N304,
  P142/143, SA73, SH207, UM154/155, VU334

"The Gift of Love" (Matt)
  C526, CG440, G693, P335, UM408, VU372

"Spirit of God, Descend upon My Heart" (Matt)
  C265, CG243, EL800, G688, N290, P326, SA290, SH277,
  UM500 (PD), VU378

"Where Charity and Love Prevail" (Matt)
  CG264, E581, EL359, G316, N396, SH271, UM549

"Lord, Whose Love Through Humble Service" (Matt)
  C461, CG650, E610, EL712, P427, SH239, UM581

"Healer of Our Every Ill" (Matt)
  C506, EL612, G795, S2213, SH339, VU619

"In Remembrance of Me" 25156 (Matt, Comm.)
  C403, CG462, G521, S2254, SH667

Additional Contemporary and Modern Suggestions

"Oh, I Know the Lord's Laid His Hands on Me" (Deut)
  S2139

"The Steadfast Love of the Lord" 21590 (Pss)

"One Thing Remains" 5508444 (Pss)

"How Great Are You, Lord" 2888576 (Pss)

"Beautiful Savior" 2492216 (Pss)

"Our God Saves" 4972837 (Pss)

"Fill Us with Your Love, O Lord" (Pss)
  WS3005

"Everlasting God" 4556538 (Pss)

"I Sing Praises to Your Name" 17061 (Matt)

"Jesus, Name above All Names" 21291 (Matt)

"To Know You More" 1767420 (Matt)

"More Like You" 2145051 (Matt)

"The Family Prayer Song" 1680466 (Matt)

"Make Me a Channel of Your Peace" 6399315 (Matt)

"No Sweeter Name" 4447984 (Matt)

"More Love, More Power" 60661 (Matt)

"You're Worthy of My Praise" 487976 (Matt)

"Refresh My Heart" 917518 (Matt)

"Let It Be Said of Us" 1855882 (Matt)

"Rise Up and Praise Him" 2060552 (Matt)

"Just Let Me Say" 1406413 (Matt)

"Take This Life" 2563365 (Matt)

"Purify My Heart" 1314323 (Matt)

"Love the Lord" 4572938 (Matt)

Vocal Solos

"Make Me a Channel of Your Peace" (Matt)
  V-3 (2)   p. 25
  V-3 (3)   p. 28

"The Gift of Love" (Matt)
  V-8   p. 120

Anthems

"Sacrifice of Praise" (1 Thess)
Joseph M. Martin; Lorenz 10/5164L
SATB, keyboard, opt brass and perc. (https://bit.ly/L-5164)

"Lord, I Want to Be a Christian" (Matt)
Jalonda Robertson; World Library (GIA) 001265
SATB, piano (https://bit.ly/G-1265)

Other Suggestions

Visuals:
  O   Portrait or bust of Moses, tears
  P   Tall grass, morning/evening, rejoicing, hands at
           work/praise
  E   Nurturing, caring for children
  G   Images of loving God, neighbor, self, worship, service
           to others, nurture, Matt 22:37, 38

Prayer: C571 or C443 (Matt) or UM268 (Deut)

Response: C523, EL642, G205, S2179. *Ubi Caritas* ("Live in
  Charity") (Matt)

Scripture Response: C56, CG341, E416, EL879, G14, P473, N28,
  SA14, SH21, UM92 (PD), VU226, stanza 4. "For the Beauty
  of the Earth" (Matt)

Benediction: G753, S2171, SA608, SH616 VU684. "Make Me a
  Channel of Your Peace" (Matt)

Alternate Lessons: Lev 19:1-2, 15-18; Ps 1 (See p. 3.)

Theme Ideas: Compassion, God: Glory of God, God: Providence /
  God our Help, Journey, Love / Great Commandment

Revelation 7:9-17

[9]After this I looked, and there was a great multitude that no one could count, from every nation, from all tribes and peoples and languages, standing before the throne and before the Lamb, robed in white, with palm branches in their hands. [10]They cried out in a loud voice, saying,

"Salvation belongs to our God who is seated on the throne
and to the Lamb!"

[11]And all the angels stood around the throne and around the elders and the four living creatures, and they fell on their faces before the throne and worshiped God, [12]singing,

"Amen! Blessing and glory and wisdom
and thanksgiving and honor
and power and might
be to our God forever and ever! Amen."

[13]Then one of the elders addressed me, saying, "Who are these, robed in white, and where have they come from?" [14]I said to him, "Sir, you are the one who knows." Then he said to me, "These are they who have come out of the great ordeal; they have washed their robes and made them white in the blood of the Lamb.

[15]For this reason they are before the throne of God
and worship him day and night within his temple,
and the one who is seated on the throne will shelter
them.
[16]They will hunger no more and thirst no more;
the sun will not strike them,
nor any scorching heat,
[17]for the Lamb at the center of the throne will be their
shepherd,
and he will guide them to springs of the water of life,
and God will wipe away every tear from their eyes."

Psalm 34:1-10, 22 (N644, P187, UM769)

I will bless the Lord at all times;
his praise shall continually be in my mouth.
[2]My soul makes its boast in the Lord;
let the humble hear and be glad.
[3]O magnify the Lord with me,
and let us exalt his name together.
[4]I sought the Lord, and he answered me
and delivered me from all my fears.
[5]Look to him, and be radiant,
so your faces shall never be ashamed.
[6]This poor soul cried and was heard by the Lord
and was saved from every trouble.
[7]The angel of the Lord encamps
around those who fear him and delivers them.
[8]O taste and see that the Lord is good;
happy are those who take refuge in him.
[9]O fear the Lord, you his holy ones,
for those who fear him have no want.
[10]The young lions suffer want and hunger,
but those who seek the Lord lack no good thing.
. . . .
[22]The Lord redeems the life of his servants;
none of those who take refuge in him will be condemned.

1 John 3:1-3

See what love the Father has given us, that we should be called children of God, and that is what we are. The reason the world does not know us is that it did not know him. [2]Beloved, we are God's children now; what we will be has not yet been revealed. What we do know is this: when he is revealed, we will be like him, for we will see him as he is. [3]And all who have this hope in him purify themselves, just as he is pure.

Matthew 5:1-12

When Jesus saw the crowds, he went up the mountain, and after he sat down, his disciples came to him. [2]And he began to speak and taught them, saying:
[3]"Blessed are the poor in spirit, for theirs is the kingdom of heaven.
[4]"Blessed are those who mourn, for they will be comforted.
[5]"Blessed are the meek, for they will inherit the earth.
[6]"Blessed are those who hunger and thirst for righteousness, for they will be filled.
[7]"Blessed are the merciful, for they will receive mercy.
[8]"Blessed are the pure in heart, for they will see God.
[9]"Blessed are the peacemakers, for they will be called children of God.
[10]"Blessed are those who are persecuted for the sake of righteousness, for theirs is the kingdom of heaven.
[11]"Blessed are you when people revile you and persecute you and utter all kinds of evil against you falsely on my account. [12]Rejoice and be glad, for your reward is great in heaven, for in the same way they persecuted the prophets who were before you."

Primary Hymns and Songs for the Day
"For All the Saints" (Rev, 1 John, Matt, All Saints) (O)
　　C637, CG567, E287, EL422, G326, N299, P526, SA253,
　　SH231, UM711 (PD), VU705
　　　　　H-3　　Hbl-58; Chr-65; Org-152
　　　　　S-1　　#314-318. Various treatments
"Ye Servants of God" (Rev) (O) or (C)
　　C110, CG420, E535, EL825 (PD), G299, N305, P477, SA97,
　　UM181 (PD), VU342
　　　　　C110　Descant (Ye Servants only)
　　　　　H-3　　Hbl-90, 105; Chr-221; Desc-49; Org-51
　　　　　S-2　　#71-74. Introduction and harmonizations
"We Praise You, O God, Our Redeemer" (Rev)
　　CG356, EL870, G612, N420, VU218
　　　　　H-3　　Chr-206; Desc-61; Org-68
　　　　　S-1　　#192-194. Various treatments
"Rejoice, Ye Pure in Heart" (Pss, 1 Thess)
　　C15, CG312, E556/557, EL873/874, G804, N55/71,
　　P145/146, UM160/161
　　　　　H-3　　Chr-166; Desc-102
"Bring Many Names" (1 John)
　　C10, G760, N11, S2047, VU268
"I Sing a Song of the Saints of God" (1 John, Matt, All Saints)
　　E293, G730, N295, P364, UM712 (PD)
　　　　　H-3　　Chr-107
　　　　　S-2　　#68. Flute descant
"Love Divine, All Loves Excelling" (Rev) (C)
　　C517, CG281, E657, EL631, G366, N43, P376, SA262,
　　SH353/354, UM384 (PD), VU333
　　　　　H-3　　Hbl-46; Chr-26, 134; Desc-53; Org-56
　　　　　S-1　　#168-171. Various treatments

Additional Hymn Suggestions
"This Is the Feast of Victory" (Rev, Comm.)
　　E417/418, G513, P594, UM638, VU904
"Rejoice in God's Saints" (Rev, All Saints)
　　C476, EL418, G732, UM708
"Come, We That Love the Lord" (Rev)
　　CG549, E392, N379, SA831, UM732, VU715
"Marching to Zion" (Rev)
　　C707, CG550, EL625, N382, SA831, UM733, VU714
"All Who Hunger" (Rev, Pss, Matt, Comm.)
　　C419, CG303, EL461, G509, S2126, VU460
"Taste and See" (Pss, Comm.)
　　EL493, G520, S2267, SH691
"Gather Us In" (Matt) (O)
　　C284, EL532, G401, S2236, SH393
"Take Up Thy Cross" (Matt)
　　E675, EL667, G718, N204, P393, SH605, UM415, VU561
"O for a World" (Matt)
　　C683, G372, N575, P386, VU697
"How Lovely, Lord, How Lovely" (All Saints)
　　C285, CG50, G402, P207, S2042, VU801 Ps 84
"For the Bread Which You Have Broken" (All Saints, Comm.)
　　C411, EL494, G516, P508/P509, UM614/UM615, VU470

Additional Contemporary and Modern Suggestions
"How Great Is Our God" 4348399 (Rev)
　　CG322, SH458, WS3003
"We Fall Down" 2437367 (Rev, All Saints)
　　G368, WS3187
"Blessing, Honour and Glory" 1001179 (Rev)
"Hallelujah to the Lamb" 2316323 (Rev)
"We Will Worship the Lamb of Glory" 208409 (Rev)
"We Declare Your Majesty" 121483 (Rev)
"To Him Who Sits on the Throne" 20429 (Rev)
"My Tribute" 11218 (Rev)
　　AH4080, C39, CG574, N14, SH434, UM99

"Shepherd Me, O God" (Rev, All Saints)
　　EL780, G473, S2058, SH365
"In the Lord I'll Be Ever Thankful" (Rev)
　　G654, S2195, SH316
"Joy Comes with the Dawn" (Rev)
　　S2210, VU166
"Holy Ground" 21198 (Rev)
　　C112, G406, S2272, SA400
"Hungry" ("Falling on My Knees") 2650364 (Rev, Pss)
"Feed Us, Lord" 4636207 (Rev, Pss, Comm.)
　　G501, WS3167
"How Majestic Is Your Name" 26007 (Pss)
　　C63, CG326, G613, S2023, SA90
"Better Is One Day" 1097451 (Pss)
"You Who Are Thirsty" 814453 (Pss, Matt)
"Think about His Love" 16299 (Pss, 1 John)
"Behold, What Manner of Love" 1596 (1 John)
"Love Moves You" ("Love Alone") 5775514 (1 John)
"Celebrate Love" 155246 (1 John)
"He Came Down" 4679219 (1 John)
　　EL253, G137, S2085, SH88
"I Have a Hope" 5087587 (1 John)
"Jesus We Love You" 7030068 (1 John)
"Santo, Santo, Santo" ("Holy, Holy, Holy") (1 John, Matt)
　　C111, CG3, EL473, G595, N793, S2007, SH452
"Holy, Holy" 18792 (1 John, Matt)
"Open Our Eyes, Lord" 1572 (Matt)
　　CG392, S2086, SA386, SH562
"Give Thanks" (Matt)
　　C528, CG373, G647, S2036, SA364, SH489
"Open the Eyes of My Heart" 2298355 (Matt)
　　G452, SA270, SH378, WS3008
"Purify My Heart" 1314323 (Matt)
"Go in Peace" 451022 (All Saints)

Vocal Solos
"Deep River" (Rev)
　　V-3 (1)　　　p. 4
"In Bright Mansions Above" (All Saints)
　　V-4　　　　p. 39

Anthems
"For All the Saints" (All Saints)
Arr. John Purifoy; Brookfield HL-08752167
SATB, piano, opt. instruments (https://bit.ly/HL-52167)

"How Lovely Is Thy Dwelling Place" (All Saints)
Daniel Kallman; MorningStar 50-7079
SAB or SATB, piano (https://bit.ly/MSM-7079)

Other Suggestions
These scriptures and ideas may be used on Nov. 5. (NOTE: Daylight Saving Time ends on Nov. 5.)
Visuals:
　　O　　White robe, palm branches
　　P　　"Taste & See," spices to taste, abundance, rejoicing, refuge
　　E　　Images of "saints" of the congregation
　　G　　Images of people living the Beatitudes, mountain
Introit: SA148, WS3044. "Make Way" (Matt)
Canticle: C185. The Beatitudes (Matt)
Prayer: C252 or UM392 (Matt)
Response: C299, G576, S2277. "Lord, Have Mercy" (Rev)
Litany: C157 or C488 or UM713 (All Saints)
Litany and Prayer for Naming of Saints: WSL45 (All Saints)
Theme Ideas: Beatitudes / Blessings, God: Glory of God, God: Love of God, Praise

Joshua 3:7-17

[7]The Lord said to Joshua, "This day I will begin to exalt you in the sight of all Israel, so that they may know that I will be with you as I was with Moses. [8]You are the one who shall command the priests who bear the ark of the covenant, 'When you come to the edge of the waters of the Jordan, you shall stand still in the Jordan.'" [9]Joshua then said to the Israelites, "Draw near and hear the words of the Lord your God." [10]Joshua said, "By this you shall know that among you is the living God who without fail will drive out from before you the Canaanites, Hittites, Hivites, Perizzites, Girgashites, Amorites, and Jebusites: [11]the ark of the covenant of the Lord of all the earth is going to pass before you into the Jordan. [12]So now select twelve men from the tribes of Israel, one from each tribe. [13]When the soles of the feet of the priests who bear the ark of the Lord, the Lord of all the earth, come to rest in the waters of the Jordan, the waters of the Jordan flowing from above shall be cut off; they shall stand in a single heap."

[14]When the people set out from their tents to cross over the Jordan, the priests bearing the ark of the covenant were in front of the people. [15]Now the Jordan overflows all its banks throughout the time of harvest. So when those who bore the ark had come to the Jordan and the feet of the priests bearing the ark were dipped in the edge of the water, [16]the waters flowing from above stood still, rising up in a single heap far off at Adam, the city that is beside Zarethan, while those flowing toward the sea of the Arabah, the Dead Sea, were wholly cut off. Then the people crossed over opposite Jericho. [17]While all Israel were crossing over on dry ground, the priests who bore the ark of the covenant of the Lord stood firmly on dry ground in the middle of the Jordan, until the entire nation finished crossing over the Jordan.

Psalm 107:1-7, 33-37 (G653, N693, UM830)

O give thanks to the Lord, for he is good,
> for his steadfast love endures forever.
[2]Let the redeemed of the Lord say so,
> those he redeemed from trouble
[3]and gathered in from the lands,
> from the east and from the west,
> from the north and from the south.
[4]Some wandered in desert wastes,
> finding no way to an inhabited town;
[5]hungry and thirsty,
> their soul fainted within them.
[6]Then they cried to the Lord in their trouble,
> and he delivered them from their distress;
[7]he led them by a straight way,
> until they reached an inhabited town.
. . . .
[33]He turns rivers into a desert,
> springs of water into thirsty ground,
[34]a fruitful land into a salty waste,
> because of the wickedness of its inhabitants.
[35]He turns a desert into pools of water,
> a parched land into springs of water.
[36]And there he lets the hungry live,
> and they establish a town to live in;
[37]they sow fields and plant vineyards
> and get a fruitful yield.

1 Thessalonians 2:9-13

[9]You remember our labor and toil, brothers and sisters; we worked night and day so that we might not burden any of you while we proclaimed to you the gospel of God. [10]You are witnesses, and God also, how pure, upright, and blameless our conduct was toward you believers. [11]As you know, we dealt with each one of you like a father with his children, [12]urging and encouraging you and pleading that you lead a life worthy of God, who calls you into his own kingdom and glory.

[13]We also constantly give thanks to God for this, that when you received the word of God that you heard from us you accepted it not as a human word but as what it really is, God's word, which is also at work in you believers.

Matthew 23:1-12

Then Jesus said to the crowds and to his disciples, [2]"The scribes and the Pharisees sit on Moses's seat; [3]therefore, do whatever they teach you and follow it, but do not do as they do, for they do not practice what they teach. [4]They tie up heavy burdens, hard to bear, and lay them on the shoulders of others, but they themselves are unwilling to lift a finger to move them. [5]They do all their deeds to be seen by others, for they make their phylacteries broad and their fringes long. [6]They love to have the place of honor at banquets and the best seats in the synagogues [7]and to be greeted with respect in the marketplaces and to have people call them rabbi. [8]But you are not to be called rabbi, for you have one teacher, and you are all brothers and sisters. [9]And call no one your father on earth, for you have one Father, the one in heaven. [10]Nor are you to be called instructors, for you have one instructor, the Messiah. [11]The greatest among you will be your servant. [12]All who exalt themselves will be humbled, and all who humble themselves will be exalted.

[13]"But woe to you, scribes and Pharisees, hypocrites! For you lock people out of the kingdom of heaven. For you do not go in yourselves, and when others are going in you stop them. [15]Woe to you, scribes and Pharisees, hypocrites! For you cross sea and land to make a single convert, and you make the new convert twice as much a child of hell as yourselves.

[16]"Woe to you, blind guides who say, 'Whoever swears by the sanctuary is bound by nothing, but whoever swears by the gold of the sanctuary is bound by the oath.' [17]You blind fools! For which is greater, the gold or the sanctuary that has made the gold sacred? [18]And you say, 'Whoever swears by the altar is bound by nothing, but whoever swears by the gift that is on the altar is bound by the oath.' [19]How blind you are! For which is greater, the gift or the altar that makes the gift sacred? [20]So whoever swears by the altar swears by it and by everything on it, [21]and whoever swears by the sanctuary swears by it and by the one who dwells in it, [22]and whoever swears by heaven swears by the throne of God and by the one who is seated upon it.

[23]"Woe to you, scribes and Pharisees, hypocrites! For you tithe mint, dill, and cumin and have neglected the weightier matters of the law: justice and mercy and faith. It is these you ought to have practiced without neglecting the others."

Primary Hymns and Songs for the Day

"Guide Me, O Thou Great Jehovah" (Josh) (O)
   C622, CG33, E690, EL618, G65, N18/19, P281, SA27, SH51,
   UM127 (PD), VU651 (Fr.)
        H-3   Hbl-25, 51, 58; Chr-89; Desc-26; Org-23
        S-1   #76-77. Descant and harmonization

"On Jordan's Stormy Banks I Stand" (Josh)
   CG556, EL437, N598, SA542, SH368, UM724 (PD)
        H-3   Chr-155; Org-117
        S-1   #271. Orff instrument arrangement
                #272. Transposition in D major

"Lord, Whose Love Through Humble Service" (Matt)
   C461, EL712, SH239, UM581
        H-3   Hbl-14, 64; Chr-132, 203
        S-2   #22. Descant
   CG650, E610, P427

"O Master, Let Me Walk with Thee" (Matt) (C)
   C602, CG660, E659/E660, EL818, G738, N503, P357, SA667,
   SH612, UM430 (PD), VU560
        H-3   Hbl-81; Chr-147; Desc-74; Org-87
        S-2   #118. Descant

Additional Hymn Suggestions

"A Mighty Fortress Is Our God" (Josh, Pss) (O)
   C65, CG418, E687/688, EL503/504/505, G275, N439/440,
   P259/260, SA1, SH651, UM110 (PD), VU261/262/263

"He Leadeth Me: O Blessed Thought" (Josh)
   C545, CG68, SA645, SH304, UM128 (PD), VU657

"Go Down, Moses" (Josh)
   C663, E648, G52, N572, P334, SH28, UM448

"Precious Lord, Take My Hand" (Josh)
   C628, CG400, EL773, G834, N472, SH336, UM474, VU670

"Faith, While Trees Are Still in Blossom" (Josh)
   C535, UM508, VU643

"Beams of Heaven as I Go" (Josh)
   N447, UM524

"Lift Every Voice and Sing" (Josh, Pss)
   AH4055, C631, CG638, E599, EL841, G339, N593, P563,
   SH36, UM519

"You Satisfy the Hungry Heart" (Pss, Comm.)
   C429, CG468, EL484, G523, P521, SH672, UM629, VU478

"O Food to Pilgrims Given" (Pss, Comm.)
   E308/309, UM631

"Thank You, Lord" (Pss, 1 Thess)
   AH4081, C531, SH496, UM84

"Because He Lives" (Pss, 1 Thess)
   AH4070, C562, CG620, SA219, SH200, UM364

"Ask Ye What Great Thing I Know" (1 Thess, Matt)
   CG443, N49, UM163 (PD), VU338

"All Who Love and Serve Your City" (1 Thess, Matt)
   C670, E570/571, EL724, G351, P413, UM433

"Thy Word Is a Lamp" (1 Thess)
   C326, CG38, G458, UM601

"Go Forth for God" (1 Thess) (C)
   CG517, E347, UM670, VU418

"I'm Gonna Live So God Can Use Me" (1 Thess, Matt)
   C614, G700, P369, S2153, SH632, VU575

"*Jesu, Jesu*" 3049039 (Matt)
   C600, CG656, E602, EL708, G203, N498, P367, SH155,
   UM432, VU593; S-1 #63 Vocal part

"Lord, Speak to Me" (Matt)
   CG503, EL676, G722, N531, SA773, SH557, UM463, VU589

"Draw Us in the Spirit's Tether" (Matt, Comm.)
   C392, EL470, G529, N337, P504, UM632, VU479

"Love the Lord Your God" 1400093 (Matt)
   G62, S2168

"Together We Serve" (Matt, Comm.)
   G767, S2175

"As We Gather at Your Table" (Matt, Comm.)
   EL522, N332, S2268, SH411, VU457

Additional Contemporary and Modern Suggestions

"Holy Ground" 21198 (Josh)
   C112, G406, S2272, SA400

"Awesome in This Place" 847554 (Josh)

"You Who Are Thirsty" 814453 (Pss)

"How Great You Are" 6271677 (Pss)

"Shout to the North" 1562261 (Pss)
   G319, SA1009, WS3042

"Hallelujah" ("Your Love Is Amazing") 3091812 (Pss)

"Feed Us, Lord" 4636207 (Pss, Comm.)
   G501, WS3167

"Your Love, Oh Lord" 1894255 (Pss)

"In the Lord I'll Be Ever Thankful" (Pss, 1 Thess)
   G654, S2195, SH316

"Sanctuary" 24140 (1 Thess)
   G701, S2164, SH265

"We Bring the Sacrifice of Praise" 9990 (1 Thess, Matt)

"The Servant Song" (Matt)
   C490, CG289, EL659, G727, N539, S2222, SA1005, SH264,
   VU595

"Make Me a Servant" 33131 (Matt)
   CG651, S2176

"Humble Thyself in the Sight of the Lord" 26564 (Matt)

"More Love, More Power" 60661 (Matt)

"I Will Boast" 4662350 (Matt)

Vocal Solos

"Deep River" (Josh)
   V-3 (1)   p. 4

"I Couldn't Hear Nobody Pray" (Josh)
   V-7   p. 40/43

"Take My Life, and Let It Be" (Matt)
   V-3 (3)   p. 17
   V-8   p. 262

Anthems

"On Jordan's Stormy Banks" (Josh)
Arr. Carolyn Hamlin, Alfred 36814
SSATB, keyboard (https://bit.ly/A-36814)

"O Master, Let Me Walk with Thee" (Matt)
Arr. Sheldon Curry; Alfred 00-35077
SATB, keyboard, opt C-instrument (https://bit.ly/A-35077)

Other Suggestions

The scriptures and service ideas from Nov. 1 may be used today as All Saints Sunday.
Daylight Saving Time ends today.
Visuals:
   O   Flowing water
   P   Water, bubbling water, sand, grapes, wheat
   E   Man encouraging child, open Bible
   G   Christ as teacher, servanthood (bowl/pitcher/towel),
         boxes symbolizing burdens, phylacteries, chair
Prayer: UM353. Ash Wednesday (1 Thess)
Offering Prayer: WSL146 (Matt)
Alternate Lessons: Mic 3:5-12 and Ps 43 (See p. 3.)
Theme Ideas: Discipleship / Following God, God: Providence / God our Help, God: Word of God, Journey, Service / Servanthood, Thanksgiving / Gratitude

Joshua 24:1-3a, 14-25

Then Joshua gathered all the tribes of Israel to Shechem and summoned the elders, the heads, the judges, and the officers of Israel, and they presented themselves before God. [2]And Joshua said to all the people, "Thus says the LORD, the God of Israel: Long ago your ancestors—Terah and his sons Abraham and Nahor—lived beyond the Euphrates and served other gods. [3]Then I took your father Abraham from beyond the River and led him through all the land of Canaan and made his offspring many. . . .

[14]"Now, therefore, revere the LORD and serve him in sincerity and in faithfulness; put away the gods that your ancestors served beyond the River and in Egypt and serve the LORD. [15]Now if you are unwilling to serve the LORD, choose this day whom you will serve, whether the gods your ancestors served in the region beyond the River or the gods of the Amorites in whose land you are living, but as for me and my household, we will serve the LORD." [16]Then the people answered, "Far be it from us that we should forsake the LORD to serve other gods, [17]for it is the LORD our God who brought us and our ancestors up from the land of Egypt, out of the house of slavery, and who did those great signs in our sight. He protected us along all the way that we went and among all the peoples through whom we passed, [18]and the LORD drove out before us all the peoples, the Amorites who lived in the land. Therefore we also will serve the LORD, for he is our God."

[19]But Joshua said to the people, "You cannot serve the LORD, for he is a holy God. He is a jealous God; he will not forgive your transgressions or your sins. [20]If you forsake the LORD and serve foreign gods, then he will turn and do you harm and consume you, after having done you good." [21]And the people said to Joshua, "No, we will serve the LORD!" [22]Then Joshua said to the people, "You are witnesses against yourselves that you have chosen the LORD, to serve him." And they said, "We are witnesses." [23]He said, "Then put away the foreign gods that are among you, and incline your hearts to the LORD, the God of Israel." [24]The people said to Joshua, "The LORD our God we will serve, and him we will obey." [25]So Joshua made a covenant with the people that day and made statutes and ordinances for them at Shechem.

Psalm 78:1-7 (G632, N669, UM799)

Give ear, O my people, to my teaching;
   incline your ears to the words of my mouth.
[2]I will open my mouth in a parable;
   I will utter dark sayings from of old,
[3]things that we have heard and known,
   that our ancestors have told us.
[4]We will not hide them from their children;
   we will tell to the coming generation
the glorious deeds of the LORD and his might
   and the wonders that he has done.
[5]He established a decree in Jacob
   and appointed a law in Israel,
which he commanded our ancestors
   to teach to their children,
[6]that the next generation might know them,
   the children yet unborn,
and rise up and tell them to their children,
[7]so that they should set their hope in God,
and not forget the works of God,
   but keep his commandments.

1 Thessalonians 4:13-18

[13]But we do not want you to be uninformed, brothers and sisters, about those who have died, so that you may not grieve as others do who have no hope. [14]For since we believe that Jesus died and rose again, even so, through Jesus, God will bring with him those who have died. [15]For this we declare to you by the word of the Lord, that we who are alive, who are left until the coming of the Lord, will by no means precede those who have died. [16]For the Lord himself, with a cry of command, with the archangel's call and with the sound of God's trumpet, will descend from heaven, and the dead in Christ will rise first. [17]Then we who are alive, who are left, will be caught up in the clouds together with them to meet the Lord in the air, and so we will be with the Lord forever. [18]Therefore encourage one another with these words.

Matthew 25:1-13

"Then the kingdom of heaven will be like this. Ten young women took their lamps and went to meet the bridegroom. [2]Five of them were foolish, and five were wise. [3]When the foolish took their lamps, they took no oil with them, [4]but the wise took flasks of oil with their lamps. [5]As the bridegroom was delayed, all of them became drowsy and slept. [6]But at midnight there was a shout, 'Look! Here is the bridegroom! Come out to meet him.' [7]Then all those young women got up and trimmed their lamps. [8]The foolish said to the wise, 'Give us some of your oil, for our lamps are going out.' [9]But the wise replied, 'No! there will not be enough for you and for us; you had better go to the dealers and buy some for yourselves.' [10]And while they went to buy it, the bridegroom came, and those who were ready went with him into the wedding banquet, and the door was shut. [11]Later the other young women came also, saying, 'Lord, lord, open to us.' [12]But he replied, 'Truly I tell you, I do not know you.' [13]Keep awake, therefore, for you know neither the day nor the hour."

Primary Hymns and Songs for the Day

"Stand Up and Bless the Lord" (Josh) (O)
    CG299, P491, SA391, UM662 (PD)
        H-3   Hbl-79; Chr-141; Desc-95; Org-143
        S-1   #306-308. Various treatments
"Let All Mortal Flesh Keep Silence" (Josh)
    C124, CG81, E324, EL490, G347, N345, P5, UM626 (PD),
    VU473 (Fr.)
        H-3   Hbl-20, 74; Chr-124; Desc-87; Org-116
        S-1   #268-269. Handbell part and descant
"Love the Lord Your God" 1400093 (Josh)
    G62, S2168
"Blessed Assurance" (1 Thess)
    AH4083, C543, CG619, EL638, G839, N473, P341, SA455,
    SH320, UM369 (PD), VU337
        H-3   Chr-39
        S-1   #24. Harmonization
"Steal Away to Jesus" (1 Thess, Matt)
    C644, G358, N599, UM704
"Rejoice, the Lord Is King" (1 Thess)
    C699, CG215, E481, EL430, G363, N303, P155, SA271,
    SH213, UM715/716, VU213
        H-3   Hbl-8, 53, 90; Chr-37; Desc-27; Org-24
        S-1   #78-80. Various treatments
"My Lord, What a Morning" (1 Thess)
    C708, EL438 (PD), G352, P449, SH356, UM719, VU708
        H-3   Chr-139
"Wake, Awake, for Night Is Flying" (Matt) (C)
    E61, EL436, G349, P17, UM720 (PD), VU711
        H-3   Chr-174, 203; Org-172

Additional Hymn Suggestions

"O God, Our Help in Ages Past" (Josh)
    C67, CG566, E680, EL632, G687, N25, P210, SA47, SH41,
    UM117 (PD), VU806
"Near to the Heart of God" (Josh)
    C581, CG383, G824, P527, UM472 (PD)
"Bless His Holy Name" 17566 (Josh)
    S2015, SA75, SH547
"Mine Eyes Have Seen the Glory" (Josh, 1 Thess)
    C705, CG439, EL890, G354, N610, SA263, UM717
"I'm Gonna Live So God Can Use Me" (Josh, Matt)
    C614, G700, P369, S2153, SH632, VU575
"Christ Beside Me" (Josh, Matt)
    G702, S2166
"Together We Serve" (Josh, Matt)
    G767, S2175
"When We All Get to Heaven" (1 Thess)
    CG548, SA676, UM701 (PD)
"Lo, He Comes with Clouds Descending" (1 Thess)
    CG100, E57/58, EL435, G348, P6, SA260, UM718, VU25
"When the Roll Is Called Up Yonder" (1 Thess)
    CG553, SA559, SH360
"Seek Ye First" 1352 (Matt)
    C354, CG436, E711, G175, P333, SA675, SH126, UM405,
    VU356
"I Love Thy Kingdom, Lord" (Matt)
    C274, CG262, E524, G310, N312, P441, UM540
"I Want to Be Ready" (Matt)
    N616, UM722
"Living for Jesus" (Matt)
    C610, S2149
"Tell Me the Story of Jesus" (Matt)
    SA152, SH122

Additional Contemporary and Modern Suggestions

"Surely the Presence of the Lord" 7909 (Josh)
    C263, UM328; S-2 #200. Stanzas for soloist
"To Know You More" 1767420 (Josh)
"Cry of My Heart" 844980 (Josh)
"Guide My Feet" (Josh)
    CG637, G741, N497, P354, S2208, SH54
"One God and Father of Us All" 3417678 (Josh)
"Holy Ground" 21198 (Josh)
    C112, G406, S2272, SA400
"Step by Step" 696994 (Josh)
    CG495, G743, WS3004
"Ain't Gonna Let Nobody Turn Me 'Round" (Josh)
    AH4051
"10,000 Reasons" ("Bless The Lord") 6016351 (Pss)
"You're Worthy of My Praise" 487976 (Josh)
"I Give You My Heart" 1866132 (Josh)
"Every Move I Make" 1595726 (Josh)
"Freedom Is Coming" 4194244 (Josh, 1 Thess, Matt)
    G359, S2192, SA29
"Awesome God" 41099 (Pss)
    G616, S2040
"My Hope Is In You" 6070957 (1 Thess)
"Words" 6437497 (1 Thess)
"The Battle Belongs to the Lord" 21583 (1 Thess)
"I Believe In Jesus" 61282 (1 Thess)
"O Freedom" (1 Thess, Matt)
"This Kingdom" 1650898 (1 Thess, Matt)
"I See the Lord" 1406176 (1 Thess, Matt)
"The Heavens Shall Declare" 904033 (1 Thess, Matt)
"We Will Dance" 1034438 (1 Thess, Matt)
"Holy Darkness" (Matt)
    WS3141
"Already Here" (Matt)
    AH4028

Vocal Solos

"Here I Am" (Josh)
    V-1   p. 19
"My Lord, What a Morning" (1 Thess)
    V-3 (1)   p. 39

Anthems

"This Is My Song" (1 Thess)
Tom Fettke; Shawnee Press 35029701
SATB, piano (https://bit.ly/SP-9701)

"Keep Your Lamps!" (Matt)
arr. Andre Thomas; Hinshaw Music HMC-577
SATB with conga drums (https://bit.ly/H-577)

Other Suggestions

Visuals:
    O   "Choose this day whom you will serve," "As for me and
         my household . . . ," servanthood (bowl / pitcher /
         towel)
    P   Christ as teacher, open Bible
    E   Trumpet, clouds, resurrection, encouragement
    G   Ten lamps, oil, wedding garments, bouquet, clock set
         at 12:00
Call to Worship: C708, EL438 (PD), G352, P449, SH356, UM719,
    VU708, refrain. "My Lord, What a Morning" (1 Thess)
Call to Prayer: C644, G358, N599, UM704, refrain. "Steal Away to
    Jesus" (1 Thess)
Alternate Lessons: Wis 6:12-16 or Amos 5:18-24; Wis 6:17-20 or Ps 70
Theme Ideas: Covenant, Faithfulness, Jesus: Return and Reign,
    Patience, Priorities, Waiting

Judges 4:1-7

The Israelites again did what was evil in the sight of the LORD, after Ehud died. [2]So the LORD sold them into the hand of King Jabin of Canaan, who reigned in Hazor; the commander of his army was Sisera, who lived in Harosheth-ha-goiim. [3]Then the Israelites cried out to the LORD for help, for he had nine hundred chariots of iron and had oppressed the Israelites cruelly twenty years.

[4]At that time Deborah, a prophet, wife of Lappidoth, was judging Israel. [5]She used to sit under the palm of Deborah between Ramah and Bethel in the hill country of Ephraim, and the Israelites came up to her for judgment. [6]She sent and summoned Barak son of Abinoam from Kedesh in Naphtali and said to him, "The LORD, the God of Israel, commands you, 'Position yourself at Mount Tabor, taking ten thousand from the tribe of Naphtali and the tribe of Zebulun. [7]I will draw out Sisera, the general of Jabin's army, to meet you by the Wadi Kishon with his chariots and his troops, and I will give him into your hand.'"

Psalm 123 (G788, N705)

To you I lift up my eyes,
    O you who are enthroned in the heavens!
[2]As the eyes of servants
    look to the hand of their master,
as the eyes of a maid
    to the hand of her mistress,
so our eyes look to the LORD our God,
    until he has mercy upon us.
[3]Have mercy upon us, O LORD, have mercy upon us,
    for we have had more than enough of contempt.
[4]Our soul has had more than its fill
    of the scorn of those who are at ease,
    of the contempt of the proud.

1 Thessalonians 5:1-11

Now concerning the times and the seasons, brothers and sisters, you do not need to have anything written to you. [2]For you yourselves know very well that the day of the Lord will come like a thief in the night. [3]When they say, "There is peace and security," then sudden destruction will come upon them, as labor pains come upon a pregnant woman, and there will be no escape! [4]But you, brothers and sisters, are not in darkness, for that day to surprise you like a thief; [5]for you are all children of light and children of the day; we are not of the night or of darkness. [6]So, then, let us not fall asleep as others do, but let us keep awake and be sober, [7]for those who sleep sleep at night, and those who are drunk get drunk at night. [8]But since we belong to the day, let us be sober and put on the breastplate of faith and love and for a helmet the hope of salvation. [9]For God has destined us not for wrath but for obtaining salvation through our Lord Jesus Christ, [10]who died for us, so that whether we are awake or asleep we may live with him. [11]Therefore encourage one another and build up each other, as indeed you are doing.

Matthew 25:14-30

[14]"For it is as if a man, going on a journey, summoned his slaves and entrusted his property to them; [15]to one he gave five talents, to another two, to another one, to each according to his ability. Then he went away. At once [16]the one who had received the five talents went off and traded with them and made five more talents. [17]In the same way, the one who had the two talents made two more talents. [18]But the one who had received the one talent went off and dug a hole in the ground and hid his master's money. [19]After a long time the master of those slaves came and settled accounts with them. [20]Then the one who had received the five talents came forward, bringing five more talents, saying, 'Master, you handed over to me five talents; see, I have made five more talents.' [21]His master said to him, 'Well done, good and trustworthy slave; you have been trustworthy in a few things; I will put you in charge of many things; enter into the joy of your master.' [22]And the one with the two talents also came forward, saying, 'Master, you handed over to me two talents; see, I have made two more talents.' [23]His master said to him, 'Well done, good and trustworthy slave; you have been trustworthy in a few things; I will put you in charge of many things; enter into the joy of your master.' [24]Then the one who had received the one talent also came forward, saying, 'Master, I knew that you were a harsh man, reaping where you did not sow and gathering where you did not scatter, [25]so I was afraid, and I went and hid your talent in the ground. Here you have what is yours.' [26]But his master replied, 'You wicked and lazy slave! You knew, did you, that I reap where I did not sow and gather where I did not scatter? [27]Then you ought to have invested my money with the bankers, and on my return I would have received what was my own with interest. [28]So take the talent from him, and give it to the one with the ten talents. [29]For to all those who have, more will be given, and they will have an abundance, but from those who have nothing, even what they have will be taken away. [30]As for this worthless slave, throw him into the outer darkness, where there will be weeping and gnashing of teeth.'"

Primary Hymns and Songs for the Day

"Immortal, Invisible, God Only Wise" (1 Thess)
　C66, CG58, E423, EL834, G12, N1, P263, SA37, UM103 (PD), VU264
　　　H-3　Hbl-15, 71; Chr-65; Desc-93; Org-135
　　　S-1　#300. Harmonization
"Jesus, Thou Joy of Loving Hearts" (1 Thess)
　C101, CG394, G494, N329, P510, SA340, SH688, VU472
　　　H-3　Hbl-73; Chr-208; Desc-89; Org-119
"God, Whose Giving Knows No Ending" (1 Thess, Matt)
　C606, CG671, G716, N565, P422
　　　H-3　Hbl-14, 64; Chr-132, 203
　　　S-2　#22. Descant
"Take My Life, and Let It Be" (Matt)
　C609, G697, P391
　　　H-3　Chr-34, 177; Desc-51; Org-53
　　　S-2　#78-80. Various treatments
　CG490, E707, EL583/EL685, N448, SA623, SH627/628, UM399 (PD), VU506
"Because You Live, O Christ" (Matt)
　G249, N231, P105
"We Praise You, O God, Our Redeemer" (Matt)
　CG356, EL870, G612, N420, VU218
　　　H-3　Chr-206; Desc-61; Org-68
　　　S-1　#192-194. Various treatments
"Soon and Very Soon" 11249 (1 Thess) (C)
　CG562, EL439, G384, SH357, UM706, S-2 #187. Piano arr.
　　　S-2　#187. Piano arrangement

Additional Hymn Suggestions

"Joyful, Joyful, We Adore Thee" (Judg) (O)
　C2, CG310, E376, EL836, G611, N4, P464, SA39, SH390, UM89 (PD), VU232
"God Hath Spoken By the Prophets" (Judg)
　CG32 UM108
"La Palabra Del Señor Es Recta" ("Righteous and Just Is the Word of Our Lord") (Judg)
　G40, UM107, SH4
"O Morning Star, How Fair and Bright" (1 Thess)
　C105, E497, EL308, G827, N158, P69, UM247, VU98
"Jesus, Keep Me Near the Cross" (1 Thess)
　C587, CG642, EL335, N197, SA178, UM301 (PD), VU142
"Holy God, We Praise Thy Name" (1 Thess) (O)
　CG9, E366, EL414, G4, N276, P460, SH431, UM79, VU894
"Pues Si Vivimos" ("When We Are Living") (1 Thess)
　C536, CG265, EL639, G822, N499, P400, SH299, UM356, VU581
"I Want to Walk as a Child of the Light" (1 Thess)
　CG96, E490, EL815, G377, SH352, UM206
"Together We Serve" (1 Thess, Matt)
　G767, S2175
"Lead Me, Guide Me" (1 Thess)
　C583, CG403, EL768, G740, S2214, SH582
"Gather Us In" (1 Thess) (O)
　C284, EL532, G401, S2236, SH393
"God Who Stretched the Spangled Heavens" (Matt)
　C651, CG21, E580, EL771, G24, N556, P268, UM150
"All Who Love and Serve Your City" (Matt)
　C670, E570/571, EL724, G351, P413, UM433
"Lord, Whose Love Through Humble Service" (Matt) (C)
　C461, CG650, E610, EL712, P427, SH239, UM581
"I'm Gonna Live So God Can Use Me" (Matt)
　C614, G700, P369, S2153, SH632, VU575

Additional Contemporary and Modern Suggestions

"Kyrie Eleison" ("Lord, Have Mercy") (Pss)
　EL152, SH519, UM482/UM483/UM484, WS3133
"Freedom Is Coming" 4194244 (1 Thess)
　G359, S2192, SA29
"Light of the World" 73342 (1 Thess)

"Siyahamba" ("We Are Marching") 1321512 (1 Thess)
　C442, CG155, EL866, G853, N526, S2235, SA903, SH717, VU646
"Praise Him" 684779 (1 Thess)
"Walking in the Light of God" (1 Thess)
　WS3163
"Awaken" 5491647 (1 Thess)
"Shine on Us" 1754646 (1 Thess)
"Hear Our Praises" 2543402 (1 Thess)
"Everyday" 2798154 (1 Thess)
"Song for the Nations" 20340 (1 Thess)
"Relentless" 6428743 (1 Thess)
"Here I Am to Worship" 3266032 (1 Thess)
　CG297, SA114, SH395, WS3177
"My Life Is in You, Lord" 17315 (Matt)
　S2032
"Lord, Be Glorified" 26368 (Matt)
　EL744, G468, S2150, SA593, SH420
"Glory To God Forever" 5384338 (Matt)
"Let It Be Said of Us" 1855882 (Matt)
"When It's All Been Said and Done" 2788353 (Matt)
"Nobody" 7121827 (Matt)

Vocal Solos

"I Will Lift Up Mine Eyes" (Pss)
　　V-1　　　　p. 27
"Redeeming Grace" (1 Thess, Matt)
　　V-4　　　　p. 47
"Take My Life, and Let It Be" (Matt)
　　V-3 (3)　　p. 17
　　V-8　　　　p. 262
"Fit for a King" (Matt, Stewardship)
　　V-10　　　 p. 32

Anthems

"Have Mercy Upon Us" (Miserere nostri, Domine) (Pss)
G. P. Palestrina; ECS Publishing 1269
SATB a cappella (https://bit.ly/E-1269)

"We Praise You, O God, Our Redeemer" (Matt)
Lloyd Larson; Beckenhorst BP1666
SATB, piano (https://bit.ly/BP-1666)

Other Suggestions

For Thanksgiving Sunday, see Thanksgiving Day suggestions.
Visuals:
　O　Manacles
　P　Hand
　E　Robber's mask, light/dark, awake/asleep, lantern
　G　Three piles of coins (large, medium, small, bank bag, time/talent survey, nos. 1, 2, and 5 (nos. 10, 4, and 1)
Matthew parable lends itself well to a stewardship emphasis.
Many Nov. 12 suggestions related to 1 Thess are also appropriate with today's reading from 1 Thess.
Introit: C699, CG215, E481, EL430, G363, N303, P155, SA271, SH213, UM715/716, VU213, stanza 1. "Rejoice, the Lord Is King" (Judg)
Response: C299, G576, S2277. "Kyrie" or S2277. "Lord, Have Mercy" (Pss)
Prayer: UM403. For True Life (1 Thess, Matt)
Prayer: UM481. Prayer of Saint Francis (Pss)
Offering Prayer: WSL112. "With money, time, talents" (Matt)
Alternate Lessons: Zeph 1:7, 12-18; Ps 90:1-12
Theme Ideas: God: Kingdom of God, God: Word of God, Humility, Jesus: Return and Reign, Patience, Stewardship, Waiting, Wisdom

Deuteronomy 8:7-18

[7]For the LORD your God is bringing you into a good land, a land with flowing streams, with springs and underground waters welling up in valleys and hills, [8]a land of wheat and barley, of vines and fig trees and pomegranates, a land of olive oil and honey, [9]a land where you may eat bread without scarcity, where you will lack nothing, a land whose stones are iron and from whose hills you may mine copper. [10]You shall eat your fill and bless the LORD your God for the good land that he has given you.

[11]"Take care that you do not forget the LORD your God by failing to keep his commandments, his ordinances, and his statutes that I am commanding you today. [12]When you have eaten your fill and have built fine houses and live in them [13]and when your herds and flocks have multiplied and your silver and gold is multiplied and all that you have is multiplied, [14]then do not exalt yourself, forgetting the LORD your God, who brought you out of the land of Egypt, out of the house of slavery, [15]who led you through the great and terrible wilderness, an arid wasteland with poisonous snakes and scorpions. He made water flow for you from flint rock. [16]He fed you in the wilderness with manna that your ancestors did not know, to humble you and to test you and in the end to do you good. [17]Do not say to yourself, 'My power and the might of my own hand have gotten me this wealth.' [18]But remember the LORD your God, for it is he who gives you power to get wealth, so that he may confirm his covenant that he swore to your ancestors, as he is doing today.

Psalm 65 (G38, N661, P200/201, SH492, UM789)

Praise is due to you,
　　O God, in Zion,
and to you shall vows be performed,
　　[2]O you who answer prayer!
To you all flesh shall come.
[3]When deeds of iniquity overwhelm us,
　　you forgive our transgressions.
[4]Happy are those whom you choose and bring near
　　to live in your courts.
We shall be satisfied with the goodness of your house,
　　your holy temple.
[5]By awesome deeds you answer us with deliverance,
　　O God of our salvation;
you are the hope of all the ends of the earth
　　and of the farthest seas.
[6]By your strength you established the mountains;
　　you are girded with might.
[7]You silence the roaring of the seas,
　　the roaring of their waves,
　　the tumult of the peoples.
[8]Those who live at earth's farthest bounds are awed by your
　　　　signs;
you make the gateways of the morning and the evening shout
　　　　for joy.
[9]You visit the earth and water it;
　　you greatly enrich it;
the river of God is full of water;
　　you provide the people with grain,
　　for so you have prepared it.
[10]You water its furrows abundantly,
　　settling its ridges,
softening it with showers,
　　and blessing its growth.
[11]You crown the year with your bounty;
　　your wagon tracks overflow with richness.
[12]The pastures of the wilderness overflow;
　　the hills gird themselves with joy;
[13]the meadows clothe themselves with flocks;
　　the valleys deck themselves with grain;
　　they shout and sing together for joy.

2 Corinthians 9:6-15

[6]The point is this: the one who sows sparingly will also reap sparingly, and the one who sows bountifully will also reap bountifully. [7]Each of you must give as you have made up your mind, not regretfully or under compulsion, for God loves a cheerful giver. [8]And God is able to provide you with every blessing in abundance, so that by always having enough of everything, you may share abundantly in every good work. [9]As it is written,
　　"He scatters abroad; he gives to the poor;
　　　　his righteousness endures forever."
[10]He who supplies seed to the sower and bread for food will supply and multiply your seed for sowing and increase the harvest of your righteousness. [11]You will be enriched in every way for your great generosity, which will produce thanksgiving to God through us, [12]for the rendering of this ministry not only supplies the needs of the saints but also overflows with many thanksgivings to God. [13]Through the testing of this ministry you glorify God by your obedience to the confession of the gospel of Christ and by the generosity of your partnership with them and with all others, [14]while they long for you and pray for you because of the surpassing grace of God that he has given you. [15]Thanks be to God for his indescribable gift!

Luke 17:11-19

[11]On the way to Jerusalem Jesus was going through the region between Samaria and Galilee. [12]As he entered a village, ten men with a skin disease approached him. Keeping their distance, [13]they called out, saying, "Jesus, Master, have mercy on us!" [14]When he saw them, he said to them, "Go and show yourselves to the priests." And as they went, they were made clean. [15]Then one of them, when he saw that he was healed, turned back, praising God with a loud voice. [16]He prostrated himself at Jesus's feet and thanked him. And he was a Samaritan. [17]Then Jesus asked, "Were not ten made clean? So where are the other nine? [18]Did none of them return to give glory to God except this foreigner?" [19]Then he said to him, "Get up and go on your way; your faith has made you well."

Primary Hymns and Songs for the Day

"Come, Ye Thankful People, Come" (2 Cor, Thanks.) (O)
   C718, CG372, E290, EL693, G367, N422, P551, SA9, SH355,
   UM694 (PD), VU516
         H-3   Hbl-54; Chr-58; Desc-94; Org-137
         S-1   #302-303. Harmonizations with descant
"From All That Dwell Below the Skies" (Deut, Pss)
   C49, CG330, E380, G327, N27, P229, UM101 (PD)
         H-3   Hbl-44; Chr-21; Desc-66; Org-73
         S-1   #198-204. Various treatments
"For the Beauty of the Earth" (Deut, Pss, Thanks.)
   C56, CG341, E416, EL879, G14, P473, N28, SA14, SH21,
   UM92 (PD), VU226
         H-3   Chr-33, 65; Desc-30; Org-29
         S-1   #93-96. Various treatments
   CG341, E416, VU226
"To Bless the Earth" (Pss)
   G38, P200 (PD), VU783
"In the Midst of New Dimensions" (2 Cor)
   G315, N391, S2238
"God of the Fertile Fields" (2 Cor)
   C695, CG668, G714
         H-3   Hbl-28, 53; Chr-56; Desc-57; Org-63
         S-1   #185-186. Descant and harmonization
"Now Thank We All Our God" (Deut, Thanks.) (C)
   C715, CG371, E396/397, EL839/840, G643, N419, P555,
   SA45, SH485, UM102 (PD), VU236 (Fr.)
         H-3   Hbl-78; Chr-140; Desc-81; Org-98
         S-1   #252-254. Various treatments

Additional Hymn Suggestions

"Praise to the Lord, the Almighty" (Deut, Thanks.) (O)
   C25, CG319, E390, EL858 (PD) and 859, G35, N22, P482,
   SA56, SH453, UM139, VU220 (Fr.) and VU221
"What Gift Can We Bring" (Deut)
   CG533, N370, UM87
"For the Fruits of This Creation" (Deut)
   C714, E424, CG376, EL679, G36, N425, P553, SA15, UM97,
   VU227
"All Things Bright and Beautiful" (Deut, Pss, Thanks.)
   C61, CG23, E405, G20, N31, P267, SA3, SH1, UM147 (PD),
   VU291
"Praise Our God Above" ("Harvest Song") (Deut, Pss, Thanks.)
   N424, P480, S2061
Una Espiga ("Sheaves of Summer") (Pss, Comm.)
   C396, G532, N338, UM637
"The Trees of the Field" 20546 (Pss) (C)
   G80, S2279, VU884
Sois la Semilla ("You Are the Seed") (2 Cor)
   C478, N528, UM583
"O For a Thousand Tongues to Sing" (Luke)
   C5, CG332, E493, EL886, G610, N42, P466, SA89, SH439,
   UM57 (PD), VU326 (See also WS3001)
"I'll Praise My Maker While I've Breath" (Luke)
   C20, CG336, E429 (PD), G806, P253, UM60, VU867
"Praise, My Soul, The King of Heaven" (Luke, Thanks.)
   C23, CG337, E410, EL864/865, G619/620, P478/479, SA55,
   SH418, UM66 (PD), VU240
"Awake, O Sleeper" (Luke)
   E547, EL452, UM551, VU566
"An Outcast among Outcasts" (Luke)
   N201, S2104
"Father, We Thank You" (Thanks., Comm.)
   E303/E302, EL478, SH686, UM563/565
"I Come with Joy" (Thanks., Comm.)
   C420, CG456, E304, EL482, G515, N349, P507, SH682,
   UM617, VU477

Additional Contemporary and Modern Suggestions

"I Will Give Thanks" 6266091 (Psalm 65, Luke, Thanks.)
"Give Thanks" (2 Cor, Thanks.)
   C528, CG373, G647, S2036, SA364, SH489
"Come! Come! Everybody Worship" 1327592 (2 Cor)
"Lord, Be Glorified" 26368 (2 Cor)
   EL744, G468, S2150, SA593, SH420
"Grace Alone" 2335524 (2 Cor)
   CG43, S2162, SA699.
"Be Glorified" 429226 (2 Cor)
"Be Glorified" 2732646 (2 Cor)
"He Is Able" 115420 (2 Cor)
"In the Lord I'll Be Ever Thankful" (2 Cor, Luke)
   G654, S2195, SH316
"Jesus Be Praised" 2014931 (Luke)
"Thank You, Lord" 865000 (Luke, Thanks.)
   AH4081, C531, SH496, UM84
"Something Beautiful" 18060 (Luke)
"Blessed Be Your Name" 3798438 (Luke, Thanks.)
   SH449, WS3002
"I Thank You, Jesus" (Luke)
   AH4079, C116, N41, WS3037
"Amazing Grace" ("My Chains Are Gone") 4768151 (Luke)
"Grateful" 7023348 (Luke, Thanks.)

Vocal Solos

"Alive and Breathing" (Luke, Thanks.)
   V-9   p. 4
"I Just Came to Praise the Lord" (Luke, Thanks.)
   V-8   p. 294
"Now Thank We All Our God" (Thanks.)
   V-6   p. 8

Anthems

"Our Grateful Praise!" (Deut, Pss, Thanks.)
Arr. Lloyd Larson; Lorenz 10/5193L
SATB, piano, opt brass and percussion (https://bit.ly/L-5193)

"Come, Ye Thankful People, Come" (2 Cor, Thanks.)
Arr. Jantz A. Black; Hope C6366
SATB, piano (https://bit.ly/C-6366)

Other Suggestions

Visuals:
   O   Flowing water, wheat, barley, figs, etc.
   P   Cornucopia with fruit, vegetables, grains; water, sheep,
             sea, mountains
   E   Seed, bread, people in ministry, 2 Cor 9:15
   G   Nos. 1 and 9, healing, praise, Luke 17:19b
Litany of Praise: WSL56. "Come on!" (Luke, Thanks.)
Litany: C716. "A Thanksgiving" (Deut, Thanks.)
Canticle: UM74. "Canticle of Thanksgiving" (See S-1, p. 374.)
Response: S2275. *Kyrie* (Luke)
Offering Prayer: WSL118. "O Lord, you know" (Deut)
Thanksgiving Prayers: N859, UM74.
Communion Hymn: N783. "As the Grains of Wheat"
Theme Ideas: Creation, God: Glory of God, Praise, Stewardship,
   Thanksgiving / Gratitude

Ezekiel 34:11-16, 20-24

[11]For thus says the Lord God: I myself will search for my sheep and will sort them out. [12]As shepherds sort out their flocks when they are among scattered sheep, so I will sort out my sheep. I will rescue them from all the places to which they have been scattered on a day of clouds and thick darkness. [13]I will bring them out from the peoples and gather them from the countries and bring them into their own land, and I will feed them on the mountains of Israel, by the watercourses, and in all the inhabited parts of the land. [14]I will feed them with good pasture, and the mountain heights of Israel shall be their pasture; there they shall lie down in good grazing land, and they shall feed on rich pasture on the mountains of Israel. [15]I myself will be the shepherd of my sheep, and I will make them lie down, says the Lord God. [16]I will seek the lost, and I will bring back the strays, and I will bind up the injured, and I will strengthen the weak, but the fat and the strong I will destroy. I will feed them with justice. . . .

[20]Therefore, thus says the Lord God to them: I myself will judge between the fat sheep and the lean sheep. [21]Because you pushed with flank and shoulder and butted at all the weak animals with your horns until you scattered them far and wide, [22]I will save my flock, and they shall no longer be ravaged, and I will judge between sheep and sheep.

[23]I will set up over them one shepherd, my servant David, and he shall feed them; he shall feed them and be their shepherd. [24]And I the Lord will be their God, and my servant David shall be prince among them; I the Lord have spoken.

Psalm 100 (G385, N688, UM821)

Make a joyful noise to the Lord, all the earth.
   [2]Serve the Lord with gladness;
      come into his presence with singing.
[3]Know that the Lord is God.
   It is he who made us, and we are his;
      we are his people and the sheep of his pasture.
[4]Enter his gates with thanksgiving
   and his courts with praise.
   Give thanks to him; bless his name.
[5]For the Lord is good;
   his steadfast love endures forever
   and his faithfulness to all generations.

Ephesians 1:15-23

[15]I have heard of your faith in the Lord Jesus and your love toward all the saints, and for this reason [16]I do not cease to give thanks for you as I remember you in my prayers, [17]that the God of our Lord Jesus Christ, the Father of glory, may give you a spirit of wisdom and revelation as you come to know him, [18]so that, with the eyes of your heart enlightened, you may perceive what is the hope to which he has called you, what are the riches of his glorious inheritance among the saints, [19]and what is the immeasurable greatness of his power for us who believe, according to the working of his great power. [20]God put this power to work in Christ when he raised him from the dead and seated him at his right hand in the heavenly places, [21]far above all rule and authority and power and dominion and above every name that is named, not only in this age but also in the age to come. [22]And he has put all things under his feet and has made him the head over all things for the church, [23]which is his body, the fullness of him who fills all in all.

Matthew 25:31-46

[31]"When the Son of Man comes in his glory and all the angels with him, then he will sit on the throne of his glory. [32]All the nations will be gathered before him, and he will separate people one from another as a shepherd separates the sheep from the goats, [33]and he will put the sheep at his right hand and the goats at the left. [34]Then the king will say to those at his right hand, 'Come, you who are blessed by my Father, inherit the kingdom prepared for you from the foundation of the world, [35]for I was hungry and you gave me food, I was thirsty and you gave me something to drink, I was a stranger and you welcomed me, [36]I was naked and you gave me clothing, I was sick and you took care of me, I was in prison and you visited me.' [37]Then the righteous will answer him, 'Lord, when was it that we saw you hungry and gave you food or thirsty and gave you something to drink? [38]And when was it that we saw you a stranger and welcomed you or naked and gave you clothing? [39]And when was it that we saw you sick or in prison and visited you?' [40]And the king will answer them, 'Truly I tell you, just as you did it to one of the least of these brothers and sisters of mine, you did it to me.' [41]Then he will say to those at his left hand, 'You who are accursed, depart from me into the eternal fire prepared for the devil and his angels, [42]for I was hungry and you gave me no food, I was thirsty and you gave me nothing to drink, [43]I was a stranger and you did not welcome me, naked and you did not give me clothing, sick and in prison and you did not visit me.' [44]Then they also will answer, 'Lord, when was it that we saw you hungry or thirsty or a stranger or naked or sick or in prison and did not take care of you?' [45]Then he will answer them, 'Truly I tell you, just as you did not do it to one of the least of these, you did not do it to me.' [46]And these will go away into eternal punishment but the righteous into eternal life."

Primary Hymns and Songs for the Day
"All People That on Earth Do Dwell" (Pss) (O)
CG18, CG331, E377/378, EL883, G385, N7, P220, SA350,
SH416, UM75 (PD), VU822 (Fr.)
- H-3 Hbl-45; Chr-24; Desc-84, 85; Org-107
- S-1 #257-259. Various treatments
- S-2 #140. Descant

"Savior, Like a Shepherd Lead Us" (Eze, Pss)
C558, CG405, E708, EL789, G187, N252, P387, SH538, UM381
- H-3 Chr-167; Org-15
- S-2 #29. Harmonization

"The Church's One Foundation" (Eph)
C272, CG246, E525, EL654, G321, N386, P442, SH233,
UM545/546, VU332 (Fr.)
- H-3 Hbl-94; Chr-180; Desc-16; Org-9
- S-1 #25-26. Descant and harmonization

"Open My Eyes, that I May See" (Eph)
C586, CG395, G451, P324, SH583, UM454, VU371
- H-3 Chr-157; Org-108

"Crown Him with Many Crowns" (Eph) (C)
C234, CG223. E494, EL855, G268, N301, P151, SA358,
SH208, UM327 (PD), VU211
- H-3 Hbl-55; Chr-60; Desc-30; Org-27
- S-1 #86-88. Various treatments

Additional Hymn Suggestions
"Praise, My Soul, the King of Heaven" (Eze, Christ the King)
C23, CG337, E410, EL864/865, G619/620, P478/479, SA55,
SH418, UM66 (PD), VU240

"The King of Love My Shepherd Is" (Eze)
CG64, E645, EL502, G802, P171, SA61, SH359, UM138 (PD),
VU273

"Come, Holy Spirit, Heavenly Dove" (Eze)
C248, E510, G279, N281, P126

"You, Lord, are Both Lamb and Shepherd" (Eze)
G274, SH210, VU210, WS3043

"Praise God, from Whom All Blessings Flow" (Pss)
C47, CG706/707, EL884/885, P591, UM95 (PD)

"Come, Thou Almighty King" (Pss, Eph, Christ the King)
C27, CG2, E365, EL408, G2, N275, P139, SA283, SH388,
UM61 (PD), VU314

"All Creatures of Our God and King" (Pss, Christ the King)
C22, CG307, E400, EL835, G15, N17, P455, SA2, SH16,
UM62, VU217 (Fr.)

"O Worship the King" (Eph, Christ the King)
C17, CG52, E388, EL842, G41, N26, P476, SA52, SH2, UM73
(PD), VU235

"Holy God, We Praise Thy Name" (Eph)
CG9, E366, EL414, G4, N276, P460, SH431, UM79, VU894

"Rejoice, the Lord Is King" (Eph)
C699, CG215, E481, EL430, G363, N303, P155, SA271,
SH213, UM715/716, VU213

"Come, Share the Lord" (Eph, Matt, Christ the King, Comm.)
C408, CG459, G510, S2269, VU469

"All Who Hunger" (Matt, Comm.)
C419, CG303, EL461, G509, S2126, VU460

"Together We Serve" (Matt)
G767, S2175

"In Remembrance of Me" 25156 (Matt, Comm.)
C403, CG462, G521, S2254, SH667

"As We Gather at Your Table" (Matt, Comm.)
EL522, N332, S2268, SH411, VU457

"O for a World" (Matt)
C683, G372, N575, P386, VU697

"Through All the World, a Hungry Christ" (Matt)
N587

"Spirit of Jesus, If I Love My Neighbor" (Matt)
N590

Additional Contemporary and Modern Suggestions
"You Are My Hiding Place" 21442 (Eze)
C554, S2055, SH46

"Shepherd Me, O God" (Eze)
EL780, G473, S2058, SH365

"All Things Are Possible" 2245140 (Eze)

"The King of Love My Shepherd Is" 7023979 (Eze)

"Forevermore" 5466830 (Pss)

"One Thing Remains" 5508444 (Pss)

"Grateful" 7023348 (Pss)

"Hallelujah" ("Your Love Is Amazing") 3091812 (Pss)

"Praise, Praise, Praise the Lord" (Pss)
EL875, G390, S2035

"I Will Enter His Gates" 1493 (Pss)

"Forever" 3148428 (Pss, Eph)

"Open the Eyes of My Heart" 2298355 (Eph)
G452, SA270, SH378, WS3008

"Give Me Jesus" (Eph)
CG546, EL770, N409, SH306, WS3140

"No Sweeter Name" 4447984 (Eph)

"What A Beautiful Name" 7068424 (Eph)

"Cornerstone" 6158927 (Eph)

"People Need the Lord" 18084 (Matt)

"King of Kings" 23952 (Christ the King)

"Come, Emmanuel" 3999938 (Christ the King)

"Prepare Ye the Way" 5286041 (Christ the King)

Vocal Solos
"He Shall Feed His Flock Like a Shepherd" (Eze)
- V-2

"God, Our Ever Faithful Shepherd" (Eze, Matt)
- V-4 p. 15

"Reach Out to Your Neighbor" (Matt)
- V-8 p. 372

"Praise to the Lord, the Almighty" (Christ the King)
- V-6 p. 18

"Crown Him, the Risen King" (Christ the King)
- V-10 p. 55

Anthems
"Jubilate Deo!" (Pss)
Vicki Tucker Courtney; Brilee Music BL956
3-part mixed, piano (https://bit.ly/BL-956)

"When the Poor Ones" (Matt)
Arr. David Cherwien, MorningStar 50-5425
SATB, guitar or piano (https://bit.ly/M-5425)

Other Suggestions
Visuals:
- O   Sheep, good shepherd
- P   Instruments, worship, singing
- E   Portraits of Christ or local church "saints," church history
- G   Christ descending, angels, food, drink, clothes, visitation, medicine bag, prison ministry, Bible, crown, rich fabric, Christ as king

Call to Worship: EL819, G388, S2274, SH405. *Uyai Mose* ("Come, All You People") (Pss)

Response: CG314, E402/403, G636, P468, S41, UM93. "Let All the World in Every Corner Sing" (Pss)

Canticle: G385, N688, P220, UM74 or UM91 (Pss)

Prayer: C473. Be God's Kindness (Matt)

Alternate Lessons: Eze 31:11-16, 20-24; Ps 95:1-7a

Theme Ideas: God our Shepherd, Praise, Thanksgiving, Faithfulness, Wisdom, Glory of God, Power of God, Kingdom of God, Service/Servanthood, Priorities

Isaiah 64:1-9

O that you would tear open the heavens and come down,
  so that the mountains would quake at your presence—
[2]as when fire kindles brushwood
  and the fire causes water to boil—
to make your name known to your adversaries,
  so that the nations might tremble at your presence!
[3]When you did awesome deeds that we did not expect,
  you came down; the mountains quaked at your presence.
[4]From ages past no one has heard,
  no ear has perceived,
no eye has seen any God besides you,
  who works for those who wait for him.
[5]You meet those who gladly do right,
  those who remember you in your ways.
But you were angry, and we sinned;
  because you hid yourself we transgressed.
[6]We have all become like one who is unclean,
  and all our righteous deeds are like a filthy cloth.
We all fade like a leaf,
  and our iniquities, like the wind, take us away.
[7]There is no one who calls on your name
  or attempts to take hold of you,
for you have hidden your face from us
  and have delivered us into the hand of our iniquity.
[8]Yet, O Lord, you are our Father;
  we are the clay, and you are our potter;
  we are all the work of your hand.
[9]Do not be exceedingly angry, O Lord,
  and do not remember iniquity forever.
  Now consider, we are all your people.

Psalm 80:1-7, 17-19 (G355, N672, P206, SH72, UM801)

[1]Give ear, O Shepherd of Israel,
  you who lead Joseph like a flock!
You who are enthroned upon the cherubim, shine forth
  [2]before Ephraim and Benjamin and Manasseh.
Stir up your might,
  and come to save us!
[3]Restore us, O God;
  let your face shine, that we may be saved.
[4]O Lord God of hosts,
  how long will you be angry with your people's prayers?
[5]You have fed them with the bread of tears
  and given them tears to drink in full measure.
[6]You make us the scorn of our neighbors;
  our enemies laugh among themselves.
[7]Restore us, O God of hosts;
  let your face shine, that we may be saved.
. . . .
[17]But let your hand be upon the one at your right hand,
  the one whom you made strong for yourself.
[18]Then we will never turn back from you;
  give us life, and we will call on your name.
[19]Restore us, O Lord God of hosts;
  let your face shine, that we may be saved.

1 Corinthians 1:3-9

[3]Grace to you and peace from God our Father and the Lord Jesus Christ.
[4]I give thanks to my God always for you because of the grace of God that has been given you in Christ Jesus, [5]for in every way you have been enriched in him, in speech and knowledge of every kind—[6]just as the testimony of Christ has been strengthened among you—[7]so that you are not lacking in any gift as you wait for the revealing of our Lord Jesus Christ. [8]He will also strengthen you to the end, so that you may be blameless on the day of our Lord Jesus Christ. [9]God is faithful, by whom you were called into the partnership of his Son, Jesus Christ our Lord.

Mark 13:24-37

[24]"But in those days, after that suffering,
  the sun will be darkened,
  and the moon will not give its light,
[25]and the stars will be falling from heaven,
  and the powers in the heavens will be shaken.
[26]"Then they will see 'the Son of Man coming in clouds' with great power and glory. [27]Then he will send out the angels and gather the elect from the four winds, from the ends of the earth to the ends of heaven.
[28]"From the fig tree learn its lesson: as soon as its branch becomes tender and puts forth its leaves, you know that summer is near. [29]So also, when you see these things taking place, you know that he is near, at the very gates. [30]Truly I tell you, this generation will not pass away until all these things have taken place. [31]Heaven and earth will pass away, but my words will not pass away.
[32]"But about that day or hour no one knows, neither the angels in heaven nor the Son, but only the Father. [33]Beware, keep alert, for you do not know when the time will come. [34]It is like a man going on a journey, when he leaves home and puts his slaves in charge, each with his work, and commands the doorkeeper to be on the watch. [35]Therefore, keep awake, for you do not know when the master of the house will come, in the evening or at midnight or at cockcrow or at dawn, [36]or else he may find you asleep when he comes suddenly. [37]And what I say to you I say to all: Keep awake."

Primary Hymns and Songs for the Day

"People, Look East" (Mark) (O)
  C142, CG90, EL248, G105, P12, UM202, VU9
    H-3   Hbl-87; Chr-159
    S-2   #26. Flute descant
"Just as I Am, Without One Plea" (Isa)
  C339, CG500, E693, EL592, G442, N207, P370, SA503,
  SH500, UM357 (PD), VU508
"O God of Every Nation" (Isa)
  C680, CG46, E607, EL713, G756, P289, UM435, VU677
"Change My Heart, O God" 1565 (Isa)
  EL801, G695, S2152, SA409, SH507
"Have Thine Own Way, Lord" (Isa, 1 Cor 1)
  C588, CG493, SA705, SH626, UM382 (PD)
    S-2   #2. Instrumental descant
"Great Is Thy Faithfulness" (Isa, 1 Cor)
  AH4011, C86, CG48, EL733, G39, N423, P276, SA26, SH48,
  UM140, VU288
    H-3   Chr-87; Desc-39; Org-39
    S-2   #59. Piano arrangement
"Creator of the Stars of Night" (1 Cor)
  C127, E60, EL245, G84, N111, P4, SH74, UM692 (PD)
    H-3   Hbl-14, 54; Chr-60; Org-20
    S-2   #41. Handbell arrangement
"Mine Eyes Have Seen the Glory" (Mark)
  C705, CG439, EL890, G354, N610, SA263, UM717
    H-3   Hbl-93; Chr-135; Desc-18; Org-13
    S-1   #40. Refrain descant
"Soon and Very Soon" 11249 (Mark) (C)
  CG562, EL439, G384, SH357, UM706, S-2 #187. Piano arr.
    S-2   #187. Piano arrangement

Additional Hymn Suggestions

"Prepare the Way of the Lord" (Isa)
  C121, G95, UM207, VU10
"Come, Thou Long-Expected Jesus" (Pss, Mark)
  C125, CG83, E66, EL254, G82/83, N122, P1/2, SA104, SH64,
  UM196 (PD), VU2
"O Morning Star, How Fair and Bright" (Pss, Mark)
  C105, E497, EL308, G827, N158, P69, UM247, VU98
"I Know Whom I Have Believed" (1 Cor, Mark)
  CG588, SA843, SH529, UM714 (PD)
"Awake, O Sleeper" (Mark)
  E547, EL452, UM551, VU566
"Lo, He Comes with Clouds Descending" (Mark)
  CG100, E57/58, EL435, G348, P6, SA260, UM718, VU25
"My Lord, What a Morning" (Mark)
  C708, EL438 (PD), G352, P449, SH356, UM719, VU708
"Wake, Awake, for Night Is Flying" (Mark)
  E61, EL436, G349, P17, UM720 (PD), VU711
"I Want to Be Ready" (Mark)
  N616, UM722
"O Day of God, Draw Nigh" (Mark, Advent)
  C700, E601, N611, P452, UM730 (PD), VU688/689
"Wait for the Lord" (Mark, Advent)
  CG644, EL262, G90, SH580, VU22, WS3049
"Let All Mortal Flesh Keep Silence" (Mark, Comm.)
  C124, CG81, E324, EL490, G347, N345, P5, UM626 (PD),
  VU473 (Fr.)
"Thou Didst Leave Thy Throne" (Advent)
  CG165, S2100, SA153, SH86

Additional Contemporary and Modern Suggestions

"Awesome God" 41099 (Isa)
  G616, S2040
"Open Our Eyes, Lord" 1572 (Isa)
  CG392, S2086, SA386, SH562
"Water, River, Spirit, Grace" (Isa, Baptism)
  C366, S2253
"Open the Eyes of My Heart" 2298355 (Isa)
  G452, SA270, SH378, WS3008
"The Power of Your Love" 917491 (Isa)
"The Potter's Hand" 2449771 (Isa)
"Jesus, Lover of My Soul" 1198817 (Isa)
"I Have a Hope" 5087587 (Isa)
"Come True Light" 5767773 (Isa, Pss, Advent)
"Song of Hope" ("Heaven Come Down") 5111477 (Isa, Mark)
"Shine, Jesus, Shine" 30426 (Pss, Advent)
  CG156, EL671, G192, S2173, SA261, SH102
"He Who Began a Good Work in You" 15238 (1 Cor)
"Let the Peace of God Reign" 1839987 (1 Cor)
"There's Something About That Name" 14064 (Mark)
  C115, SA80, UM171
"Freedom Is Coming" 4194244 (Mark)
  G359, S2192, SA29
"Come, O Redeemer, Come" 2069663 (Mark, Advent)
"Holy Darkness" (Mark)
  WS3141
"Already Here" (Mark)
  AH4028
"Awaken" 5491647 (Mark)
"Ancient of Days" 798108 (Mark)
"No Greater Love" 930887 (Mark)
"Did You Feel the Mountains Tremble?" 1097028 (Mark)

Vocal Solos

"Patiently Have I Waited" (Isa, Advent)
  V-4   p. 24
"The Blessing" (Pss)
  V-9   p. 10
"But Who May Abide" (Isa, Mark)
  V-2
"My Lord, What a Morning" (Mark)
  V-3 (1)   p. 39

Anthems

"Waiting" (Mark)
Joel Raney; Hope C6325
SATB, piano, opt. instruments (https://bit.ly/C-6325)

"Come, My Light" (Advent)
Anne Krentz Organ; Augsburg 9780800675813
2-part mixed, piano (https://bit.ly/AEC-2-30)

Other Suggestions

Visuals:
  O   Fire, volcanic imagery, dirty cloth, leaf, potter, potter's
        wheel, lump of clay, water
  P   Angels, water (tears), dried leaves, rough cloth (bur-
        lap), shepherd
  E   Portrait of Christ, pile of gifts, 1 Cor 1:9
  G   Eclipse of sun/moon, stars, angels, fig tree, alarm
        clock, crowing rooster
Introit: CG99, WS3048. "View the Present through the Promise"
  (Advent)
Response: S2090. "Light the Advent Candle" (Advent)
Canticle: UM205. Canticle of Light and Darkness (Pss) See S-1,
  p. 383.
Opening Prayer: WSL1 (Mark, Advent)
Prayers: C19 (Advent)
Prayer: WSL57 (Isa)
Response: CG644, EL262, VU22. "Wait for the Lord" (Isa)
Offering Prayer: WSL125 (Advent)
Theme Ideas: Faithfulness, God: Kingdom of God, Preparation,
  Redemption / Salvation, Waiting

Isaiah 40:1-11

Comfort, O comfort my people,
  says your God.
²Speak tenderly to Jerusalem,
  and cry to her
that she has served her term,
  that her penalty is paid,
that she has received from the Lord's hand
  double for all her sins.
³A voice cries out:
"In the wilderness prepare the way of the Lord;
  make straight in the desert a highway for our God.
⁴Every valley shall be lifted up,
  and every mountain and hill be made low;
the uneven ground shall become level,
  and the rough places a plain.
⁵Then the glory of the Lord shall be revealed,
  and all flesh shall see it together,
  for the mouth of the Lord has spoken."
⁶A voice says, "Cry out!"
  And I said, "What shall I cry?"
All flesh is grass;
  their constancy is like the flower of the field.
⁷The grass withers; the flower fades,
  when the breath of the Lord blows upon it;
  surely the people are grass.
⁸The grass withers; the flower fades,
  but the word of our God will stand forever.
⁹Get you up to a high mountain,
  O Zion, herald of good news;
lift up your voice with strength,
  O Jerusalem, herald of good news;
  lift it up, do not fear;
say to the cities of Judah,
  "Here is your God!"
¹⁰See, the Lord God comes with might,
  and his arm rules for him;
his reward is with him
  and his recompense before him.
¹¹He will feed his flock like a shepherd;
  he will gather the lambs in his arms
and carry them in his bosom
  and gently lead the mother sheep.

Psalm 85:1-2, 8-13 (G449, N676, UM806)

Lord, you were favorable to your land;
  you restored the fortunes of Jacob.
²You forgave the iniquity of your people;
  you pardoned all their sin. *Selah*
. . . .
⁸Let me hear what God the Lord will speak,
  for he will speak peace to his people,
  to his faithful, to those who turn to him in their hearts.
⁹Surely his salvation is at hand for those who fear him,
  that his glory may dwell in our land.
¹⁰Steadfast love and faithfulness will meet;
  righteousness and peace will kiss each other.
¹¹Faithfulness will spring up from the ground,
  and righteousness will look down from the sky.
¹²The Lord will give what is good,
  and our land will yield its increase.
¹³Righteousness will go before him
  and will make a path for his steps.

2 Peter 3:8-15a

⁸But do not ignore this one fact, beloved, that with the Lord one day is like a thousand years, and a thousand years are like one day. ⁹The Lord is not slow about his promise, as some think of slowness, but is patient with you, not wanting any to perish but all to come to repentance. ¹⁰But the day of the Lord will come like a thief, and then the heavens will pass away with a loud noise, and the elements will be destroyed with fire, and the earth and everything that is done on it will be disclosed. ¹¹Since all these things are to be destroyed in this way, what sort of persons ought you to be in leading lives of holiness and godliness, ¹²waiting for and hastening the coming of the day of God, because of which the heavens will be set ablaze and destroyed and the elements will melt with fire? ¹³But, in accordance with his promise, we wait for new heavens and a new earth, where righteousness is at home. ¹⁴Therefore, beloved, while you are waiting for these things, strive to be found by him at peace, without spot or blemish, ¹⁵and regard the patience of our Lord as salvation.

Mark 1:1-8

The beginning of the good news of Jesus Christ. ²As it is written in the prophet Isaiah,
  "See, I am sending my messenger ahead of you,
    who will prepare your way,
  ³the voice of one crying out in the wilderness:
    'Prepare the way of the Lord;
    make his paths straight,' "
⁴so John the baptizer appeared in the wilderness, proclaiming a baptism of repentance for the forgiveness of sins. ⁵And the whole Judean region and all the people of Jerusalem were going out to him and were baptized by him in the River Jordan, confessing their sins. ⁶Now John was clothed with camel's hair, with a leather belt around his waist, and he ate locusts and wild honey. ⁷He proclaimed, "The one who is more powerful than I is coming after me; I am not worthy to stoop down and untie the strap of his sandals. ⁸I have baptized you with water, but he will baptize you with the Holy Spirit."

Primary Hymns and Songs for the Day

"O Come, O Come, Emmanuel" (Isa, Pss, Mark) (O)
    C119, CG79, E56, EL257, G88, N116, P9, SA117, SH73,
    UM211, VU1 (Fr.)
            H-3   Hbl-14, 79; Chr-141; Org-168
            S-1   #342. Handbell accompaniment
"Lo, How a Rose E'er Blooming" (Isa)
    C160, CG105, E81, EL272, G129, N127, P48 (PD), UM216,
    VU8
            S-2   #56. Male chorus arrangement
                   #57. Two-octave handbell arrangement
"Who Would Think That What Was Needed" (Isa)
    G138, N153
"Spirit Divine, Attend Our Prayers" (Isa)
    E509, G407, P325, SA210, VU385
"Isaiah the Prophet Has Written of Old" (Isa)
    G77, N108, P337, VU680
"Lift Up Your Heads, Ye Mighty Gates" (Pss, 2 Pet)
    C129, G93, N117, P8, UM213 (PD)
            H-3   Hbl-91; Chr-176; Desc-101; Org-167
            S-1   #334-335. Descant and harmonization
"Lord, Make Us More Holy" (2 Pet)
    G313, N75 (PD), P536
"Angels from the Realms of Glory" (Mark)
    C149, CG126, E93, EL275, G143, N126, P22, SA100, SH99,
    UM220 (PD), VU36
            H-3   Chr-30, 48, 62; Desc-89; Org-121
            S-1   #280. Descant and harmonization
"Wild and Lone the Prophet's Voice" (Mark)
    G163, P409, S2089
"Lord, I Want to Be a Christian" (2 Pet) (C)
    C589, CG507, G729, N454, P372 (PD), SH621, UM402
            H-3   Chr-130

Additional Hymn Suggestions

"People, Look East" (Isa, Advent)
    C142, CG90, EL248, G105, P12, UM202, VU9
"Soon and Very Soon" 11249 (Isa)
    CG562, EL439, G384, SH357, UM706, S-2 #187. Piano arr.
"I Love You, Lord" 25266 (Isa)
    CG362, G627, S2068, SA369, SH417
"Come, Thou Long-Expected Jesus" (Isa, Mark) (O)
    C125, CG83, E66, EL254, G82/83, N122, P1/2, SA104, SH64,
    UM196 (PD), VU2
"Hail to the Lord's Anointed" (Isa, Mark)
    C140, CG98, E311, EL311, G149, N104, P205, SH112, UM203, VU30
"Prepare the Way of the Lord" (Isa, Mark)
    C121, G95, UM207, VU10
"Blessed Be the God of Israel" (Isa, Mark)
    C135, CG88, E444, EL250/552, G109, P602, UM209, VU901
"O Day of Peace that Dimly Shines" (Pss)
    C711, E597, EL711, G373, P450, UM729, VU682
"O God Our Help in Ages Past" (2 Pet)
    C67, CG566, E680, EL632, G687, N25, P210, SA47, SH41,
    UM117 (PD), VU806
"I Know Whom I Have Believed" (2 Pet)
    CG588, SA843, SH529, UM714 (PD)
"O Day of God, Draw Nigh" (2 Pet, Advent)
    C700, E601, N611, P452, UM730 (PD), VU688/689
"Freedom Is Coming" 4194244 (2 Peter)
    G359, S2192, SA29
"God Be with You Till We Meet Again" (Mark) (C)
    C434, CG523, EL536, G541/542, N81, P540, SA1027,
    UM672/673, VU422/423
"Let All Mortal Flesh Keep Silence" (Comm., Advent)
    C124, CG81, E324, EL490, G347, N345, P5, UM626, VU473
"In the Singing" (Comm., Advent)
    EL466, G533, S2255

Additional Contemporary and Modern Suggestions

"Alleluia" 16811 (Isa, Mark)
    C106, N765, SH699, UM186
"Dios Está Aquí" ("God Is Here Today") 3170575 (Isa)
    G411, S2049, SH382
"O Lord, Your Tenderness" 38136 (Isa)
"Gentle Shepherd" 15609 (Isa)
"Let It Rise" 2240585 (Isa)
"Rise Up and Praise Him" 2060552 (Isa)
"How Great Are You, Lord" 2888576 (Isa, Pss)
"Salvation Is Here" 4451327 (Isa, Pss)
"He Came Down" 4679219 (Isa, Pss, Advent)
    EL253, G137, S2085, SH88
"Make Way" 121074 (Isa, Mark)
"God Will Make a Way" 458620 (Isa, Mark)
"Prepare Ye the Way" 5286041 (Isa, Mark)
"O Freedom" (2 Pet)
"Promises" 6454250 (2 Pet)
"Song of Hope" 5111477 (2 Pet, Advent)
"While We Are Waiting, Come" 27525 (2 Pet, Advent)
    G92
"Jesus, Name above All Names" 21291 (Mark)
"Emmanuel, Emmanuel" 12949 (Advent)
    C134, CG120, UM204

Vocal Solos

"Comfort Ye"
"Every Valley"
"O Thou That Tellest Good Tidings to Zion" (Isa)
    V-2
"He Shall Feed His Flock Like a Shepherd" (Isa)
    V-2
    V-8   p. 334
"Come Thou Long Expected Jesus" (Isa, Mark)
    V-3 (3)   p. 50
    V-10   p. 11
"Into the Sea" ("It's Gonna Be OK") (2 Pet)
    V-9   p. 48

Anthems

"Come, Messiah!" (Isa, Advent)
Lloyd Larson; Lorenz 10/5161L
SATB, piano, opt. oboe and percussion (https://bit.ly/L-5161)

"O Come, O Come, Emmanuel" (Isa, Pss, Mark)
Arr. Brenda E. Austin; Hope C6334
SATB, piano, opt. handbells (https://bit.ly/C-6334)

Other Suggestions

Visuals:
    O   God's outstretched hand, Bible, straight highway,
             wilderness, places of solitude, city streets, prairies,
             mountaintop, shepherd carrying a lamb, sheep
    P   Kiss, images of peace, reconciliation
    E   Fire, upheaval / peace, calm
    G   Wilderness, water, rough fabric, leather, honeycomb,
             sandals, fire/dove (Holy Spirit)
Litany: C120, UM211. Advent Antiphons (Pss, Mark)
Responsive Psalm: SH71. *Salmo*/Psalm 85:8-13 (Pss)
Canticle: UM205. "Canticle of Light and Darkness" (Isa). See
    S-1, p. 383.
Canticle: C123. "The Coming of God" (Pss, Mark, Advent)
Prayer: UM201. Advent.
Offering Prayer: WSL152 (Mark, Advent)
Theme Ideas: God: Shepherd, Journey, Patience, Preparation,
    Waiting

Isaiah 61:1-4, 8-11

The spirit of the Lord GOD is upon me
  because the LORD has anointed me;
he has sent me to bring good news to the oppressed,
  to bind up the brokenhearted,
to proclaim liberty to the captives
  and release to the prisoners,
²to proclaim the year of the LORD's favor
  and the day of vengeance of our God,
  to comfort all who mourn,
³to provide for those who mourn in Zion—
  to give them a garland instead of ashes,
the oil of gladness instead of mourning,
  the mantle of praise instead of a faint spirit.
They will be called oaks of righteousness,
  the planting of the LORD, to display his glory.
⁴They shall build up the ancient ruins;
  they shall raise up the former devastations;
they shall repair the ruined cities,
  the devastations of many generations.
. . . .
⁸For I, the LORD, love justice,
  I hate robbery and wrongdoing;
I will faithfully give them their recompense,
  and I will make an everlasting covenant with them.
⁹Their descendants shall be known among the nations
  and their offspring among the peoples;
all who see them shall acknowledge
  that they are a people whom the LORD has blessed.
¹⁰I will greatly rejoice in the LORD;
  my whole being shall exult in my God,
for he has clothed me with the garments of salvation;
  he has covered me with the robe of righteousness,
as a bridegroom decks himself with a garland
  and as a bride adorns herself with her jewels.
¹¹For as the earth brings forth its shoots
  and as a garden causes what is sown in it to spring up,
so the Lord GOD will cause righteousness and praise
  to spring up before all the nations.

Psalm 126 (G73, N707, P237, UM847)

When the LORD restored the fortunes of Zion,
  we were like those who dream.
²Then our mouth was filled with laughter
  and our tongue with shouts of joy;
then it was said among the nations,
  "The LORD has done great things for them."
³The LORD has done great things for us,
  and we rejoiced.
⁴Restore our fortunes, O LORD,
  like the watercourses in the Negeb.
⁵May those who sow in tears
  reap with shouts of joy.
⁶Those who go out weeping,
  bearing the seed for sowing,
shall come home with shouts of joy,
  carrying their sheaves.

1 Thessalonians 5:16-24

¹⁶Rejoice always, ¹⁷pray without ceasing, ¹⁸give thanks in all circumstances, for this is the will of God in Christ Jesus for you. ¹⁹Do not quench the Spirit. ²⁰Do not despise prophecies, ²¹but test everything; hold fast to what is good; ²²abstain from every form of evil.

²³May the God of peace himself sanctify you entirely, and may your spirit and soul and body be kept sound and blameless at the coming of our Lord Jesus Christ. ²⁴The one who calls you is faithful, and he will do this.

John 1:6-8, 19-28

⁶There was a man sent from God whose name was John. ⁷He came as a witness to testify to the light, so that all might believe through him. ⁸He himself was not the light, but he came to testify to the light. . . .

¹⁹This is the testimony given by John when the Jews sent priests and Levites from Jerusalem to ask him, "Who are you?" ²⁰He confessed and did not deny it, but he confessed, "I am not the Messiah." ²¹And they asked him, "What then? Are you Elijah?" He said, "I am not." "Are you the prophet?" He answered, "No." ²²Then they said to him, "Who are you? Let us have an answer for those who sent us. What do you say about yourself?" ²³He said,

  "I am the voice of one crying out in the wilderness,
    'Make straight the way of the Lord,'"
  as the prophet Isaiah said.

²⁴Now they had been sent from the Pharisees. ²⁵They asked him, "Why, then, are you baptizing if you are neither the Messiah, nor Elijah, nor the prophet?" ²⁶John answered them, "I baptize with water. Among you stands one whom you do not know, ²⁷the one who is coming after me; I am not worthy to untie the strap of his sandal." ²⁸This took place in Bethany across the Jordan where John was baptizing.

Primary Hymns and Songs for the Day

"Come, Thou Long-Expected Jesus" (Isa, John) (O)
C125, CG83, E66, EL254, G82/83, N122, P1/2, SA104, SH64, UM196 (PD), VU2
    H-3   Hbl-46; Chr-26, 134; Desc-53; Org-56
    S-1   #168-171. Various treatments
"Gather Us In" (Isa, John) (O)
C284, EL532, G401, S2236, SH393
"Hail to the Lord's Anointed" (Isa, Pss)
N104, UM203
    H-3   Hbl-16, 22, 68; Chr-101; Desc-37
    S-1   #114. Descant
         #115. Harmonization
C140, CG98, EL311, G149, P205, SH112, VU30
"On Jordan's Bank the Baptist's Cry" (Isa, John)
E76, EL249, G96, N115, P10, SA120, SH77, VU20
"When God Restored Our Common Life" (Pss)
G74, S2182
"Savior of the Nations, Come" (John)
E54, EL263, G102, P14 (PD), SH67, UM214
    H-3   Chr-168; Org-100
"Hark! the Herald Angels Sing" (John) (C)
C150, CG127, E87, EL270, G119, N144, P31, SA108, SH94, UM240 (PD), VU48
    H-3   Hbl-26, 67; Chr-91; Desc-75; Org-89
    S-1   #234-236. Harmonizations and descant

Additional Hymn Suggestions

"O For a Thousand Tongues to Sing" (Isa) (O)
C5, CG332, E493, EL886, G610, N42, P466, SA89, SH439, UM57 (PD), VU326 (See also WS3001)
"Holy, Holy, Holy! Lord God Almighty" (Isa)
C4, CG1, E362, EL413, G1, N277, P138, SA31, SH450, UM64/65, VU315
"Tell Out, My Soul" (Isa)
CG94, E437/E438, SA393, UM200
"Rejoice, Ye Pure in Heart" (Pss, 1 Thess) (O)
C15, CG312, E556/557, EL873/874, G804, N55/71, P145/146, UM160/161
"Jesus Shall Reign" (1 Thess)
C95, CG158, E544, EL434, G265, N300, P423, SA258, SH209, UM157 (PD), VU330
"Softly and Tenderly Jesus Is Calling" (1 Thess)
C340, CG474, EL608 (PD), G418, N449, SA435, SH601, UM348
"Christ, Whose Glory Fills the Skies" (John)
EL553, G662, P462/463, SA249, UM173, VU336
"Send Your Word" (John)
N317, UM195
"I Want to Walk as a Child of the Light" (John)
CG96, E490, EL815, G377, SH352, UM206
"Lead Me, Lord" (John)
C593, N774, UM473 (PD), VU662
"Lead Me, Guide Me" (John)
C583, CG403, EL768, G740, S2214, SH582
"Wild and Lone the Prophet's Voice" (John, Advent)
G163, P409, S2089

Additional Contemporary and Modern Suggestions

"Hosanna! Hosanna!" 1388919 (Isa)
"Santo, Santo, Santo" ("Holy, Holy, Holy") (Isa)
C111, CG3, EL473, G595, N793, S2007, SH452
"Holy, Holy" 18792 (Isa)
"Veni Sancte Spiritus" ("Holy Spirit, Come to Us") (Isa, Advent)
EL406, G281, S2118
"O Lord, Your Tenderness" 38136 (Isa)
"From Ashes to Beauty" 5288953 (Isa)
"Come, Emmanuel" 3999938 (Isa, Pss, Advent)

"Let Us Build a House Where Love Can Dwell" (Isa, Pss)
EL641, G301, SH228 (See also WS3152)
"Make Way" 121074 (Isa, John, Advent)
"Shout to the Lord" 1406918 (Pss)
CG348, EL821, S2074, SA264, SH426
"Jubilate Servite" ("Come, Rejoice in God") (1 Thess)
"Sanctuary" 24140 (1 Thess)
G701, S2164, SH265
"Canto de Esperanza" ("Song of Hope") (1 Thess)
G765, P432, S2186, SH721, VU424
"Lord, Listen to Your Children Praying" 22829 (1 Thess)
C305, CG389, G469, S2193, SH577, VU400
"In the Lord I'll Be Ever Thankful" (1 Thess)
G654, S2195, SH316
"Yesu Tawa Pano" ("Jesus, We Are Here") (1 Thess)
EL529, G392, S2273, SH611
"Forever" 3148428 (1 Thess)
CG53, SA363, WS3023
"I Will Give Thanks" 6266091 (1 Thess)
"Prepare the Way of the Lord" (John)
C121, G95, UM207, VU10
"Jesus, Name above All Names" 21291 (John)
S2071, SA82
"Light of the World" 73342 (John)
"Behold, What Manner of Love" 1596 (John)
"Arise, Shine" 13797 (John)
"Glory in the Highest" 4822451 (John)
"Come True Light" 5767773 (John)

Vocal Solos

"Great Things" (Isa)
    V-9   p. 36
"Rejoice Greatly, O Daughter of Zion" (Pss)
    V-2
"Now Thank We All Our God" (Pss, 1 Thess)
    V-6   p. 8

Anthems

"Advent Jubilate" (Isa, Pss, John)
Arr. Victoria Schwarz: Shawnee Press 00292336
SATB, piano, opt. flute (https://bit.ly/SP-2336)

"I Want to Walk as a Child of the Light" (John)
Arr. Tom Trenney; Pavane HL 00268934
SATB, piano (https://bit.ly/HL-68934)

Other Suggestions

Visuals:
    O   Garland, oil, mantel, oak tree, rich garments/jewelry
    P   Praise, tears of joy, sheaves of wheat
    E   Praying hands, 1 Thess 5:16, 17
    G   Water/baptism, light, John 1:23 (Christ candle)
Introit: C142, CG90, EL248, G105, P12, UM202, VU9, stanza 3. "People, Look East" (Advent)
Canticle: UM205. "Canticle of Light and Darkness" (John)
Call to Prayer: EL406, G281, S2118. "Holy Spirit, Come to Us" (Isa)
Prayer of Confession: UM201. Advent (Isa, John)
Prayer: C591 or UM489. "For God's Gifts" (John)
Response: C593, N774, UM473 (PD), VU662. "Lead Me, Lord" (John)
Offering Prayer: WSL136 (Advent)
Benediction: WSL165 (1 Thess)
Theme Ideas: Holy Spirit, Joy, Justice, Light, Preparation

2 Samuel 7:1-11, 16

Now when the king was settled in his house and the LORD had given him rest from all his enemies around him, [2]the king said to the prophet Nathan, "See now, I am living in a house of cedar, but the ark of God stays in a tent." [3]Nathan said to the king, "Go, do all that you have in mind, for the LORD is with you."

[4]But that same night the word of the LORD came to Nathan, [5]"Go and tell my servant David: Thus says the LORD: Are you the one to build me a house to live in? [6]I have not lived in a house since the day I brought up the people of Israel from Egypt to this day, but I have been moving about in a tent and a tabernacle. [7]Wherever I have moved about among all the people of Israel, did I ever speak a word with any of the tribal leaders of Israel, whom I commanded to shepherd my people Israel, saying, 'Why have you not built me a house of cedar?' [8]Now therefore thus you shall say to my servant David: Thus says the LORD of hosts: I took you from the pasture, from following the sheep to be prince over my people Israel, [9]and I have been with you wherever you went and have cut off all your enemies from before you, and I will make for you a great name, like the name of the great ones of the earth. [10]And I will appoint a place for my people Israel and will plant them, so that they may live in their own place and be disturbed no more, and evildoers shall afflict them no more, as formerly, [11]from the time that I appointed judges over my people Israel, and I will give you rest from all your enemies. Moreover, the LORD declares to you that the LORD will make you a house. . . .

[16]Your house and your kingdom shall be made sure forever before me; your throne shall be established forever."

Luke 1:46b-55

[46b]"My soul magnifies the Lord,
     [47]and my spirit rejoices in God my Savior,
[48]for he has looked with favor on the lowly state of his servant.
     Surely from now on all generations will call me blessed,
[49]for the Mighty One has done great things for me,
     and holy is his name;
[50]indeed, his mercy is for those who fear him
     from generation to generation.
[51]He has shown strength with his arm;
     he has scattered the proud in the imagination of their hearts.
[52]He has brought down the powerful from their thrones
     and lifted up the lowly;
[53]he has filled the hungry with good things
     and sent the rich away empty.
[54]He has come to the aid of his child Israel,
     in remembrance of his mercy,
[55]according to the promise he made to our ancestors,
     to Abraham and to his descendants forever."

Romans 16:25-27

[25]Now to God who is able to strengthen you according to my gospel and the proclamation of Jesus Christ, according to the revelation of the mystery that was kept secret for long ages [26]but is now disclosed and through the prophetic writings is made known to all the gentiles, according to the command of the eternal God, to bring about the obedience of faith—[27]to the only wise God, through Jesus Christ, to whom be the glory forever! Amen.

Luke 1:26-38

[26]In the sixth month the angel Gabriel was sent by God to a town in Galilee called Nazareth, [27]to a virgin engaged to a man whose name was Joseph, of the house of David. The virgin's name was Mary. [28]And he came to her and said, "Greetings, favored one! The Lord is with you." [29]But she was much perplexed by his words and pondered what sort of greeting this might be. [30]The angel said to her, "Do not be afraid, Mary, for you have found favor with God. [31]And now, you will conceive in your womb and bear a son, and you will name him Jesus. [32]He will be great and will be called the Son of the Most High, and the Lord God will give to him the throne of his ancestor David. [33]He will reign over the house of Jacob forever, and of his kingdom there will be no end." [34]Mary said to the angel, "How can this be, since I am a virgin?" [35]The angel said to her, "The Holy Spirit will come upon you, and the power of the Most High will overshadow you; therefore the child to be born will be holy; he will be called Son of God. [36]And now, your relative Elizabeth in her old age has also conceived a son, and this is the sixth month for her who was said to be barren. [37]For nothing will be impossible with God." [38]Then Mary said, "Here am I, the servant of the Lord; let it be with me according to your word." Then the angel departed from her.

Primary Hymns and Songs for the Day
"O Come, O Come, Emmanuel" (2 Sam) (O)
    C119, CG79, E56, EL257, G88, N116, P9, SA117, SH73,
    UM211, VU1(Fr.)
        H-3   Hbl-14, 79; Chr-141; Org-168
        S-1   #342. Handbell accompaniment
"Hail to the Lord's Anointed" (2 Sam, Luke) (O)
    N104, UM203
        H-3   Hbl-16, 22, 68; Chr-101; Desc-37
        S-1   #114. Descant
               #115. Harmonization
    C140, CG98, EL311, G149, P205, SH112, VU30
"Blessed Be the God of Israel" (2 Sam)
    C135, CG88, E444, EL250/552, G109, P602, UM209, VU901
        H-3   Hbl-70; Chr-103, 174; Desc-76; Org-90
"It Came Upon the Midnight Clear" (2 Sam, Rom, Luke)
    C153, CG132, E89, EL282, G123, N131, P38, SA111, SH89,
    UM218 (PD), VU44
        H-3   Hbl-72; Chr-113; Desc-22; Org-19
        S-2   #39. Descant
"That Boy-Child of Mary" (2 Sam, Luke)
    EL293, G139, P55, UM241
        H-3   Chr-179
        S-1   #45. Guitar/autoharp chords
        S-2   #28. Flute descant
"Of the Father's Love Begotten" (Rom)
    C104, CG113, E82, EL295, G108, N118, P309, SA119, SH81,
    UM184, VU61
        H-3   Hbl-14, 85; Chr-155; Org-29
        S-1   #92. Handbell arrangement
"My Soul Gives Glory to My God" (Luke)
    C130, EL251, G99, N119, P600, UM198, VU899
        H-3   Chr-139, 145; Desc-77
        S-1   #241-242. Orff arr. and descant
"Canticle of the Turning" (Luke)
    EL723, G100, SH68
"To a Maid Engaged to Joseph" (Luke)
    G98, P19, UM215, VU14
"Jesus, the Light of the World" 6363190 (Luke)
    WS3056 (See also AH4038, CG129, G127, N160, SH103)
"Hark! the Herald Angels Sing" (Luke) (C)
    C150, CG127, E87, EL270, G119, N144, P31, SA108, SH94,
    UM240 (PD), VU48
        C150 Descant
        H-3   Hbl-26, 67; Chr-91; Desc-75; Org-89
        S-1   #234-236. Harmonizations and descant

Additional Hymn Suggestions
"O Come, O Come, Emmanuel" (2 Sam)
    C119, CG79, E56, EL257, G88, N116, P9, SA117, SH73,
    UM211, VU1(Fr.)
"Come, Thou Long-Expected Jesus" (Luke) (O)
    C125, CG83, E66, EL254, G82/83, N122, P1/2, SA104, SH64,
    UM196 (PD), VU2
"Tell Out, My Soul" (Luke)
    CG94, E437/E438, SA393, UM200
"Savior of the Nations, Come" (Luke)
    E54, EL263, G102, P14 (PD), SH67, UM214
"Il Est Né" ("He Is Born") (Luke)
    CG106, UM228, VU50 (Fr.)
"O Come, All Ye Faithful" (Luke) (O)
    C148, CG103, E83, EL283, G133, N135, P41, SA116, SH96,
    UM234 (PD), VU60 (Fr.)
"Once in Royal David's City" (Luke)
    C165, CG104, E102, EL269, G140, N145, P49, SA121, UM250
    (PD), VU62
"The Snow Lay on the Ground" (Luke)
    E110, G116, S2093, P57

"The Virgin Mary Had a Baby Boy" 2957081 (Luke)
    AH4037, S2098, SA127, VU73
"Joseph Dearest, Joseph Mine" (Luke)
    N105, S2099

Additional Contemporary and Modern Suggestions
"The Family Prayer Song" 1680466 (2 Sam)
"All Things Are Possible" 2245140 (2 Sam, Luke)
"He Is Able" 115420 (Rom)
"Guide My Feet" (Rom)
    CG637, G741, N497, P354, S2208, SH54
"God Is the Strength of My Heart" 80919 (Rom)
"You Are My All in All" 825356 (Rom, Luke)
    CG571, G519, SH335, WS3040
"Praise to the Lord" (Luke)
    EL844, S2029, VU835
"Gloria a Dios" ("Glory to God") (Luke)
    CG320, EL164, G585, S2033, SH381
"How Great You Are" 6271677 (Luke)
"Shout to the North" 1562261 (Luke)
    G319, SA1009, WS3042
"Make Way" 121074 (Luke, Advent)
"Glory To God Forever" 5384338 (Luke)
"Great and Mighty Is He" 66665 (Luke)
"This Kingdom" 1650898 (Luke)
"Holy Spirit, Rain Down" 2405227 (Luke)
"Good to Me" 313480 (Luke)
"My Savior Lives" 4882965 (Luke)
"From Ashes to Beauty" 5288953 (Luke)
"Daughter of God" 4509781 (Luke)

Vocal Solos
"Behold, A Virgin Shall Conceive" (Luke)
    V-2
"Sing of Mary, Pure and Lowly" (Luke)
    V-5 (1)   p. 21
"Great Things" (Luke)
    V-9   p. 36
"Sleep, Little Baby" (Luke, Christmas)
    V-10   p. 27

Anthems
"Emmanuel" (2 Sam)
Arr. Larry Shackley; Lorenz 10/5189L
SATB, keyboard, opt. rhythm section (https://bit.ly/L-5189)

"Joy To the World" (Luke, Christmas)
Arr. Dan Forrest; Beckenhorst BP2263
SATB, piano 4-hands, opt. orchestra (https://bit.ly/BP-2263)

Other Suggestions
Visuals:
    O   Cedar, crown, tent, ark of the covenant (chest)
    G   Luke 1:46b, food, hungry being fed
    E   Open Bible, Christ, servant, obedience
    G   Luke 1:28-56, angel, Mary, annunciation, servant imag-
         ery, Luke 1:38
As an alternative to reading the Luke passage, have the choir lead the
    congregation in singing C130, G99, N119, P600, UM198, VU899,
    "My Soul Gives Glory to My God."
Additional Magnificat Settings: C131, CG91, E269, EL314, G100,
    SH68, N732, UM199, VU898 (Luke)
Canticle: UM199. "Canticle of Mary" (Luke) (See S-1, p. 382.)
Movement or dance can enhance the Luke songs and readings.
Offering Prayer: WSL135 or WSL148 (Luke, Advent)
Theme Ideas: God: Love of God, God: Promises, Holy Spirit,
    Justice, Praise

Isaiah 9:2-7

²The people who walked in darkness
 have seen a great light;
those who lived in a land of deep darkness—
 on them light has shined.
³You have multiplied exultation;
 you have increased its joy;
they rejoice before you
 as with joy at the harvest,
 as people exult when dividing plunder.
⁴For the yoke of their burden
 and the bar across their shoulders,
 the rod of their oppressor,
 you have broken as on the day of Midian.
⁵For all the boots of the tramping warriors
 and all the garments rolled in blood
 shall be burned as fuel for the fire.
⁶For a child has been born for us,
 a son given to us;
authority rests upon his shoulders,
 and he is named
Wonderful Counselor, Mighty God,
 Everlasting Father, Prince of Peace.
⁷Great will be his authority,
 and there shall be endless peace
for the throne of David and his kingdom.
 He will establish and uphold it
with justice and with righteousness
 from this time onward and forevermore.
The zeal of the LORD of hosts will do this.

Psalm 96 (G304, N684, P216/217, SH648, UM815)

O sing to the LORD a new song;
 sing to the LORD, all the earth.
²Sing to the LORD; bless his name;
 tell of his salvation from day to day.
³Declare his glory among the nations,
 his marvelous works among all the peoples.
⁴For great is the LORD and greatly to be praised;
 he is to be revered above all gods.
⁵For all the gods of the peoples are idols,
 but the LORD made the heavens.
⁶Honor and majesty are before him;
 strength and beauty are in his sanctuary.
⁷Ascribe to the LORD, O families of the peoples,
 ascribe to the LORD glory and strength.
⁸Ascribe to the LORD the glory due his name;
 bring an offering, and come into his courts.
⁹Worship the LORD in holy splendor;
 tremble before him, all the earth.
¹⁰Say among the nations, "The LORD is king!
 The world is firmly established; it shall never be moved.
 He will judge the peoples with equity."
¹¹Let the heavens be glad, and let the earth rejoice;
 let the sea roar and all that fills it;
 ¹²let the field exult and everything in it.
Then shall all the trees of the forest sing for joy
 ¹³before the LORD, for he is coming,
 for he is coming to judge the earth.
He will judge the world with righteousness
 and the peoples with his truth.

Titus 2:11-14

¹¹For the grace of God has appeared, bringing salvation to all, ¹²training us to renounce impiety and worldly passions and in the present age to live lives that are self-controlled, upright, and godly, ¹³while we wait for the blessed hope and the manifestation of the glory of our great God and Savior, Jesus Christ. ¹⁴He it is who gave himself for us that he might redeem us from all iniquity and purify for himself a people of his own who are zealous for good deeds.

Luke 2:1-20

In those days a decree went out from Caesar Augustus that all the world should be registered. ²This was the first registration and was taken while Quirinius was governor of Syria. ³All went to their own towns to be registered. ⁴Joseph also went from the town of Nazareth in Galilee to Judea, to the city of David called Bethlehem, because he was descended from the house and family of David. ⁵He went to be registered with Mary, to whom he was engaged and who was expecting a child. ⁶While they were there, the time came for her to deliver her child. ⁷And she gave birth to her firstborn son and wrapped him in bands of cloth and laid him in a manger, because there was no place in the guest room.

⁸Now in that same region there were shepherds living in the fields, keeping watch over their flock by night. ⁹Then an angel of the Lord stood before them, and the glory of the Lord shone around them, and they were terrified. ¹⁰But the angel said to them, "Do not be afraid, for see, I am bringing you good news of great joy for all the people: ¹¹to you is born this day in the city of David a Savior, who is the Messiah, the Lord. ¹²This will be a sign for you: you will find a child wrapped in bands of cloth and lying in a manger." ¹³And suddenly there was with the angel a multitude of the heavenly host, praising God and saying,

 ¹⁴"Glory to God in the highest heaven,
  and on earth peace among those whom he favors!"

¹⁵When the angels had left them and gone into heaven, the shepherds said to one another, "Let us go now to Bethlehem and see this thing that has taken place, which the Lord has made known to us." ¹⁶So they went with haste and found Mary and Joseph and the child lying in the manger. ¹⁷When they saw this, they made known what had been told them about this child, ¹⁸and all who heard it were amazed at what the shepherds told them, ¹⁹and Mary treasured all these words and pondered them in her heart. ²⁰The shepherds returned, glorifying and praising God for all they had heard and seen, just as it had been told them.

Primary Hymns and Songs for the Day
"O Come, All Ye Faithful" (Isa, Luke) (O)
   See especially stanzas 1, 3, and 4.
   C148, CG103, E83, EL283, G133, N135, P41, SA116, SH96,
   UM234 (PD), VU60 (Fr.)
      H-3   Hbl-78; Desc-12; Org-2
      S-1   #7-13. Various treatments
"Born in the Night, Mary's Child" (Isa)
   G158, N152, P30, VU95
      H-3   Chr-44
"On Christmas Night" (Isa, Titus, Luke)
   CG133, EL274, G112, N143, WS3064
"O Little Town of Bethlehem" (Luke)
   C144, CG107, E78/79, EL279, G121, N133, P43/44, SA118,
   SH80, UM230, VU64
      H-3   Hbl-81; Chr-145; Desc-95; Org-141
      S-1   #304. Harmonization
"Angels We Have Heard on High" (Luke) (festive close)
   C155, CG125, E96, EL289, G113, P23, N125, SH93, UM238,
   VU38 (Fr.)
      C155   Descant
      H-3   Hbl-47; Chr-31; Desc-43; Org-45
"Silent Night, Holy Night" (Luke) (quiet close)
   C145, CG134, E111, EL281, G122, N134, P60, SA124, SH83,
   UM239 (PD), VU67 (Fr.)
      H-3   Hbl-92; Chr-171; Desc-99; Org-159
      S-1   #322. Descant
            #323. Guitar/Autoharp chords
      S-2   #167. Handbell arrangement

Additional Hymn Suggestions
"In the Singing" (Titus, Comm.)
   EL466, G533, S2255
"Away in a Manger" (Luke)
   C147, CG110/111, E101, EL277, G114/115, N124, P24/P25,
   SA102, SH79, UM217, VU69
"What Child Is This" (Luke)
   C162, CG148, E115, EL296, G145, N148, P53, SH105, UM219
   (PD), VU74
"Good Christian Friends, Rejoice" (Luke)
   C164, CG122, E107, EL288, G132, N129, P28, UM224, VU35
"Infant Holy, Infant Lowly" (Luke)
   C163, CG139, EL276, G128, P37, UM229, VU58
"While Shepherds Watched Their Flocks" (Luke)
   C154, E94/E95, CG123, G117/118, P58, SA132, UM236,
   VU75
"Hark! the Herald Angels Sing" (Luke)
   C150, CG127, E87, EL270, G119, N144, P31, SA108, SH94,
   UM240 (PD), VU48
"Love Came Down at Christmas" (Luke)
   CG147, E84, N165, UM242
"The First Noel" (Luke)
   C151, CG124, E109, EL300, G147, N139, P56, SA126, UM245
   (PD), VU90 (Fr.) and VU91
"On This Day Earth Shall Ring" (Luke)
   E92, G141, P46, UM248 (PD)
"Go, Tell It on the Mountain" (Luke)
   C167, CG143, E99, EL290, G136, N154, P29, SA106, SH90,
   UM251, VU43
"Like a Child" (Luke)
   C133, S2092, VU366
"The Snow Lay on the Ground" (Luke)
   E110, G116, S2093, P57
"Rise Up, Shepherd, and Follow" (Luke)
   G135, P50, S2096, VU70
"Still, Still, Still" (Luke)
   CG117, G124, P47, VU47, WS3066
"From Heaven Above" (Luke)
   C146, CG128, E80, EL268, G111, N130, P54, VU72

Additional Contemporary and Modern Suggestions
"His Name Is Wonderful" 1122230 (Isa)
   CG343, SH454, UM174
"O-So-So" ("Come Now, O Prince of Peace") (Isa)
   EL247, G103, S2232, SH235
"Light of the World" 73342 (Isa)
"How Majestic Is Your Name" 26007 (Isa)
   C63, CG326, G613, S2023, SA90
"Jesus, Name above All Names" 21291 (Isa)
"Love Has Come" (Isa, Titus, Luke)
   EL292, G110, WS3059
"Jesus, Jesus, Oh, What a Wonderful Child" 4206259 (Isa, Luke)
   EL297, G126, N136, WS3060
"I Sing Praises to Your Name" 17061 (Pss)
"Shout to the Lord" 1406918 (Pss)
   CG348, EL821, S2074, SA264, SH426
"Lord, I Lift Your Name on High" 117947 (Luke)
   AH4071, CG606, EL857, S2088, SA379, SH205
"Amen, Amen" (Luke)
   N161, P299, S2072
"Welcome to Our World" 2317391 (Luke)
"Glory To God Forever" 5384338 (Luke)
"Peace in the Manger" 7104263 (Luke)
"What Love Has Done" 5836965 (Luke, Christmas)

Vocal Solos
"Hark! The Herald Angels Sing" (Pss, Luke)
   V-1   p. 13
"O Holy Night" (Luke)
   V-8   p. 93
"In the First Light" (Luke)
   V-5(1)   p. 28
"Sleep, Little Baby" (Luke)
   V-10   p. 27
"Go, Tell It on the Mountain" (Christmas)
   V-3 (1)   p. 10

Anthems
"It Came Upon a Midnight Clear" (Luke)
Arr. Marianne Forman; Beckenhorst BP2277
SATB, piano, opt. violin (https://bit.ly/BP-2277)

"Shepherd Song" (Luke)
Molly Ijames; Lorenz 10/5188L
Unison or Two-part, keyboard (https://bit.ly/L-5188)

Other Suggestions
Visuals:
   O   Joy, praise, Isa 9:6b
   P   Musical notes, sea, field, trees, branches upraised,
           Ps 96:12b
   E   Titus 2:11, Christ child, manger
   G   Christ child, manger, Mary, Joseph, shepherds/angels,
           peace, joy, Luke 2:14, 19
Introit: C166, E114, EL284, G142, N151, P61, UM244, VU71,
   stanzas 1 and 4 "'Twas in the Moon of Wintertime" (Luke,
   Christmas)
Introit: CG320, EL164, G585, S2033, SH381. *"Gloria"* (Luke)
Canticle: N757, UM82 "Canticle of God's Glory" (Luke)
Readings: C152, CG108 (Luke)
Response: EL293, G139, P55, UM241, stanzas 2 and 5. "That
   Boy-Child of Mary" (Luke)
Call to Offering: WS3063. "If I Could Visit Bethlehem" (Luke)
Offering Prayer: WSL149. "Gracious God" (Christmas)
Theme Ideas: God: Promises, Light, Praise

Isaiah 61:10–62:3

[10]I will greatly rejoice in the LORD;
  my whole being shall exult in my God,
for he has clothed me with the garments of salvation;
  he has covered me with the robe of righteousness,
as a bridegroom decks himself with a garland
  and as a bride adorns herself with her jewels.
[11]For as the earth brings forth its shoots
  and as a garden causes what is sown in it to spring up,
so the Lord GOD will cause righteousness and praise
  to spring up before all the nations.
62 For Zion's sake I will not keep silent,
  and for Jerusalem's sake I will not rest,
until her vindication shines out like the dawn
  and her salvation like a burning torch.
[2]The nations shall see your vindication
  and all the kings your glory,
and you shall be called by a new name
  that the mouth of the LORD will give.
[3]You shall be a beautiful crown in the hand of the LORD
  and a royal diadem in the hand of your God.

Psalm 148 (G17, N721, P256, UM861)

Praise the LORD!
Praise the LORD from the heavens;
  praise him in the heights!
[2]Praise him, all his angels;
  praise him, all his host!
[3]Praise him, sun and moon;
  praise him, all you shining stars!
[4]Praise him, you highest heavens
  and you waters above the heavens!
[5]Let them praise the name of the LORD,
  for he commanded and they were created.
[6]He established them forever and ever;
  he fixed their bounds, which cannot be passed.
[7]Praise the LORD from the earth,
  you sea monsters and all deeps,
[8]fire and hail, snow and frost,
  stormy wind fulfilling his command!
[9]Mountains and all hills,
  fruit trees and all cedars!
[10]Wild animals and all cattle,
  creeping things and flying birds!
[11]Kings of the earth and all peoples,
  princes and all rulers of the earth!
[12]Young men and women alike,
  old and young together!
[13]Let them praise the name of the LORD,
  for his name alone is exalted;
  his glory is above earth and heaven.
[14]He has raised up a horn for his people,
  praise for all his faithful,
  for the people of Israel who are close to him.
Praise the LORD!

Galatians 4:4-7

[4]But when the fullness of time had come, God sent his Son, born of a woman, born under the law, [5]in order to redeem those who were under the law, so that we might receive adoption as children. [6]And because you are children, God has sent the Spirit of his Son into our hearts, crying, "Abba! Father!" [7]So you are no longer a slave but a child, and if a child then also an heir through God.

Luke 2:22-40

[22]When the time came for their purification according to the law of Moses, they brought him up to Jerusalem to present him to the Lord [23](as it is written in the law of the Lord, "Every first-born male shall be designated as holy to the Lord"), [24]and they offered a sacrifice according to what is stated in the law of the Lord, "a pair of turtledoves or two young pigeons."

[25]Now there was a man in Jerusalem whose name was Simeon; this man was righteous and devout, looking forward to the consolation of Israel, and the Holy Spirit rested on him. [26]It had been revealed to him by the Holy Spirit that he would not see death before he had seen the Lord's Messiah. [27]Guided by the Spirit, Simeon came into the temple, and when the parents brought in the child Jesus to do for him what was customary under the law, [28]Simeon took him in his arms and praised God, saying,

[29]"Master, now you are dismissing your servant in peace,
  according to your word,
[30]for my eyes have seen your salvation,
  [31]which you have prepared in the presence of all peoples,
  [32]a light for revelation to the gentiles
  and for glory to your people Israel."

[33]And the child's father and mother were amazed at what was being said about him. [34]Then Simeon blessed them and said to his mother Mary, "This child is destined for the falling and the rising of many in Israel and to be a sign that will be opposed [35]so that the inner thoughts of many will be revealed—and a sword will pierce your own soul, too."

[36]There was also a prophet, Anna the daughter of Phanuel, of the tribe of Asher. She was of a great age, having lived with her husband seven years after her marriage, [37]then as a widow to the age of eighty-four. She never left the temple but worshiped there with fasting and prayer night and day. [38]At that moment she came and began to praise God and to speak about the child to all who were looking for the redemption of Jerusalem.

[39]When they had finished everything required by the law of the Lord, they returned to Galilee, to their own town of Nazareth. [40]The child grew and became strong, filled with wisdom, and the favor of God was upon him.

Primary Hymns and Songs for the Day
"All Creatures of Our God and King" (Pss) (O)
    C22, CG307, E400, EL835, G15, N17, P455, SA2, SH16,
    UM62, VU217 (Fr.)
        H-3   Hbl-44; Chr-21; Desc-66; Org-73
        S-1   #198-204. Various treatments
"Hark! the Herald Angels Sing" (Isa, Gal, Luke) (O)
    C150, CG127, E87, EL270, G119, N144, P31, SA108, SH94,
    UM240 (PD), VU48
        C150 Descant
        H-3   Hbl-26, 67; Chr-91; Desc-75; Org-89
        S-1   #234-236. Harmonizations and descant
"Jesus, the Light of the World" 6363190 (Gal, Luke)
    WS3056 (See also AH4038, CG129, G127, N160, SH103)
"Wash, O God, Our Sons and Daughters" (Gal, Baptism)
    C365, EL445, G490, SH669, UM605, VU442
        H-3   Hbl-14, 64; Chr-132, 203
        S-2   #22. Descant
"Baptized in Water" (Gal, Baptism)
    CG449, E294, EL456, G482, P492, S2248, SH666
        H-3   Hbl-77; Chr-136; Desc-21; Org-16
        S-1   #50-51. Flute and vocal descants
"Away in a Manger" (Luke, Christmas)
    C147, CG110/111, E101, EL277, G114/115, N124, P24/P25,
    SA102, SH79, UM217, VU69
        H-3   Org-21
"Lord, Dismiss Us with Thy Blessing" (Luke) (C)
    C439, E344, EL545, G546, N77, P538, UM671 (PD), VU425
        H-3   Chr-75, 116, 130; Desc-98; Org-151

Additional Hymn Suggestions
"I Sing the Almighty Power of God" (Isa, Gal)
    C64, CG19, E398, G32, N12, P288 (PD), SA36, UM152 (PD),
    VU231 (PD)
"Hail to the Lord's Anointed" (Isa)
    C140, CG98, EL311, G149, N104, P205, SH112, UM203, VU30
"Lo, How a Rose E'er Blooming" (Isa)
    C160, CG105, E81, EL272, G129, N127, P48 (PD), UM216, VU8
"Deck Thyself, My Soul, with Gladness" (Isa)
    E339, EL488/EL489, G514, P506, UM612 (PD), VU463
"God Who Stretched the Spangled Heavens" (Gal)
    C651, CG21, E580, EL771, G24, N556, P268, UM150
"Savior of the Nations, Come" (Gal)
    E54, EL263, G102, P14 (PD), SH67, UM214
"Because He Lives" (Gal)
    AH4070, C562, CG620, SA219, SH200, UM364
"Once in Royal David's City" (Gal, Luke)
    C165, CG104, E102, EL269, G140, N145, P49, SA121, UM250
    (PD), VU62
"I Want to Walk as a Child of the Light" (Luke)
    CG96, E490, EL815, G377, SH352, UM206
"What Child Is This" (Luke, Christmas)
    C162, CG148, E115, EL296, G145, N148, P53, SH105, UM219
    (PD), VU74
"That Boy-Child of Mary" (Luke, Christmas)
    EL293, G139, P55, UM241
"Sing of Mary, Pure and Lowly" (Luke)
    C184, E277, UM272
"Our Parent, by Whose Name" (Luke)
    E587, EL640, UM447, VU555
"Let Us Now Depart in Thy Peace" (Luke)
    C444, UM668
"Like a Child" (Luke, Christmas)
    C133, S2092, VU366
"Joseph Dearest, Joseph Mine" (Luke, Christmas)
    N105, S2099
"Lord of All Hopefulness" (Luke)
    CG678, E482, EL765, G683, S2197, SA772, SH464
"Gather Us In" (Luke)
    C284, EL532, G401, S2236, SH393

Additional Contemporary and Modern Suggestions
"Honor and Praise" 1867485 (Pss)
"Let Everything That Has Breath" 2430979 (Pss)
"God of Wonders" 3118757 (Pss)
"Glory in the Highest" 4822451 (Pss, Christmas)
"Praise You" 863806 (Pss, Luke)
"Santo, Santo, Santo" ("Holy, Holy, Holy") (Gal, Comm.)
    C111, CG3, EL473, G595, N793, S2007, SH452
"Holy, Holy" 18792 (Gal, Comm.)
    P140, S2039
"What Love Has Done" 5836965 (Gal, Christmas)
"Lord, I Lift Your Name on High" 117947 (Gal, Luke)
    AH4071, CG606, EL857, S2088, SA379, SH205
"All Hail King Jesus" 12877 (Luke)
"Jesus, Name above All Names" 21291 (Luke)
"The Virgin Mary Had a Baby Boy" 2957081 (Luke, Christmas)
    AH4037, S2098, SA127, VU73
"Shine, Jesus, Shine" 30426 (Luke)
    CG156, EL671, G192, S2173, SA261, SH102
"Jesus, Jesus, Oh, What a Wonderful Child" 4206259 (Luke,
    Christmas)
    EL297, G126, N136, WS3060
"Stand in Awe" (Luke)
"Go Now in Peace" (Luke)
    C437, SH722, UM665, VU964; S-1 #146 Orff arr.

Vocal Solos
"Sing a Song of Joy" (Pss)
    V-4   p. 2
"Sing for Christ Is Born" (Luke, Christmas)
    V-10   p. 16

Anthems
"Song of Simeon" (Luke)
Stephan Casurella; Concordia 984210
Unison, organ, opt. descant (https://bit.ly/C-984210)

"Jesus, Oh, What a Wonderful Child" (Luke, Christmas)
Arr. Lloyd Larson; Hope C-5898
Two-part mixed, piano (https://bit.ly/C-5898)

Other Suggestions
*You may also choose to use Watch Night (Dec. 31) scriptures for
    this service or even celebrate Epiphany Sunday using January 6
    scriptures.*
Visuals:
    O   Wedding garments, crown, garland, Spring garden
    P   Celestial imagery, nature imagery, all ages of people
           praising
    E   Clock, open manacles, children's toys
    G   Baby, elderly man/woman, Christ candle
Introit: C166, E114, EL284, G142, N151, P61, UM244, VU71,
    stanzas 2 and 4. "'Twas in the Moon of Wintertime" (Christmas)
Settings of Song of Simeon: C156, N734, N805-N808, P604/
    P605, SH78, UM225, VU902/VU903 (Luke)
Prayer of Confession: WSL43. "We often act" (Gal)
Prayer: WSL69. "Creator God, how great" (Pss)
Prayer: UM231 (Gal) or C1 (Pss)
Sung Benediction: WS3182 (See also EL313). "Benediction
    Hymn" (Luke)
See Christmas Eve for additional Christmas carols.
Theme Ideas: Children / Family of God, God: Promises, Joy,
    Light, Praise

Ecclesiastes 3:1-13

For everything there is a season and a time for every matter under heaven:

²a time to be born and a time to die;
a time to plant and a time to pluck up what is planted;
³a time to kill and a time to heal;
a time to break down and a time to build up;
⁴a time to weep and a time to laugh;
a time to mourn and a time to dance;
⁵a time to throw away stones and a time to gather stones together;
a time to embrace and a time to refrain from embracing;
⁶a time to seek and a time to lose;
a time to keep and a time to throw away;
⁷a time to tear and a time to sew;
a time to keep silent and a time to speak;
⁸a time to love and a time to hate;
a time for war and a time for peace.

⁹What gain have the workers from their toil? ¹⁰I have seen the business that God has given to everyone to be busy with. ¹¹He has made everything suitable for its time; moreover, he has put a sense of past and future into their minds, yet they cannot find out what God has done from the beginning to the end. ¹²I know that there is nothing better for them than to be happy and enjoy themselves as long as they live; ¹³moreover, it is God's gift that all should eat and drink and take pleasure in all their toil.

Psalm 8 (G25, N624, P162/163, SH6, UM743)

O Lord, our Sovereign,
how majestic is your name in all the earth!
You have set your glory above the heavens.
²Out of the mouths of babes and infants
you have founded a bulwark because of your foes,
to silence the enemy and the avenger.
³When I look at your heavens, the work of your fingers,
the moon and the stars that you have established;
⁴what are humans that you are mindful of them,
mortals that you care for them?
⁵Yet you have made them a little lower than God
and crowned them with glory and honor.
⁶You have given them dominion over the works of your hands;
you have put all things under their feet,
⁷all sheep and oxen,
and also the beasts of the field,
⁸the birds of the air, and the fish of the sea,
whatever passes along the paths of the seas.
⁹O Lord, our Sovereign,
how majestic is your name in all the earth!

Revelation 21:1-6a

Then I saw a new heaven and a new earth, for the first heaven and the first earth had passed away, and the sea was no more. ²And I saw the holy city, the new Jerusalem, coming down out of heaven from God, prepared as a bride adorned for her husband. ³And I heard a loud voice from the throne saying,

"See, the home of God is among mortals.
He will dwell with them;
they will be his peoples,
and God himself will be with them and be their God;
⁴he will wipe every tear from their eyes.
Death will be no more;
mourning and crying and pain will be no more,
for the first things have passed away."

⁵And the one who was seated on the throne said, "See, I am making all things new." Also he said, "Write this, for these words are trustworthy and true." ⁶Then he said to me, "It is done! I am the Alpha and the Omega, the Beginning and the End."

Matthew 25:31-46

³¹"When the Son of Man comes in his glory and all the angels with him, then he will sit on the throne of his glory. ³²All the nations will be gathered before him, and he will separate people one from another as a shepherd separates the sheep from the goats, ³³and he will put the sheep at his right hand and the goats at the left. ³⁴Then the king will say to those at his right hand, 'Come, you who are blessed by my Father, inherit the kingdom prepared for you from the foundation of the world, ³⁵for I was hungry and you gave me food, I was thirsty and you gave me something to drink, I was a stranger and you welcomed me, ³⁶I was naked and you gave me clothing, I was sick and you took care of me, I was in prison and you visited me.' ³⁷Then the righteous will answer him, 'Lord, when was it that we saw you hungry and gave you food or thirsty and gave you something to drink? ³⁸And when was it that we saw you a stranger and welcomed you or naked and gave you clothing? ³⁹And when was it that we saw you sick or in prison and visited you?' ⁴⁰And the king will answer them, 'Truly I tell you, just as you did it to one of the least of these brothers and sisters of mine, you did it to me.' ⁴¹Then he will say to those at his left hand, 'You who are accursed, depart from me into the eternal fire prepared for the devil and his angels, ⁴²for I was hungry and you gave me no food, I was thirsty and you gave me nothing to drink, ⁴³I was a stranger and you did not welcome me, naked and you did not give me clothing, sick and in prison and you did not visit me.' ⁴⁴Then they also will answer, 'Lord, when was it that we saw you hungry or thirsty or a stranger or naked or sick or in prison and did not take care of you?' ⁴⁵Then he will answer them, 'Truly I tell you, just as you did not do it to one of the least of these, you did not do it to me.' ⁴⁶And these will go away into eternal punishment but the righteous into eternal life."

Primary Hymns and Songs for the Day
"For the Beauty of the Earth" (Eccl) (O)
    C56, CG341, E416, EL879, G14, P473, N28, SA14, SH21,
    UM92 (PD), VU226
        H-3   Chr-33, 65; Desc-30; Org-29
        S-1   #93-96. Various treatments
"Sing Praise to God Who Reigns Above" (Eccl) (O)
    C6, CG315, E408, EL871, G645, N6, P483, UM126 (PD), VU216
        H-3   Hbl-92; Chr-173; Desc-76; Org-91
        S-1   #237. Descant
"Great Is Thy Faithfulness" (Eccl)
    AH4011, C86, CG48, EL733, G39, N423, P276, SA26, SH48,
    UM140, VU288
        H-3   Chr-87; Desc-39; Org-39
        S-2   #59. Piano arrangement
"Many and Great, O God" (Eccl)
    C58, CG28, E385, EL837, G21, N3, N341, P271 (PD), SH5,
    UM148, VU308
        H-3   Hbl-76; Chr-135; Desc-63; Org-70
        S-2   #104. Performance note
"O God, in a Mysterious Way" (Eccl)
    CG39, E677, G30, N412, P270, SA17, SH47
"O God, Our Help in Ages Past" (Eccl, Pss) (O) or (C)
    C67, CG566, E680, EL632, G687, N25, P210, SA47, SH41,
    UM117 (PD), VU806
        H-3   Hbl-80, 87; Chr-143; Desc-93; Org-132
        S-1   #293-296. Various treatments
"How Great Thou Art" (Pss)
    AH4015, C33, CG323, EL856, G625, N35, P467, SA49, SH14,
    UM77, VU238 (Fr.)
        H-3   Chr-103; Org-105
        S-1   #163. Harmonization
"For the Healing of the Nations" (Rev)
    C668, CG698, G346, N576, SA1000, UM428, VU678
"Rejoice! Rejoice, Believers" (Rev)
    E68, EL244, G362, P15
"O Holy City, Seen of John" (Rev)
    E582/583, G374, N613, P453, UM726, VU709
        H-3   Chr-139, 145; Desc-77
        S-1   #241-242. Orff arr. and descant
"Morning Has Broken" (Matt)
    C53, CG27, E8, EL556, G664, SA44, SH465, UM145, VU409
"Hymn of Promise" (Eccl) (C)
    C638, CG545, G250, N433, UM707, VU703
        H-3   Chr-112; Org-117
        S-1   #270. Descant

Additional Hymn Suggestions
"Come, Ye Disconsolate" (Rev)
    C502, EL607, SH342, UM510 (PD)
"We Shall Overcome" (Rev)
    AH4047/4048, C630, G379, N570, UM533
"We've a Story to Tell to the Nations" (Rev, Matt)
    C484, CG427, SA943, UM569 (PD)
"All Who Hunger" (Rev, Matt, Comm.)
    C419, CG303, EL461, G509, S2126, VU460
"There's a Spirit in the Air" (Matt)
    C257, P433, N294, UM192, VU582
"Hail to the Lord's Anointed" (Matt)
    C140, CG98, EL311, G149, N104, P205, SH112, UM203, VU30
"Where Cross the Crowded Ways of Life" (Matt)
    C665, CG657, E609, EL719, G343, N543, UM427, VU681
"Cuando el Pobre" ("When the Poor Ones") (Matt)
    C662, EL725, G762, P407, SH240, UM434, VU702
"You Satisfy the Hungry Heart" (Matt, Comm.)
    C429, CG468, EL484, G523, P521, SH672, UM629, VU478
"In Remembrance of Me" 25156 (Matt, Comm.)
    C403, CG462, G521, S2254, SH667
"As We Gather at Your Table" (Matt, Comm.)
    EL522, N332, S2268, SH411, VU457

Additional Contemporary and Modern Suggestions
"In His Time" 25981 (Eccl)
"I Could Sing of Your Love Forever" 1043199 (Eccl)
"Be Glorified" 2732646 (Eccl, Matt)
"How Majestic Is Your Name" 26007 (Pss)
    C63, CG326, G613, S2023, SA90
"Hallelujah" ("Your Love Is Amazing") 3091812 (Pss)
"God of Wonders" 3118757 (Pss)
"Across the Lands" 3709898 (Pss)
"Soon and Very Soon" 11249 (Rev)
    CG562, EL439, G384, SH357, UM706, S-2 #187. Piano arr.
"Spirit Song" 27824 (Rev)
    C352, SH409, UM347
"There's Something About That Name" 14064 (Rev)
    C115, SA80, UM171
"Hallelujah to the Lamb" 2316323 (Rev)
"We Will Worship the Lamb of Glory" 208409 (Rev)
"Holy and Anointed One" 164361 (Rev)
"Did You Feel the Mountains Tremble?" 1097028 (Rev)
"I See the Lord" 1406176 (Rev, Matt)
"Song of Hope" 5111477 (Rev)
"To Him Who Sits on the Throne" 20429 (Rev, Matt)
"You Who Are Thirsty" 814453 (Rev, Matt)
"People Need the Lord" 18084 (Matt)
"Song for the Nations" 20340 (Rev, Matt)
"Peace in the Manger" 7104263 (Matt, Christmas)

Vocal Solos
"I Will Sing of Thy Great Mercies" (Eccl)
    V-4   p. 43
"Oh What a Beautiful City"
    V-7   p. 72/77
"Alive and Breathing" (Rev, New Year)
    V-9   p. 4
"A Covenant Prayer" (New Year, Covenant Service)
    V-1   p. 6

Anthems
"Hymn of Promise" (Eccl)
Natalie Sleeth; Hope A580
Two-part, keyboard (https://bit.ly/H-A580)

"Mighty Are Your Works" (Pss)
Mozart/Hopson; Selah Publishing 410-808
Two-part mixed, keyboard (https://bit.ly/410-808)

Other Suggestions
*These scriptures may also be used on December 31 in place of 1st
Sunday After Christmas lections.*
Visuals:
    O   Clock, many images from text
    P   Infants, all ages, outer space, nature
    E   Butterfly, chrysalis, bride, portrait of Christ
    G   Shepherd, sheep, goats, ministries to others
Opening Prayer: WSL64 (Pss, Covenant Renewal)
Canticle: C702 or UM734 (Rev)
Prayer: UM607 (New Year)
Prayer: C68. Ancient Jewish Prayer (Eccl)
Benediction or Sending Words: WSL169 (Matt)
Sung Benediction: C518, N417, UM383, stanza 4. "This Is a Day
    of New Beginnings" (Rev)
Theme Ideas: Covenant, God: Glory of God, God: God's Time,
    Justice, New Creation, Patience, Service / Servanthood

Isaiah 60:1-6

Arise, shine, for your light has come,
  and the glory of the LORD has risen upon you.
[2]For darkness shall cover the earth
  and thick darkness the peoples,
but the LORD will arise upon you,
  and his glory will appear over you.
[3]Nations shall come to your light
  and kings to the brightness of your dawn.
[4]Lift up your eyes and look around;
  they all gather together; they come to you;
your sons shall come from far away,
  and your daughters shall be carried in their nurses' arms.
[5]Then you shall see and be radiant;
  your heart shall thrill and rejoice,
because the abundance of the sea shall be brought to you;
  the wealth of the nations shall come to you.
[6]A multitude of camels shall cover you,
  the young camels of Midian and Ephah;
  all those from Sheba shall come.
They shall bring gold and frankincense
  and shall proclaim the praise of the LORD.

Psalm 72:1-7, 10-14 (G149, N667, P204/205, UM795)

Give the king your justice, O God,
  and your righteousness to a king's son.
[2]May he judge your people with righteousness
  and your poor with justice.
[3]May the mountains yield prosperity for the people,
  and the hills, in righteousness.
[4]May he defend the cause of the poor of the people,
  give deliverance to the needy,
  and crush the oppressor.
[5]May he live while the sun endures
  and as long as the moon, throughout all generations.
[6]May he be like rain that falls on the mown grass,
  like showers that water the earth.
[7]In his days may righteousness flourish
  and peace abound, until the moon is no more.
. . . .
[10]May the kings of Tarshish and of the isles
  render him tribute;
may the kings of Sheba and Seba
  bring gifts.
[11]May all kings fall down before him,
  all nations give him service.
[12]For he delivers the needy when they call,
  the poor and those who have no helper.
[13]He has pity on the weak and the needy
  and saves the lives of the needy.
[14]From oppression and violence he redeems their life,
  and precious is their blood in his sight.

Ephesians 3:1-12

This is the reason that I, Paul, am a prisoner for Christ Jesus for the sake of you gentiles, [2]for surely you have already heard of the commission of God's grace that was given me for you [3]and how the mystery was made known to me by revelation, as I wrote above in a few words, [4]a reading of which will enable you to perceive my understanding of the mystery of Christ. [5]In former generations this mystery was not made known to humankind, as it has now been revealed to his holy apostles and prophets by the Spirit: [6]that is, the gentiles have become fellow heirs, members of the same body, and sharers in the promise in Christ Jesus through the gospel.

[7]Of this gospel I have become a servant according to the gift of God's grace that was given me by the working of his power. [8]Although I am the very least of all the saints, this grace was given to me to bring to the gentiles the news of the boundless riches of Christ [9]and to make everyone see what is the plan of the mystery hidden for ages in God, who created all things, [10]so that through the church the wisdom of God in its rich variety might now be made known to the rulers and authorities in the heavenly places. [11]This was in accordance with the eternal purpose that he has carried out in Christ Jesus our Lord, [12]in whom we have access in boldness and confidence through faith in him.

Matthew 2:1-12

In the time of King Herod, after Jesus was born in Bethlehem of Judea, magi from the east came to Jerusalem, [2]asking, "Where is the child who has been born king of the Jews? For we observed his star in the east and have come to pay him homage." [3]When King Herod heard this, he was frightened, and all Jerusalem with him, [4]and calling together all the chief priests and scribes of the people, he inquired of them where the Messiah was to be born. [5]They told him, "In Bethlehem of Judea, for so it has been written by the prophet:
  [6]'And you, Bethlehem, in the land of Judah,
    are by no means least among the rulers of Judah,
  for from you shall come a ruler
    who is to shepherd my people Israel.'"
[7]Then Herod secretly called for the magi and learned from them the exact time when the star had appeared. [8]Then he sent them to Bethlehem, saying, "Go and search diligently for the child, and when you have found him, bring me word so that I may also go and pay him homage." [9]When they had heard the king, they set out, and there, ahead of them, went the star that they had seen in the east, until it stopped over the place where the child was. [10]When they saw that the star had stopped, they were overwhelmed with joy. [11]On entering the house, they saw the child with Mary his mother, and they knelt down and paid him homage. Then, opening their treasure chests, they offered him gifts of gold, frankincense, and myrrh. [12]And having been warned in a dream not to return to Herod, they left for their own country by another road.

Primary Hymns and Songs for the Day
"The First Noel" (Matt) (O)
    C151, CG124, E109, EL300, G147, N139, P56, SA126, UM245 (PD), VU90 (Fr.) and VU91
        H-3   Hbl-95; Chr-182; Desc-100; Org-161
        S-1   #328-330. Various treatments
"Awake! Awake, and Greet the New Morn" (Isa)
    C138, EL242, G107, N107, SH66
"Arise, Your Light Is Come" (Isa)
    EL314, G744, N164, P411, VU79
"Break Forth, O Beauteous Heavenly Light" (Isa)
    E91, G130, N140, P26, UM223, VU83
"O Morning Star, How Fair and Bright" (Isa, Eph, Matt)
    C105, E497, EL308, G827, N158, P69, UM247, VU98
        H-3   Chr-147; Desc-104; Org-183
"As with Gladness Men of Old" (Matt)
    C173, CG150, E119, EL302, G150, N159, P63 (PD), SA101, SH106, VU81
        H-3   Chr-33, 65; Desc-30; Org-29
        S-1   #93-96. Various treatments
"What Star Is This, with Beams So Bright" (Matt)
    E124, G152, P68
        H-3   Chr-19
"In Bethlehem a Newborn Boy" (Matt)
    E246, G153, P35 (PD), VU77
"Sing of God Made Manifest" (Matt)
    C176, G156
"What Child Is This" (Matt)
    C162, CG148, E115, EL296, G145, N148, P53, SH105, UM219 (PD), VU74
        H-3   Hbl-102; Chr-210; Desc-46; Org-47
        S-1   #150. Guitar chords
"On This Day Earth Shall Ring" (Matt)
    E92, G141, P46, UM248 (PD)
        H-3   Hbl-20, 86; Chr-156; Org-114
        S-1   #267. Handbell part
"Rise Up, Shepherd, and Follow" (Matt)
    G135, P50, S2096, VU70
"Siyahamba" ("We Are Marching") 1321512 (Matt)
    C442, CG155, EL866, G853, N526, S2235, SA903, SH717, VU646
"We Three Kings" (Matt) (C)
    C172, CG151, E128, G151, P66, SA129, SH107, UM254 (PD)
        H-3   Chr-208; Org-65

Additional Hymn Suggestions
"Rise, Shine, You People" (Isa)
    EL665, UM187
"This Little Light of Mine" (Isa)
    N525, SH257, UM585 (See also AH4150, EL677, N524)
"You are the Light" 6238098 (Isa, Matt)
"Hail to the Lord's Anointed" (Pss)
    C140, CG98, EL311, G149, N104, P205, SH112, UM203, VU30
"Go, Tell It on the Mountain" (Eph, Matt) (C)
    C167, CG143, E99, EL290, G136, N154, P29, SA106, SH90, UM251, VU43
"What Gift Can We Bring" (Matt)
    CG533, N370, UM87
"Lo, How a Rose E'er Blooming" (Matt)
    C160, CG105, E81, EL272, G129, N127, P48 (PD), UM216, VU8
"De Tierra Lejana Venimos" ("From a Distant Home") (Matt)
    P64, SH110, UM243, VU89
"This Is a Day of New Beginnings" (New Year, Comm.)
    C518, N417, UM383
"Star-Child" (Matt)
    CG145, S2095
"The Virgin Mary Had a Baby Boy" 2957081 (Matt)
    AH4037, S2098, SA127, VU73
"A Place at the Table" (Matt, Comm.)
    G769, WS3149

Additional Contemporary and Modern Suggestions
"Come True Light" 5767773 (Isa)
"Shine, Jesus, Shine" 30426 (Isa, Epiphany)
    CG156, EL671, G192, S2173, SA261, SH102
"Mighty to Save" 4591782 (Isa)
"Jesus, the Light of the World" 6363190 (Isa, Epiphany)
"Here I Am to Worship" 3266032 (Isa, Epiphany)
    CG297, SA114, SH395, WS3177
"Arise, Shine" 13797 (Isa)
"Let It Rise" 2240585 (Isa)
"Shine on Us" 1754646 (Isa, Epiphany)
"You are the Light" 6238098 (Isa, Epiphany)
"Bless His Holy Name" 17566 (Pss)
"Blessed Be the Name" 265239 (Pss)
"Everlasting God" 4556538 (Pss)
"Grace Alone" 2335524 (Eph)
    CG43, S2162, SA699.
"Honor and Praise" 1867485 (Matt, Epiphany)
"All Hail King Jesus" 12877 (Matt, Epiphany)
"Alleluia" 16811 (Matt, Epiphany)
    C106, N765, SH699, UM186
"What A Beautiful Name" 7068424 (Matt)
"What Love Has Done" 5836965 (Matt, Christmas)

Vocal Solos
"O Thou That Tellest Good Tidings to Zion" (Isa)
"The People That Walked in Darkness" (Isa)
    V-2
"Go, Tell It on the Mountain" (Eph, Matt)
    V-3 (1)   p. 10
"Behold that Star!" (Matt, Epiphany)
    V-3 (1)   p. 34
"A Scottish Christmas Song" (Matt)
    V-4   p. 4
"Jesus, What a Wonderful Child" (Matt, Epiphany)
(with "Go Tell It on the Mountain")
    V-5 (1)   p. 48
"Fit for a King" (Matt, Epiphany)
    V-10   p. 32

Anthems
"The Journey of the Magi" (Matt, Epiphany)
Arr. K. Lee Scott; MorningStar MSM-50-1106
SAB, keyboard (https://bit.ly/M-1106)

"Light of the World" (Matt, Epiphany)
Karen Marrolli, MorningStar 50-2620
SATB, violin, piano (https://bit.ly/M-2620)

Other Suggestions
These scriptures and ideas can be used on Sunday, December 31 as Epiphany Sunday.
Visuals:
    O   Light, gold, frankincense, crown
    P   Deliverance, poor and needy being helped, sun, moon, rain, kings, gifts
    E   Manacles, towel, bowl/pitcher (servant)
    G   Kings, gold, frankincense, myrrh (gifts), star
Introit: EL406, G281, S2118. "Holy Spirit, Come to Us" (Pss)
Canticle: UM225. Canticle of Simeon (Matt) See S-1, p. 386.
Prayer: UM255 (Epiphany, Matt)
For additional ideas, see *The Abingdon Worship Annual 2024.*
Theme Ideas: God: Promises, Inclusion, Journey, Light, Righteousness, Stewardship, Unity

Genesis 1:1-5

When God began to create the heavens and the earth, [2]the earth was complete chaos, and darkness covered the face of the deep, while a wind from God swept over the face of the waters. [3]Then God said, "Let there be light," and there was light. [4]And God saw that the light was good, and God separated the light from the darkness. [5]God called the light Day, and the darkness he called Night. And there was evening and there was morning, the first day.

Psalm 29 (G259, N638, P180, UM761)

Ascribe to the Lord, O heavenly beings,
　　ascribe to the Lord glory and strength.
[2]Ascribe to the Lord the glory of his name;
　　worship the Lord in holy splendor.
[3]The voice of the Lord is over the waters;
　　the God of glory thunders,
　　the Lord, over mighty waters.
[4]The voice of the Lord is powerful;
　　the voice of the Lord is full of majesty.
[5]The voice of the Lord breaks the cedars;
　　the Lord breaks the cedars of Lebanon.
[6]He makes Lebanon skip like a calf
　　and Sirion like a young wild ox.
[7]The voice of the Lord flashes forth flames of fire.
[8]The voice of the Lord shakes the wilderness;
　　the Lord shakes the wilderness of Kadesh.
[9]The voice of the Lord causes the oaks to whirl
　　and strips the forest bare,
　　and in his temple all say, "Glory!"
[10]The Lord sits enthroned over the flood;
　　the Lord sits enthroned as king forever.
[11]May the Lord give strength to his people!
　　May the Lord bless his people with peace!

Acts 19:1-7

While Apollos was in Corinth, Paul passed through the interior regions and came to Ephesus, where he found some disciples. [2]He said to them, "Did you receive the Holy Spirit when you became believers?" They replied, "No, we have not even heard that there is a Holy Spirit." [3]Then he said, "Into what, then, were you baptized?" They answered, "Into John's baptism." [4]Paul said, "John baptized with the baptism of repentance, telling the people to believe in the one who was to come after him, that is, in Jesus." [5]On hearing this, they were baptized in the name of the Lord Jesus. [6]When Paul had laid his hands on them, the Holy Spirit came upon them, and they spoke in tongues and prophesied, [7]altogether there were about twelve of them.

Mark 1:4-11

[4]so John the baptizer appeared in the wilderness, proclaiming a baptism of repentance for the forgiveness of sins. [5]And the whole Judean region and all the people of Jerusalem were going out to him and were baptized by him in the River Jordan, confessing their sins. [6]Now John was clothed with camel's hair, with a leather belt around his waist, and he ate locusts and wild honey. [7]He proclaimed, "The one who is more powerful than I is coming after me; I am not worthy to stoop down and untie the strap of his sandals. [8]I have baptized you with water, but he will baptize you with the Holy Spirit."

[9]In those days Jesus came from Nazareth of Galilee and was baptized by John in the Jordan. [10]And just as he was coming up out of the water, he saw the heavens torn apart and the Spirit descending like a dove upon him. [11]And a voice came from the heavens, "You are my Son, the Beloved; with you I am well pleased."

Primary Hymns and Songs for the Day

"I Sing the Almighty Power of God" (Gen, Pss) (O)
    C64, G32, N12, P288 (PD), SA36
        H-3   Hbl-16, 22, 68; Chr-101; Desc-37
        S-1   #115. Harmonization
    CG19, E398, UM152 (PD)
        H-3   Hbl-44; Chr-21; Desc-40; Org-40
        S-1   #131-132. Introduction and descant
    VU231 (PD)
"Crashing Waters at Creation" (Gen, Mark)
    EL455, G476, N326, VU449
"Loving Spirit" (Gen, Acts, Mark, Baptism)
    C244, EL397, G293, P323, S2123, VU387
"When Jesus Came to Jordan" (Mark)
    CG152, EL305, P72, SH113, UM252
        H-3   Chr-211
"Spirit Song" 27824 (Mark)
    C352, SH409, UM347
"Down Galilee's Slow Roadways" (Mark)
    G164
"Wild and Lone the Prophet's Voice" (Mark)
    G163, P409, S2089
        H-3   Hbl-72; Chr-116, 205; Desc-11; Org-2
        S-1   #6. Descant
"Take Me to the Water" (Mark, Baptism)
    AH4045, C367, G480, N322, SH665, WS3165
"Breathe on Me, Breath of God" (C)
    C254, CG235, E508, G286, N292, P316, SA294, SH224/273,
    UM420 (PD), VU382 (Fr.)
        H-3   Hbl-49; Chr-45; Desc-101; Org-166

Additional Hymn Suggestions

"All Things Bright and Beautiful" (Gen)
    C61, CG23, E405, G20, N31, P267, SA3, SH1, UM147 (PD),
    VU291
"God Created Heaven and Earth" (Gen)
    EL738, N33, P290, UM151, VU251
"O Breath of Life" (Gen)
    C250, SA818, UM543, VU202, WS3146
"Wind Who Makes All Winds That Blow" (Gen)
    C236, CG226, N271, P131, UM538, VU196
"God the Sculptor of the Mountains" (Gen)
    EL736, G5, S2060
"Spirit, Spirit of Gentleness" (Gen, Mark)
    C249, EL396, G291, N286, P319, S2120, VU375
"Praise and Thanksgiving Be to God" (Pss, Acts, Mark, Baptism)
    CG453, EL458, UM604, VU441
"Wash, O God, Our Sons and Daughters" (Acts)
    C365, EL445, G490, SH669, UM605, VU442
"This Is the Spirit's Entry Now" (Acts, Mark)
    EL448, UM608, VU451
"Come, Holy Ghost, Our Souls Inspire" (Acts, Mark)
    E503/504, N268, G278, P125, UM651, VU201
"Wonder of Wonders" (Acts, Mark, Baptism)
    C378, G489, N328, P499, S2247
"Baptized in Water" (Acts, Mark, Baptism)
    CG449, E294, EL456, G482, P492, S2248, SH666
"Blessed Be the God of Israel" (Mark)
    C135, CG88, E444, EL250/552, G109, P602, UM209, VU901
"Shall We Gather at the River" (Mark, Baptism)
    C701, CG561, EL423, G375, N597, SA546, SH366, UM723,
    VU710
"At the Font We Start Our Journey" (Mark)
    N308, S2114

Additional Contemporary and Modern Suggestions

"Across the Lands" 3709898 (Gen)
    SH654, WS3032
"Ah, Lord God" 17896 (Gen)
"Forevermore" 5466830 (Gen)
"What A Beautiful Name" 7068424 (Gen, Mark)
"Thou Art Worthy" 14789 (Gen, Mark)
    C114, S2041
"Veni Sancte Spiritus" ("Holy Spirit, Come to Us") (Gen, Baptism)
    EL406, G281, S2118
"God of Wonders" 3118757 (Gen, Pss)
"Please Enter My Heart, Hosanna" 2485371 (Acts)
"Somos Uno en Cristo" ("We Are One in Christ Jesus") 6368975
    (Acts)
    C493, EL643, G322, S2229, SH227
"Yesu Tawa Pano" ("Jesus, We Are Here") (Acts)
    EL529, G392, S2273, SH611
"Jesus, Name above All Names" 21291 (Mark)
    S2071, SA82
"Wade in the Water" (Mark)
    AH4046, C371, EL459 (PD), S2107
"Water, River, Spirit, Grace" (Mark)
    C366, S2253
Great and Mighty Is He" 66665 (Mark)
"Holy Spirit, Rain Down" 2405227 (Mark)

Vocal Solos

"Brighter than the Sun" (Acts, Mark, Baptism)
    V-5 (1)   p. 57
"Waterlife" (Acts, Mark, Baptism)
    V-5 (3)   p. 17
"I've Just Come from the Fountain" (Acts, Mark, Baptism)
    V-7   p. 54/59

Anthems

"Shall We Gather at the River" (Mark, Baptism)
Arr. David Lantz; Beckenhorst BP2269
SATB, piano (https://bit.ly/BP-2269)

"Down Galilee's Slow Roadways" (Mark, Baptism)
Michael Burkhardt; MorningStar 50-2111
SATB, organ (https://bit.ly/MSM-50-2111)

Other Suggestions

Visuals:
    O   Light/darkness, water, wind, evening/morning
    P   Ps 29:2b, 11a, *b*; water, cedar, skipping calf, wind (bent
            trees)
    E   Dove, symbols of the Holy Spirit, water, baptism
    G   Sandals, water, dove, 1:8, 11b
This is an excellent day to celebrate baptisms or baptism renewal.
Introit: C53, CG27, E8, EL556, G664, SA44, SH465, UM145,
    VU409, stanza 1. "Morning Has Broken" (Gen)
Opening Prayer: WSL42 (Gen, Baptism)
Call to Prayer: G283, S2124/S2125, VU383, SH223, WS3091/
    WS2092. "Come, Holy Spirit" (Gen)
Prayer: C698. Prayer of a Native American (Gen)
Prayer: WSL12. "Great God of waves" (Mark, Baptism)
Prayer: WSL50. "O God whose love" (Gen, Mark, Baptism)
Prayer: UM146, UM253 (Baptism, Mark)
Call to Baptism: CG451, S2252. "Come, Be Baptized"
Baptism Response: EL211, G491, SH663, UM609, VU452. "You
    Have Put On Christ" (Acts)
Response: C261, CG241, G408, N293, P398, SH410, UM334.
    "Sweet, Sweet Spirit" (Acts, Mark)
For additional ideas, see The Abingdon Worship Annual 2024.
Theme Ideas: Baptism, Creation, God: Glory of God, God: Love
    of God, Holy Spirit, Journey

1 Samuel 3:1-10 (11-20)

Now the boy Samuel was ministering to the LORD under Eli. The word of the LORD was rare in those days; visions were not widespread.

[2]At that time Eli, whose eyesight had begun to grow dim so that he could not see, was lying down in his room; [3]the lamp of God had not yet gone out, and Samuel was lying down in the temple of the LORD, where the ark of God was. [4]Then the LORD called, "Samuel! Samuel!" and he said, "Here I am!" [5]and ran to Eli and said, "Here I am, for you called me." But he said, "I did not call; lie down again." So he went and lay down. [6]The LORD called again, "Samuel!" Samuel got up and went to Eli and said, "Here I am, for you called me." But he said, "I did not call, my son; lie down again." [7]Now Samuel did not yet know the LORD, and the word of the LORD had not yet been revealed to him. [8]The LORD called Samuel again, a third time. And he got up and went to Eli and said, "Here I am, for you called me." Then Eli perceived that the LORD was calling the boy. [9]Therefore Eli said to Samuel, "Go, lie down, and if he calls you, you shall say, 'Speak, LORD, for your servant is listening.'" So Samuel went and lay down in his place.

[10]Now the LORD came and stood there, calling as before, "Samuel! Samuel!" And Samuel said, "Speak, for your servant is listening." ([11]Then the LORD said to Samuel, "See, I am about to do something in Israel that will make both ears of anyone who hears of it tingle. [12]On that day I will fulfill against Eli all that I have spoken concerning his house, from beginning to end. [13]For I have told him that I am about to punish his house forever for the iniquity that he knew, because his sons were blaspheming God, and he did not restrain them. [14]Therefore I swear to the house of Eli that the iniquity of Eli's house shall not be expiated by sacrifice or offering forever."

[15]Samuel lay there until morning; then he opened the doors of the house of the LORD. Samuel was afraid to tell the vision to Eli. [16]But Eli called Samuel and said, "Samuel, my son." He said, "Here I am." [17]Eli said, "What was it that he told you? Do not hide it from me. May God do so to you and more also, if you hide anything from me of all that he told you." [18]So Samuel told him everything and hid nothing from him. Then he said, "It is the LORD; let him do what seems good to him."

[19]As Samuel grew up, the LORD was with him and let none of his words fall to the ground. [20]And all Israel from Dan to Beersheba knew that Samuel was a trustworthy prophet of the LORD.)

Psalm 139:1-6, 13-18 (G28, N715, P248, UM854)

O LORD, you have searched me and known me.
[2]You know when I sit down and when I rise up;
    you discern my thoughts from far away.
[3]You search out my path and my lying down
    and are acquainted with all my ways.
[4]Even before a word is on my tongue,
    O LORD, you know it completely.
[5]You hem me in, behind and before,
    and lay your hand upon me.
[6]Such knowledge is too wonderful for me;
    it is so high that I cannot attain it.
. . . .
[13]For it was you who formed my inward parts;
    you knit me together in my mother's womb.
[14]I praise you, for I am fearfully and wonderfully made.
    Wonderful are your works;
    that I know very well.
[15]My frame was not hidden from you,
    when I was being made in secret,
    intricately woven in the depths of the earth.
[16]Your eyes beheld my unformed substance.

In your book were written
    all the days that were formed for me,
    when none of them as yet existed.
[17]How weighty to me are your thoughts, O God!
    How vast is the sum of them!
[18]I try to count them—they are more than the sand;
    I come to the end—I am still with you.

1 Corinthians 6:12-20

[12]"All things are permitted for me," but not all things are beneficial. "All things are permitted for me," but I will not be dominated by anything. [13]"Food is meant for the stomach and the stomach for food," and God will destroy both one and the other. The body is meant not for sexual immorality but for the Lord and the Lord for the body. [14]And God raised the Lord and will also raise us by his power. [15]Do you not know that your bodies are members of Christ? Should I therefore take the members of Christ and make them members of a prostitute? Never! [16]Do you not know that whoever is united to a prostitute becomes one body with her? For it is said, "The two shall be one flesh." [17]But anyone united to the Lord becomes one spirit with him. [18]Shun sexual immorality! Every sin that a person commits is outside the body, but the sexually immoral person sins against the body itself. [19]Or do you not know that your body is a temple of the Holy Spirit within you, which you have from God, and that you are not your own? [20]For you were bought with a price; therefore glorify God in your body.

John 1:43-51

[43]The next day Jesus decided to go to Galilee. He found Philip and said to him, "Follow me." [44]Now Philip was from Bethsaida, the city of Andrew and Peter. [45]Philip found Nathanael and said to him, "We have found him about whom Moses in the Law and also the Prophets wrote, Jesus son of Joseph from Nazareth." [46]Nathanael said to him, "Can anything good come out of Nazareth?" Philip said to him, "Come and see." [47]When Jesus saw Nathanael coming toward him, he said of him, "Here is truly an Israelite in whom there is no deceit!" [48]Nathanael asked him, "Where did you get to know me?" Jesus answered, "I saw you under the fig tree before Philip called you." [49]Nathanael replied, "Rabbi, you are the Son of God! You are the King of Israel!" [50]Jesus answered, "Do you believe because I told you that I saw you under the fig tree? You will see greater things than these." [51]And he said to him, "Very truly, I tell you, you will see heaven opened and the angels of God ascending and descending upon the Son of Man."

Primary Hymns and Songs for the Day
"Open My Eyes, that I May See" (1 Sam) (O)
    C586, CG395, G451, P324, SH583, UM454, VU371
        H-3   Chr-157; Org-108
"Awake, My Soul, and with the Sun" (1 Sam)
    E11, EL557 (PD), G663, P456, SA4
"God of Our Life" (1 Sam, Pss)
    C713, G686, N366, P275
"Lord, Speak to Me" (1 Sam, John)
    CG503, EL676, G722, N531, SA773, SH557, UM463, VU589
        H-3   Hbl-75; Chr-131; Desc-22; Org-18
        S-1   #52. Descant
"I Was There to Hear Your Borning Cry" (Pss)
    C75, EL732, G488, N351, S2051, VU644
"Guide My Feet" (Pss, MLK Day)
    CG637, G741, N497, P354, S2208, SH54
        H-3   Hbl-66; Chr-89
"Lord, Be Glorified" 26368 (1 Cor)
    EL744, G468, S2150, SA593, SH420
"Sanctuary" 24140 (1 Cor)
    G701, S2164, SH265
"Christ Beside Me" (2 Cor)
    G702, S2166
        H-3   Hbl-77; Chr-136; Desc-21; Org-16
        S-1   #50-51. Flute and vocal descants
"Sacred the Body" (1 Cor)
    G27, S2228
        H-3   Chr-201
"Take My Life, and Let It Be" (1 Sam, 1 Cor) (C)
    C609, CG490, E707, EL583/EL685, G697, P391, N448, SA623, SH627/628, UM399 (PD), VU506
"Here I Am, Lord" (1 Sam, John) (C)
    C452, CG482, EL574, G69, SA1002, SH608, UM593, VU509
        H-3   Chr-97; Org-54

Additional Hymn Suggestions
"Come, Thou Fount of Every Blessing" (1 Sam)
    AH4086, C16, CG295/559, E686, EL807, G475, N459, P356, SA830, SH394, UM400 (PD), VU559
"Be Thou My Vision" (1 Sam, 1 Cor, John)
    C595, CG71, E488, EL793, G450, N451, P339, SA573, SH640, UM451, VU642
"Lord, You Give the Great Commission" (1 Sam, John) (C)
    C459, CG651, S2176, EL579, G298, P429, UM584, VU512
"Precious Lord, Take My Hand" (Pss, MLK Day)
    C628, CG400, EL773, G834, N472, SH336, UM474, VU670
"O Master, Let Me Walk with Thee" (Pss, 1 Cor, John)
    C602, CG660, E659/E660, EL818, G738, N503, P357, SA667, SH612, UM430 (PD), VU560
"To God Be the Glory" (1 Cor)
    C72, CG349, G634, P485, SA279, SH545, UM98 (PD)
"Have Thine Own Way, Lord" (1 Cor)
    C588, CG493, SA705, SH626, UM382 (PD)
"A Charge to Keep I Have" (1 Cor)
    AH4117, CG623, SA946, SH634, UM413 (PD)
"Come, Let Us with Our Lord Arise" (1 Cor)
    E49, S2084
"Built on a Rock" (1 Cor)
    C273, CG247, EL652, WS3147
"He Leadeth Me: O Blessed Thought" (John) (C)
    C545, CG68, SA645, SH304, UM128 (PD), VU657
"I Know Whom I Have Believed" (John) (C)
    CG588, SA843, SH529, UM714 (PD)
"God Made from One Blood" (MLK Day)
    C500, CG686, N427, S2170, VU554

Additional Contemporary and Modern Suggestions
"Oh, I Know the Lord's Laid His Hands on Me" (1 Sam, Pss, John, MLK Day)
    S2139
"God Is Speaking" (1 Sam, John)
    WS3025
"Somebody's Knockin' at Your Door" (1 Sam, John)
    G728, P382, SH597, WS3095
"Lead Me, Lord" 1609045 (1 Sam, John)
"A Wilderness Wandering People" 7068566 (1 Sam, MLK Day)
"He Knows My Name" 2151368 (1 Sam, Pss)
"In the Secret" 1810119 (Pss)
"The Potter's Hand" 2449771 (Pss)
"These Hands" 3251827 (Pss)
"Wonderfully Made" 5768239 (Pss)
"House of God" (1 Cor)
    WS3132
"Be Glorified" 429226 (1 Cor)
"Be Glorified" 2732646 (1 Cor)
"Cry of My Heart" 844980 (John)
"Come Just As You Are" 1189479 (John)
"Just to Be with You" 5585120 (John)
"Step by Step" 696994 (John)
    CG495, G743, WS3004
Somlandela ("We Will Follow") (John)
    WS3160
"All of Me" 6290160 (John)

Vocal Solos
"Be Thou My Vision" (1 Sam, 1 Cor, John)
    V-6   p. 13
"Chosen of the Lord" (1 Sam, John)
    V-8   p. 34
"Here I Am" (1 Sam, John)
    V-1   p. 19
"Take My Life, and Let It Be" (1 Cor)
    V-3 (3)   p. 17
    V-8   p. 262
"Say I Won't" (John)
    V-9   p. 80

Anthems
"O Lord, You Know Me Completely" (1 Sam, Pss)
Hal Hopson; Choristers Guild CGA-833
Unison/Two-part, keyboard (https://bit.ly/CG833)

"Somebody's Knockin' " (1 Sam, John)
Arr. Joseph Martin, Hope C6276
SATB, piano, opt. Unison choir (https://bit.ly/C-6276)

Other Suggestions
This day may include observances of Martin Luther King Jr. Day.
Visuals:
    O   Listening, service to others, 3:4b, 5b, 9b
    P   Hand, newborn child, hour glass
    E   Unity, various body shapes and sizes, circle of hands, 1 Cor 6:19
    G   John 1:43c, "Come and see," invitation, fig tree, mission
Introit: WS3150. "Father, We Have Heard You Calling" (1 Sam, John)
Litanies: C451 (1 Cor), C157 or C664 (ML King Jr. Day)
Prayer: C19. "Prayer of an African Girl" (1 Sam, Epiphany)
Responsive Prayer: WSL77 (John, MLK Day)
Response: N161, P299, S2072. "Amen, Amen" (John, MLK Day)
Theme Ideas: Discipleship / Following God, God: Call of God / Listening, God: Providence / God our Help, Service / Servanthood, Wisdom

Jonah 3:1-5, 10

The word of the LORD came to Jonah a second time, saying, [2]"Get up, go to Nineveh, that great city, and proclaim to it the message that I tell you." [3]So Jonah set out and went to Nineveh, according to the word of the LORD. Now Nineveh was an exceedingly large city, a three days' walk across. [4]Jonah began to go into the city, going a day's walk. And he cried out, "Forty days more, and Nineveh shall be overthrown!" [5]And the people of Nineveh believed God; they proclaimed a fast, and everyone, great and small, put on sackcloth. . . .

[10]When God saw what they did, how they turned from their evil ways, God changed his mind about the calamity that he had said he would bring upon them, and he did not do it.

Psalm 62:5-12 (G790, N659, P197, UM787)

[5]For God alone my soul waits in silence,
    for my hope is from him.
[6]He alone is my rock and my salvation,
    my fortress; I shall not be shaken.
[7]On God rests my deliverance and my honor;
    my mighty rock, my refuge is in God.
[8]Trust in him at all times, O people;
    pour out your heart before him;
God is a refuge for us.   *Selah*
[9]Those of low estate are but a breath;
    those of high estate are a delusion;
    in the balances they go up;
    they are together lighter than a breath.
[10]Put no confidence in extortion,
    and set no vain hopes on robbery;
    if riches increase, do not set your heart on them.
[11]Once God has spoken;
    twice have I heard this:
that power belongs to God,
    [12]and steadfast love belongs to you, O Lord.
For you repay to all
    according to their work.

1 Corinthians 7:29-31

[29]I mean, brothers and sisters, the appointed time has grown short; from now on, let even those who have wives be as though they had none, [30]and those who mourn as though they were not mourning, and those who rejoice as though they were not rejoicing, and those who buy as though they had no possessions, [31]and those who deal with the world as though they had no dealings with it. For the present form of this world is passing away.

Mark 1:14-20

[14]Now after John was arrested, Jesus came to Galilee proclaiming the good news of God [15]and saying, "The time is fulfilled, and the kingdom of God has come near; repent, and believe in the good news."

[16]As Jesus passed along the Sea of Galilee, he saw Simon and his brother Andrew casting a net into the sea, for they were fishers. [17]And Jesus said to them, "Follow me, and I will make you fishers of people." [18]And immediately they left their nets and followed him. [19]As he went a little farther, he saw James son of Zebedee and his brother John, who were in their boat mending the nets. [20]Immediately he called them, and they left their father Zebedee in the boat with the hired men and followed him.

Primary Hymns and Songs for the Day

"Blessed Be the God of Israel" (Jonah, Mark) (O)
　　C135, CG88, E444, EL250/552, G109, P602, UM209, VU901
　　　　H-3　　Hbl-70; Chr-42, 103; Desc-76; Org-90
"Rock of Ages, Cleft for Me" (Jonah, Pss)
　　C214, E685, EL623, G438, N596, SA671, SH301, UM361
　　(PD)
　　　　H-3　　Chr-167; Org-164
　　　　S-2　　#179. Harmonization
"Dear Lord and Father of Mankind" (Jonah, Mark)
　　(Alternate Text: "Dear God, Creator good and kind.")
　　C594, CG413, E652/563, G169, N502, P345, SA456, UM358
　　(PD), VU608
　　　　H-3　　Hbl-56; Chr-61; Org-124
　　　　S-2　　#151. Introduction
　　　　　　　 #152. Violin descant
"In God Alone" (Pss, 1 Cor)
　　G814, WS3135
"Hope of the World" (Pss, 1 Cor)
　　C538, E472, G734; N46, P360, UM178, VU215
　　　　H-3　　Chr-100
"Abide with Me" (1 Cor)
　　C636, CG543, E662, EL629, G836, N99, P543, SA529, SH475,
　　UM700 (PD), VU436
"Change My Heart, O God" 1565 (1 Cor)
　　EL801, G695, S2152, SA409, SH507
"You Walk along Our Shoreline" (Mark)
　　CG476, G170, N504
"O Jesus, I Have Promised" (Mark)
　　C612, E655, EL810, G724/725, N493, P388/389, SA613,
　　SH623, UM396 (PD), VU120
　　　　S-2　　#9. Descant
"I Have Decided to Follow Jesus" (Mark)
　　C344, CG497, S2129, SH610
"Jesus Calls Us" (Mark) (C)
　　C337, EL696, G720, N172, SA653, SH604, UM398, VU562
　　　　H-3　　Chr-115
　　　　S-2　　#65. Harmonization
　　CG486, E549/550, N171
"Blest Be the Tie That Binds" (1 Cor) (C)
　　C433, CG267, EL656, G306, N393, P438, SA812, SH701,
　　UM557 (PD), VU602
　　　　H-3　　Hbl-49; Chr-14; Desc-27; Org-25

Additional Hymn Suggestions

"For the Healing of the Nations" (Jonah)
　　C668, CG698, G346, N576, SA1000, UM428, VU678
"O God Beyond All Praising" (Jonah)
　　CG366, EL880, S2009, VU256
"Trust and Obey" (Jonah, Pss)
　　C556, CG509, SA690, SH636, UM467 (PD)
"It's Me, It's Me, O Lord" (Jonah, 1 Cor)
　　C579, N519, UM352
"Taste and See" (Pss, Comm.)
　　EL493, G520, S2267, SH691
"Come, We That Love the Lord" (1 Cor)
　　CG549, E392, N379, SA831, UM732, VU715
"God of Grace and God of Glory" (1 Cor, Mark) (O)
　　C464, CG285, E594/595, EL705, G307, N436, P420, SA814,
　　SH250, UM577, VU686
"Lord of the Dance" (Mark)
　　G157, P302, SA141, UM261, VU352
"Softly and Tenderly Jesus Is Calling" (Mark)
　　C340, CG474, EL608 (PD), G418, N449, SA435, SH601,
　　UM348
"Tú Has Venido a la Orilla" ("Lord, You Have Come to the
　　Lakeshore") (Mark)
　　C342, EL817, G721, N173, P377, SH599, UM344, VU563

"I Sing a Song of the Saints of God" (Mark)
　　E293, G730, N295, P364, UM712 (PD)
"The Summons" (Mark)
　　CG473, EL798, G726, S2130, SA695, SH598, VU567

Additional Contemporary and Modern Suggestions

"Came to My Rescue" 4705190 (Jonah)
"Psalm 62" ("My Soul Finds Rest") 5040902 (Jonah, Pss)
"I Will Call upon the Lord" 11263 (Jonah, Pss)
　　G621, S2002
"Give Thanks" (Pss)
　　C528, CG373, G647, S2036, SA364, SH489
"Praise Him" 684779 (Pss)
"Who Can Satisfy My Soul Like You?" 208492 (Pss)
"Rock of Ages" 2240547 (Pss)
"Cornerstone" 6158927 (Pss, Mark)
"Praise the Name of Jesus" 12712 (Pss, Mark)
"Amen, Amen" (Mark)
　　N161, P299, S2072
"Cry of My Heart" 844980 (Mark)
"You're Worthy of My Praise" 487976 (Mark)
"Step by Step" 696994 (Mark)
　　CG495, G743, WS3004
"Somlandela" ("We Will Follow") (Mark)
"Jesus, Lover of My Soul" ("It's All about You") 1545484 (Mark)
"Lead Me, Lord" 1609045 (Mark)
"Every Move I Make" 1595726 (Mark)
"Everyday" 2798154 (Mark)
"All of Me" 6290160 (Mark)
"Nobody" 7121827 (Mark)

Vocal Solos

"Didn't My Lord Deliver Daniel" (Jonah)
　　V-7　　p. 14/19
"Here I Am" (Jonah, Mark)
　　V-1　　p. 19

Anthems

"Change My Heart, O God" (1 Cor)
Espinosa/Raney; Hope C5750
SATB, piano (https://bit.ly/C-5750)

"Lord of the Dance" (Mark)
Arr. Neil Harmon; MorningStar 50-4365
SATB, keyboard or Orff and flute (https://bit.ly/MSM-50-4365)

Other Suggestions

Visuals:
　　O　　Sackcloth, empty plate, no. 40
　　P　　Large rock, refuge, symbols of power, Ps 62:11
　　E　　Ticking alarm clock
　　G　　Sackcloth, fish/net, fishing, nets left behind, disci-
　　　　　　pling, multiple images of people
Introit: WS3150. "Father, We Have Heard You Calling" (Jonah,
　　Mark)
Call to Confession: UM366. For Guidance.
Offering Prayer: WSL113. "Loving God, faithful and gracious"
　　(Jonah, Mark)
Response: UM587. "Bless Thou the Gifts" (Jonah, Mark)
Sung Benediction: WS3180. "As We Part For The Towns And
　　Cities" (Jonah, Mark)
See The Abingdon Worship Annual 2024 *for additional worship
　　resources.*
Theme Ideas: Discipleship / Following God, God: Call of God
　　/ Listening, God: Providence / God our Help, Preparation,
　　Sin and Forgiveness

Deuteronomy 18:15-20

[15]"The LORD your God will raise up for you a prophet like me from among your own people; you shall heed such a prophet. [16]This is what you requested of the LORD your God at Horeb on the day of the assembly when you said, 'Let me not hear again the voice of the LORD my God or see this great fire any more, lest I die.' [17]Then the LORD replied to me, 'They are right in what they have said. [18]I will raise up for them a prophet like you from among their own people; I will put my words in the mouth of the prophet, who shall speak to them everything that I command. [19]Anyone who does not heed the words that the prophet shall speak in my name, I myself will hold accountable. [20]But any prophet who presumes to speak in my name a word that I have not commanded the prophet to speak or who speaks in the name of other gods, that prophet shall die.'"

Psalm 111 (G652, N696, UM832)

Praise the LORD!
I will give thanks to the LORD with my whole heart,
   in the company of the upright, in the congregation.
[2]Great are the works of the LORD,
   studied by all who delight in them.
[3]Full of honor and majesty is his work,
   and his righteousness endures forever.
[4]He has gained renown by his wonderful deeds;
   the LORD is gracious and merciful.
[5]He provides food for those who fear him;
   he is ever mindful of his covenant.
[6]He has shown his people the power of his works,
   in giving them the heritage of the nations.
[7]The works of his hands are faithful and just;
   all his precepts are trustworthy.
[8]They are established forever and ever,
   to be performed with faithfulness and uprightness.
[9]He sent redemption to his people;
   he has commanded his covenant forever.
Holy and awesome is his name.
[10]The fear of the LORD is the beginning of wisdom;
   all those who practice it have a good understanding.
His praise endures forever.

1 Corinthians 8:1-13

Now concerning food sacrificed to idols: we know that "all of us possess knowledge." Knowledge puffs up, but love builds up. [2]Anyone who claims to know something does not yet have the necessary knowledge, [3]but anyone who loves God is known by him.

[4]Hence, as to the eating of food offered to idols, we know that "no idol in the world really exists" and that "there is no God but one." [5]Indeed, even though there may be so-called gods in heaven or on earth—as in fact there are many gods and many lords—[6]yet for us there is one God, the Father, from whom are all things and for whom we exist, and one Lord, Jesus Christ, through whom are all things and through whom we exist.

[7]It is not everyone, however, who has this knowledge. Since some have become so accustomed to idols until now, they still think of the food they eat as food offered to an idol, and their conscience, being weak, is defiled. [8]"Food will not bring us close to God." We are no worse off if we do not eat and no better off if we do. [9]But take care that this liberty of yours does not somehow become a stumbling block to the weak. [10]For if others see you, who possess knowledge, eating in the temple of an idol, might they not, since their conscience is weak, be encouraged to the point of eating food sacrificed to idols? [11]So by your knowledge the weak brother or sister for whom Christ died is destroyed. [12]But when you thus sin against brothers and sisters and wound their conscience when it is weak, you sin against Christ. [13]Therefore, if food is a cause of their falling, I will never again eat meat, so that I may not cause one of them to fall.

Mark 1:21-28

[21]They went to Capernaum, and when the Sabbath came, he entered the synagogue and taught. [22]They were astounded at his teaching, for he taught them as one having authority and not as the scribes. [23]Just then there was in their synagogue a man with an unclean spirit, [24]and he cried out, "What have you to do with us, Jesus of Nazareth? Have you come to destroy us? I know who you are, the Holy One of God." [25]But Jesus rebuked him, saying, "Be quiet and come out of him!" [26]And the unclean spirit, convulsing him and crying with a loud voice, came out of him. [27]They were all amazed, and they kept on asking one another, "What is this? A new teaching—with authority! He commands even the unclean spirits, and they obey him." [28]At once his fame began to spread throughout the surrounding region of Galilee.

Primary Hymns and Songs for the Day

"Christ, Whose Glory Fills the Skies" (Mark) (O)
    EL553, G662, P462/463, SA249, UM173, VU336
"Lord, Speak to Me" (Deut)
    CG503, EL676, G722, N531, SA773, SH557, UM463, VU589
        H-3   Hbl-75; Chr-131; Desc-22; Org-18
        S-1   #52. Descant
"All Creatures of Our God and King" (1 Cor)
    C22, CG307, E400, EL835, G15, N17, P455, SA2, SH16,
    UM62, VU217 (Fr.)
        H-3   Hbl-44; Chr-21; Desc-66; Org-73
        S-1   #198-204. Various treatments
"Be Thou My Vision" (1 Cor)
    C595, CG71, E488, EL793, G450, N451, P339, SA573, SH640,
    UM451, VU642
        H-3   Hbl-15, 48; Chr-36; Org-153
        S-1   #319. Arr. for organ and voices in canon
"Where Charity and Love Prevail" (1 Cor)
    CG264, EL359, G316, N396, SH271
        H-3   Hbl-104; Chr-112, 219; Desc-95; Org-143
        S-2   #162. Harmonization
    E581, UM549
"Guide Me, O Thou Great Jehovah" (Deut) (C)
    C622, CG33, E690, EL618, G65, N18/19, P281, SA27, SH51,
    UM127 (PD), VU651 (Fr.)
        H-3   Hbl-25, 51, 58; Chr-89; Desc-26; Org-23
        S-1   #76-77. Descant and harmonization

Additional Hymn Suggestions

"God Hath Spoken By the Prophets" (Deut) (O)
    CG32 UM108
"We Sing to You, O God" (Deut)
    EL791, N9, S2001
"We Sing of Your Glory" (Deut)
    EL849, S2011, SH622
"Christ Is the World's Light" (1 Cor)
    CG154, UM188
"Pues Si Vivimos" ("When We Are Living") (1 Cor)
    C536, CG265, EL639, G822, N499, P400, SH299, UM356,
    VU581
"Forgive Our Sins as We Forgive" (1 Cor)
    CG694 E674, EL605, G444, P347, SH504, UM390, VU364
"Help Us Accept Each Other" (1 Cor)
    C487, G754, N388, P358, UM560
"God Made from One Blood" (1 Cor)
    C500, CG686, N427, S2170, VU554
"Together We Serve" (1 Cor)
    G767, S2175
"Sacred the Body" (1 Cor)
    G27, S2228
"Baptized in Water" (1 Cor, Baptism)
    CG449, E294, EL456, G482, P492, S2248, SH666
"Healer of Our Every Ill" (1 Cor, Mark)
    C506, EL612, G795, S2213, SH339, VU619
"O Christ, the Healer" (1 Cor, Mark)
    C503. EL610, G793, N175, P380, UM265
"Draw Us in the Spirit's Tether" (1 Cor, Comm.)
    C392, EL470, G529, N337, P504, UM632, VU479
"Heal Me, Hands of Jesus" (Mark)
    C504, CG541, UM262, VU621
"Silence, Frenzied, Unclean Spirit" (Mark)
    C186, G180/181, N176, UM264, VU620
"An Outcast among Outcasts" (Mark)
    N201, S2104
"You Satisfy the Hungry Heart" (Comm.)
    C429, CG468, EL484, G523, P521, SH672, UM629, VU478

Additional Contemporary and Modern Suggestions

"Awesome God" 41099 (Deut, Pss, Mark)
    G616, S2040
"Majesty" 1527 (Deut, Mark)
    CG346, SA382, SH212, UM176
"Thank You, Lord" 865000 (Pss)
    AH4081, C531, SH496, UM84
"Great Is the Lord" 1149 (Pss)
    CG325, G614, S2022, SH459
"How Majestic Is Your Name" 26007 (Pss)
    C63, CG326, G613, S2023, SA90
"In the Lord I'll Be Ever Thankful" (Pss)
    G654, S2195, SH316
"Famous One" 3599431 (Pss)
"Because of Your Love" 4662501 (Pss)
"Desert Song" 5060793 (Pss)
"What a Mighty God We Serve" 11823 (Pss, Mark)
"What a Mighty God We Serve" 2245023 (Pss, Mark)
"Through It All" 18211 (Pss, Mark)
    C555, UM507
"Make Us One" 695737 (1 Cor)
"Bind Us Together" 1228 (1 Cor)
"I Believe In Jesus" 61282 (1 Cor)
"People Need the Lord" 18084 (Mark)
"Mighty to Save" 4591782 (Mark)
"We Walk His Way" (Mark)
"No Sweeter Name" 4447984 (Mark)
"There Is None Like You" 674545 (Mark)
"Good to Me" 313480 (Mark)
"You Have Saved Us" 5548514 (Mark)
"Able" 1256560 (Mark)
"The Dark Is Not Your Time" 7132934 (Mark)

Vocal Solos

"Where Shall My Wondering Soul Begin?" (Mark)
    V-1   p. 59
"Jesus Is Lord of All" (Mark)
    V-8   p. 254
"In Jesus' Name" (Mark)
    V-8   p. 188

Anthems

"Be Thou My Vision" (1 Cor)
Mary McDonald; Hope C5985
SATB, piano, opt. orchestra (https://bit.ly/C5985)

"Hymn to Christ the Light" (Mark)
Zebulon M. Highben; Augsburg 9781506447315
SATB a cappella (https://bit.ly/AF-47315)

Other Suggestions

Visuals:
    O   Bust or painting of Moses, fire, prophets, pulpit, open
            Bible
    P   Praise, food, hands, justice, Ps 111:9c, 10a, c
    E   Building, no. 1 (God, Lord), 1 Cor 8:1b, food, stum-
            bling blocks, books, healing, Christ, love
    G   Christ sitting and teaching, healing, others teaching,
            healing, Mark 1:24b, open Bible
Prayer: C394 or UM564. "For Unity" (1 Cor)
Prayer: C505 or C508 (Mark)
Response: AH4081, C531, SH496, UM84. "Thank You, Lord"
    (Pss)
Theme Ideas: Discipleship / Following God, God: Call of God
    / Listening, God: Power of God , Healing, Jesus: Body of
    Christ, Praise, Sin and Forgiveness

Isaiah 40:21-31

[21]Have you not known? Have you not heard?
  Has it not been told you from the beginning?
  Have you not understood from the foundations of the earth?
[22]It is he who sits above the circle of the earth,
  and its inhabitants are like grasshoppers,
who stretches out the heavens like a curtain
  and spreads them like a tent to live in,
[23]who brings princes to naught
  and makes the rulers of the earth as nothing.
[24]Scarcely are they planted, scarcely sown,
  scarcely has their stem taken root in the earth,
when he blows upon them, and they wither,
  and the tempest carries them off like stubble.
[25]To whom, then, will you compare me,
  or who is my equal? says the Holy One.
[26]Lift up your eyes on high and see:
  Who created these?
He who brings out their host and numbers them,
  calling them all by name;
because he is great in strength,
  mighty in power,
  not one is missing.
[27]Why do you say, O Jacob,
  and assert, O Israel,
"My way is hidden from the LORD,
  and my right is disregarded by my God"?
[28]Have you not known? Have you not heard?
The LORD is the everlasting God,
  the Creator of the ends of the earth.
He does not faint or grow weary;
  his understanding is unsearchable.
[29]He gives power to the faint
  and strengthens the powerless.
[30]Even youths will faint and be weary,
  and the young will fall exhausted,
[31]but those who wait for the LORD shall renew their strength;
  they shall mount up with wings like eagles;
they shall run and not be weary;
  they shall walk and not faint.

Psalm 147:1-11, 20c (G657, P255, UM859)

Praise the LORD!
How good it is to sing praises to our God,
  for he is gracious, and a song of praise is fitting.
[2]The LORD builds up Jerusalem;
  he gathers the outcasts of Israel.
[3]He heals the brokenhearted
  and binds up their wounds.
[4]He determines the number of the stars;
  he gives to all of them their names.
[5]Great is our Lord and abundant in power;
  his understanding is beyond measure.
[6]The LORD lifts up the downtrodden;
  he casts the wicked to the ground.
[7]Sing to the LORD with thanksgiving;
  make melody to our God on the lyre.
[8]He covers the heavens with clouds,
  prepares rain for the earth,
  makes grass grow on the hills.
[9]He gives to the animals their food
  and to the young ravens when they cry.
[10]His delight is not in the strength of the horse
  nor his pleasure in the speed of a runner,
[11]but the LORD takes pleasure in those who fear him,
  in those who hope in his steadfast love.
. . . .
[20c]Praise the LORD!

1 Corinthians 9:16-23

[16]If I proclaim the gospel, this gives me no ground for boasting, for an obligation is laid on me, and woe to me if I do not proclaim the gospel! [17]For if I do this of my own will, I have a wage, but if not of my own will, I am entrusted with a commission. [18]What then is my wage? Just this: that in my proclamation I may make the gospel free of charge, so as not to make full use of my rights in the gospel.

[19]For though I am free with respect to all, I have made myself a slave to all, so that I might gain all the more. [20]To the Jews I became as a Jew, in order to gain Jews. To those under the law I became as one under the law (though I myself am not under the law) so that I might gain those under the law. [21]To those outside the law I became as one outside the law (though I am not outside God's law but am within Christ's law) so that I might gain those outside the law. [22]To the weak I became weak, so that I might gain the weak. I have become all things to all people, that I might by all means save some. [23]I do it all for the sake of the gospel, so that I might become a partner in it.

Mark 1:29-39

[29]As soon as they left the synagogue, they entered the house of Simon and Andrew, with James and John. [30]Now Simon's mother-in-law was in bed with a fever, and they told him about her at once. [31]He came and took her by the hand and lifted her up. Then the fever left her, and she began to serve them.

[32]That evening, at sunset, they brought to him all who were sick or possessed by demons. [33]And the whole city was gathered around the door. [34]And he cured many who were sick with various diseases and cast out many demons, and he would not permit the demons to speak, because they knew him.

[35]In the morning, while it was still very dark, he got up and went out to a deserted place, and there he prayed. [36]And Simon and his companions hunted for him. [37]When they found him, they said to him, "Everyone is searching for you." [38]He answered, "Let us go on to the neighboring towns, so that I may proclaim the message there also, for that is what I came out to do." [39]And he went throughout all Galilee, proclaiming the message in their synagogues and casting out demons.

Primary Hymns and Songs for the Day

"Sing Praise to God Who Reigns Above" (Isa, Pss) (O)
  C6, CG315, E408, EL871, G645, N6, P483, UM126 (PD),
  VU216
        H-3   Hbl-92; Chr-126, 173; Desc-76; Org-91
        S-1   #237. Descant
"Arise, Your Light Is Come" (Isa)
  EL314, G744, N164, P411, VU79
"God of Our Life" (Isa)
  C713, G686, N366, P275
"O God, in a Mysterious Way" (Isa)
  CG39, E677, G30, N412, P270, SA17, SH47
        H-3   Chr-76; Desc-31
"From All That Dwell Below the Skies" (Isa)
  C49, CG330, E380, G327, N27, P229, UM101 (PD)
"On Eagle's Wings" (Isa)
  C77, CG51, EL787, G43, N775, SH318, UM143, VU807/808
        S-2   #143 Stanzas for soloist
"Immortal, Invisible, God Only Wise" (Pss, 1 Cor)
  C66, CG58, E423, EL834, G12, N1, P263, SA37, UM103 (PD),
  VU264
        H-3   Hbl-15, 71; Chr-65; Desc-93; Org-135
        S-1   #300. Harmonization
"There Is a Balm in Gilead" (Mark, Black History)
  AH4110, C501, CG74, E676, EL614 (PD), G792, N553, P394,
  SH340, UM375, VU612
"Precious Lord, Take My Hand" (Mark, Black History)
  C628, CG400, EL773, G834, N472, SH336, UM474, VU670
        H-3   Chr-164; Org-116
"Healer of Our Every Ill" (Mark)
  C506, EL612, G795, S2213, SH339, VU619
"We Cannot Measure How You Heal" (Mark)
  CG540, G797, SH341, VU613, WS3139
        S-2   #33-37. Various treatments
"In the Midst of New Dimensions" (Isa) (C)
  G315, N391, S2238

Additional Hymn Suggestions

"My Faith Looks Up to Thee" (Isa)
  C576, CG407, E691, EL759, G829, P383, SA726, UM452, VU663
"God of the Ages" (Isa)
  C725, CG62, E718, G331, N592, P262, SA19, UM698
"We Sing to You, O God" (Isa)
  EL791, N9, S2001
"O Holy Spirit, Root of Life" (Isa)
  C251, EL399, N57, S2121, VU379
"Make Me a Captive, Lord" (1 Cor) (C)
  P378, SA724, SH639, UM421
"O Zion, Haste" (1 Cor)
  C482, CG479, E539, EL668, UM573 (PD)
"Make Me a Channel of Your Peace" (1 Cor) (C)
  G753, S2171, SA608, SH616 VU684
"Lord of the Dance" (1 Cor, Mark)
  G157, P302, SA141, UM261, VU352
"We've a Story to Tell to the Nations" (1 Cor, Mark) (C)
  C484, CG427, SA943, UM569 (PD)
"He Touched Me" (Mark)
  C564, SA475, UM367
"Take Time to Be Holy" (Mark)
  C572, SA790, UM395 (PD), VU672
"I'm So Glad Jesus Lifted Me" (Mark, Black History)
  C529, EL860 (PD), N474, S2151

Additional Contemporary and Modern Suggestions

"Everlasting God" 4556538 (Isa)
"Still" 3940963 (Isa)
"This is My Story" 7046375 (Isa)
"The Power of Your Love" 917491 (Isa)

"Eagle's Wings" 2478168 (Isa)
"Your Love, Oh Lord" 1894255 (Isa)
"Our God Saves" 4972837 (Isa)
"Forevermore" 5466830 (Isa)
"I Will Rise" 5183450 (Isa)
"Great and Mighty Is He" 66665 (Isa, Pss)
"How Great Are You, Lord" 2888576 (Isa, Pss)
"Good to Me" 313480 (Isa, Mark)
"People Need the Lord" 18084 (Isa, Mark)
"Great Is the Lord" 1149 (Pss)
  CG325, G614, S2022, SH459
"Awesome Is the Lord Most High" 4674159 (Pss)
"You Have Saved Us" 5548514 (Pss, Mark)
"Make Me a Channel of Your Peace" 6399315 (1 Cor)
"Song for the Nations" 20340 (1 Cor, Mark)
"Oh Lord, You're Beautiful" 14514 (Mark)
"Amen, Amen" (Mark, Black History)
  N161, P299, S2072
"Here Is Bread, Here Is Wine" 983717 (Mark, Comm.)
"No Sweeter Name" 4447984 (Mark)
"My Redeemer Lives" 2397964 (Mark)
"There Is None Like You" 674545 (Mark)
"Turn Your Eyes upon Jesus" 15960 (Mark)
  CG472, SA445, UM349

Vocal Solos

"On Eagle's Wings" (Isa)
  V-3 (2)   p. 2
  V-3 (3)   p. 4
"Who You Are to Me" (Isa)
  V-9   p. 124
"There is a Balm in Gilead" (Mark, Black History)
  V-3 (1)   p. 29

Anthems

"Hope in Me" (Isa)
Terre Johnson; MorningStar MSM-50-2014
SATB, piano and clarinet (https://bit.ly/MS-2014)

"If We Wait for the Lord" (Isa)
Manuel/Hodges; Shawnee Press 00295395
Unison/opt. 2-part treble, piano (https://bit.ly/SP-5395)

Other Suggestions

This day may include an observance of Scout Sunday.
*February is Black History Month, which can be reflected in your
  choice of music and liturgy.*
Visuals:
  O   Helping the powerless, exhausted youth, Isa 40:31
  P   Praising, singing, healing, stars, stringed instruments
        (lyre), rain clouds, grass, birds, love
  E   Proclamation, ordination certificate, manacles (slave)
  G   Helping older woman up, healing, sundown/early
        dawn
Consider a service of healing (Mark)
Call to Prayer: C503. EL610, G793, N175, P380, UM265, stanza 1.
  O Christ, the Healer (Mark)
Intercessory Prayer: UM457. For the Sick (Mark)
Prayer: C332. "God of Wondrous Darkness" (Isa, Mark)
Scripture Response: C588, CG493, SA705, SH626, UM382,
  stanza 3. "Have Thine Own Way, Lord" (Pss, Mark)
Response: C30, CG316, EL846, G598, N760, S2067, SH596,
  VU431. *Amen Siakudumisa* ("Amen, We Praise Your Name,
  O God") (Pss, Black History)
Benediction: S2281. "May You Run and Not Be Weary" 807099 (Isa)
Theme Ideas: Faithfulness, Faithfulness, God: Faithfulness, God:
  Glory of God, God: Providence / God our Help, Healing,
  Praise

2 Kings 2:1-12

Now when the LORD was about to take Elijah up to heaven by a whirlwind, Elijah and Elisha were on their way from Gilgal. ²Elijah said to Elisha, "Stay here, for the LORD has sent me as far as Bethel." But Elisha said, "As the LORD lives and as you yourself live, I will not leave you." So they went down to Bethel. ³The company of prophets who were in Bethel came out to Elisha and said to him, "Do you know that today the LORD will take your master away from you?" And he said, "Yes, I know; keep silent."

⁴Elijah said to him, "Elisha, stay here, for the LORD has sent me to Jericho." But he said, "As the LORD lives and as you yourself live, I will not leave you." So they came to Jericho. ⁵The company of prophets who were at Jericho drew near to Elisha and said to him, "Do you know that today the LORD will take your master away from you?" And he answered, "Yes, I know; keep silent."

⁶Then Elijah said to him, "Stay here, for the LORD has sent me to the Jordan." But he said, "As the LORD lives and as you yourself live, I will not leave you." So the two of them went on. ⁷Fifty men of the company of prophets also went and stood at some distance from them, as they both were standing by the Jordan. ⁸Then Elijah took his mantle and rolled it up and struck the water; the water was parted to the one side and to the other, and the two of them crossed on dry ground.

⁹When they had crossed, Elijah said to Elisha, "Tell me what I may do for you before I am taken from you." Elisha said, "Please let me inherit a double share of your spirit." ¹⁰He responded, "You have asked a hard thing, yet if you see me as I am being taken from you, it will be granted you; if not, it will not." ¹¹As they continued walking and talking, a chariot of fire and horses of fire separated the two of them, and Elijah ascended in a whirlwind into heaven. ¹²Elisha kept watching and crying out, "Father, father! The chariots of Israel and its horsemen!" But when he could no longer see him, he grasped his own clothes and tore them in two pieces.

Psalm 50:1-6 (G13, N656, UM783)

The mighty one, God the LORD,
    speaks and summons the earth
    from the rising of the sun to its setting.
²Out of Zion, the perfection of beauty,
    God shines forth.
³Our God comes and does not keep silent;
    before him is a devouring fire
    and a mighty tempest all around him.
⁴He calls to the heavens above
    and to the earth, that he may judge his people:
⁵"Gather to me my faithful ones,
    who made a covenant with me by sacrifice!"
⁶The heavens declare his righteousness,
    for God himself is judge. *Selah*

2 Corinthians 4:3-6

³And even if our gospel is veiled, it is veiled to those who are perishing. ⁴In their case the god of this world has blinded the minds of the unbelievers, to keep them from seeing clearly the light of the gospel of the glory of Christ, who is the image of God. ⁵For we do not proclaim ourselves; we proclaim Jesus Christ as Lord and ourselves as your slaves for Jesus's sake. ⁶For it is the God who said, "Light will shine out of darkness," who has shone in our hearts to give the light of the knowledge of the glory of God in the face of Christ.

Mark 9:2-9

²Six days later, Jesus took with him Peter and James and John and led them up a high mountain apart, by themselves. And he was transfigured before them, ³and his clothes became dazzling bright, such as no one on earth could brighten them. ⁴And there appeared to them Elijah with Moses, who were talking with Jesus. ⁵Then Peter said to Jesus, "Rabbi, it is good for us to be here; let us set up three tents: one for you, one for Moses, and one for Elijah." ⁶He did not know what to say, for they were terrified. ⁷Then a cloud overshadowed them, and from the cloud there came a voice, "This is my Son, the Beloved; listen to him!" ⁸Suddenly when they looked around, they saw no one with them any more, but only Jesus.

⁹As they were coming down the mountain, he ordered them to tell no one about what they had seen, until after the Son of Man had risen from the dead.

Primary Hymns and Songs for the Day

"Christ, Whose Glory Fills the Skies" (Mark) (O)
    EL553, G662, P462/463, SA249, UM173, VU336
        H-3   Hbl-51; Chr-206; Desc-89; Org-120
        S-1   #278-279. Harmonizations
"Source and Sovereign, Rock and Cloud" (2 Kgs, Pss, 2 Cor, Mark)
    C12, G11, UM113
"God Is Here" (2 Cor)
    C280, CG298, EL526, G409, N70, P461, UM660
        H-3   Hbl-61; Chr-132; Org-2
        S-1   #4-5. Instrumental and vocal descants
"O Splendor of God's Glory Bright" (2 Cor)
    E5, EL559, G666, N87, P474, UM679 (PD), VU413
        H-3   Chr-19
"Sing of God Made Manifest" (Mark)
    C176, G156
"O Wondrous Sight! O Vision Fair" (Mark)
    E137, UM258 (PD)
        H-3   Hbl-93; Chr-84; Desc-102; Org-175
        S-2   #191. Harmonization
        S-2   #191. Harmonization
    EL316 (PD), G189, N184, P75
"Swiftly Pass the Clouds of Glory" (Mark)
    G190, P73, S2102
"We Have Come at Christ's Own Bidding" (Mark)
    N182, S2103
        H-3   Hbl-46; Chr-26, 134; Desc-53; Org-56
        S-1   #168-171. Various treatments
    CG162, G191, VU104
"Holy Ground" 21198 (Mark)
    C112, G406, S2272, SA400
"Jesus, Take Us to the Mountain" (Mark)
    N183, G193
"Swing Low, Sweet Chariot" (2 Kgs, Black History) (C)
    C643, G825, UM703
        H-3   Chr-177
"Shine, Jesus, Shine" 30426 (2 Cor, Mark) (C)
    CG156, EL671, G192, S2173, SA261, SH102
        H-3   Chr-171

Additional Hymn Suggestions

"Hail to the Lord's Anointed" (2 Kgs, Mark) (O)
    C140, CG98, EL311, G149, N104, P205, SH112, UM203, VU30
"Steal Away to Jesus" (2 Kgs, Mark, Black History)
    C644, G358, N599, UM704
"I Want to Walk as a Child of the Light" (2 Cor)
    CG96, E490, EL815, G377, SH352, UM206
"Be Thou My Vision" (2 Cor)
    C595, CG71, E488, EL793, G450, N451, P339, SA573, SH640, UM451, VU642
"Open My Eyes, That I May See" (2 Cor)
    C586, CG395, G451, P324, SH583, UM454, VU371
"This Little Light of Mine" (2 Cor)
    See also AH4150
    N525, SH257, UM585 (See also AH4150, EL677, N524)
"Christ Beside Me" (2 Cor)
    G702, S2166
"Jesus Shall Reign" (Mark)
    C95, CG158, E544, EL434, G265, N300, P423, SA258, SH209, UM157 (PD), VU330
"Christ, Upon the Mountain Peak" (Mark)
    E129/130, EL317, P74, UM260, VU102
"I Stand Amazed in the Presence" (Mark)
    CG576, SA466, SH537, UM371 (PD)
"Mine Eyes Have Seen the Glory" (Mark, Transfiguration)
    C705, CG439, EL890, G354, N610, SA263, UM717

"As We Gather at Your Table" (Mark, Comm.)
    EL522, N332, S2268, SH411, VU457
"You, Lord, are Both Lamb and Shepherd" (Transfiguration)
    G274, SH210, VU210, WS3043

Additional Contemporary and Modern Suggestions

"Praise to the Lord" (Pss)
    EL844, S2029, VU835
"From the Rising of the Sun" (Pss)
    G670, S2024, SH469
"Dios Está Aquí" ("God Is Here Today") 3170575 (Pss, Transfiguration)
    G411, S2049, SH382
"What a Mighty God We Serve" 11823 (Pss)
"What a Mighty God We Serve" 2245023 (Pss)
"How Great Is Our God" 4348399 (Pss)
    CG322, SH458, WS3003
"I Will Not Forget You" 2694306 (Pss)
"Shine on Us" 1754646 (2 Cor)
"Mighty to Save" 4591782 (2 Cor)
"Walking in the Light of God" (2 Cor)
"Turn Your Eyes upon Jesus" 15960 (Mark)
    CG472, SA445, UM349
"Yesu Tawa Pano" ("Jesus, We Are Here") (Mark)
    EL529, G392, S2273, SH611
"We Declare Your Majesty" 121483 (Mark, Transfiguration)
"He Is Exalted" 17827 (Mark, Transfiguration)
    AH4082, CG342, S2070, SH423
"Open Our Eyes, Lord" 1572 (Mark, Transfiguration)
    CG392, S2086, SA386, SH562
"Honor and Praise" 1867485 (Transfiguration)
"All Hail King Jesus" 12877 (Transfiguration)
"Jesus, the Light of the World" 6363190 (Transfiguration)
    WS3056 (See also AH4038, CG129, G127, N160, SH103)
"Great and Mighty Is He" 66665 (Transfiguration)
"Awesome in This Place" 847554 (Transfiguration)

Vocal Solos

"Ride Up in the Chariot" (2 Kgs)
    V-7   p. 82/86
"Shine, Jesus, Shine" (2 Cor, Transfiguration)
    V-3 (2)   p. 48
"I Saw the Lord, and All Beside Was Darkness" (Mark)
    V-8   p. 268

Anthems

"Shine on Us" (Mark)
Arr. Victoria Schwarz; Shawnee Press HL-35031917
SATB, keyboard, opt. harp (https://bit.ly/SP-1917)

"Holy Ground" (Mark)
Ken Medema; Hope GC980
SATB, piano (https://bit.ly/Hope-980)

Other Suggestions

Visuals:
    O   Light, whirlwind, fire, mantel/stole, generations
    P   Sunrise/set, fire, scales of justice, Ps 50:6a
    E   Manacles, light/darkness, Christ
    G   White robe, cloud, transfigured Christ, Elijah, Moses
Introit: S2005. "Arise, Shine" (2 Kgs, Mark)
Call to Prayer: S2202. "Come Away with Me" (Mark)
Prayer: C591, UM489, or UM259 (1 Cor, Mark)
Response: SH556, WS3137. "Lord Jesus Christ, Your Light Shines" (Mark)
Closing Prayer: WSL13 (Transfiguration)
Theme Ideas: God: Glory of God, God: Mystery of God, Holy Spirit, Light

Joel 2:1-2, 12-17

Blow the trumpet in Zion;
    sound the alarm on my holy mountain!
Let all the inhabitants of the land tremble,
    for the day of the LORD is coming, it is near—
²a day of darkness and gloom,
    a day of clouds and thick darkness!
Like blackness spread upon the mountains,
    a great and powerful army comes;
their like has never been from of old,
    nor will be again after them
    in ages to come.
. . . .

¹²Yet even now, says the LORD,
    return to me with all your heart,
with fasting, with weeping, and with mourning;
    ¹³rend your hearts and not your clothing.
Return to the LORD your God,
    for he is gracious and merciful,
slow to anger, abounding in steadfast love,
    and relenting from punishment.
¹⁴Who knows whether he will not turn and relent
    and leave a blessing behind him,
a grain offering and a drink offering
    for the LORD your God?
¹⁵Blow the trumpet in Zion;
    consecrate a fast;
call a solemn assembly;
    ¹⁶gather the people.
Consecrate the congregation;
    assemble the aged;
gather the children,
    even infants at the breast.
Let the bridegroom leave his room
    and the bride her canopy.
¹⁷Between the vestibule and the altar,
    let the priests, the ministers of the LORD, weep.
Let them say, "Spare your people, O LORD,
    and do not make your heritage a mockery,
    a byword among the nations.
Why should it be said among the peoples,
    'Where is their God?' "

Psalm 51:1-17 (UM785)

Have mercy on me, O God,
    according to your steadfast love;
according to your abundant mercy,
    blot out my transgressions.
²Wash me thoroughly from my iniquity,
    and cleanse me from my sin.
³For I know my transgressions,
    and my sin is ever before me.
⁴Against you, you alone, have I sinned
    and done what is evil in your sight,
so that you are justified in your sentence
    and blameless when you pass judgment.
⁵Indeed, I was born guilty,
    a sinner when my mother conceived me.
⁶You desire truth in the inward being;
    therefore teach me wisdom in my secret heart.
⁷Purge me with hyssop, and I shall be clean;
    wash me, and I shall be whiter than snow.
⁸Let me hear joy and gladness;
    let the bones that you have crushed rejoice.
⁹Hide your face from my sins,
    and blot out all my iniquities.
¹⁰Create in me a clean heart, O God,
    and put a new and right spirit within me.
¹¹Do not cast me away from your presence,
    and do not take your holy spirit from me.

¹²Restore to me the joy of your salvation,
    and sustain in me a willing spirit.
¹³Then I will teach transgressors your ways,
    and sinners will return to you.
¹⁴Deliver me from bloodshed, O God,
    O God of my salvation,
    and my tongue will sing aloud of your deliverance.
¹⁵O Lord, open my lips,
    and my mouth will declare your praise.
¹⁶For you have no delight in sacrifice;
    if I were to give a burnt offering, you would not be pleased.
¹⁷The sacrifice acceptable to God is a broken spirit;
    a broken and contrite heart, O God, you will not despise.

2 Corinthians 5:20b–6:10

²⁰ᵇwe entreat you on behalf of Christ: be reconciled to God. ²¹For our sake God made the one who knew no sin to be sin, so that in him we might become the righteousness of God.

6 As we work together with him, we entreat you also not to accept the grace of God in vain. ²For he says,
    "At an acceptable time I have listened to you,
        and on a day of salvation I have helped you."
Look, now is the acceptable time; look, now is the day of salvation! ³We are putting no obstacle in anyone's way, so that no fault may be found with our ministry, ⁴but as servants of God we have commended ourselves in every way: in great endurance, afflictions, hardships, calamities, ⁵beatings, imprisonments, riots, labors, sleepless nights, hunger; ⁶in purity, knowledge, patience, kindness, holiness of spirit, genuine love, ⁷truthful speech, and the power of God; with the weapons of righteousness for the right hand and for the left; ⁸in honor and dishonor, in ill repute and good repute. We are treated as impostors and yet are true, ⁹as unknown and yet are well known, as dying and look—we are alive, as punished and yet not killed, ¹⁰as sorrowful yet always rejoicing, as poor yet making many rich, as having nothing and yet possessing everything.

Matthew 6:1-6, 16-21

"Beware of practicing your righteousness before others in order to be seen by them, for then you have no reward from your Father in heaven.

²"So whenever you give alms, do not sound a trumpet before you, as the hypocrites do in the synagogues and in the streets, so that they may be praised by others. Truly I tell you, they have received their reward. ³But when you give alms, do not let your left hand know what your right hand is doing, ⁴so that your alms may be done in secret, and your Father who sees in secret will reward you.

⁵"And whenever you pray, do not be like the hypocrites, for they love to stand and pray in the synagogues and at the street corners, so that they may be seen by others. Truly I tell you, they have received their reward. ⁶But whenever you pray, go into your room and shut the door and pray to your Father who is in secret, and your Father who sees in secret will reward you. . . .

¹⁶"And whenever you fast, do not look somber, like the hypocrites, for they mark their faces to show others that they are fasting. Truly I tell you, they have received their reward. ¹⁷But when you fast, put oil on your head and wash your face, ¹⁸so that your fasting may be seen not by others but by your Father who is in secret, and your Father who sees in secret will reward you.

¹⁹"Do not store up for yourselves treasures on earth, where moth and rust consume and where thieves break in and steal, ²⁰but store up for yourselves treasures in heaven, where neither moth nor rust consumes and where thieves do not break in and steal. ²¹For where your treasure is, there your heart will be also."

Primary Hymns and Songs for the Day
"There's a Wideness in God's Mercy" (Joel)
    C73, CG41, E470, EL587/88G435, N23, P298, SH526, UM121, VU271
"O Master, Let Me Walk with Thee" (Joel, Lent)
    C602, CG660, E659/E660, EL818, G738, N503, P357, SA667, SH612, UM430 (PD), VU560
        H-3   Hbl-81; Chr-147; Desc-74; Org-87
        S-2   #118. Descant
"Jesus, the Very Thought of Thee" (2 Cor)
    C102, CG386, E642, EL754, G629, N507, P310, SA85, UM175
        H-3   Hbl-66, 73; Chr-90; Desc-92; Org-131
        S-1   #291-292. Descant and harmonization
"What Wondrous Love Is This" (2 Cor)
    C200, CG171, E439, EL666, G215, N223, P85, SA207, SH177, UM292, VU147 (Fr.)
        H-3   Hbl-102; Chr-212; Org-185
        S-1   #347. Harmonization
"Lead On, O King Eternal" (2 Cor)
    C632, CG63, E555, EL805, G269, N573, P447/ P448, SA964, UM580
        H-3   Hbl-74; Chr-123; Desc-64; Org-71
        S-1   #9-197. Various treatments
"The Glory of These Forty Days" (Matt)
    E143, EL320, G165, P87
"Forty Days and Forty Nights" (Matt)
    C179, E150, G167, N205, P77, SH116, VU114
"Come and Find the Quiet Center" (Matt)
    C575, S2128, VU374
"More Love to Thee, O Christ" (Matt) (C)
    C527, CG365, G828, N456, P359, UM453 (PD)
        H-3   Org-94

Additional Hymn Suggestions
"Lord, Who Throughout These Forty Days" (Joel, Matt)
    C180, CG169, E142, EL319, G166, N211, P81, UM269
"Sing My Tongue, the Glorious Battle" (Joel)
    E165/166, EL355/356, G225, N220, UM296
"Alas! and Did My Savior Bleed" (2 Cor)
    AH4067, C204, CG182/595, EL337, G212, N199/200, P78, SA159, UM294/359, SH172/173
"Lead On, O Cloud of Presence" (2 Cor, Lent)
    C633, S2234, VU421
"Love Divine, All Loves Excelling" (2 Cor, Matt)
    C517, CG281, E657, EL631, G366, N43, P376, SA262, SH353/354, UM384 (PD), VU333
"It's Me, It's Me, O Lord" (Matt, Black History)
    C579, N519, UM352
"Just as I Am, Without One Plea" (Matt)
    C339, CG500, E693, EL592, G442, N207, P370, SA503, SH500, UM357 (PD), VU508
"Take Time to Be Holy" (Matt)
    C572, SA790, UM395 (PD), VU672
"Lord, I Want to Be a Christian" (Matt) (C)
    C589, CG507, G729, N454, P372 (PD), SH621, UM402
"Near to the Heart of God" (Matt)
    C581, CG383, G824, P527, UM472 (PD)
"Prayer Is the Soul's Sincere Desire" (Matt)
    CG391, N508, SA784, UM492
"Sweet Hour of Prayer" (Matt)
    C570, CG412, N505, SA787, SH578, UM496 (PD)
"Since Jesus Came into My Heart" (Matt)
    C614, S2140, SA907
"The Lord's Prayer" (Matt, Lent)
    C307-C310, G464, P589, S2278, SH595, UM271, WS3068/3069/3071

Additional Contemporary and Modern Suggestions
"Cornerstone" 6158927 (Joel, Lent)
"Because of Your Love" 4662501 (Joel, Pss)
"Open Our Eyes, Lord" 1572 (Pss)
    CG392, S2086, SA386, SH562

"Give Me a Clean Heart" 314764 (Pss)
    AH4125, C515, N188, S2133
Confitemini Domino ("Come and Fill Our Hearts") (Pss)
    EL538, G466, S2157
"Open the Eyes of My Heart" 2298355 (Pss)
    G452, SA270, SH378, WS3008
"Hosanna" 4785835 (Pss)
"Purify My Heart" 1314323 (Pss)
"Better Than A Hallelujah" 5622564 (Pss)
"Today" 5775617 (Pss)
"Refiner's Fire" 426298 (Pss)
"The Power of Your Love" 917491 (Pss)
"I Give You My Heart" 1866132 (Pss)
"Give Us Clean Hands" 2060208 (Pss)
"Grace Like Rain" 3689877 (Pss)
"How Great Is the Love" 5521823 (Pss)
"You Are My Hiding Place" 21442 (Pss, Matt)
    C554, S2055, SH46
"Jesus Messiah" 5183443 (2 Cor, Lent)
"Lord, Listen to Your Children Praying" 22829 (Matt)
    C305, CG389, G469, S2193, SH577, VU400
"You Are My All in All" 825356 (Matt)
    CG571, G519, SH335, WS3040
"When It's All Been Said and Done" 2788353 (Matt)
"From Ashes to Beauty" 5288953 (Ash Wednesday)
"Beauty for Ashes" 4414735 (Ash Wednesday)
"Take These Ashes" (Ash Wednesday)

Vocal Solos
"If with All Your Hearts" (Recitative & Aria from *Elijah*) (Joel)
    V-8   p. 277
"A Contrite Heart" (Pss)
    V-4   p. 10
"Give Me Jesus" (Pss, Matt, Lent)
    V-3 (1)   p. 53
    V-7   p. 24/28
    V-8   p. 256

Anthems
"O God, Have Mercy" (Pss)
Arr. Lloyd Pfautsch; Hinshaw HMC1875
SATB a cappella (https://bit.ly/H-1875)

"Dust I Am" (Ash Wednesday)
Mark Miller; Hinshaw HMC2600
SATB, piano (https://bit.ly/H-2600)

Other Suggestions
Visuals:
    O   Black cloth, grain, wine, trumpet, empty plate
    P   Water, snow, rejoicing, Ps 51:10, 15, 17, heart
    E   Clock, calendar with today's date, rejoicing, black/gold
    G   Praying hands, oil/water, closed door, empty plate, rust
Introit: EL529, G392, S2273, SH611. "Jesus, We Are Here" (Matt)
Call to Prayer: CG399, EL751, G471, S2200, SH311/517. "O Lord, Hear My Prayer" (Matt)
Responsive Reading: CG166. (Lent)
Response: S2275, or N784 (Pss)
Prayer: C574, N846 or UM353 (Pss)
Prayer: C456, C567, or N769 (Matt)
Theme Ideas: Light, Prayer, Priorities, Reconciliation, Repentance, Sin and Forgiveness

Genesis 9:8-17

[8]Then God said to Noah and to his sons with him, [9]"As for me, I am establishing my covenant with you and your descendants after you [10]and with every living creature that is with you, the birds, the domestic animals, and every animal of the earth with you, as many as came out of the ark. [11]I establish my covenant with you, that never again shall all flesh be cut off by the waters of a flood, and never again shall there be a flood to destroy the earth." [12]God said, "This is the sign of the covenant that I make between me and you and every living creature that is with you, for all future generations: [13]I have set my bow in the clouds, and it shall be a sign of the covenant between me and the earth. [14]When I bring clouds over the earth and the bow is seen in the clouds, [15]I will remember my covenant that is between me and you and every living creature of all flesh, and the waters shall never again become a flood to destroy all flesh. [16]When the bow is in the clouds, I will see it and remember the everlasting covenant between God and every living creature of all flesh that is on the earth." [17]God said to Noah, "This is the sign of the covenant that I have established between me and all flesh that is on the earth."

Psalm 25:1-10 (G420, N635, P178, SH575, UM756)

To you, O Lord, I lift up my soul.
[2]O my God, in you I trust;
    do not let me be put to shame;
    do not let my enemies exult over me.
[3]Do not let those who wait for you be put to shame;
    let them be ashamed who are wantonly treacherous.
[4]Make me to know your ways, O Lord;
    teach me your paths.
[5]Lead me in your truth and teach me,
    for you are the God of my salvation;
    for you I wait all day long.
[6]Be mindful of your mercy, O Lord, and of your steadfast love,
    for they have been from of old.
[7]Do not remember the sins of my youth or my transgressions;
    according to your steadfast love remember me,
    for the sake of your goodness, O Lord!
[8]Good and upright is the Lord;
    therefore he instructs sinners in the way.
[9]He leads the humble in what is right
    and teaches the humble his way.
[10]All the paths of the Lord are steadfast love and faithfulness,
    for those who keep his covenant and his decrees.

1 Peter 3:18-22

[18]For Christ also suffered for sins once for all, the righteous for the unrighteous, in order to bring you to God. He was put to death in the flesh but made alive in the spirit, [19]in which also he went and made a proclamation to the spirits in prison, [20]who in former times did not obey, when God waited patiently in the days of Noah, during the building of the ark, in which a few, that is, eight lives, were saved through water. [21]And baptism, which this prefigured, now saves you—not as a removal of dirt from the body but as an appeal to God for a good conscience, through the resurrection of Jesus Christ, [22]who has gone into heaven and is at the right hand of God, with angels, authorities, and powers made subject to him.

Mark 1:9-15

[9]In those days Jesus came from Nazareth of Galilee and was baptized by John in the Jordan. [10]And just as he was coming up out of the water, he saw the heavens torn apart and the Spirit descending like a dove upon him. [11]And a voice came from the heavens, "You are my Son, the Beloved; with you I am well pleased."

[12]And the Spirit immediately drove him out into the wilderness. [13]He was in the wilderness forty days, tested by Satan, and he was with the wild beasts, and the angels waited on him.

[14]Now after John was arrested, Jesus came to Galilee proclaiming the good news of God [15]and saying, "The time is fulfilled, and the kingdom of God has come near; repent, and believe in the good news."

Primary Hymns and Songs for the Day

"Lord, Who Throughout These Forty Days" (Mark) (O)
UM269
H-3   Chr-106; Desc-65; Org-72
S-2   #105. Flute/violin descant
#106. Harmonization
C180, CG169, E142, EL319, G166, N211, P81

"This Is My Father's World" (Gen, 1 Peter) (O)
C59, E651, CG17, EL824 (PD), G370, P293, SA66, SH17,
UM144, VU296
H-3   Hbl-31, 99; Chr-87, 102, 197; Org-159
S-1   #326. Transposition in D major

"O Love That Wilt Not Let Me Go" (Gen)
Especially stanzas 1-3.
C540, CG631, G833, N485, P384, SA616, SH314, UM480,
VU658
H-3   Chr-146; Org-142

"Wash, O God, Our Sons and Daughters" (1 Pet, Mark)
C365, EL445, G490, SH669, UM605, VU442
H-3   Hbl-14, 64; Chr-132, 203
S-2   #22. Descant

"The Glory of These Forty Days" (Mark)
E143, EL320, G165, P87

"Forty Days and Forty Nights" (Mark)
C179, E150, G167, N205, P77, SH116, VU114

"Touch the Earth Lightly" (Gen) (C)
C693, EL739, G713, N569, VU307, WS3129

"O Love, How Deep" (Mark) (C)
E448/449, EL322, G618, N209, P83, SH115, UM267, VU348
H-3   Org-145
S-1   #82-84. Various treatments

Additional Hymn Suggestions

"God of the Sparrow" (Gen)
C70, EL740, G22, N32, P272, UM122, VU229

"All Things Bright and Beautiful" (Gen)
C61, CG23, E405, G20, N31, P267, SA3, SH1, UM147 (PD),
VU291

"Womb of Life" (Gen)
C14, G3, N274, S2046

"Loving Spirit" (Gen, Mark, Baptism)
C244, EL397, G293, P323, S2123, VU387

"As the Deer" 1431 (1 Pet)
CG49, G626/778, S2025, SA571, VU766

"Wonder of Wonders" (1 Pet, Mark, Baptism)
C378, G489, N328, P499, S2247

"Baptized in Water" (1 Pet, Mark, Baptism)
CG446, E294, EL456, G482, P492, S2248, SH666

"Hope of the World" (Mark)
C538, E472, G734, N46, P360, UM178, VU215

"When Jesus Came to Jordan" (Mark)
CG152, EL305, P72, SH113, UM252

"Spirit Song" 27824 (1 Pet, Mark)
C352, SH409, UM347

"Shall We Gather at the River" (Mark, Baptism)
C701, CG561, EL423, G375, N597, SA546, SH366, UM723,
VU710

"Wild and Lone the Prophet's Voice" (Mark, Lent)
G163, P409, S2089

"Jesus Walked This Lonesome Valley" (Mark)
C211, P80, S2112

"She Comes Sailing on the Wind" (Mark)
S2122, VU380

Additional Contemporary and Modern Suggestions

"God of Wonders" 3118757 (Gen, Pss)

"Cornerstone" 6158927 (Gen)

"Promises" 6454250 (Gen, Mark)

"Jesus, Remember Me" (Gen)
C569, CG393, EL616, G227, P599, SH175, UM488, VU148

"Great Is the Lord" 1149 (Pss)
CG325, G614, S2022, SH459

"To Know You More" 1767420 (Pss)

"Cry of My Heart" 844980 (Pss)

"More Like You" 2145051 (Pss)

"One Thing Remains" 5508444 (Pss)

"In the Secret" 1810119 (Pss)

"I Could Sing of Your Love Forever" 1043199 (Pss)

"Hungry" ("Falling on My Knees") 2650364 (Pss, Lent)

"Lead Me, Lord" 1609045 (Pss)

"How Great Is the Love" 5521823 (Pss, Lent)

"Gentle Shepherd" 15609 (Pss, Mark, Lent)

"God Will Make a Way" 458620 (Pss, Mark)

"Knowing You" 1045238 (Pss, Mark)

"Jesus, Name above All Names" 21291 (1 Pet, Mark)

"I've Just Come from the Fountain" (1 Pet, Mark)

"Wade in the Water" (Mark)
AH4046, C371, EL459 (PD), S2107

"Spirit of God" (Mark)

"Holy Ground" 21198 (Mark, Lent)
C112, G406, S2272, SA400

"We Walk His Way" (Mark, Lent)

"Down to the River to Pray" 4369457 (Mark)

Vocal Solos

"God Will Make a Way" (with "He Leadeth Me") (Pss, Lent)
V-3 (2)   p. 9

"I've Just Come from the Fountain" (Mark)
V-7   p. 54/59

Anthems

"I Never Touched a Rainbow" (Gen)
Ruth Artman; Choristers Guild CGA355
Unison/two-part, piano (https://bit.ly/CG-355)

"The Glory of These Forty Days" (Mark)
Arr. Hal Hopson; GIA Publications G-9242
SATB, *a cappella* (https://bit.ly/G-9242)

Other Suggestions

Visuals:
O   Water, Noah's ark, animals, rainbow
P   Praying hands, Ps 25:1, 9a
E   Baptism, cross, resurrection, open Bible, see (Gen),
prison
G   Rocks, sand, bones, Holy Spirit, no. 40, wild animals,
angels, dove

Introit: UM292, stanza 1. "What Wondrous Love Is This"
C200, CG171, E439, EL666, G215, N223, P85, SA207, SH177,
UM292, VU147 (Fr.)

Response: "Lord, Have Mercy" (Pss)
C299, S2277

Prayer: WSL16, UM253 (Mark)

Scripture Response: UM368, stanza 3. "My Hope Is Built" (Gen)
AH4105, C537, CG590, EL596/597, G353, N403, P379,
SA662, SH324, UM368 (PD)

Call to Baptism: S2050, stanza 1. "Mothering God, You Gave Me
Birth" (Gen, Mark)
C83, N467, S2050, VU320

Theme Ideas: Baptism, Covenant, Discipleship / Following God,
God: Promises, Holy Spirit, Journey, Sin and Forgiveness

Genesis 17:1-7, 15-16

When Abram was ninety-nine years old, the LORD appeared to Abram and said to him, "I am God Almighty; walk before me, and be blameless. [2]And I will make my covenant between me and you and will make you exceedingly numerous." [3]Then Abram fell on his face, and God said to him, [4]"As for me, this is my covenant with you: You shall be the ancestor of a multitude of nations. [5]No longer shall your name be Abram, but your name shall be Abraham, for I have made you the ancestor of a multitude of nations. [6]I will make you exceedingly fruitful, and I will make nations of you, and kings shall come from you. [7]I will establish my covenant between me and you and your offspring after you throughout their generations, for an everlasting covenant, to be God to you and to your offspring after you. . . .

[15]God said to Abraham, "As for Sarai your wife, you shall not call her Sarai, but Sarah shall be her name. [16]I will bless her and also give you a son by her. I will bless her, and she shall give rise to nations; kings of peoples shall come from her."

Psalm 22:23-31 (G631, N632, UM 752)

[23]You who fear the LORD, praise him!
　　All you offspring of Jacob, glorify him;
　　stand in awe of him, all you offspring of Israel!
[24]For he did not despise or abhor
　　the affliction of the afflicted;
he did not hide his face from me
　　but heard when I cried to him.
[25]From you comes my praise in the great congregation;
　　my vows I will pay before those who fear him.
[26]The poor shall eat and be satisfied;
　　those who seek him shall praise the LORD.
　　May your hearts live forever!
[27]All the ends of the earth shall remember
　　and turn to the LORD,
and all the families of the nations
　　shall worship before him.
[28]For dominion belongs to the LORD,
　　and he rules over the nations.
[29]To him, indeed, shall all who sleep in the earth bow down;
　　before him shall bow all who go down to the dust,
　　and I shall live for him.
[30]Posterity will serve him;
　　future generations will be told about the Lord
[31]and proclaim his deliverance to a people yet unborn,
　　saying that he has done it.

Romans 4:13-25

[13]For the promise that he would inherit the world did not come to Abraham or to his descendants through the law but through the righteousness of faith. [14]For if it is the adherents of the law who are to be the heirs, faith is null and the promise is void. [15]For the law brings wrath, but where there is no law, neither is there transgression.

[16]For this reason the promise depends on faith, in order that it may rest on grace, so that it may be guaranteed to all his descendants, not only to the adherents of the law but also to those who share the faith of Abraham (who is the father of all of us, [17]as it is written, "I have made you the father of many nations"), in the presence of the God in whom he believed, who gives life to the dead and calls into existence the things that do not exist. [18]Hoping against hope, he believed that he would become "the father of many nations," according to what was said, "So shall your descendants be." [19]He did not weaken in faith when he considered his own body, which was already as good as dead (for he was about a hundred years old), and the barrenness of Sarah's womb. [20]No distrust made him waver concerning the promise of God, but he grew strong in his faith as he gave glory to God, [21]being fully convinced that God was able to do what he had promised. [22]Therefore "it was reckoned to him as righteousness." [23]Now the words, "it was reckoned to him," were written not for his sake alone [24]but for ours also. It will be reckoned to us who believe in him who raised Jesus our Lord from the dead, [25]who was handed over for our trespasses and was raised for our justification.

Mark 8:31-38

[31]Then he began to teach them that the Son of Man must undergo great suffering and be rejected by the elders, the chief priests, and the scribes and be killed and after three days rise again. [32]He said all this quite openly. And Peter took him aside and began to rebuke him. [33]But turning and looking at his disciples, he rebuked Peter and said, "Get behind me, Satan! For you are setting your mind not on divine things but on human things."

[34]He called the crowd with his disciples and said to them, "If any wish to come after me, let them deny themselves and take up their cross and follow me. [35]For those who want to save their life will lose it, and those who lose their life for my sake, and for the sake of the gospel, will save it. [36]For what will it profit them to gain the whole world and forfeit their life? [37]Indeed, what can they give in return for their life? [38]Those who are ashamed of me and of my words in this adulterous and sinful generation, of them the Son of Man will also be ashamed when he comes in the glory of his Father with the holy angels."

Primary Hymns and Songs for the Day

"The God of Abraham Praise" (Gen, Pss, Mark) (O)
  C24, CG45, E401, EL831, G49, N24, P488, SH50, UM116
  (PD), VU255
        H-3   Hbl-62, 95; Chr-59; Org-77
        S-1   #211. Harmonization
"We've Come This Far by Faith" (Gen, Rom, Mark) (O)
  AH4042, C533, EL633, G656, SH58
"O Word of God Incarnate" (Gen, Rom, Mark)
  C322, E632, EL514, G459, N315, P327, UM598 (PD), VU499
        H-3   Hbl-86; Chr-153; Org-95
        S-1   #243. Harmonization
"I Have Decided to Follow Jesus" (Mark)
  C344, CG497, S2129, SH610
"The Summons" (Mark)
  CG473, EL798, G726, S2130, SA695, SH598, VU567
        H-3   Chr-220
"Open the Eyes of My Heart" 2298355 (Mark)
  G452, SA270, SH378, WS3008
"Be Still, My Soul" (Gen, Rom, Mark) (C)
  C566, CG57, G819, N488, SH330, UM534, VU652
        H-3   Chr-36
"Take Up Thy Cross" (Mark) (C)
  E675, EL667, G718, N204, P393, SH605, UM415, VU561

Additional Hymn Suggestions

"Deep in the Shadows of the Past" (Gen)
  G50, N320, P330, S2246
"Be Thou My Vision" (Gen, Rom)
  C595, CG71, E488, EL793, G450, N451, P339, SA573, SH640,
  UM451, VU642
"Hope of the World" (Rom)
  C538, E472, G734, N46, P360, UM178, VU215
"Standing on the Promises" (Rom)
  AH4057, C552, CG625, G838, SA522, SH45, UM374 (PD)
"Faith of Our Fathers" (Rom)
  C635, CG645, EL812/813, N381, UM710 (PD), VU580
"There Are Some Things I May Not Know" (Rom)
  N405, S2147
"We Walk by Faith" (Rom)
  CG634, E209, EL635, G817, N256, P399, S2196, SH660
"In the Singing" (Rom, Comm.)
  EL466, G533, S2255
"Lord of the Dance" (Mark)
  G157, P302, SA141, UM261, VU352
"Beneath the Cross of Jesus" (Mark)
  C197, CG184, E498, EL338, G216, N190, P92, SA161, SH166,
  UM297 (PD), VU135
"Forth in Thy Name, O Lord" (Mark) (C)
  SA642, UM438 (PD), VU416
"The Church of Christ, in Every Age" (Mark)
  C475, EL729, G320, N306, P421, UM589, VU601
"My Song Is Love Unknown" (Mark, Lent)
  E458, EL343, G209, N222, P76, S2083, SA149, VU143
"Swiftly Pass the Clouds of Glory" (Mark)
  G190, P73, S2102
"Living for Jesus" (Mark)
  C610, S2149

Additional Contemporary and Modern Suggestions

"Step by Step" 696994 (Gen)
  CG495, G743, WS3004
"El-Shaddai" 26856 (Gen)
  UM123, S-2 #54 Verses for Vocal Solo
"Daughter of God" 4509781 (Gen)
"Be Still and Know That I Am God" (Gen, Rom, Mark)
  G414, N743, S2057, SH55
"Be Still and Know" 2758912 (Gen, Rom, Mark)

"Nobody" 7121827 (Gen, Mark)
"Give Thanks" (Pss)
  C528, CG373, G647, S2036, SA364, SH489
"My Tribute" 11218 (Rom)
  AH4080, C39, CG574, N14, SH434, UM99; V-8 p. 5. Vocal
  Solo
"O How He Loves You and Me" 15850 (Rom)
  CG600, S2108, SH535
"Canto de Esperanza" ("Song of Hope") (Rom) (C)
  G765, P432, S2186, SH721, VU424
"Sing Alleluia to the Lord" (Rom)
  C32, S2258, SH685
"There Is a Redeemer" 11483 (Rom, Lent)
  CG377, G443, SA204, SH495
"Grace Like Rain" 3689877 (Rom)
"Somlandela" ("We Will Follow") (Mark)
  WS3160
"Knowing You" 1045238 (Mark, Lent)
"Let It Be Said of Us" 1855882 (Mark)
"The Wonderful Cross" 3148435 (Mark, Lent)
"I Stand Amazed" 769450 (Mark, Lent)
"Take This Life" 2563365 (Mark, Lent)
"I Come to the Cross" 1965249 (Mark, Lent)
"Every Move I Make" 1595726 (Mark)
"Everyday" 2798154 (Mark)
"One Way" 4222082 (Mark)
"Take Up Our Cross" 5358955 (Mark)
"Just to Be with You" 5585120 (Mark, Lent)

Vocal Solos

"Redeeming Grace" (Rom)
  V-4   p. 47
"Christ Living Within You" (Mark)
  V-8   p. 177
"Lead Me to Calvary" (Mark, Lent)
  V-8   p. 226

Anthems

"Take Up Your Cross" (Mark)
Thomas Keesecker; MorningStar 50-3062
SATB, piano (https://bit.ly/MSM-50-3062)

"And Are We Yet Alive?" (Mark)
Mark Miller; Choristers Guild CGA1638
SATB, piano (https://bit.ly/CG-1638)

Other Suggestions

Visuals:
  O   Elderly man/woman, people of all nations, covenant
  P   Praising, hungry being fed, people of all nations,
       deliverance
  E   Elderly person holding a child, all nations,
       resurrection
  G   Wooden cross, crucifix, resurrection, sandals (follow)
Introit: 292, stanza 1. "What Wondrous Love Is This."
  C200, CG171, E439, EL666, G215, N223, P85, SA207, SH177,
  UM292, VU147 (Fr.)
Prayer of Confession: WSL90 (Mark)
Response: S2277. "Lord, Have Mercy" (Mark, Lent)
  C299, S2277
Prayer: UM268 or UM403 (Mark)
Benediction or Sending Words: WSL164 (Gen)
Benediction: WS3183. "As We Go" (Mark)
Theme Ideas: Covenant, Cross, Discipleship / Following God,
  God: Promises

Exodus 20:1-17

Then God spoke all these words,

[2]"I am the Lord your God, who brought you out of the land of Egypt, out of the house of slavery; [3]you shall have no other gods before me.

[4]"You shall not make for yourself an idol, whether in the form of anything that is in heaven above or that is on the earth beneath or that is in the water under the earth. [5]You shall not bow down to them or serve them, for I the Lord your God am a jealous God, punishing children for the iniquity of parents to the third and the fourth generation of those who reject me [6]but showing steadfast love to the thousandth generation of those who love me and keep my commandments.

[7]"You shall not make wrongful use of the name of the Lord your God, for the Lord will not acquit anyone who misuses his name.

[8]"Remember the Sabbath day and keep it holy. [9]Six days you shall labor and do all your work. [10]But the seventh day is a Sabbath to the Lord your God; you shall not do any work—you, your son or your daughter, your male or female slave, your livestock, or the alien resident in your towns. [11]For in six days the Lord made heaven and earth, the sea, and all that is in them, but rested the seventh day; therefore the Lord blessed the Sabbath day and consecrated it.

[12]"Honor your father and your mother, so that your days may be long in the land that the Lord your God is giving you.

[13]"You shall not murder.

[14]"You shall not commit adultery.

[15]"You shall not steal.

[16]"You shall not bear false witness against your neighbor.

[17]"You shall not covet your neighbor's house; you shall not covet your neighbor's wife, male or female slave, ox, donkey, or anything that belongs to your neighbor."

Psalm 19 (G690, N630, P166/167, SH559, UM750)

The heavens are telling the glory of God,
    and the firmament proclaims his handiwork.
[2]Day to day pours forth speech,
    and night to night declares knowledge.
[3]There is no speech, nor are there words;
    their voice is not heard;
[4]yet their voice goes out through all the earth
    and their words to the end of the world.
In the heavens he has set a tent for the sun,
    [5]which comes out like a bridegroom from his wedding
        canopy,
    and like a strong man runs its course with joy.
[6]Its rising is from the end of the heavens
    and its circuit to the end of them,
    and nothing is hid from its heat.
[7]The law of the Lord is perfect,
    reviving the soul;
the decrees of the Lord are sure,
    making wise the simple;
[8]the precepts of the Lord are right,
    rejoicing the heart;
the commandment of the Lord is clear,
    enlightening the eyes;
[9]the fear of the Lord is pure,
    enduring forever;
the ordinances of the Lord are true
    and righteous altogether.
[10]More to be desired are they than gold,
    even much fine gold;
sweeter also than honey
    and drippings of the honeycomb.
[11]Moreover, by them is your servant warned;
    in keeping them there is great reward.

[12]But who can detect one's own errors?
    Clear me from hidden faults.
[13]Keep back your servant also from the insolent;
    do not let them have dominion over me.
Then I shall be blameless
    and innocent of great transgression.
[14]Let the words of my mouth and the meditation of my heart
    be acceptable to you,
    O Lord, my rock and my redeemer.

---

1 Corinthians 1:18-25

[18]For the message about the cross is foolishness to those who are perishing, but to us who are being saved it is the power of God. [19]For it is written,

    "I will destroy the wisdom of the wise,
        and the discernment of the discerning I will thwart."

[20]Where is the one who is wise? Where is the scholar? Where is the debater of this age? Has not God made foolish the wisdom of the world? [21]For since, in the wisdom of God, the world did not know God through wisdom, God decided, through the foolishness of the proclamation, to save those who believe. [22]For Jews ask for signs and Greeks desire wisdom, [23]but we proclaim Christ crucified, a stumbling block to Jews and foolishness to gentiles, [24]but to those who are the called, both Jews and Greeks, Christ the power of God and the wisdom of God. [25]For God's foolishness is wiser than human wisdom, and God's weakness is stronger than human strength.

John 2:13-22

[13]The Passover of the Jews was near, and Jesus went up to Jerusalem. [14]In the temple he found people selling cattle, sheep, and doves and the money changers seated at their tables. [15]Making a whip of cords, he drove all of them out of the temple, with the sheep and the cattle. He also poured out the coins of the money changers and overturned their tables. [16]He told those who were selling the doves, "Take these things out of here! Stop making my Father's house a marketplace!" [17]His disciples remembered that it was written, "Zeal for your house will consume me." [18]The Jews then said to him, "What sign can you show us for doing this?" [19]Jesus answered them, "Destroy this temple, and in three days I will raise it up." [20]The Jews then said, "This temple has been under construction for forty-six years, and will you raise it up in three days?" [21]But he was speaking of the temple of his body. [22]After he was raised from the dead, his disciples remembered that he had said this, and they believed the scripture and the word that Jesus had spoken.

Primary Hymns and Songs for the Day

"Christ Is Made the Sure Foundation" (1 Cor, John) (O)
C275, E518, EL645, G394, P416, SA246, SH225, UM559, VU325
H-3 Chr-49; Desc-103; Org-180
S-1 #346. Descant
CG248, N400, P417
"God the Sculptor of the Mountains" (Exod, 1 Cor, John) (O)
EL736, G5, S2060
"How Great Thou Art" (Exod, Pss, 1 Cor)
AH4015, C33, CG323, EL856, G625, N35, P467, SA49, SH14, UM77, VU238 (Fr.)
H-3 Chr-103; Org-105
S-1 #163. Harmonization
"In the Cross of Christ I Glory" (1 Cor)
C207, CG183, E441, EL324, G213, N193, P84, SA174, UM295
H-3 Hbl-72; Chr-113; Desc-89; Org-119
S-1 #276-277. Harmonization with descant
"Lift High the Cross" (1 Cor, John)
C108, CG415, E473, EL660, G826, N198, P371, SH162, UM159, VU151
"Lord, I Want to Be a Christian" (1 Cor, John) (C)
C589, CG507, G729, N454, P372 (PD), SH621, UM402
H-3 Chr-130
"Where Charity and Love Prevail" (Exod, 1 Cor, John)
CG264, EL359, G316, N396, SH271
H-3 Hbl-71; Chr-111-112; Desc-95; Org-143
S-2 #162. Harmonization
E581, UM549

Additional Hymn Suggestions

"Forgive Our Sins as We Forgive" (Exod)
CG694 E674, EL605, G444, P347, SH504, UM390, VU364
"Every Time I Feel the Spirit" (Exod)
C592, G66, N282, P315, UM404
"Spirit, Spirit of Gentleness" (Exod)
C249, EL396, G291, N286, P319, S2120, VU375
"Love the Lord Your God" 1400093 (Exod)
G62, S2168
"How Firm a Foundation" (Exod, Pss, John)
C618, CG425, E636/637, EL796, G463, N407, P361, SA804, SH291, UM529 (PD), VU660
"Take Time to Be Holy" (Exod, John)
C572, SA790, UM395 (PD), VU672
"Cantemos al Señor" ("Let's Sing unto the Lord") (Pss)
C60, EL555, G669, N39, SH432, UM149
"Let Us with a Joyful Mind" (Pss)
E389, G31, N16, P244, S2012, SA42, VU234
"Praise the Source of Faith and Learning" (Pss, 1 Cor, John)
N411, S2004
"Sing, My Tongue, the Glorious Battle" (1 Cor)
E165/166, EL355/356, G225, N220, UM296
"The Old Rugged Cross" (1 Cor)
C548, CG185, N195, SA191, SH165, UM504 (PD)
"God of Grace and God of Glory" (1 Cor)
C464, CG285, E594/595, EL705, G307, N436, P420, SA814, SH250, UM577, VU686
"God the Sculptor of the Mountains" (1 Cor)
EL736, G5, S2060
"Beneath the Cross of Jesus" (1 Cor, John)
C197, CG184, E498, EL338, G216, N190, P92, SA161, SH166, UM297 (PD), VU135
"Here, O Lord, Your Servants Gather" (1 Cor, John, Comm.)
C278, EL530, G311, N72, P465, UM552, VU362
"Lord of the Dance" (John)
G157, P302, SA141, UM261, VU352
"Where Cross the Crowded Ways of Life" (John)
C665, CG657, E609, EL719, G343, N543, UM427, VU681
"All Who Love and Serve Your City" (John)
C670, E570/571, EL724, G351, P413, UM433

"For the Bread Which You Have Broken" (John, Comm.)
C411, E340/E341, EL494, G516, P508/P509, UM614/UM615, VU470
"Bread of the World" (John, Comm.)
C387, E301, G499, N346, P502, UM624, VU461
"Come to the Table of Grace" 7034746 (John, Comm.)
G507, WS3168

Additional Contemporary and Modern Suggestions

"Every Time I Feel the Spirit" (Exod)
C592, G66, N282, P315, UM404
"Honor and Praise" 1867485 (Exod)
"Forevermore" 5466830 (Exod)
"Love the Lord" 4572938 (Exod)
"I Will Call upon the Lord" 11263 (Pss)
G621, S2002
"God of Wonders" 3118757 (Pss)
"All Heaven Declares" 120556 (Pss)
"The Heavens Shall Declare" 904033 (Pss)
"Beautiful Savior" 2492216 (Pss, 1 Cor)
"Rock of Ages" 2240547 (Pss, John)
"More Precious than Silver" 11335 (Pss, John)
"Shout to the North" 1562261 (1 Cor)
G319, SA1009, WS3042
"The Wonderful Cross" 3148435 (1 Cor, Lent)
"Here at the Cross" 7046292 (1 Cor, Lent)
"Let It Be Said of Us" 1855882 (1 Cor)
"Good to Me" 313480 (1 Cor)
"I Will Boast" 4662350 (1 Cor)
"You Are My All in All" 825356 (1 Cor, John)
CG571, G519, SH335, WS3040
"Sanctuary" 24140 (John)
G701, S2164, SH265

Vocal Solos

"The Heavens Declare His Glory" (Pss)
V-8 p. 248
"A Contrite Heart" (Pss, Lent)
V-4 p. 10
"Ah, Holy Jesus" (John)
V-6 p. 24

Anthems

"How Great Thou Art & Majesty" (Exod, Pss, 1 Cor)
Arr. Joel Raney; Hope C6234
Two-Part Mixed, piano, opt. 4-hands (https://bit.ly/C-6234)

"Where Charity and Love Prevail" (Exod, 1 Cor, John)
Arr. William A. McNair; Augsburg 9781506452555
SATB, keyboard (https://bit.ly/AF-52555)

Other Suggestions

Visuals:
O Tablet/ten commandments, open manacles
P Celestial images, tent, wedding canopy, bridegroom, runner
E Wooden cross, clown or jester, (stumbling) block
G Animals, whip, overturned table, spilled coins, cross
Introit: S2271. "Come! Come! Everybody Worship" (Exod)
Canticle: UM112. "Canticle of Wisdom" (1 Cor)
Prayer for Illumination: WSL71 (Exod, Pss)
Prayer: UM268. Lent (Exod)
Prayer: UM429. For Our Country (1 Cor, John)
Theme Ideas: Covenant, Creation, Cross, God: Word of God, Holy Spirit, Jesus: Prophet, Priorities, Wisdom, Worship

Numbers 21:4-9

4From Mount Hor they set out by the way to the Red Sea, to go around the land of Edom, but the people became discouraged on the way. 5The people spoke against God and against Moses, "Why have you brought us up out of Egypt to die in the wilderness? For there is no food and no water, and we detest this miserable food." 6Then the LORD sent poisonous serpents among the people, and they bit the people, so that many Israelites died. 7The people came to Moses and said, "We have sinned by speaking against the LORD and against you; pray to the LORD to take away the serpents from us." So Moses prayed for the people. 8And the LORD said to Moses, "Make a poisonous serpent, and set it on a pole, and everyone who is bitten shall look at it and live." 9So Moses made a serpent of bronze and put it upon a pole, and whenever a serpent bit someone, that person would look at the serpent of bronze and live.

Psalm 107:1-3, 17-22 (G653, N693, UM830)

1O give thanks to the LORD, for he is good,
 for his steadfast love endures forever.
2Let the redeemed of the LORD say so,
 those he redeemed from trouble
3and gathered in from the lands,
 from the east and from the west,
 from the north and from the south.
. . . .
17Some were sick through their sinful ways
 and because of their iniquities endured affliction;
18they loathed any kind of food,
 and they drew near to the gates of death.
19Then they cried to the LORD in their trouble,
 and he saved them from their distress;
20he sent out his word and healed them
 and delivered them from destruction.
21Let them thank the LORD for his steadfast love,
 for his wonderful works to humankind.
22And let them offer thanksgiving sacrifices
 and tell of his deeds with songs of joy.

Ephesians 2:1-10

You were dead through the trespasses and sins 2in which you once walked, following the course of this world, following the ruler of the power of the air, the spirit that is now at work among those who are disobedient. 3All of us once lived among them in the passions of our flesh, doing the will of flesh and senses, and we were by nature children of wrath, like everyone else, 4but God, who is rich in mercy, out of the great love with which he loved us 5even when we were dead through our trespasses, made us alive together with Christ—by grace you have been saved—6and raised us up with him and seated us with him in the heavenly places in Christ Jesus, 7so that in the ages to come he might show the immeasurable riches of his grace in kindness toward us in Christ Jesus. 8For by grace you have been saved through faith, and this is not your own doing; it is the gift of God—9not the result of works, so that no one may boast. 10For we are what he has made us, created in Christ Jesus for good works, which God prepared beforehand so that we may walk in them.

John 3:14-21

14And just as Moses lifted up the serpent in the wilderness, so must the Son of Man be lifted up, 15that whoever believes in him may have eternal life.

16"For God so loved the world that he gave his only Son, so that everyone who believes in him may not perish but may have eternal life.

17"Indeed, God did not send the Son into the world to condemn the world but in order that the world might be saved through him. 18Those who believe in him are not condemned, but those who do not believe are condemned already because they have not believed in the name of the only Son of God. 19And this is the judgment, that the light has come into the world, and people loved darkness rather than light because their deeds were evil. 20For all who do evil hate the light and do not come to the light, so that their deeds may not be exposed. 21But those who do what is true come to the light, so that it may be clearly seen that their deeds have been done in God."

Primary Hymns and Songs for the Day

"God Is Here" (Eph, John) (O)
    C280, CG298, EL526, G409, N70, P461, UM660
        H-3   Hbl-61; Chr-132; Org-2
        S-1   #4-5. Instrumental and vocal descants
"Come, Ye Sinners, Poor and Needy" (Num, Eph, John) (O)
    CG471, G415, UM340
        S-1   #283. Choral harmonization
"There Is a Balm in Gilead" (Num, Eph, John)
    AH4110, C501, CG74, E676, EL614 (PD), G792, N553, P394,
    SH340, UM375, VU612
        H-3   Chr-194
        S-2   #21. Descant
"For the Healing of the Nations" (Num, Eph, John)
    C668, CG698, G346, N576, SA1000, UM428, VU678
"To God Be the Glory" (Eph, John)
    C72, CG349, G634, P485, SA279, SH545, UM98 (PD)
        S-2   #176. Piano arrangement
"Lead Me, Guide Me" (Num, Eph, John)
    C583, CG403, EL768, G740, S2214, SH582
"I Want to Walk as a Child of the Light" (John) (C)
    CG96, E490, EL815, G377, SH352, UM206
        S-2   #91. Descant

Additional Hymn Suggestions

"If Thou But Suffer God to Guide Thee" (Num)
    C565, CG76, E635, EL769, G816, N410, P282, SA40, SH326,
    UM142 (PD), VU285 (Fr.) and VU286
"You Are My All in All" 825356 (Num, Eph, John)
    CG571, G519, SH335, WS3040
"We Cannot Measure How You Heal" (Num, Eph, John)
    CG540, G797, SH341, VU613, WS3139
"Give Thanks" (Num, Pss)
    C528, CG373, G647, S2036, SA364, SH489
"Amazing Grace" (Eph, Comm.)
    AH4091, C546, CG587, E671, EL779, G649, N547/548, P280,
    SA453, SH523, UM378 (PD), VU266 (Fr.)
"Just as I Am, Without One Plea" (Eph)
    C339, CG500, E693, EL592, G442, N207, P370, SA503,
    SH500, UM357 (PD), VU508
"Rock of Ages, Cleft for Me" (Eph)
    C214, E685, EL623, G438, N596, SA671, SH301, UM361
"Savior, Like a Shepherd Lead Us" (Eph)
    C558, CG405, E708, EL789, G187, N252, P387, SH538,
    UM381 (PD)
"Lord God, Your Love Has Called Us Here" (Eph)
    EL358. P353, SA335, UM579
"We Walk by Faith" (Eph)
    CG634, E209, EL635, G817, N256, P399, S2196, SH660
"In the Singing" (Eph, Comm.)
    EL466, G533, S2255
"Goodness Is Stronger than Evil" (Num, Eph, John)
    EL721, G750, S2219
"What Wondrous Love Is This" (John)
    C200, CG171, E439, EL666, G215, N223, P85, SA207, SH177,
    UM292, VU147 (Fr.)
"Because He Lives" (John)
    AH4070, C562, CG620, SA219, SH200, UM364
"Come, Let Us with Our Lord Arise" (John)
    E49, S2084
"He Came Down" 4679219 (John)
    EL253, G137, S2085, SH88
"O Holy Spirit, Root of Life" (John)
    C251, EL399, N57, S2121, VU379
"Living for Jesus" (John)
    C610, S2149

Additional Contemporary and Modern Suggestions

"Song for the Nations" 20340 (Num, Eph, John)
"Grateful" 7023348 (Pss)
"We Bring the Sacrifice of Praise" 9990 (Pss)
"Shout to the North" 1562261 (Pss)
    G319, SA1009, WS3042
"You Are Good" 3383788 (Pss)
    AH4018, SH455, WS3014
"One Thing Remains" 5508444 (Pss)
"Hallelujah" ("Your Love Is Amazing") 3091812 (Pss, Eph, John)
"We Fall Down" 2437367 (Eph)
    G368, WS3187
"God Is Good All the Time" 1729073 (Eph)
"Majesty" 1527 (Eph)
    CG346, SA382, SH212, UM176
"Grace Like Rain" 3689877 (Eph)
"Psalm 62" ("My Soul Finds Rest") 5040902 (Eph)
"Love Moves You" ("Love Alone") 5775514 (Eph, John)
"Celebrate Love" 155246 (Eph, John)
"Sing Alleluia to the Lord" (Eph, John)
    C32, S2258, SH685
"Lord, I Lift Your Name on High" 117947 (John, Lent)
    AH4071, CG606, EL857, S2088, SA379, SH205
"O How He Loves You and Me" 15850 (John)
    CG600, S2108, SH535
"There Is a Redeemer" 11483 (John)
    CG377, G443, SA204, SH495
"No Greater Love" 930887 (John)
"I Could Sing of Your Love Forever" 1043199 (John)
"You Are My King" ("Amazing Love") 2456623 (John)
"I Come to the Cross" 1965249 (John, Lent)

Vocal Solos

"There is a Balm in Gilead" (Num, Eph, John)
    V-3 (1)   p. 29
"And Can It Be That I Should Gain" (Eph)
    V-1   p. 29
"Redeeming Grace" (Eph)
    V-4   p. 47
"Love Moved First" (Eph, John)
    V-9   p. 56

Anthems

"God So Loved the World" (John)
Bill Wolaver; Choristers Guild CGAMB100
Unison, piano (https://bit.ly/CGAMB100)

"For God So Loved the World" (John)
Melchior Franck; Augsburg 978-1-5064-5245-6
SATB a cappella (https://bit.ly/AF-52456)

Other Suggestions

Daylight Saving Time begins today.
This day may include an observance of Girl Scout Sunday.
Visuals:
    O   Bronze serpent on a pole, wilderness, empty bowl/cup
    P   Ps 107:2, map or globe, praying hands, thanksgiving,
           singing
    E   Death (black), resurrection, gift, life preserver (salva-
           tion)
    G   Light/darkness, wooden cross, crucifix, John 3:16, life
           preserver
Song of Assurance: S2141. "There's a Song" (Eph)
Prayer: WSL17. "A wilderness beckons" (Num, Lent)
Poem: UM58 or UM342 (Eph)
Offering Prayer: WSL110 (John)
Theme Ideas: God: Love of God, God: Providence / God our
    Help, Grace, Journey, Sin and Forgiveness, Thanksgiving /
    Gratitude

Jeremiah 31:31-34

[31]The days are surely coming, says the LORD, when I will make a new covenant with the house of Israel and the house of Judah. [32]It will not be like the covenant that I made with their ancestors when I took them by the hand to bring them out of the land of Egypt—a covenant that they broke, though I was their husband, says the LORD. [33]But this is the covenant that I will make with the house of Israel after those days, says the LORD: I will put my law within them, and I will write it on their hearts, and I will be their God, and they shall be my people. [34]No longer shall they teach one another or say to each other, "Know the LORD," for they shall all know me, from the least of them to the greatest, says the LORD, for I will forgive their iniquity and remember their sin no more.

Psalm 51:1-12 (G421, N657, P195/196, UM785)

Have mercy on me, O God,
    according to your steadfast love;
according to your abundant mercy,
    blot out my transgressions.
[2]Wash me thoroughly from my iniquity,
    and cleanse me from my sin.
[3]For I know my transgressions,
    and my sin is ever before me.
[4]Against you, you alone, have I sinned
    and done what is evil in your sight,
so that you are justified in your sentence
    and blameless when you pass judgment.
[5]Indeed, I was born guilty,
    a sinner when my mother conceived me.
[6]You desire truth in the inward being;
    therefore teach me wisdom in my secret heart.
[7]Purge me with hyssop, and I shall be clean;
    wash me, and I shall be whiter than snow.
[8]Let me hear joy and gladness;
    let the bones that you have crushed rejoice.
[9]Hide your face from my sins,
    and blot out all my iniquities.
[10]Create in me a clean heart, O God,
    and put a new and right spirit within me.
[11]Do not cast me away from your presence,
    and do not take your holy spirit from me.
[12]Restore to me the joy of your salvation,
    and sustain in me a willing spirit.

Hebrews 5:5-10

[5]So also Christ did not glorify himself in becoming a high priest but was appointed by the one who said to him,
    "You are my Son;
        today I have begotten you";
[6]as he says also in another place,
    "You are a priest forever,
        according to the order of Melchizedek."
[7]In the days of his flesh, Jesus offered up prayers and supplications, with loud cries and tears, to the one who was able to save him from death, and he was heard because of his reverent submission. [8]Although he was a Son, he learned obedience through what he suffered, [9]and having been made perfect, he became the source of eternal salvation for all who obey him, [10]having been designated by God a high priest according to the order of Melchizedek.

John 12:20-33

[20]Now among those who went up to worship at the festival were some Greeks. [21]They came to Philip, who was from Bethsaida in Galilee, and said to him, "Sir, we wish to see Jesus." [22]Philip went and told Andrew, then Andrew and Philip went and told Jesus. [23]Jesus answered them, "The hour has come for the Son of Man to be glorified. [24]Very truly, I tell you, unless a grain of wheat falls into the earth and dies, it remains just a single grain, but if it dies it bears much fruit. [25]Those who love their life lose it, and those who hate their life in this world will keep it for eternal life. [26]Whoever serves me must follow me, and where I am, there will my servant be also. Whoever serves me, the Father will honor.

[27]"Now my soul is troubled. And what should I say: 'Father, save me from this hour'? No, it is for this reason that I have come to this hour. [28]Father, glorify your name." Then a voice came from heaven, "I have glorified it, and I will glorify it again." [29]The crowd standing there heard it and said that it was thunder. Others said, "An angel has spoken to him." [30]Jesus answered, "This voice has come for your sake, not for mine. [31]Now is the judgment of this world; now the ruler of this world will be driven out. [32]And I, when I am lifted up from the earth, will draw all people to myself." [33]He said this to indicate the kind of death he was to die.

Primary Hymns and Songs for the Day

"At the Name of Jesus" (Heb, John) (O)
      CG424, E435, EL416, G264, SA74, SH657, UM168, VU335
"O Love That Wilt Not Let Me Go" (Jer)
      C540, CG631, G833, N485, P384, SA616, SH314, UM480,
      VU658
            H-3   Chr-146; Org-142
"Change My Heart, O God" 1565 (Jer, Pss)
      EL801, G695, S2152, SA409, SH507
"Near to the Heart of God" (Jer, Heb)
      C581, CG383, G824, P527, UM472 (PD)
            S-1   #230. Performance note
"My Song Is Love Unknown" (Jer, Heb, John)
      E458, EL343, G209, N222, P76, S2083, SA149, VU143
"Lord, Be Glorified" 26368 (Jer, Heb, John, Comm.)
      EL744, G468, S2150, SA593, SH420
"Lord, Dismiss Us with Thy Blessing" (Heb, John) (C)
      C439, E344, EL545, G546, N77, P538, UM671 (PD), VU425
            H-3   Chr-75, 116, 130; Desc-98; Org-151
"O Jesus, I Have Promised" (John)
      C612, E655, EL810, G724/725, N493, P388/389, SA613,
      SH623, UM396 (PD), VU120
            S-2   #9. Descant
"Take Up Thy Cross" (John) (C)
      E675, EL667, G718, N204, P393, SH605, UM415, VU561

Additional Hymn Suggestions

"Here I Am, Lord" (Jer)
      C452, CG482, EL574, G69, SA1002, SH608, UM593, VU509
"God the Sculptor of the Mountains" (Jer, Comm.)
      EL736, G5, S2060
"Wonder of Wonders" (Jer, Baptism)
      C378, G489, N328, P499, S2247
"Give Me a Clean Heart" 314764 (Jer, Pss)
      AH4125, C515, N188, S2133
"This Is a Day of New Beginnings" (Jer, John)
      C518, N417, UM383
"Ah, Holy Jesus" (Heb)
      C210, E158, EL349, G218, N218, P93, UM289, VU138
"Jesus Shall Reign" (Heb, John)
      C95, CG158, E544, EL434, G265, N300, P423, SA258, SH209,
      UM157 (PD), VU330
"Lift High the Cross" (John)
      C108, CG415, E473, EL660, G826, N198, P371, SH162,
      UM159, VU151
"Beneath the Cross of Jesus" (John)
      C197, CG184, E498, EL338, G216, N190, P92, SA161, SH166,
      UM297 (PD), VU135
"Where He Leads Me" (John)
      C346, SA693, UM338 (PD)
"Jesus Calls Us" (John)
      C337, CG486, E549/550, EL696, G720, N171/172, SA653,
      SH604, UM398, VU562
"Mothering God, You Gave Me Birth" (John)
      C83, N467, S2050, VU320
"I Have Decided to Follow Jesus" (John)
      C344, CG497, S2129, SH610
"Healer of Our Every Ill" (John)
      C506, EL612, G795, S2213, SH339, VU619

Additional Contemporary and Modern Suggestions

"The Potter's Hand" 2449771 (Jer)
"Before the Throne of God Above" 2306412 (Jer, Heb)
"You Have Saved Us" 5548514 (Jer, Heb)
"Refresh My Heart" 917518 (Jer, Pss)
"Purified" 3409710 (Jer, Pss)
"Set A Fire" 5911299 (Jer, Pss)
"I Give You My Heart" 1866132 (Jer, Pss)

"Please Enter My Heart, Hosanna" 2485371 (Jer, Pss, John)
"*Confitemini Domino*" ("Come and Fill Our Hearts") (Jer, John)
      EL538, G466, S2157
"Depth of Mercy" 5412781 (Pss)
"Purify My Heart" 1314323 (Pss)
"Hosanna" 4785835 (Pss, Lent)
      SH361, WS3188
"Here at the Cross" 7046292 (Pss, Lent)
"The Power of Your Love" 917491 (Pss)
"In the Secret" 1810119 Pss)
"Refiner's Fire" 426298 (Pss)
"Give Us Clean Hands" 2060208 (Pss)
"Because of Your Love" 4662501 (Pss)
"Give Me Jesus" (Pss, John)
      CG546, EL770, N409, SH306, WS3140
"Today" 5775617 (Pss, John)
"Restored" 5894615 (Pss, John)
"Take My Life" 1617154 (Pss, John)
"Glory To God Forever" 5384338 (Pss, John)
"Jesus Messiah" 5183443 (Heb, Lent)
"That's Why We Praise Him" 2668576 (Heb)
"Glorify Thy Name" 1383 (John)
      CG8, S2016, SA582, SH427
"Open Our Eyes, Lord" 1572 (Pss, John)
      CG392, S2086, SA386, SH562
"He Came Down" 4679219 (John)
      EL253, G137, S2085, SH88
"Lord, I Lift Your Name on High" 117947 (John, Lent)
      AH4071, CG606, EL857, S2088, SA379, SH205
"The Servant Song" 72673 (John)
      C490, CG289, EL659, G727, N539, S2222, SA1005, SH264,
      VU595
"We Want to See Jesus Lifted High" 1033408 (John)

Vocal Solos

"Turn My Heart to You" (Pss)
      V-5 (2)   p. 14
"Give Me Jesus" (Pss, John)
      V-3 (1)   p. 53
      V-7   p. 24/28
      V-8   p. 256

Anthems

"My Song Is Love Unknown" (Jer, Heb, John)
Arr. Molly Ijames; Beckenhorst BP1977
SATB, piano (https://bit.ly/BP-1977)

"Create in Me" (Pss)
Michael Larkin; MorningStar 50-3486
SATB, piano (https://bit.ly/M-3486)

Other Suggestions

Visuals:
      O   Heart, Exodus, open Bible, love at work
      P   Water, bones, Ps 51:7b, 10; rejoicing
      E   Miter/chasuble, praying hands, crucifix, cross
      G   Clock or hourglass, Crucifixion, bowl/pitcher/towel
            (service)
Introit: C200, CG171, E439, EL666, G215, N223, P85, SA207,
      SH177, UM292, VU147 (Fr.), stanza 1. "What Wondrous Love
      Is This."
Response: C299, S2277. "Lord, Have Mercy" (Jer, Lent)
Scripture Response: C542, CG406, E699, G440, N546, P303,
      SA257, SH542/543, UM479, VU669, stanza 4. "Jesus, Lover
      of My Soul" (Jer)
Theme Ideas: Covenant, God: Promises, Jesus: Jesus our Savior,
      Resurrection, Service / Servanthood, Sin and Forgiveness

PALMS READINGS
Mark 11:1-11

When they were approaching Jerusalem, at Bethphage and Bethany, near the Mount of Olives, he sent two of his disciples [2]and said to them, "Go into the village ahead of you, and immediately as you enter it you will find tied there a colt that has never been ridden; untie it and bring it. [3]If anyone says to you, 'Why are you doing this?' just say this: 'The Lord needs it and will send it back here immediately.' " [4]They went away and found a colt tied near a door, outside in the street. As they were untying it, [5]some of the bystanders said to them, "What are you doing, untying the colt?" [6]They told them what Jesus had said, and they allowed them to take it. [7]Then they brought the colt to Jesus and threw their cloaks on it, and he sat on it. [8]Many people spread their cloaks on the road, and others spread leafy branches that they had cut in the fields. [9]Then those who went ahead and those who followed were shouting,

"Hosanna!
Blessed is the one who comes in the name of the Lord!
[10]Blessed is the coming kingdom of our ancestor David!
Hosanna in the highest heaven!"

[11]Then he entered Jerusalem and went into the temple, and when he had looked around at everything, as it was already late, he went out to Bethany with the twelve.

Psalm 118:1-2, 19-29 (N700, P230/231/232, UM839)
O give thanks to the LORD, for he is good;
his steadfast love endures forever!
[2]Let Israel say,
"His steadfast love endures forever."
. . . .
[19]Open to me the gates of righteousness,
that I may enter through them
and give thanks to the LORD.
[20]This is the gate of the LORD;
the righteous shall enter through it.
[21]I thank you that you have answered me
and have become my salvation.
[22]The stone that the builders rejected
has become the chief cornerstone.
[23]This is the LORD's doing;
it is marvelous in our eyes.
[24]This is the day that the LORD has made;
let us rejoice and be glad in it.
[25]Save us, we beseech you, O LORD!
O LORD, we beseech you, give us success!
[26]Blessed is the one who comes in the name of the LORD.
We bless you from the house of the LORD.
[27]The LORD is God,
and he has given us light.
Bind the festal procession with branches,
up to the horns of the altar.
[28]You are my God, and I will give thanks to you;
you are my God; I will extol you.
[29]O give thanks to the LORD, for he is good,
for his steadfast love endures forever.

PASSION READINGS
Isaiah 50:4-9a
[4]The Lord GOD has given me
a trained tongue,
that I may know how to sustain
the weary with a word.
Morning by morning he wakens,
wakens my ear
to listen as those who are taught.
[5]The Lord GOD has opened my ear,
and I was not rebellious;
I did not turn backward.

[6]I gave my back to those who struck me
and my cheeks to those who pulled out the beard;
I did not hide my face
from insult and spitting.
[7]The Lord GOD helps me;
therefore I have not been disgraced;
therefore I have set my face like flint,
and I know that I shall not be put to shame;
[8]he who vindicates me is near.
Who will contend with me?
Let us stand in court together.
Who are my adversaries?
Let them confront me.
[9]It is the Lord GOD who helps me;
who will declare me guilty?

Psalm 31:9-16 (G811, N641, P182/183, SH515, UM764)
[9]Be gracious to me, O LORD, for I am in distress;
my eye wastes away from grief,
my soul and body also.
[10]For my life is spent with sorrow
and my years with sighing;
my strength fails because of my misery,
and my bones waste away.
[11]I am the scorn of all my adversaries,
a horror to my neighbors,
an object of dread to my acquaintances;
those who see me in the street flee from me.
[12]I have passed out of mind like one who is dead;
I have become like a broken vessel.
[13]For I hear the whispering of many—
terror all around!—
as they scheme together against me,
as they plot to take my life.
[14]But I trust in you, O LORD;
I say, "You are my God."
[15]My times are in your hand;
deliver me from the hand of my enemies and persecutors.
[16]Let your face shine upon your servant;
save me in your steadfast love.

Philippians 2:5-11
[5]Let the same mind be in you that was in Christ Jesus,
[6]who, though he existed in the form of God,
did not regard equality with God
as something to be grasped,
[7]but emptied himself,
taking the form of a slave,
assuming human likeness.
And being found in appearance as a human,
[8]he humbled himself
and became obedient to the point of death—
even death on a cross.
[9]Therefore God exalted him even more highly
and gave him the name
that is above every other name,
[10]so that at the name given to Jesus
every knee should bend,
in heaven and on earth and under the earth,
[11]and every tongue should confess
that Jesus Christ is Lord,
to the glory of God the Father.

Mark 14:1–15:47 or Mark 15:1-39 (40-47)
It was two days before the Passover and the Festival of Unleavened Bread. The chief priests and the scribes were looking for a way to arrest Jesus by stealth and kill him, [2]for they said, "Not during the festival, or there may be a riot among the people."

[3]While he was at Bethany in the house of Simon the leper, as he sat at the table, a woman came with an alabaster jar of very costly ointment of nard, and she broke open the jar and poured the ointment on his head. [4]But some were there who said to one another in anger, "Why was the ointment wasted in this way? [5]For this ointment could have been sold for more than three hundred denarii and the money given to the poor." And they scolded her. [6]But Jesus said, "Let her alone; why do you trouble her? She has performed a good service for me. [7]For you always have the poor with you, and you can show kindness to them whenever you wish, but you will not always have me. [8]She has done what she could; she has anointed my body beforehand for its burial. [9]Truly I tell you, wherever the good news is proclaimed in the whole world, what she has done will be told in remembrance of her."

[10]Then Judas Iscariot, who was one of the twelve, went to the chief priests in order to betray him to them. [11]When they heard it, they were greatly pleased and promised to give him money. So he began to look for an opportunity to betray him.

[12]On the first day of Unleavened Bread, when the Passover lamb is sacrificed, his disciples said to him, "Where do you want us to go and make the preparations for you to eat the Passover?" [13]So he sent two of his disciples, saying to them, "Go into the city, and a man carrying a jar of water will meet you; follow him, [14]and wherever he enters, say to the owner of the house, 'The Teacher asks: Where is my guest room where I may eat the Passover with my disciples?' [15]He will show you a large room upstairs, furnished and ready. Make preparations for us there." [16]So the disciples set out and went to the city and found everything as he had told them, and they prepared the Passover meal.

[17]When it was evening, he came with the twelve. [18]And when they had taken their places and were eating, Jesus said, "Truly I tell you, one of you will betray me, one who is eating with me." [19]They began to be distressed and to say to him one after another, "Surely, not I?" [20]He said to them, "It is one of the twelve, one who is dipping bread into the bowl with me. [21]For the Son of Man goes as it is written of him, but woe to that one by whom the Son of Man is betrayed! It would have been better for that one not to have been born."

[22]While they were eating, he took a loaf of bread, and after blessing it he broke it, gave it to them, and said, "Take; this is my body." [23]Then he took a cup, and after giving thanks he gave it to them, and all of them drank from it. [24]He said to them, "This is my blood of the covenant, which is poured out for many. [25]Truly I tell you, I will never again drink of the fruit of the vine until that day when I drink it new in the kingdom of God."

[26] When they had sung the hymn, they went out to the Mount of Olives. [27]And Jesus said to them, "You will all fall away, for it is written,

'I will strike the shepherd,
    and the sheep will be scattered.'

[28]"But after I am raised up, I will go before you to Galilee." [29]Peter said to him, "Even though all fall away, I will not." [30]Jesus said to him, "Truly I tell you, this day, this very night, before the cock crows twice, you will deny me three times." [31]But he said vehemently, "Even though I must die with you, I will not deny you." And all of them said the same.

[32]They went to a place called Gethsemane, and he said to his disciples, "Sit here while I pray." [33]He took with him Peter and James and John and began to be distressed and agitated. [34]And he said to them, "My soul is deeply grieved, even to death; remain here, and keep awake." [35]And going a little farther, he threw himself on the ground and prayed that, if it were possible, the hour might pass from him. [36]He said, "Abba, Father, for you all things are possible; remove this cup from me, yet not what I want but what you want." [37]He came and found them sleeping, and he said to Peter, "Simon, are you asleep? Could you not keep awake one hour? [38]Keep awake and pray that you may not come into the time of trial; the spirit indeed is willing, but the flesh is weak." [39]And again he went away and prayed, saying the same words. [40]And once more he came and found them sleeping, for their eyes were very heavy, and they did not know what to say to him. [41]He came a third time and said to them, "Are you still sleeping and taking your rest? Enough! The hour has come; the Son of Man is betrayed into the hands of sinners. [42]Get up, let us be going. Look, my betrayer is at hand."

[43]Immediately, while he was still speaking, Judas, one of the twelve, arrived, and with him there was a crowd with swords and clubs, from the chief priests, the scribes, and the elders. [44]Now the betrayer had given them a sign, saying, "The one I will kiss is the man; arrest him and lead him away under guard." [45]So when he came, he went up to him at once and said, "Rabbi!" and kissed him. [46]Then they laid hands on him and arrested him. [47]But one of those who stood near drew his sword and struck the slave of the high priest, cutting off his ear. [48]Then Jesus said to them, "Have you come out with swords and clubs to arrest me as though I were a rebel? [49]Day after day I was with you in the temple teaching, and you did not arrest me. But let the scriptures be fulfilled." [50]All of them deserted him and fled.

[51]A certain young man was following him, wearing nothing but a linen cloth. They caught hold of him, [52]but he left the linen cloth and ran off naked.

[53]They took Jesus to the high priest, and all the chief priests, the elders, and the scribes were assembled. [54]Peter had followed him at a distance, right into the courtyard of the high priest, and he was sitting with the guards, warming himself at the fire. [55]Now the chief priests and the whole council were looking for testimony against Jesus to put him to death, but they found none. [56]For many gave false testimony against him, and their testimony did not agree. [57]Some stood up and gave false testimony against him, saying, [58]"We heard him say, 'I will destroy this temple that is made with hands, and in three days I will build another, not made with hands.'" [59]But even on this point their testimony did not agree. [60]Then the high priest stood up before them and asked Jesus, "Have you no answer? What is it that they testify against you?" [61]But he was silent and did not answer. Again the high priest asked him, "Are you the Messiah, the Son of the Blessed One?" [62]Jesus said, "I am, and

'you will see the Son of Man
    seated at the right hand of the Power'
    and 'coming with the clouds of heaven.'"

[63]Then the high priest tore his clothes and said, "Why do we still need witnesses? [64]You have heard his blasphemy! What is your decision?" All of them condemned him as deserving death. [65]Some began to spit on him, to blindfold him, and to strike him, saying to him, "Prophesy!" The guards also took him and beat him.

[66]While Peter was below in the courtyard, one of the female servants of the high priest came by. [67]When she saw Peter warming himself, she stared at him and said, "You also were with Jesus, the man from Nazareth." [68]But he denied it, saying, "I do not know or understand what you are talking about." And he went out into the forecourt. Then the cock crowed. [69]And the female servant, on seeing him, began again to say to the bystanders, "This man is one of them." [70]But again he denied it. Then after a little while the bystanders again said to Peter, "Certainly you are one of them, for you are a Galilean, and you talk like one." [71]But he began to curse, and he swore an oath, "I do not know this man you are talking about." [72]At that moment the cock crowed for the second time. Then Peter remembered that Jesus had said to him, "Before the cock crows twice, you will deny me three times." And he broke down and wept.

15 As soon as it was morning, the chief priests held a consultation with the elders and scribes and the whole council. They bound Jesus, led him away, and handed him over to Pilate. [2]Pilate asked him, "Are you the King of the Jews?" He answered him, "You say so." [3]Then the chief priests accused him of many things. [4]Pilate asked him again, "Have you no answer? See how many charges they bring against you." [5]But Jesus made no further reply, so that Pilate was amazed.

[6]Now at the festival he used to release a prisoner for them, anyone for whom they asked. [7]Now a man called Barabbas was in prison with the insurrectionists who had committed murder during the insurrection. [8]So the crowd came and began to ask Pilate to do for them according to his custom. [9]Then he answered them, "Do you want me to release for you the King of the Jews?" [10]For he realized that it was out of jealousy that the chief priests had handed him over. [11]But the chief priests stirred up the crowd to have him release Barabbas for them instead. [12]Pilate spoke to them again, "Then what do you wish me to do with the man you call the King of the Jews?" [13]They shouted back, "Crucify him!" [14]Pilate asked them, "Why, what evil has he done?" But they shouted all the more, "Crucify him!" [15]So Pilate, wishing to satisfy the crowd, released Barabbas for them, and after flogging Jesus he handed him over to be crucified.

[16]Then the soldiers led him into the courtyard of the palace (that is, the governor's headquarters), and they called together the whole cohort. [17]And they clothed him in a purple cloak, and after twisting some thorns into a crown they put it on him. [18]And they began saluting him, "Hail, King of the Jews!" [19]They struck his head with a reed, spat upon him, and knelt down in homage to him. [20]After mocking him, they stripped him of the purple cloak and put his own clothes on him. Then they led him out to crucify him.

[21]They compelled a passer-by, who was coming in from the country, to carry his cross; it was Simon of Cyrene, the father of Alexander and Rufus. [22]Then they brought Jesus to the place called Golgotha (which means Place of a Skull). [23]And they offered him wine mixed with myrrh, but he did not take it. [24]And they crucified him and divided his clothes among them, casting lots to decide what each should take.

[25]It was nine o'clock in the morning when they crucified him. [26]The inscription of the charge against him read, "The King of the Jews." [27]And with him they crucified two rebels, one on his right and one on his left. [29]Those who passed by derided him, shaking their heads and saying, "Aha! You who would destroy the temple and build it in three days, [30]save yourself, and come down from the cross!" [31]In the same way the chief priests, along with the scribes, were also mocking him among themselves and saying, "He saved others; he cannot save himself. [32]Let the Messiah, the King of Israel, come down from the cross now, so that we may see and believe." Those who were crucified with him also taunted him.

[33]When it was noon, darkness came over the whole land until three in the afternoon. [34]At three o'clock Jesus cried out with a loud voice, "Eloi, Eloi, lema sabachthani?" which means, "My God, my God, why have you forsaken me?" [35]When some of the bystanders heard it, they said, "Listen, he is calling for Elijah." [36]And someone ran, filled a sponge with sour wine, put it on a stick, and gave it to him to drink, saying, "Wait, let us see whether Elijah will come to take him down." [37]Then Jesus gave a loud cry and breathed his last. [38]And the curtain of the temple was torn in two, from top to bottom. [39]Now when the centurion who stood facing him saw that in this way he breathed his last, he said, "Truly this man was God's Son!"

[40]There were also women looking on from a distance. Among them were Mary Magdalene, and Mary the mother of James the younger and of Joses, and Salome, [41]who followed him when he was in Galilee and ministered to him, and there were many other women who had come up with him to Jerusalem.

[42]When evening had come, and since it was the day of Preparation, that is, the day before the Sabbath, [43]Joseph of Arimathea, a respected member of the council who was also himself waiting expectantly for the kingdom of God, went boldly to Pilate and asked for the body of Jesus. [44]Then Pilate wondered if he were already dead, and summoning the centurion he asked him whether he had been dead for some time. [45]When he learned from the centurion that he was dead, he granted the body to Joseph. [46]Then Joseph bought a linen cloth and, taking down the body, wrapped it in the linen cloth and laid it in a tomb that had been hewn out of rock. He then rolled a stone against the door of the tomb. [47]Mary Magdalene and Mary the mother of Joses saw where the body was laid.

Primary Hymns and Songs for the Day
"Hosanna, Loud Hosanna" (Palms Gospel) (O)
  CG172, G197, N213, P89, SH146, UM278 (PD), VU123
    H-3   Hbl-16, 22, 68; Chr-101; Desc-37
    S-1   #115. Harmonization
"All Glory, Laud, and Honor" (Palms Gospel)
  C192, CG175, E154/ E155, EL344, G196, N216/N217, P88,
  SA135, SH143, UM280 (PD), VU122
    H-3   Hbl-45; Chr-22; Desc-96; Org-144
    S-1   #309-310. Harmonization with descant
"Mantos y Palmas" ("Filled with Excitement") (Palms Gospel)
  G199, N214, SH144, UM279
    S-2   #90. Performance note
           #89. Harm.
"O Love, How Deep" (Passion Gospel)
  E448/449, EL322, G618, N209, P83, SH115, UM267, VU348
    H-3   Org-145
    S-1   #82-84. Various treatments
"Sing, My Tongue, the Glorious Battle" (Passion)
  E165/166, EL355/356, G225, N220, UM296
"When I Survey the Wondrous Cross" (Passion) (C)
  C195, CG186, EL803, G223, N224, P101, SH163/164, UM298
    H-3   Hbl-6, 102; Chr-213; Desc-49; Org-49
    S-1   #155. Descant
  E474, G224, P100, SA208, UM299 (PD), VU149 (Fr.)
    H-3   Hbl-47; Chr-76, 214; Desc-90; Org-127
    S-1   #288. Transposition to E-flat major

Additional Hymn Suggestions
"Tell Me the Stories of Jesus" (Palms Gospel)
  C190, SA151, UM277 (PD), VU357
"My Song Is Love Unknown" (Palm Sunday)
  E458, EL343, G209, N222, P76, S2083, SA149, VU143
"He Never Said a Mumbalin' Word" (Isa, Passion)
  C208, EL350, G219, P95 (PD), UM291, VU141
"At the Name of Jesus" (Phil)
  CG424, E435, EL416, G264, SA74, SH657, UM168, VU335
"Precious Name" (Phil)
  C625, SA92, UM536 (PD)
"Lift High the Cross" (Passion Gospel) (O) or (C)
  C108, CG415, E473, EL660, G826, N198, P371, SH162,
  UM159, VU151
"O Sacred Head, Now Wounded" (Passion Gospel)
  C202, CG191, E168/169, EL351/352, G221, N226, P98,
  SA190, SH168, UM286, VU145 (Fr.)
"Were You There" (Passion Gospel)
  C198, CG192, E172, EL353, G228, N229, P102, SA206,
  SH176, UM288, VU144
"Lord, Whose Love Through Humble Service" (Passion)
  C461, CG650, E610, EL712, P427, SH239, UM581
"The Bread of Life for All Is Broken" (Passion, Comm.)
  E342, N333, UM633
"An Outcast among Outcasts" (Passion Gospel)
  N201, S2104
"Why Has God Forsaken Me?" (Passion Gospel)
  G809, P406, S2110, VU154

Additional Contemporary and Modern Suggestions
"Open the Eyes of My Heart" 2298355 (Isa, Phil)
  G452, SA270, SH378, WS3008
"This Is the Day" 32754 (Ps 118) (O)
  AH4149, C286, N84, SA398, SH379, UM657, VU412
"I Will Enter His Gates" 1493 (Ps 118) (O)
"Today Is the Day" 5200924 (Ps 118)
"One Thing Remains" 5508444 (Ps 118)
"I Will Give Thanks" 6266091 (Ps 118)
"Grateful" 7023348 (Ps 118)
"All Hail King Jesus" 12877 (Palms Gospel)

"King of Kings" 23952 (Palm Sunday)
  S2075, VU167
"The King of Glory Comes" (Palm Sunday)
  CG177, S2091, SH206
"Hosanna! Hosanna!" 1388919 (Palms Gospel)
"Please Enter My Heart, Hosanna" 2485371 (Palms Gospel)
"Hosanna" 4785835 (Palms Gospel)
"Adoremus te Christe" ("We Adore You, Jesus Christ") (Palm/
  Passion)
  WS3083
"Forever" 3148428 (Ps 118)
  CG53, SA363, WS3023
"Make Way" 121074 (Ps 118)
"He Is Exalted" 17827 (Phil)
  AH4082, CG342, S2070, SH423
"Jesus, Name above All Names" 21291 (Phil)
"He Is Lord" 1515225 (Phil)
  C117, CG208, SA222, SH657, UM177
"What A Beautiful Name" 7068424 (Phil)
"No Sweeter Name" 4447984 (Phil)
"You are the Light" 6238098 (Phil)
"Jesus Messiah" 5183443 (Phil, Passion Gospel)
"O Praise The Name" 7037787 (Passion Gospel)
"Jesus We Love You" 7030068 (Passion Gospel)
"Lord of the Dance" (Passion Gospel)
  G157, P302, SA141, UM261, VU352
"Nohu pū" ("Stay with Me") (Passion Gospel)
  EL348, G204, S2198, SH157
"The Power of the Cross" 4490766 (Passion, Holy Week)
  CG190, WS3085

Vocal Solos
"Open the Gates of the Temple" (Palm Sunday, Holy Week)
(with "I Know That My Redeemer Liveth" coda)
  V-8   p. 202
"Ride On, Ride On in Majesty!" (Palms Gospel)
  V-5 (2)   p. 57

Anthems
"Jesus the King" (Mark, Palms)
Lloyd Larson; Beckenhorst BP1234
SAB, piano (https://bit.ly/BP-1234)

"O Vos Omnes" (Mark, Passion)
Pablo Casals; Tetra/Continuo BC0011C
SATB divisi, a cappella (https://bit.ly/BC0011C)

Other Suggestions
Visuals:

Palms Gospel	Colt, palms, cloaks, Hosanna
Ps 118	Gates, cornerstone, Ps 118:24, 26a, 29
O	Jesus teaching, Christ's passion, flint
Ps 13	Praying hands, grief, broken pottery
E	Manacles, wooden cross, crucifix, resurrection, Phil 2:9, 10
Passion Gospel	Perfume bottle, water jar, cup/bread/wine, cock crowing, sword, bowl of water, wooden cross, placard, purple cloak, sponge/vinegar, torn curtain, shroud, hourglass

For additional Passion ideas, consult Good Friday suggestions.
Introit: UM658. "This Is the Day" (Ps 118)
Call to Worship: WSL21 (Palms)
Canticle: UM167. "Canticle of Christ's Obedience" (Phil) (See
  S-1, p. 381.)
Prayer: UM281. Palm/Passion Sunday
Theme Ideas: Communion, Humility, Jesus: Crucifixion, Jesus:
  Mind of Christ, Lament, Praise, Thanksgiving / Gratitude

Exodus 12:1-4, (5-10), 11-14

The LORD said to Moses and Aaron in the land of Egypt, [2]"This month shall mark for you the beginning of months; it shall be the first month of the year for you. [3]Tell the whole congregation of Israel that on the tenth of this month they are to take a lamb for each family, a lamb for each household. [4]If a household is too small for a whole lamb, it shall join its closest neighbor in obtaining one; the lamb shall be divided in proportion to the number of people who eat of it. ([5]Your lamb shall be without blemish, a year-old male; you may take it from the sheep or from the goats. [6]You shall keep it until the fourteenth day of this month; then the whole assembled congregation of Israel shall slaughter it at twilight. [7]They shall take some of the blood and put it on the two doorposts and the lintel of the houses in which they eat it. [8]They shall eat the lamb that same night; they shall eat it roasted over the fire with unleavened bread and bitter herbs. [9]Do not eat any of it raw or boiled in water but roasted over the fire, with its head, legs, and inner organs. [10]You shall let none of it remain until the morning; anything that remains until the morning you shall burn with fire.) [11]This is how you shall eat it: your loins girded, your sandals on your feet, and your staff in your hand, and you shall eat it hurriedly. It is the Passover of the LORD. [12]I will pass through the land of Egypt that night, and I will strike down every firstborn in the land of Egypt, from human to animal, and on all the gods of Egypt I will execute judgments: I am the LORD. [13]The blood shall be a sign for you on the houses where you live: when I see the blood, I will pass over you, and no plague shall destroy you when I strike the land of Egypt.

[14]"This day shall be a day of remembrance for you. You shall celebrate it as a festival to the LORD; throughout your generations you shall observe it as a perpetual ordinance."

Psalm 116:1-4, 12-19 (N699, P228, SH344, UM837)

I love the LORD because he has heard
   my voice and my supplications.
[2]Because he inclined his ear to me,
   therefore I will call on him as long as I live.
[3]The snares of death encompassed me;
   the pangs of Sheol laid hold on me;
   I suffered distress and anguish.
[4]Then I called on the name of the LORD,
   "O LORD, I pray, save my life!"
. . . .
[12]What shall I return to the LORD
   for all his bounty to me?
[13]I will lift up the cup of salvation
   and call on the name of the LORD;
[14]I will pay my vows to the LORD
   in the presence of all his people.
[15]Precious in the sight of the LORD
   is the death of his faithful ones.
[16]O LORD, I am your servant;
   I am your servant, the child of your serving girl.
   You have loosed my bonds.
[17]I will offer to you a thanksgiving sacrifice
   and call on the name of the LORD.
[18]I will pay my vows to the LORD
   in the presence of all his people,
[19]in the courts of the house of the LORD,
   in your midst, O Jerusalem.
Praise the LORD!

1 Corinthians 11:23-26

[23]For I received from the Lord what I also handed on to you, that the Lord Jesus on the night when he was betrayed took a loaf of bread, [24]and when he had given thanks, he broke it and said, "This is my body that is for you. Do this in remembrance of me." [25]In the same way he took the cup also, after supper, saying, "This cup is the new covenant in my blood. Do this, as often as you drink it, in remembrance of me." [26]For as often as you eat this bread and drink the cup, you proclaim the Lord's death until he comes.

John 13:1-17, 31b-35

Now before the festival of the Passover, Jesus knew that his hour had come to depart from this world and go to the Father. Having loved his own who were in the world, he loved them to the end. [2]The devil had already decided that Judas son of Simon Iscariot would betray Jesus. And during supper [3]Jesus, knowing that the Father had given all things into his hands and that he had come from God and was going to God, [4]got up from supper, took off his outer robe, and tied a towel around himself. [5]Then he poured water into a basin and began to wash the disciples' feet and to wipe them with the towel that was tied around him. [6]He came to Simon Peter, who said to him, "Lord, are you going to wash my feet?" [7]Jesus answered, "You do not know now what I am doing, but later you will understand." [8]Peter said to him, "You will never wash my feet." Jesus answered, "Unless I wash you, you have no share with me." [9]Simon Peter said to him, "Lord, not my feet only but also my hands and my head!" [10]Jesus said to him, "One who has bathed does not need to wash, except for the feet, but is entirely clean. And you are clean, though not all of you." [11]For he knew who was to betray him; for this reason he said, "Not all of you are clean."

[12]After he had washed their feet, had put on his robe, and had reclined again, he said to them, "Do you know what I have done to you? [13]You call me Teacher and Lord, and you are right, for that is what I am. [14]So if I, your Lord and Teacher, have washed your feet, you also ought to wash one another's feet. [15]For I have set you an example, that you also should do as I have done to you. [16]Very truly, I tell you, slaves are not greater than their master, nor are messengers greater than the one who sent them. [17]If you know these things, you are blessed if you do them. . . .

[31b]"Now the Son of Man has been glorified, and God has been glorified in him. [32]If God has been glorified in him, God will also glorify him in himself and will glorify him at once. [33]Little children, I am with you only a little longer. You will look for me, and as I said to the Jews so now I say to you, 'Where I am going, you cannot come.' [34]I give you a new commandment, that you love one another. Just as I have loved you, you also should love one another."

Primary Hymns and Songs for the Day

"What Wondrous Love Is This" (Exod, 1 Cor, John) (O)
    C200, CG171, E439, EL666, G215, N223, P85, SA207, SH177,
    UM292, VU147 (Fr.)
        H-3   Hbl-102; Chr-212; Org-185
        S-1   #347. Harmonization
"O Love That Wilt Not Let Me Go" (Exod, 1 Cor, John)
    C540, CG631, G833, N485, P384, SA616, SH314, UM480, VU658
        H-3   Chr-146; Org-142
"Here, O Lord, Your Servants Gather" (Exod, John, Comm.)
    C278, EL530, G311, N72, P465, UM552, VU362
        S-1   #333. Orff arrangement
        S-2   #178. Flute descant
"In Remembrance of Me" 25156 (1 Cor, John, Comm.)
    C403, CG462, G521, S2254, SH667
"Lord, Be Glorified" 26368 (John, Footwashing)
    EL744, G468, S2150, SA593, SH420
"Jesus, We Are Here" (John)
    EL529, G392, S2273, SH611
"Jesu, Jesu" 3049039 (John) (C)
        S-1   #63 Vocal part
    C600, CG656, E602, EL708, G203, N498, P367, SH155,
    UM432, VU593; S-1 #63 Vocal part
"Abide with Me" (Exod, John) (C)
    C636, CG543, E662, EL629, G836, N99, P543, SA529, SH475,
    UM700 (PD), VU436

Additional Hymn Suggestions

"Go Down, Moses" (Exod)
    C663, E648, G52, N572, P334, SH28, UM448
"Deep in the Shadows of the Past" (Exod)
    G50, N320, P330, S2246
"Nada Te Turbe" ("Nothing Can Trouble") (Exod, John)
    CG73, G820, N772, S2054, SH292, VU290
"For the Bread Which You Have Broken" (1 Cor)
    C411, E340/E341, EL494, G516, P508/P509, UM614/
    UM615, VU470
"Let Us Break Bread Together" (1 Cor, Comm.)
    AH4140, C425, CG461, EL471 (PD), G525, N330, P513,
    SH674, UM618, VU480
"Una Espiga" ("Sheaves of Summer") (1 Cor, John, Comm.)
    C396, G532, N338, UM637
"Bread of the World" (John, Comm.)
    C387, E301, G499, N346, P502, UM624, VU461
"O Love, How Deep" (John)
    E448/449, EL322, G618, N209, P83, SH115, UM267, VU348
"O Jesus, I Have Promised" (John)
    C612, E655, EL810, G724/725, N493, P388/389, SA613,
    SH623, UM396 (PD), VU120
"O Master, Let Me Walk with Thee" (John)
    C602, CG660, E659/E660, EL818, G738, N503, P357, SA667,
    SH612, UM430 (PD), VU560
"Where Charity and Love Prevail" (John)
    CG264, E581, EL359, G316, N396, SH271, UM549
"Lord God, Your Love Has Called Us Here" (John)
    EL358. P353, SA335, UM579
"Lord, Whose Love Through Humble Service" (John)
    C461, CG650, E610, EL712, P427, SH239, UM581
"Together We Serve" (John)
    G767, S2175
"Ubi Caritas" ("Live in Charity") (John, Footwashing)
    C523, EL642, G205, S2179
"Healer of Our Every Ill" (John)
    C506, EL612, G795, S2213, SH339, VU619
"As We Gather at Your Table" (John, Comm.)
    EL522, N332, S2268, SH411, VU457
"Let Us Build a House Where Love Can Dwell" (John)
    EL641, G301, SH228 (See also WS3152)

Additional Contemporary and Modern Suggestions

"Fill My Cup, Lord" 15946 (Pss, Comm.)
    C351, UM641 (refrain only), WS3093
"I Will Call upon the Lord" 11263 (Pss)
    G621, S2002
"We Bring the Sacrifice of Praise" 9990 (Pss)
"I Love You, Lord" 25266 (Pss)
    CG362, G627, S2068, SA369, SH417
"I Stand Amazed" 769450 (Pss, Lent)
"I Will Not Forget You" 2694306 (Pss)
"Beautiful Savior" 2492216 (Pss, Holy Week)
"Take Our Bread" (1 Cor, Comm.)
    C413, UM640
"Broken for Me" (1 Cor, Comm.)
"Communion" 4586072 (1 Cor, Comm.)
"We Remember We Believe" 5767711 (1 Cor, Comm.)
"Jesus Messiah" 5183443 (1 Cor, Holy Week, Comm.)
"For Us" 7119349 (John)
"Make Me a Servant" 33131 (John)
    CG651, S2176
"The Servant Song" 72673 (John)
    C490, CG289, EL659, G727, N539, S2222, SA1005, SH264,
    VU595
"They'll Know We Are Christians" 26997 (John)
    AH4074, C494, CG272, G300, S2223, SH232
"Nohu pū" ("Stay with Me") (Holy Thursday)
    EL348, G204, S2198, SH157
"One Bread, One Body" (Comm.)
    C393, EL496, G530, SH678, UM620, VU467

Vocal Solos

"In Remembrance" (1 Cor, John, Comm.)
    V-5 (2)   p. 7
"Wondrous Love" (John)
    V-6   p. 47
"O the Deep, Deep Love of Jesus" (John, Comm.)
    V-8   p. 247
"This Is My Commandment" (John)
    V-8   p. 284
"He Breaks the Bread, He Pours the Wine" (John, Comm.)
    V-10   p. 43

Anthems

"I Heard the Voice of Jesus Say" (John, Holy Thursday)
John Helgen; Choristers Guild CGA1177
SAB, piano (https://bit.ly/CG-1177)

"When Twilight Comes" (John, Holy Thursday)
Arr. Robert Buckley Farlee; Augsburg 9780800675578
2-part mixed, piano (https://bit.ly/AF-75578)

Other Suggestions

Visuals:
    O   Lamb, sandals, staff, Passover meal
    P   Cup or goblet, open manacles
    E   Bread/wine/pottery chalice, Passover meal
    G   Passover meal, outer garment, towel/basin/water/
            pitcher, 12 disciples, Last Supper, stripping of the
            altar, darkness
Introit: EL641, G301, SH228 (See also WS3152). "Let Us Build a
    House Where Love Can Dwell" (John)
Prayer: UM283. Holy Thursday (John, 1 Cor)
Offering Prayer: WSL154 (John)
Blessing: John 13:34
Theme Ideas: Communion, Faithfulness, Passover,
    Remembrance, Service / Servanthood

Isaiah 52:13–53:12

¹³See, my servant shall prosper;
  he shall be exalted and lifted up
  and shall be very high.
¹⁴Just as there were many who were astonished at him
    —so marred was his appearance, beyond human semblance,
  and his form beyond that of mortals—
¹⁵so he shall startle many nations;
  kings shall shut their mouths because of him,
for that which had not been told them they shall see,
  and that which they had not heard they shall contemplate.
53 Who has believed what we have heard?
  And to whom has the arm of the LORD been revealed?
²For he grew up before him like a young plant
  and like a root out of dry ground;
he had no form or majesty that we should look at him,
  nothing in his appearance that we should desire him.
³He was despised and rejected by others;
  a man of suffering and acquainted with infirmity,
and as one from whom others hide their faces
  he was despised, and we held him of no account.
⁴Surely he has borne our infirmities
  and carried our diseases,
yet we accounted him stricken,
  struck down by God, and afflicted.
⁵But he was wounded for our transgressions,
  crushed for our iniquities;
upon him was the punishment that made us whole,
  and by his bruises we are healed.
⁶All we like sheep have gone astray;
  we have all turned to our own way,
and the LORD has laid on him
  the iniquity of us all.
⁷He was oppressed, and he was afflicted,
  yet he did not open his mouth;
like a lamb that is led to the slaughter
  and like a sheep that before its shearers is silent,
  so he did not open his mouth.
⁸By a perversion of justice he was taken away.
  Who could have imagined his future?
For he was cut off from the land of the living,
  stricken for the transgression of my people.
⁹They made his grave with the wicked
  and his tomb with the rich,
although he had done no violence,
  and there was no deceit in his mouth.
¹⁰Yet it was the will of the LORD to crush him with affliction.
  When you make his life an offering for sin,
he shall see his offspring and shall prolong his days;
  through him the will of the LORD shall prosper.
¹¹Out of his anguish he shall see;
  he shall find satisfaction through his knowledge.
The righteous one, my servant, shall make many righteous,
  and he shall bear their iniquities.
¹²Therefore I will allot him a portion with the great,
  and he shall divide the spoil with the strong,
because he poured out himself to death
  and was numbered with the transgressors,
yet he bore the sin of many
  and made intercession for the transgressors.

Psalm 22 (G631, N632, SH178, UM752)

My God, my God, why have you forsaken me?
  Why are you so far from helping me, from the words of my
    groaning?
²O my God, I cry by day, but you do not answer;
  and by night but find no rest.
³Yet you are holy,
  enthroned on the praises of Israel.

⁴In you our ancestors trusted;
  they trusted, and you delivered them.
⁵To you they cried and were saved;
  in you they trusted and were not put to shame.
⁶But I am a worm and not human,
  scorned by others and despised by the people.
⁷All who see me mock me;
  they sneer at me; they shake their heads;
⁸"Commit your cause to the LORD; let him deliver—
  let him rescue the one in whom he delights!"
⁹Yet it was you who took me from the womb;
  you kept me safe on my mother's breast.
¹⁰On you I was cast from my birth,
  and since my mother bore me you have been my God.
¹¹Do not be far from me,
  for trouble is near,
  and there is no one to help.
¹²Many bulls encircle me;
  strong bulls of Bashan surround me;
¹³they open wide their mouths at me,
  like a ravening and roaring lion.
¹⁴I am poured out like water,
  and all my bones are out of joint;
my heart is like wax;
  it is melted within my breast;
¹⁵my mouth is dried up like a potsherd,
  and my tongue sticks to my jaws;
  you lay me in the dust of death.
¹⁶For dogs are all around me;
  a company of evildoers encircles me;
  they bound my hands and feet.
¹⁷I can count all my bones.
They stare and gloat over me;
¹⁸they divide my clothes among themselves,
  and for my clothing they cast lots.
¹⁹But you, O LORD, do not be far away!
  O my help, come quickly to my aid!
²⁰Deliver my soul from the sword,
  my life from the power of the dog!
  ²¹Save me from the mouth of the lion!
From the horns of the wild oxen you have rescued me.
²²I will tell of your name to my brothers and sisters;
  in the midst of the congregation I will praise you:
²³You who fear the LORD, praise him!
  All you offspring of Jacob, glorify him;
  stand in awe of him, all you offspring of Israel!
²⁴For he did not despise or abhor
  the affliction of the afflicted;
he did not hide his face from me
  but heard when I cried to him.
²⁵From you comes my praise in the great congregation;
  my vows I will pay before those who fear him.
²⁶The poor shall eat and be satisfied;
  those who seek him shall praise the LORD.
  May your hearts live forever!
²⁷All the ends of the earth shall remember
  and turn to the LORD,
and all the families of the nations
  shall worship before him.
²⁸For dominion belongs to the LORD,
  and he rules over the nations.
²⁹To him, indeed, shall all who sleep in the earth bow down;
  before him shall bow all who go down to the dust,
  and I shall live for him.
³⁰Posterity will serve him;
  future generations will be told about the Lord
³¹and proclaim his deliverance to a people yet unborn,
  saying that he has done it.

Hebrews 10:16-25

[16]"This is the covenant that I will make with them
    after those days, says the Lord:
I will put my laws in their hearts,
    and I will write them on their minds,"
[17]and he adds,
 "I will remember their sins and their lawless deeds no more."
[18]Where there is forgiveness of these, there is no longer any offering for sin.

[19]Therefore, my brothers and sisters, since we have confidence to enter the sanctuary by the blood of Jesus, [20]by the new and living way that he opened for us through the curtain (that is, through his flesh), [21]and since we have a great priest over the house of God, [22]let us approach with a true heart in full assurance of faith, with our hearts sprinkled clean from an evil conscience and our bodies washed with pure water. [23]Let us hold fast to the confession of our hope without wavering, for he who has promised is faithful. [24]And let us consider how to provoke one another to love and good deeds, [25]not neglecting to meet together, as is the habit of some, but encouraging one another, and all the more as you see the Day approaching.

John 18:1–19:42

After Jesus had spoken these words, he went out with his disciples across the Kidron Valley to a place where there was a garden, which he and his disciples entered. [2]Now Judas, who betrayed him, also knew the place because Jesus often met there with his disciples. [3]So Judas brought a detachment of soldiers together with police from the chief priests and the Pharisees, and they came there with lanterns and torches and weapons. [4]Then Jesus, knowing all that was to happen to him, came forward and asked them, "Whom are you looking for?" [5]They answered, "Jesus of Nazareth." Jesus replied, "I am he." Judas, who betrayed him, was standing with them. [6]When Jesus said to them, "I am he," they stepped back and fell to the ground. [7]Again he asked them, "Whom are you looking for?" And they said, "Jesus of Nazareth." [8]Jesus answered, "I told you that I am he. So if you are looking for me, let these people go." [9]This was to fulfill the word that he had spoken, "I did not lose a single one of those whom you gave me." [10]Then Simon Peter, who had a sword, drew it, struck the high priest's slave, and cut off his right ear. The slave's name was Malchus. [11]Jesus said to Peter, "Put your sword back into its sheath. Am I not to drink the cup that the Father has given me?"

[12]So the soldiers, their officer, and the Jewish police arrested Jesus and bound him. [13]First they took him to Annas, who was the father-in-law of Caiaphas, the high priest that year. [14]Caiaphas was the one who had advised the Jews that it was better to have one person die for the people.

[15]Simon Peter and another disciple followed Jesus. Since that disciple was known to the high priest, he went with Jesus into the courtyard of the high priest, [16]but Peter was standing outside at the gate. So the other disciple, who was known to the high priest, went out, spoke to the woman who guarded the gate, and brought Peter in. [17]The woman said to Peter, "You are not also one of this man's disciples, are you?" He said, "I am not." [18]Now the slaves and the police had made a charcoal fire because it was cold, and they were standing around it and warming themselves. Peter also was standing with them and warming himself.

[19]Then the high priest questioned Jesus about his disciples and about his teaching. [20]Jesus answered, "I have spoken openly to the world; I have always taught in synagogues and in the temple, where all the Jews come together. I have said nothing in secret. [21]Why do you ask me? Ask those who heard what I said to them; they know what I said." [22]When he had said this, one of the police standing nearby struck Jesus on the face, saying, "Is that how you answer the high priest?" [23]Jesus answered, "If I have spoken wrongly, testify to the wrong. But if I have spoken rightly, why do you strike me?" [24]Then Annas sent him bound to Caiaphas the high priest.

[25]Now Simon Peter was standing and warming himself. They asked him, "You are not also one of his disciples, are you?" He denied it and said, "I am not." [26]One of the slaves of the high priest, a relative of the man whose ear Peter had cut off, asked, "Did I not see you in the garden with him?" [27]Again Peter denied it, and at that moment the cock crowed.

[28]Then they took Jesus from Caiaphas to Pilate's headquarters. It was early in the morning. They themselves did not enter the headquarters, so as to avoid ritual defilement and to be able to eat the Passover. [29]So Pilate went out to them and said, "What accusation do you bring against this man?" [30]They answered, "If this man were not a criminal, we would not have handed him over to you." [31]Pilate said to them, "Take him yourselves and judge him according to your law." The Jews replied, "We are not permitted to put anyone to death." [32](This was to fulfill what Jesus had said when he indicated the kind of death he was to die.)

[33]Then Pilate entered the headquarters again, summoned Jesus, and asked him, "Are you the King of the Jews?" [34]Jesus answered, "Do you ask this on your own, or did others tell you about me?" [35]Pilate replied, "I am not a Jew, am I? Your own nation and the chief priests have handed you over to me. What have you done?" [36]Jesus answered, "My kingdom does not belong to this world. If my kingdom belonged to this world, my followers would be fighting to keep me from being handed over to the Jews. But as it is, my kingdom is not from here." [37]Pilate asked him, "So you are a king?" Jesus answered, "You say that I am a king. For this I was born, and for this I came into the world, to testify to the truth. Everyone who belongs to the truth listens to my voice." [38]Pilate asked him, "What is truth?"

After he had said this, he went out to the Jews again and told them, "I find no case against him. [39]But you have a custom that I release someone for you at the Passover. Do you want me to release for you the King of the Jews?" [40]They shouted in reply, "Not this man but Barabbas!" Now Barabbas was a rebel.

19 Then Pilate took Jesus and had him flogged. [2]And the soldiers wove a crown of thorns and put it on his head, and they dressed him in a purple robe. [3]They kept coming up to him, saying, "Hail, King of the Jews!" and striking him on the face. [4]Pilate went out again and said to them, "Look, I am bringing him out to you to let you know that I find no case against him." [5]So Jesus came out wearing the crown of thorns and the purple robe. Pilate said to them, "Behold the man!" [6]When the chief priests and the police saw him, they shouted, "Crucify him! Crucify him!" Pilate said to them, "Take him yourselves and crucify him; I find no case against him." [7]The Jews answered him, "We have a law, and according to that law he ought to die because he has claimed to be the Son of God."

[8]Now when Pilate heard this, he was more afraid than ever. [9]He entered his headquarters again and asked Jesus, "Where are you from?" But Jesus gave him no answer. [10]Pilate therefore said to him, "Do you refuse to speak to me? Do you not know that I have power to release you and power to crucify you?" [11]Jesus answered him, "You would have no power over me unless it had been given you from above; therefore the one who handed me over to you is guilty of a greater sin." [12]From then on Pilate tried to release him, but the Jews cried out, "If you release this man, you are no friend of Caesar. Everyone who claims to be a king sets himself against Caesar."

[13]When Pilate heard these words, he brought Jesus outside and sat on the judge's bench at a place called The Stone Pavement, or in Hebrew Gabbatha. [14]Now it was the day of Preparation for the Passover, and it was about noon. He said to the Jews, "Here is your King!" [15]They cried out, "Away with him! Away with him! Crucify him!" Pilate asked them, "Shall I crucify your King?" The chief priests answered, "We have no king but Caesar." [16]Then he handed him over to them to be crucified.

So they took Jesus, [17]and carrying the cross by himself he went out to what is called the Place of the Skull, which in Hebrew is called Golgotha. [18]There they crucified him and with him two others, one on either side, with Jesus between them. [19]Pilate also had an inscription written and put on the cross. It read, "Jesus of Nazareth, the King of the Jews." [20]Many of the Jews read this inscription because the place where Jesus was crucified was near the city, and it was written in Hebrew, in Latin, and in Greek. [21]Then the chief priests of the Jews said to Pilate, "Do not write, 'The King of the Jews,' but, 'This man said, I am King of the Jews.'" [22]Pilate answered, "What I have written I have written." [23]When the soldiers had crucified Jesus, they took his clothes and divided them into four parts, one for each soldier. They also took his tunic; now the tunic was seamless, woven in one piece from the top. [24]So they said to one another, "Let us not tear it but cast lots for it to see who will get it." This was to fulfill what the scripture says,

"They divided my clothes among themselves,
    and for my clothing they cast lots."

[25]And that is what the soldiers did.

Meanwhile, standing near the cross of Jesus were his mother, and his mother's sister, Mary the wife of Clopas, and Mary Magdalene. [26]When Jesus saw his mother and the disciple whom he loved standing beside her, he said to his mother, "Woman, here is your son." [27]Then he said to the disciple, "Here is your mother." And from that hour the disciple took her into his own home.

[28]After this, when Jesus knew that all was now finished, he said (in order to fulfill the scripture), "I am thirsty." [29]A jar full of sour wine was standing there. So they put a sponge full of the wine on a branch of hyssop and held it to his mouth. [30]When Jesus had received the wine, he said, "It is finished." Then he bowed his head and gave up his spirit.

[31]Since it was the day of Preparation, the Jews did not want the bodies left on the cross during the Sabbath, especially because that Sabbath was a day of great solemnity. So they asked Pilate to have the legs of the crucified men broken and the bodies removed. [32]Then the soldiers came and broke the legs of the first and of the other who had been crucified with him. [33]But when they came to Jesus and saw that he was already dead, they did not break his legs. [34]Instead, one of the soldiers pierced his side with a spear, and at once blood and water came out. [35](He who saw this has testified so that you also may believe. His testimony is true, and he knows that he tells the truth, so that you also may continue to believe.) [36]These things occurred so that the scripture might be fulfilled, "None of his bones shall be broken." [37]And again another passage of scripture says, "They will look on the one whom they have pierced."

[38]After these things, Joseph of Arimathea, who was a disciple of Jesus, though a secret one because of his fear of the Jews, asked Pilate to let him take away the body of Jesus. Pilate gave him permission, so he came and removed his body. [39]Nicodemus, who had at first come to Jesus by night, also came, bringing a mixture of myrrh and aloes, weighing about a hundred pounds. [40]They took the body of Jesus and wrapped it with the spices in linen cloths, according to the burial custom of the Jews. [41]Now there was a garden in the place where he was crucified, and in the garden there was a new tomb in which no one had ever been laid. [42]And so, because it was the Jewish day of Preparation and the tomb was nearby, they laid Jesus there.

Primary Hymns and Songs for the Day

"When I Survey the Wondrous Cross" (John) (O)
 C195, CG186, EL803, G223, N224, P101, SH163/164, UM298
  H-3 Hbl-6, 102; Chr-213; Desc-49; Org-49
  S-1 #155. Descant
 E474, G224, P100, SA208, UM299 (PD), VU149 (Fr.)
  H-3 Hbl-47; Chr-76, 214; Desc-90; Org-127
  S-1 #288. Transposition to E-flat major
"Victim Divine" (Isa, Heb)
 S2259
"O Sacred Head, Now Wounded" (Isa, Heb, John)
 C202, CG191, E168/169, EL351/352, G221, N226, P98,
 SA190, SH168, UM286, VU145 (Fr.)
  H-3 Hbl-82; Chr-148; Desc-86; Org-111
"Were You There" (John) (C)
 C198, CG192, E172, EL353, G228, N229, P102, SA206,
 SH176, UM288, VU144
  H-3 Hbl-101; Chr-209
  S-2 #195-196. Descant and harmonization

Additional Hymn Suggestions

"You, Lord, are Both Lamb and Shepherd" (Isa)
 G274, SH210, VU210, WS3043
"I Love the Lord" 1168957 (Isa, Heb, John)
 CG613, G799, P362, N511, SH343, VU617, WS3142
"O-So-So" ("Come Now, O Prince of Peace") (Isa, Heb, John)
 EL247, G103, S2232, SH235
"He Never Said a Mumbalin' Word" (Isa, John)
 C208, EL350, G219, P95 (PD), UM291, VU141
"Why Stand So Far Away, My God?" (Pss, John)
 C671, G786, S2180
"Ah, Holy Jesus" (Heb)
 C210, E158, EL349, G218, N218, P93, UM289, VU138
"Woman in the Night" (John)
 C188, G161, UM274
"Go to Dark Gethsemane" (John)
 C196, CG180, E171, EL347, G220, N219, P97, SH171, UM290
 (PD), VU133
"Alas! and Did My Savior Bleed" (John) (O)
 AH4067, C204, CG182/595, EL337, G212, N199/200, P78,
 SA159, UM294/359, SH172/173
"In the Cross of Christ I Glory" (John) (C)
 C207, CG183, E441, EL324, G213, N193, P84, SA174, UM295
"My Song Is Love Unknown" (John, Good Friday)
 E458, EL343, G209, N222, P76, S2083, SA149, VU143
"Thou Didst Leave Thy Throne" (John)
 CG165, S2100, SA153, SH86
"When Jesus Wept" (John)
 C199, E715, G194, N192, P312, S2106, VU146
"Why Has God Forsaken Me?" (John)
 G809, P406, S2110, VU154
"Goodness Is Stronger than Evil" (Good Friday)
 EL721, G750, S2219

Additional Contemporary and Modern Suggestions

"The Power of the Cross" 4490766 (Isa, John)
 CG190, WS3085
"Our God Reigns" 8458 (Isa)
"Why Stand So Far Away, My God?" (Pss)
 C671, G786, S2180
"Before the Throne of God Above" 2306412 (Heb)
"Because of Your Love" 4662501 (Heb)
"Grace Like Rain" 3689877 (Heb)
"Jesus Messiah" 5183443 (Heb, John, Good Friday)
"Amazing Love" 192553 (Heb, John)
"The Wonderful Cross" 3148435 (Heb, John, Good Friday)
"You Are My King" ("Amazing Love") 2456623 (Heb, John)
"I Come to the Cross" 1965249 (Heb, John)

"There Is a Redeemer" 11483 (Heb, John, Good Friday)
 CG377, G443, SA204, SH495
"O How He Loves You and Me" 15850 (John)
 CG600, S2108, SH535
"How Long, O Lord" (John, Good Friday)
 G777, S2209
"Lord of the Dance" (John)
 G157, P302, SA141, UM261, VU352
"Jesus, Remember Me" (John)
 C569, CG393, EL616, G227, P599, SH175, UM488, VU148
"Jesus, We Crown You with Praise" 1453284 (John)
"O Praise The Name" 7037787 (John, Good Friday)
"Lamb of God" 16787 (Good Friday)
 EL336, G518, S2113

Vocal Solos

"He Was Despised" from *Messiah* (Isa)
"He was Cut Off Out of the Land of the Living" (recitative) (Isa)
"But Thou Didst Not Leave His Soul in Hell" (aria) (John)
 V-2
"Ah, Holy Jesus" (Isa, John)
 V-6 p. 24
"Into the Sea" ("It's Gonna Be OK") (Pss, John)
 V-9 p. 48
"The Shepherd Became a Lamb" (Heb, John)
 V-10 p. 48
"They Led Him Away" (John)
 V-8 p. 245
" 'Tis Finished! The Messiah Dies" (John, Good Friday)
 V-1 p. 63
"Lamb of God" (Good Friday)
 V-5 (2) p. 5

Anthems

"*Recordare*: Drop, Drop Slow Tears" (John)
Howard Goodall; MorningStar 56-0055
SATB, keyboard and soprano solo (https://bit.ly/MS-0055)

"My Hope Is In the Lord" (John, Good Friday)
Marianne Forman; Beckenhorst BP2192
SATB, piano (https://bit.ly/BP-2192)

Other Suggestions

Visuals: Black draping the cross, black paraments, or none
 O Plant, root, suffering, crucifix, lamb, darkness/light
 P Exodus, mother breast-feeding, water, bones, sword, dog
 E Heb 10:16b, crucifix
 G Sword, charcoal fire, cock crowing, whip, purple robe, rugged cross, tunic, crucifix, nails, Crown of thorns, ladder, sponge on branch, spear, shroud
For additional ideas, consult Palm/Passion Sunday suggestions.
Introit: S2199. "Stay with Us" (John)
Response: EL336, G518, S2113. "Lamb of God" (John)
Prayer: UM284 (John)
Psalm: SH178. Psalm 22 with stanzas of "What Wondrous Love Is This" (Pss)
Reading: UM293. "Behold the Savior of Mankind" (John)
Scripture Response: C196, CG180, E171, EL347, G220, N219, P97, SH171, UM290 (PD), VU133. "Go to Dark Gethsemane." Use this hymn to supplement the reading from John. Sing stanza 1 before beginning 18:1, stanza 2 after 19:3, stanza 3 after 19:30. Sing UM288 stanza 5 at the conclusion of the reading.
Offering Prayer: WSL155 (Good Friday)
Theme Ideas: Covenant, Cross, Grace, Jesus: Crucifixion, Jesus: Jesus our Savior, Lament

Acts 10:34-43

[34]Then Peter began to speak to them: "I truly understand that God shows no partiality, [35]but in every people anyone who fears him and practices righteousness is acceptable to him. [36]You know the message he sent to the people of Israel, preaching peace by Jesus Christ—he is Lord of all. [37]That message spread throughout Judea, beginning in Galilee after the baptism that John announced: [38]how God anointed Jesus of Nazareth with the Holy Spirit and with power; how he went about doing good and healing all who were oppressed by the devil, for God was with him. [39]We are witnesses to all that he did both in Judea and in Jerusalem. They put him to death by hanging him on a tree, [40]but God raised him on the third day and allowed him to appear, [41]not to all the people but to us who were chosen by God as witnesses and who ate and drank with him after he rose from the dead. [42]He commanded us to preach to the people and to testify that he is the one ordained by God as judge of the living and the dead. [43]All the prophets testify about him that everyone who believes in him receives forgiveness of sins through his name."

Psalm 118:1-2, 14-24 (N700, P231, UM839)

O give thanks to the LORD, for he is good;
   his steadfast love endures forever!
[2]Let Israel say,
   "His steadfast love endures forever."
. . . .
[14]The LORD is my strength and my might;
   he has become my salvation.
[15]There are glad songs of victory in the tents of the righteous:
   "The right hand of the LORD does valiantly;
[16]the right hand of the LORD is exalted;
   the right hand of the LORD does valiantly."
[17]I shall not die, but I shall live
   and recount the deeds of the LORD.
[18]The LORD has punished me severely,
   but he did not give me over to death.
[19]Open to me the gates of righteousness,
   that I may enter through them
   and give thanks to the LORD.
[20]This is the gate of the LORD;
   the righteous shall enter through it.
[21]I thank you that you have answered me
   and have become my salvation.
[22]The stone that the builders rejected
   has become the chief cornerstone.
[23]This is the LORD's doing;
   it is marvelous in our eyes.
[24]This is the day that the LORD has made;
   let us rejoice and be glad in it.

1 Corinthians 15:1-11

Now I want you to understand, brothers and sisters, the good news that I proclaimed to you, which you in turn received, in which also you stand, [2]through which also you are being saved, if you hold firmly to the message that I proclaimed to you—unless you have come to believe in vain.

[3]For I handed on to you as of first importance what I in turn had received: that Christ died for our sins in accordance with the scriptures [4]and that he was buried and that he was raised on the third day in accordance with the scriptures [5]and that he appeared to Cephas, then to the twelve. [6]Then he appeared to more than five hundred brothers and sisters at one time, most of whom are still alive, though some have died. [7]Then he appeared to James, then to all the apostles. [8]Last of all, as to one untimely born, he appeared also to me. [9]For I am the least of the apostles, unfit to be called an apostle, because I persecuted the church of God. [10]But by the grace of God I am what I am, and his grace toward me has not been in vain. On the contrary, I worked harder than any of them, though it was not I but the grace of God that is with me. [11]Whether then it was I or they, so we proclaim and so you believed.

John 20:1-18

Early on the first day of the week, while it was still dark, Mary Magdalene came to the tomb and saw that the stone had been removed from the tomb. [2]So she ran and went to Simon Peter and the other disciple, the one whom Jesus loved, and said to them, "They have taken the Lord out of the tomb, and we do not know where they have laid him." [3]Then Peter and the other disciple set out and went toward the tomb. [4]The two were running together, but the other disciple outran Peter and reached the tomb first. [5]He bent down to look in and saw the linen wrappings lying there, but he did not go in. [6]Then Simon Peter came, following him, and went into the tomb. He saw the linen wrappings lying there, [7]and the cloth that had been on Jesus's head, not lying with the linen wrappings but rolled up in a place by itself. [8]Then the other disciple, who reached the tomb first, also went in, and he saw and believed; [9]for as yet they did not understand the scripture, that he must rise from the dead. [10]Then the disciples returned to their homes.

[11]But Mary stood weeping outside the tomb. As she wept, she bent over to look into the tomb, [12]and she saw two angels in white sitting where the body of Jesus had been lying, one at the head and the other at the feet. [13]They said to her, "Woman, why are you weeping?" She said to them, "They have taken away my Lord, and I do not know where they have laid him." [14]When she had said this, she turned around and saw Jesus standing there, but she did not know that it was Jesus. [15]Jesus said to her, "Woman, why are you weeping? Whom are you looking for?" Supposing him to be the gardener, she said to him, "Sir, if you have carried him away, tell me where you have laid him, and I will take him away." [16]Jesus said to her, "Mary!" She turned and said to him in Hebrew, "Rabbouni!" (which means Teacher). [17]Jesus said to her, "Do not touch me, because I have not yet ascended to the Father. But go to my brothers and say to them, 'I am ascending to my Father and your Father, to my God and your God.'" [18]Mary Magdalene went and announced to the disciples, "I have seen the Lord," and she told them that he had said these things to her.

or Mark 16:1-8

When the Sabbath was over, Mary Magdalene and Mary the mother of James and Salome bought spices, so that they might go and anoint him. [2]And very early on the first day of the week, when the sun had risen, they went to the tomb. [3]They had been saying to one another, "Who will roll away the stone for us from the entrance to the tomb?" [4]When they looked up, they saw that the stone, which was very large, had already been rolled back. [5]As they entered the tomb, they saw a young man dressed in a white robe sitting on the right side, and they were alarmed. [6]But he said to them, "Do not be alarmed; you are looking for Jesus of Nazareth, who was crucified. He has been raised; he is not here. Look, there is the place they laid him. [7]But go, tell his disciples and Peter that he is going ahead of you to Galilee; there you will see him, just as he told you." [8]So they went out and fled from the tomb, for terror and amazement had seized them, and they said nothing to anyone, for they were afraid.

Primary Hymns and Songs for the Day
"Christ the Lord Is Risen Today" (1 Cor, John) (O)
     C216, CG194, N233, SA218, SH181, UM302 (PD), VU155/157
          C216   Descant
          H-3   Hbl-8, 51; Chr-49; Desc-31; Org-32
          S-1   #104-108. Various treatments
     G245, P113
          H-3   Hbl-72; Chr-50; Desc-69; Org-78
          S-1   #213. Descant
     EL373
"Jesus Christ Is Risen Today" (1 Cor, John) (O)
     E207, EL365 (PD), G232, P123
          H-3   Hbl-8, 51; Chr-49; Desc-31; Org-32
          S-1   #104-108. Various treatments
"Come, Ye Faithful, Raise the Strain" (Acts)
     C215, CG218, E199, EL363, G234, N230, P115, UM315 (PD),
     VU165
          H-3   Hbl-53; Chr-57; Desc-94; Org-141
          S-2   #161. Descant
"Shout to the North" 1562261 (Acts)
     G319, SA1009, WS3042
"This Is the Feast of Victory" (Acts, 1 Cor, John, Comm.)
     E417/418, G513, P594, UM638, VU904
          H-3   Chr-198
          S-1   #130. Trumpet part
          S-2   #60-61 Descant and harmonization
"To God Be the Glory" (1 Cor)
     C72, CG349, G634, P485, SA279, SH545, UM98 (PD)
"The Day of Resurrection" (1 Cor, John)
     C228, CG214, E210, EL361, G233, N245, P118, SH186,
     UM303 (PD), VU164
          H-3   Hbl-74; Chr-123; Desc-64; Org-71
          S-1   #9-197. Various treatments
"The Strife Is O'er, the Battle Done" (1 Cor)
     C221, E208, EL366, G236, N242, P119, SA233, SH193,
     UM306, VU159
          H-3   Hbl-97; Chr-191; Desc-102; Org-169
          S-1   #344. Descant idea
          S-2   #190. Descant
"Woman, Weeping in the Garden" (John, Mark)
     C223, G241
"Crown Him with Many Crowns" (John) (C)
     C234, CG223. E494, EL855, G268, N301, P151, SA358,
     SH208, UM327 (PD), VU211
          H-3   Hbl-55; Chr-60; Desc-30; Org-27
          S-1   #86-88. Various treatments

Additional Hymn Suggestions
"We Know That Christ Is Raised" (Acts, Baptism)
     E296, EL449, G485, P495, UM610, VU448
"Alleluia" (Pss)
     EL174, G587, S2043
"Christ Is Risen" (1 Cor, John, Comm.)
     C222, CG206, P104, UM307
"He Lives" (1 Cor, John)
     C226, CG622, SA847, SH198, UM310
Cristo Vive ("Christ Is Risen") (1 Cor, John)
     N235, P109, SH184, UM313
"Thine Be the Glory" (John)
     C218, CG222, EL376, G238, N253, P122, SA276, SH192,
     UM308, VU173 (Fr.)
"In the Garden" (John)
     C227, CG200, N237, UM314
"Woman in the Night" (John, Mark)
     C188, G161, UM274
"Christ Is Alive" (Mark)
     CG205, E182, EL389, G246, P108, SA217, UM318, VU158
"Up from the Grave He Arose" (Mark)
     C224, CG207, SA228, SH185, UM322 (PD)
"Because He Lives" (Mark)
     AH4070, C562, CG620, SA219, SH200, UM364

Additional Contemporary and Modern Suggestions
"Emmanuel, Emmanuel" 12949 (Acts)
     C134, CG120, UM204
"Holy and Anointed One" 164361 (Acts)
"Today Is the Day" 5200924 (Ps 118)
"One Thing Remains" 5508444 (Pss)
"I Will Enter His Gates" 1493 (Pss)
     S2270, SA337
"Grace Alone" 2335524 (1 Cor)
     CG43, S2162, SA699.
"What A Beautiful Name" 7068424 (1 Cor)
"Lord, I Lift Your Name on High" 117947 (1 Cor, John)
     AH4071, CG606, EL857, S2088, SA379, SH205
"Christ the Lord Is Risen" 230240 (John, Mark)
"Our God Reigns" 8458 (John)
"Celebrate Jesus" 16859 (John)
"Jesus Is Alive" 550652 (John)
"Alleluia" 16811 (Easter)
     C106, N765, SH699, UM186
"Halle, Halle, Halleluja" 2659190 (Easter)
     C41, CG433, EL172, G591, N236, S2026, SH694, VU958
"Amen, Amen" (Easter)
     N161, P299, S2072
"Alleluia" (Easter)
     S2078
"Blessing, Honour and Glory" 1001179 (Easter)
"That's Why We Praise Him" 2668576 (Easter)
"My Redeemer Lives" 2397964 (Easter)
"Alive Forever, Amen" 4190176 (Easter)
"See What a Morning" ("Resurrection Hymn") 4108797 (Easter)
"You Are More Than Enough" 6005063 (Easter)

Vocal Solos
"Jesus Christ is Risen Today" (John, Easter)
     V-1   p. 50
"You Keep Hope Alive" (Easter)
     V-9   p. 132
"Crown Him, the Risen King" (Easter)
     V-10   p. 55

Anthems
"Crown Him with Many Crowns" (John)
Arr. Dan Forrest; Beckenhorst BP2254
SATB, keyboard, opt. cong. and brass (https://bit.ly/BP-2254)

"Good Christian Friends, Rejoice and Sing!" (John, Easter)
arr. Jeremy Bankson; Augsburg 9781506452463
SATB, organ, opt. brass and percussion (https://bit.ly/AF-52463)

Other Suggestions
Visuals:
   Acts   crucifixion/Resurrection, Acts 10:39a
   P   Cornerstone
   E   Butterfly, empty tomb, open Bible, empty cross
   G   Basket, spices, stone, angels, shroud, risen Christ
Call to Worship: Psalm 118:19
Hymns Appropriate for Sunrise Service with Guitar:
     "Morning Has Broken" (C53, CG27, E8, EL556, G664,
     SH465, UM145, VU409) (Easter)
     "Lord of the Dance" (G157, P302, SA141, UM261, VU352)
     (Acts)
     "This Is the Day" (AH4149, C286, N84, SA398, SH379,
     UM657, VU412) (Pss)
     "Spirit Song" (C352, SH409, UM347) (Acts, John)
Theme Ideas: Grace, Inclusion, Jesus: Jesus our Savior, Praise,
     Resurrection, Thanksgiving / Gratitude

Acts 4:32-35

[32]Now the whole group of those who believed were of one heart and soul, and no one claimed private ownership of any possessions, but everything they owned was held in common. [33]With great power the apostles gave their testimony to the resurrection of the Lord Jesus, and great grace was upon them all. [34]There was not a needy person among them, for as many as owned lands or houses sold them and brought the proceeds of what was sold. [35]They laid it at the apostles' feet, and it was distributed to each as any had need.

Psalm 133 (N712, P241, UM850)

How very good and pleasant it is
  when kindred live together in unity!
[2]It is like the precious oil on the head,
  running down upon the beard,
on the beard of Aaron,
  running down over the collar of his robes.
[3]It is like the dew of Hermon,
  which falls on the mountains of Zion.
For there the Lord ordained his blessing,
  life forevermore.

1 John 1:1–2:2

We declare to you what was from the beginning, what we have heard, what we have seen with our eyes, what we have looked at and touched with our hands, concerning the word of life—[2]this life was revealed, and we have seen it and testify to it and declare to you the eternal life that was with the Father and was revealed to us—[3]what we have seen and heard we also declare to you so that you also may have fellowship with us, and truly our fellowship is with the Father and with his Son Jesus Christ. [4]We are writing these things so that our joy may be complete.

[5]This is the message we have heard from him and proclaim to you, that God is light and in him there is no darkness at all. [6]If we say that we have fellowship with him while we are walking in darkness, we lie and do not do what is true; [7]but if we walk in the light as he himself is in the light, we have fellowship with one another, and the blood of Jesus his Son cleanses us from all sin. [8]If we say that we have no sin, we deceive ourselves, and the truth is not in us. [9]If we confess our sins, he who is faithful and just will forgive us our sins and cleanse us from all unrighteousness. [10]If we say that we have not sinned, we make him a liar, and his word is not in us.

2 My little children, I am writing these things to you so that you may not sin. But if anyone does sin, we have an advocate with the Father, Jesus Christ the righteous, [2]and he is the atoning sacrifice for our sins, and not for ours only but also for the sins of the whole world.

John 20:19-31

[19]When it was evening on that day, the first day of the week, and the doors were locked where the disciples were, for fear of the Jews, Jesus came and stood among them and said, "Peace be with you." [20]After he said this, he showed them his hands and his side. Then the disciples rejoiced when they saw the Lord. [21]Jesus said to them again, "Peace be with you. As the Father has sent me, so I send you." [22]When he had said this, he breathed on them and said to them, "Receive the Holy Spirit. [23]If you forgive the sins of any, they are forgiven them; if you retain the sins of any, they are retained."

[24]But Thomas (who was called the Twin), one of the twelve, was not with them when Jesus came. [25]So the other disciples told him, "We have seen the Lord." But he said to them, "Unless I see the mark of the nails in his hands and put my finger in the mark of the nails and my hand in his side, I will not believe."

[26]A week later his disciples were again in the house, and Thomas was with them. Although the doors were shut, Jesus came and stood among them and said, "Peace be with you." [27]Then he said to Thomas, "Put your finger here and see my hands. Reach out your hand and put it in my side. Do not doubt but believe." [28]Thomas answered him, "My Lord and my God!" [29]Jesus said to him, "Have you believed because you have seen me? Blessed are those who have not seen and yet have come to believe."

[30]Now Jesus did many other signs in the presence of his disciples that are not written in this book. [31]But these are written so that you may continue to believe that Jesus is the Messiah, the Son of God, and that through believing you may have life in his name.

Primary Hymns and Songs for the Day

"Christ the Lord Is Risen Today" (John) (O)
C216, CG194, EL373, G245, N233, P113, SA218, SH181, UM302 (PD), VU155/157
     H-3   Hbl-72; Chr-50; Desc-69; Org-78
     S-1   #213-214. Trans, with Desc. in F major.

"I'm Gonna Eat at the Welcome Table" (Acts, John)
C424, G770

"¡Miren Qué Bueno!" ("O Look and Wonder") (Pss)
C292, EL649, G397, S2231, SH230, VU856

"I Want to Walk as a Child of the Light" (1 John, John)
CG96, E490, EL815, G377, SH352, UM206
     S-2   #91. Descant

"That Easter Day with Joy Was Bright" (1 John, John)
C229, CG204, E193, EL384 (PD), G254, P121
     H-3   Chr-19

"Breathe on Me, Breath of God" (John)
C254, CG235, E508, G286, N292, P316, SA294, SH224/273, UM420 (PD), VU382 (Fr.)
     H-3   Hbl-49; Chr-45; Desc-101; Org-166

"We Walk by Faith" (John)
CG634, E209, EL635, G817, N256, P399, S2196, SH660
     H-3   Chr-21

"Go, My Children, with My Blessing" (Acts, 1 John, John)
C431, EL543, G547, N82, SH710
     H-3   Chr-60, 67, 73, 79; Org-6
     S-2   #14. Descant

"Trust and Obey" (1 John) (C)
C556, CG509, SA690, SH636, UM467 (PD)
     H-3   Chr-202
     S-1   #336. Harmonization

Additional Hymn Suggestions

"Here, O Lord, Your Servants Gather" (Acts)
C278, EL530, G311, N72, P465, UM552, VU362

"Blest Be the Tie That Binds" (Acts) (C)
C433, CG267, EL656, G306, N393, P438, SA812, SH701, UM557 (PD), VU602

"Help Us Accept Each Other" (Acts)
C487, G754, N388, P358, UM560

"Come, Share the Lord" (Acts, Pss)
C408, CG459, G510, S2269, VU469

"This Is the Spirit's Entry Now" (1 John, Baptism)
EL448, UM608, VU451

"Draw Us in the Spirit's Tether" (1 John, Comm.)
C392, EL470, G529, N337, P504, UM632, VU479

"Just a Closer Walk with Thee" (1 John)
C557, EL697, G835, S2158, SH584

"Lead Me, Guide Me" (1 John)
C583, CG403, EL768, G740, S2214, SH582

"Walk with Me" (1 John, John)
S2242, VU649

"Here, O My Lord, I See Thee" (John, Comm.)
C416, CG460, E318, G517, N336, P520, UM623, VU459

"Womb of Life" (John)
C14, G3, N274, S2046

"At the Font We Start Our Journey" (John, Baptism)
N308, S2114

"I Know that My Redeemer Lives!" (John)
CG210, EL619 (PD), SA224, SH199

Additional Contemporary and Modern Suggestions

"We Are the Church" 18510 (Acts)

"Grace Alone" 2335524 (Acts)
CG43, S2162, SA699.

"They'll Know We Are Christians" 26997 (Acts, Pss)
AH4074, C494, CG272, G300, S2223, SH232

"Make Us One" 695737 (Pss)

"Light of the World" 73342 (1 John)

"Here I Am to Worship" 3266032 (1 John)
CG297, SA114, SH395, WS3177

"Santo, Santo, Santo" ("Holy, Holy, Holy") (1 John)
C111, CG3, EL473, G595, N793, S2007, SH452

"Holy, Holy" 18792 (1 John)
P140, S2039

"Celebrate Love" 155246 (1 John, Easter)

"You Are My King" ("Amazing Love") 2456623 (1 John)
SH539, WS3102

"Everyday" 2798154 (1 John)

"O Come To The Altar" 7051511 (1 John)

"My Savior Lives" 4882965 (1 John, Easter)

"Dios Está Aquí" ("God Is Here Today") 3170575 (1 John, John)
G411, S2049, SH382

"Somos el Cuerpo de Cristo" ("We Are the Body of Christ") (1 Cor)
G768, SH229, S2227

"Open Our Eyes, Lord" 1572 (John)
CG392, S2086, SA386, SH562

"Where the Spirit of the Lord Is" 27484 (John)
C264, S2119

"The Power of Your Love" 917491 (John)

"Surely the Presence of the Lord" 7909 (John)
C263, UM328; S-2 #200. Stanzas for soloist

"Dona Nobis Pacem" (John)
C297, E712, EL753, G752, UM376 (PD)

"God Is Good, All the Time" (John)
AH4010, WS3026

"Oceans" ("Where Feet May Fail") 6428767 (John)

"Here at the Cross" 7046292 (John, Easter)

Vocal Solos

"Just a Closer Walk with Thee" (1 John)
     V-8   p. 323

"Great Things" (1 John, Easter)
     V-9   p. 36

"I Know That My Redeemer Liveth" (John, Easter)
     V-2

"I Know That My Redeemer Lives" (John, Easter)
     V-5 (2)   p. 22

"Love Moved First" (John)
     V-9   p. 56

Anthems

"Umoja Tunaimba" (Acts, Pss)
Victor C. Johnson; Hope C6355
SATB, piano, opt. percussion (https://bit.ly/C-6355)

"Hine Ma Tov" (Pss)
Neil Ginsberg; Santa Barbara Music Publishing SBMP286
SATB, piano, opt. flute (https://bit.ly/SBMP-286)

Other Suggestions

Visuals:

Acts	Offering plates filled with money
P	Oil, clasped hands, dew
E	Light/darkness, water (cleansing), briefcase (advocate), 1 John 2:1b
G	Lock, wind (breath) (Holy Spirit), risen Christ, question mark, dove, peace

Introit: CG203, G252, EL374, WS3086, stanza 2. "Day of Arising" (John)

Response: C260, N288, UM503. "Let It Breathe on Me" (John)

See The Abingdon Worship Annual 2024 *for more ideas.*

Theme Ideas: Baptism, Doubt, Faith, God: Love of God, Holy Spirit, Light, Resurrection, Sin and Forgiveness, Unity

Acts 3:12-19

[12]When Peter saw it, he addressed the people, "Fellow Israelites, why do you wonder at this, or why do you stare at us, as though by our own power or piety we had made him walk? [13]The God of Abraham and Isaac and Jacob, the God of our ancestors, has glorified his servant Jesus, whom you handed over and rejected in the presence of Pilate, though he had decided to release him. [14]But you rejected the holy and righteous one and asked to have a murderer given to you, [15]and you killed the author of life, whom God raised from the dead. To this we are witnesses. [16]And by faith in his name, his name itself has made this man strong, whom you see and know, and the faith that is through Jesus has given him this perfect health in the presence of all of you.

[17]"And now, brothers and sisters, I know that you acted in ignorance, as did also your rulers. [18]In this way God fulfilled what he had foretold through all the prophets, that his Messiah would suffer. [19]Repent, therefore, and turn to God so that your sins may be wiped out."

Psalm 4 (G776, N622, P160, SH478, UM741)

Answer me when I call, O God of my right!
    You gave me room when I was in distress.
    Be gracious to me, and hear my prayer.
[2]How long, you people, shall my honor suffer shame?
    How long will you love vain words and seek after lies? *Selah*
[3]But know that the LORD has set apart the faithful for himself;
    the LORD hears when I call to him.
[4]When you are disturbed, do not sin;
    ponder it on your beds, and be silent. *Selah*
[5]Offer right sacrifices,
    and put your trust in the LORD.
[6]There are many who say, "O that we might see some good!
    Let the light of your face shine on us, O LORD!"
[7]You have put gladness in my heart
    more than when their grain and wine abound.
[8]I will both lie down and sleep in peace,
    for you alone, O LORD, make me lie down in safety.

1 John 3:1-7

See what love the Father has given us, that we should be called children of God, and that is what we are. The reason the world does not know us is that it did not know him. [2]Beloved, we are God's children now; what we will be has not yet been revealed. What we do know is this: when he is revealed, we will be like him, for we will see him as he is. [3]And all who have this hope in him purify themselves, just as he is pure.

[4]Everyone who commits sin is guilty of lawlessness; sin is lawlessness. [5]You know that he was revealed to take away sins, and in him there is no sin. [6]No one who abides in him sins; no one who sins has either seen him or known him. [7]Little children, let no one deceive you. Everyone who does what is right is righteous, just as he is righteous.

Luke 24:36b-48

[36b]Jesus himself stood among them and said to them, "Peace be with you." [37]They were startled and terrified and thought that they were seeing a ghost. [38]He said to them, "Why are you frightened, and why do doubts arise in your hearts? [39]Look at my hands and my feet; see that it is I myself. Touch me and see, for a ghost does not have flesh and bones as you see that I have." [40]And when he had said this, he showed them his hands and his feet. [41]Yet for all their joy they were still disbelieving and wondering, and he said to them, "Have you anything here to eat?" [42]They gave him a piece of broiled fish, [43]and he took it and ate in their presence.

[44]Then he said to them, "These are my words that I spoke to you while I was still with you—that everything written about me in the law of Moses, the prophets, and the psalms must be fulfilled." [45]Then he opened their minds to understand the scriptures, [46]and he said to them, "Thus it is written, that the Messiah is to suffer and to rise from the dead on the third day [47]and that repentance and forgiveness of sins is to be proclaimed in his name to all nations, beginning from Jerusalem. [48]You are witnesses of these things."

Primary Hymns and Songs for the Day
"This Joyful Eastertide" (John) (O)
    E192, EL391, G244, N232, SA234, VU177
        H-3   Hbl-48; Chr-199; Desc-102; Org-170
"I Greet Thee, Who My Sure Redeemer Art" (Acts)
    G624, N251, P457, VU393
"Great Is Thy Faithfulness" (Acts)
    AH4011, C86, CG48, EL733, G39, N423, P276, SA26, SH48,
    UM140, VU288
        H-3   Chr-87; Desc-39; Org-39
        S-2   #59. Piano arrangement
"Precious Lord, Take My Hand" (Acts)
    C628, CG400, EL773, G834, N472, SH336, UM474, VU670
        H-3   Chr-164; Org-116
"The Strife Is O'er, the Battle Done" (1 John, Luke)
    C221, E208, EL366, G236, N242, P119, SA233, SH193,
    UM306, VU159
        H-3   Hbl-97; Chr-191; Desc-102; Org-169
        S-1   #344. Descant idea
        S-2   #190. Descant
"Let Us Talents and Tongues Employ" (Luke)
    C422, CG458, EL674, G526, N347, P514, VU468
        H-3   Hbl-75; Chr-127
"Be Thou My Vision" (Acts, 1 John, Luke) (C)
    C595, CG71, E488, EL793, G450, N451, P339, SA573, SH640,
    UM451, VU642
        H-3   Hbl-15, 48; Chr-36; Org-153
        S-1   #319. Arr. for organ and voices
"Christ Is Alive" (Acts, Luke) (C)
    CG205, E182, EL389, G246, P108, SA217, UM318, VU158
        H-3   Hbl-50; Chr-47; Desc-101; Org-167
        S-1   #334-335. Descant and harmonization

Additional Hymn Suggestions
"God of Grace and God of Glory" (Acts)
    C464, CG285, E594/595, EL705, G307, N436, P420, SA814,
    SH250, UM577, VU686
"God of the Ages" (Acts)
    C725, CG62, E718, G331, N592, P262, SA19, UM698
"He Lives" (Acts, Luke)
    C226, CG622, SA847, SH198, UM310
"He Came Down" 4679219 (1 John)
    EL253, G137, S2085, SH88
"Baptized in Water" (1 John, Baptism)
    CG449, E294, EL456, G482, P492, S2248, SH666
"Jesus, the Very Thought of Thee" (1 John, Luke)
    C102, CG386, EL754, G629, N507, P310, SA85, UM175
"Alleluia, Alleluia" 32376 (Luke, Easter)
    CG196, E178, G240, P106, SA216, SH189, UM162, VU179
"Thine Be the Glory" (Luke) (O)
    C218, CG222, EL376, G238, N253, P122, SA276, SH192,
    UM308, VU173 (Fr.)
"Come, Ye Faithful, Raise the Strain" (Luke)
    C215, CG218, E199, EL363, G234, N230, P115, UM315 (PD),
    VU165
"Blessed Jesus, at Thy Word" (Luke)
    E440, EL520, G395, N74, P454, UM596 (PD), VU500
"Here, O My Lord, I See Thee" (Luke, Comm.)
    C416, CG460, E318, G517, N336, P520, UM623, VU459
"Enviado Soy de Dios" ("Sent Out in Jesus' Name") 6290823
    (Luke)
    EL538, G747, S2184, SH718
"Healer of Our Every Ill" (Luke)
    C506, EL612, G795, S2213, SH339, VU619
"The Spirit Sends Us Forth to Serve" (Luke)
    CG520, EL551, S2241
"Come, Share the Lord" (Luke, Comm.)
    C408, CG459, G510, S2269, VU469

"Day of Arising" (Luke)
    CG203, G252, EL374, WS3086
"Go to the World" (Luke)
    CG481, G295, SH720, VU420, WS3158

Additional Contemporary and Modern Suggestions
"We Bring the Sacrifice of Praise" 9990 (Pss)
"Please Enter My Heart, Hosanna" 2485371 (Pss)
"Refresh My Heart" 917518 (Pss)
"Lead Me, Lord" 1609045 (Pss)
"Santo, Santo, Santo" ("Holy, Holy, Holy") (1 John)
    C111, CG3, EL473, G595, N793, S2007, SH452
"Holy, Holy" 18792 (1 John)
    P140, S2039
"Celebrate Love" 155246 (1 John)
"Behold, What Manner of Love" 1596 (1 John)
"Love Moves You" ("Love Alone") 5775514 (1 John)
"Open the Eyes of My Heart" 2298355 (Luke)
    G452, SA270, SH378, WS3008
"Celebrate Jesus" 16859 (Luke, Easter)
"Jesus Is Alive" 550652 (Luke, Easter)
"Open Our Eyes, Lord" 1572 (Luke)
    CG392, S2086, SA386, SH562
"Confitemini Domino" ("Come and Fill Our Hearts") (Luke)
    EL538, G466, S2157
"Turn Your Eyes upon Jesus" 15960 (Luke)
    CG472, SA445, UM349

Vocal Solos
"Author Of Life Divine" (Acts)
    V-1   p. 39
"Safe Within Your Arms" (1 John 3, Luke)
    V-3 (3)   p. 44
"You Keep Hope Alive" (1 John 3, Easter)
    V-9   p. 132
"I Walked Today Where Jesus Walked" (Luke, Easter)
    V-8   p. 14

Anthems
"To Sing Once More" (Acts, 1 John, Luke)
Craig Courtney; Beckenhorst BP2267
SATB, piano (https://bit.ly/BP2267)

"Day of Arising" (Luke)
Schalk/Burkhardt; MorningStar MSM-50-4067
2-part, organ, opt. oboe or clarinet (https://bit.ly/MS-4067)

Other Suggestions
Visuals:
    Acts   Portrait of Christ crucified, risen, names given to
                Jesus, eraser (forgiveness)
    P   Praying hands, person pondering, light, rejoicing
    E   Children, risen Christ, 1 John 3:1
    G   Risen Christ, fear, broiled fish, open Bible, Luke
                24:36c, 48, witnessing
Introit: EL529, G392, S2273, SH611. "Jesus, We Are Here"
    (Luke)
Call to Prayer: C305, CG389, G469, S2193, SH577, VU400.
    "Lord, Listen to Your Children" (Pss)
Response: CG399, EL751, G471, S2200, SH311/517. "O Lord,
    Hear My Prayer" (Pss)
Response: C24, CG45, E401, EL831, G49, N24, P488, SH50,
    UM116 (PD), VU255, Stanza 1. "The God of Abraham
    Praise" (Acts)
Prayer of Thanksgiving: UM553 (Acts)
Theme Ideas: Communion, God: Guidance, God: Love of God,
    Grace, Holy Spirit, Jesus: Jesus our Savior, Repentance,
    Resurrection

Acts 4:5-12

[5]The next day their rulers, elders, and scribes assembled in Jerusalem, [6]with Annas the high priest, Caiaphas, John, and Alexander, and all who were of the high-priestly family. [7]When they had made the prisoners stand in their midst, they inquired, "By what power or by what name did you do this?" [8]Then Peter, filled with the Holy Spirit, said to them, "Rulers of the people and elders, [9]if we are being questioned today because of a good deed done to someone who was sick and are being asked how this man has been healed, [10]let it be known to all of you, and to all the people of Israel, that this man is standing before you in good health by the name of Jesus Christ of Nazareth, whom you crucified, whom God raised from the dead. [11]This Jesus is

'the stone that was rejected by you, the builders;
it has become the cornerstone.'

[12]"There is salvation in no one else, for there is no other name under heaven given among mortals by which we must be saved."

Psalm 23 (N633, P170-175, SH295/307, UM754)

The LORD is my shepherd; I shall not want.
[2]He makes me lie down in green pastures;
he leads me beside still waters;
[3]he restores my soul.
He leads me in right paths
for his name's sake.
[4]Even though I walk through the darkest valley,
I fear no evil,
for you are with me;
your rod and your staff,
they comfort me.
[5]You prepare a table before me
in the presence of my enemies;
you anoint my head with oil;
my cup overflows.
[6]Surely goodness and mercy shall follow me
all the days of my life,
and I shall dwell in the house of the LORD
my whole life long.

1 John 3:16-24

[16]We know love by this, that he laid down his life for us—and we ought to lay down our lives for the brothers and sisters. [17]How does God's love abide in anyone who has the world's goods and sees a brother or sister in need and yet refuses help?

[18]Little children, let us love not in word or speech but in deed and truth. [19]And by this we will know that we are from the truth and will reassure our hearts before him [20]whenever our hearts condemn us, for God is greater than our hearts, and he knows everything. [21]Beloved, if our hearts do not condemn us, we have boldness before God, [22]and we receive from him whatever we ask, because we obey his commandments and do what pleases him.

[23]And this is his commandment, that we should believe in the name of his Son Jesus Christ and love one another, just as he has commanded us. [24]All who obey his commandments abide in him, and he abides in them. And by this we know that he abides in us, by the Spirit that he has given us.

John 10:11-18

[11]"I am the good shepherd. The good shepherd lays down his life for the sheep. [12]The hired hand, who is not the shepherd and does not own the sheep, sees the wolf coming and leaves the sheep and runs away, and the wolf snatches them and scatters them. [13]The hired hand runs away because a hired hand does not care for the sheep. [14]I am the good shepherd. I know my own, and my own know me, [15]just as the Father knows me, and I know the Father. And I lay down my life for the sheep. [16]I have other sheep that do not belong to this fold. I must bring them also, and they will listen to my voice. So there will be one flock, one shepherd. [17]For this reason the Father loves me, because I lay down my life in order to take it up again. [18]No one takes it from me, but I lay it down of my own accord. I have power to lay it down, and I have power to take it up again. I have received this command from my Father."

Primary Hymns and Songs for the Day
"O For a Thousand Tongues to Sing" (Acts, 1 John, John)
   C5, CG332, E493, EL886, G610, N42, P466, SA89, SH439,
   UM57 (PD), VU326 (See also WS3001)
         H-3   Hbl-79; Chr-142; Desc-17; Org-12
         S-1   #33-38. Various Treatments
"The King of Love My Shepherd Is" (Pss, 1 John, John)
   CG64, E645, EL502, G802, P171, SA61, SH359, UM138 (PD),
   VU273
         H-3   Hbl-96; Chr-188, 221; Desc-93; Org-135
         S-1   #298-299. Harmonizations
"Because You Live, O Christ" (Pss, John)
   G249, N231, P105
         H-3   Hbl-48; Chr-199; Desc-102; Org-170
"Savior, Like a Shepherd Lead Us" (Pss, John)
   C558, CG405, E708, EL789, G187, N252, P387, SH538,
   UM381 (PD)
         H-3   Chr-167; Org-15
         S-2   #29. Harmonization
"Lead Me, Guide Me" (Pss)
   C583, CG403, EL768, G740, S2214, SH582
"Shepherd Me, O God" (Pss, John)
   EL780, G473, S2058, SH365
"Guide My Feet" (1 John, John)
   CG637, G741, N497, P354, S2208, SH54
"My Life Flows On" (1 John, John)
   C619, CG592, EL763, G821, N476, S2212, SA663, VU716
"I Heard the Voice of Jesus Say" (John)
   CG577, E692, EL611, G182, N489, SA424, SH127, VU626
         H-3   Hbl-15, 20, 34, 84; Chr-150; Org-67
         S-2   #100-103. Various treatments
"Christ Is Made the Sure Foundation" (Acts) (C)
   C275, E518, EL645, G394, P416, SA246, SH225, UM559,
   VU325
         H-3   Chr-49; Desc-103; Org-180
         S-1   #346. Descant
   CG248, N400, P417
"How Firm a Foundation" (Acts) (C)
   C618, CG425, E636/637, EL796, G463, N407, P361, SA804,
   SH291, UM529 (PD), VU660
         H-3   Hbl-27, 69; Chr-102; Desc-41; Org-41
         S-1   #133. Harmonization
                 #134. Performance note

Additional Hymn Suggestions
"Alleluia, Alleluia" 32376 (Acts, Easter)
   CG196, E178, G240, P106, SA216, SH189, UM162, VU179
"The Church's One Foundation" (Acts)
   C272, CG246, E525, EL654, G321, N386, P442, SH233,
   UM545/546, VU332 (Fr.)
"Healer of Our Every Ill" (Acts, 1 John)
   C506, EL612, G795, S2213, SH339, VU619
"He Leadeth Me: O Blessed Thought" (Pss) (O)
   C545, CG68, SA645, SH304, UM128 (PD), VU657
"The Lord's My Shepherd, I'll Not Want" (Pss)
   C78/79, CG65, EL778, G801, N479, P170, SA62, SH375,
   UM136, VU747/748
"Precious Lord, Take My Hand" (Pss)
   C628, CG400, EL773, G834, N472, SH336, UM474, VU670
"Send Me, Lord" (Pss)
   C447, EL809, G746, N360, SH723, UM497, VU572
"My Shepherd Will Supply My Need" (Pss)
   C80, CG66, E664, EL782 (PD), G803, N247, P172, SH44
"Abide with Me" (Pss, 1 John, John) (C)
   C636, CG543, E662, EL629, G836, N99, P543, SA529, SH475,
   UM700 (PD), VU436
"Where Charity and Love Prevail" (1 John)
   CG264, E581, EL359, G316, N396, SH271, UM549

"My Song Is Love Unknown" (1 John)
   E458, EL343, G209, N222, P76, S2083, SA149, VU143
"Here Am I" (1 John)
   C654, S2178
"I Am Thine, O Lord" (John)
   AH4087, C601, CG504, N455, SA586, UM419 (PD)

Additional Contemporary and Modern Suggestions
"Praise the Name of Jesus" 12712 (Acts)
"Grace Alone" 2335524 (Acts)
   CG43, S2162, SA699.
"Cornerstone" 6158927 (Acts)
"What A Beautiful Name" 7068424 (Acts)
"We Believe" 6367165 (Acts)
"Nada Te Turbe" ("Nothing Can Trouble") (Pss)
   CG73, G820, N772, S2054, SH292, VU290
"God Is Good All the Time" 1729073 (Pss)
"The King of Love My Shepherd Is" 7023979 (Pss)
"For Us" 7119349 (Pss, John)
"Gentle Shepherd" 15609 (Pss, John)
"Your Grace Is Enough" 4477026 (Pss)
"God Will Make a Way" 458620 (Pss)
"You Never Let Go" 4674166 (Pss)
"I Have a Hope" 5087587 (Pss)
"Jesus, Draw Me Close" 443680 (1 John)
"Ubi Caritas" ("Live in Charity") (1 John)
   C523, EL642, G205, S2179
"They'll Know We Are Christians" 26997 (1 John)
   AH4074, C494, CG272, G300, S2223, SH232
"Make Us One" 695737 (1 John)
"Bind Us Together" 1228 (1 John)
"Let It Be Said of Us" 1855882 (1 John)
"I Could Sing of Your Love Forever" 1043199 (1 John)
"His Name Is Wonderful" 1122230 (1 John)
"People Need the Lord" 18084 (1 John, John)

Vocal Solos
"How Firm a Foundation" (Acts)
   V-6   p. 31
"The Lord is My Shepherd" (Pss)
   V-5 (3)   p. 30
"God, Our Ever Faithful Shepherd" (Pss, 1 John)
   V-4   p. 15
"Famous For" ("I Believe") (Pss, John)
   V-9   p. 22

Anthems
"How Firm a Foundation" (Acts)
Arr. Craig Courtney; Beckenhorst BP2271
SATB, piano (https://bit.ly/BP-2271)

"The Lamb" (Pss)
John Ferguson; Augsburg 9781506447544
SATB, organ, opt. clarinet (https://bit.ly/AF-47544)

Other Suggestions
Visuals:
   Acts   Stone, cornerstone
   P   Shepherd, Christ as a shepherd, sheep, water, path
   E   Cross, people sacrificing for others, pitcher/bowl/
            towel
   G   Christ the Shepherd, sheep, wolf, crucifix, John 10:11
Bilingual Sung Response: SH294/613. *"El Señor es mi pastor"*
   ("The Lord is My Shepherd") (Pss)
For more ideas, see The Abingdon Worship Annual 2024.
Theme Ideas: God: Love of God, God: Shepherd, Jesus:
   Cornerstone, Jesus: Jesus our Savior, Love / Great
   Commandment

Do you have the planner you need?

We want you to have the best planner, designed to meet your specific needs. How do you know if you have the right resource? Simply complete this one-question quiz:

Do you lead worship in a United Methodist congregation?

Yes?
Use *The United Methodist Music and Worship Planner 2024–2025*
(CEB Edition—ISBN: 9781791015602; eBook– ISBN: 9781791015619)
(NRSVue Edition—ISBN: 9781791015626; eBook– ISBN: 9781791015633)

No?
Use *Prepare! An Ecumenical Music and Worship Planner 2024–2025*
(CEB Edition—ISBN: 9781791015725; eBook– ISBN: 9781791015732)
(NRSVue Edition—ISBN: 9781791015749; eBook– ISBN: 9781791015756)

**TO ORDER THESE RESOURCES, CALL COKESBURY
TOLL FREE AT 800-672-1789 OR SHOP ONLINE AT COKESBURY.COM.**

**Do you find yourself rushing at the last minute to order your new planner?
Subscribe today and receive your new *The United Methodist Music and Worship
Planner* or *Prepare!* automatically next year and every year.
Call toll free 800-672-1789 to request a subscription.**

MORE TIME TO DO WHAT YOU DO BEST

2024 worship and preaching annuals make planning easy and efficient, helping to add freshness and relevancy to worship.

The Abingdon Worship Annual 2024

The go-to worship planning resource for all who plan weekly worship. Helpful Christian Year reminders.
9781791027049;
eBook 9781791027056

The Abingdon Preaching Annual 2024

The local pastor's go-to resource for weekly sermon planning. Follows the calendar year.
9781791027063;
eBook 9781791027070

Acts 8:26-40

[26]Then an angel of the Lord said to Philip, "Get up and go toward the south to the road that goes down from Jerusalem to Gaza." (This is a wilderness road.) [27]So he got up and went. Now there was an Ethiopian eunuch, a court official of the Candace, the queen of the Ethiopians, in charge of her entire treasury. He had come to Jerusalem to worship [28]and was returning home; seated in his chariot, he was reading the prophet Isaiah. [29]Then the Spirit said to Philip, "Go over to this chariot and join it." [30]So Philip ran up to it and heard him reading the prophet Isaiah. He asked, "Do you understand what you are reading?" [31]He replied, "How can I, unless someone guides me?" And he invited Philip to get in and sit beside him. [32]Now the passage of the scripture that he was reading was this:

"Like a sheep he was led to the slaughter,
    and like a lamb silent before its shearer,
    so he does not open his mouth.
[33]In his humiliation justice was denied him.
    Who can describe his generation?
    For his life is taken away from the earth."

[34]The eunuch asked Philip, "About whom, may I ask you, does the prophet say this, about himself or about someone else?" [35]Then Philip began to speak, and starting with this scripture he proclaimed to him the good news about Jesus. [36]As they were going along the road, they came to some water, and the eunuch said, "Look, here is water! What is to prevent me from being baptized?" [38]He commanded the chariot to stop, and both of them, Philip and the eunuch, went down into the water, and Philip baptized him. [39]When they came up out of the water, the Spirit of the Lord snatched Philip away; the eunuch saw him no more and went on his way rejoicing. [40]But Philip found himself at Azotus, and as he was passing through the region he proclaimed the good news to all the towns until he came to Caesarea.

Psalm 22:25-31 (G631, N632, P168, UM752)

[25]From you comes my praise in the great congregation;
    my vows I will pay before those who fear him.
[26]The poor shall eat and be satisfied;
    those who seek him shall praise the Lord.
    May your hearts live forever!
[27]All the ends of the earth shall remember
    and turn to the Lord,
and all the families of the nations
    shall worship before him.
[28]For dominion belongs to the Lord,
    and he rules over the nations.
[29]To him, indeed, shall all who sleep in the earth bow down;
    before him shall bow all who go down to the dust,
    and I shall live for him.
[30]Posterity will serve him;
    future generations will be told about the Lord
[31]and proclaim his deliverance to a people yet unborn,
    saying that he has done it.

1 John 4:7-21

[7]Beloved, let us love one another, because love is from God; everyone who loves is born of God and knows God. [8]Whoever does not love does not know God, for God is love. [9]God's love was revealed among us in this way: God sent his only Son into the world so that we might live through him. [10]In this is love, not that we loved God but that he loved us and sent his Son to be the atoning sacrifice for our sins. [11]Beloved, since God loved us so much, we also ought to love one another. [12]No one has ever seen God; if we love one another, God abides in us, and his love is perfected in us.

[13]By this we know that we abide in him and he in us, because he has given us of his Spirit. [14]And we have seen and do testify that the Father has sent his Son as the Savior of the world. [15]God abides in those who confess that Jesus is the Son of God, and they abide in God. [16]So we have known and believe the love that God has for us.

God is love, and those who abide in love abide in God, and God abides in them. [17]Love has been perfected among us in this: that we may have boldness on the day of judgment, because as he is, so are we in this world. [18]There is no fear in love, but perfect love casts out fear; for fear has to do with punishment, and whoever fears has not reached perfection in love. [19]We love because he first loved us. [20]Those who say, "I love God," and hate a brother or sister are liars, for those who do not love a brother or sister, whom they have seen, cannot love God, whom they have not seen. [21]The commandment we have from him is this: those who love God must love their brothers and sisters also.

John 15:1-8

"I am the true vine, and my Father is the vinegrower. [2]He removes every branch in me that bears no fruit. Every branch that bears fruit he prunes to make it bear more fruit. [3]You have already been cleansed by the word that I have spoken to you. [4]Abide in me as I abide in you. Just as the branch cannot bear fruit by itself unless it abides in the vine, neither can you unless you abide in me. [5]I am the vine; you are the branches. Those who abide in me and I in them bear much fruit, because apart from me you can do nothing. [6]Whoever does not abide in me is thrown away like a branch and withers; such branches are gathered, thrown into the fire, and burned. [7]If you abide in me and my words abide in you, ask for whatever you wish, and it will be done for you. [8]My Father is glorified by this, that you bear much fruit and become my disciples.

Primary Hymns and Songs for the Day
"Gather Us In" (Acts, 1 John, Comm.) (O)
  C284, EL532, G401, S2236, SH393
"Love Divine, All Loves Excelling" (Acts, 1 John, John) (O)
  C517, CG281, E657, EL631, G366, N43, P376, SA262,
  SH353/354, UM384 (PD), VU333
    H-3 Hbl-46; Chr-26, 134; Desc-53; Org-56
    S-1 #168-171. Various treatments
"We Know That Christ Is Raised" (Acts, Baptism)
  E296, EL449, G485, P495, UM610, VU448
    H-3 Hbl-100; Chr-214; Desc-38; Org-37
    S-1 #118-127. Various treatments
"Take Me to the Water" (Acts, Baptism)
  AH4045, C367, G480, N322, SH665, WS3165
"All Who Hunger" (Acts, John, Comm.)
  C419, CG303, EL461, G509, S2126, VU460
    H-3 Chr-80; Desc-52
    S-1 #160-162. Various treatments
    S-2 #87-88. Brass and timpani
"Lord, I Want to Be a Christian" (Acts, 1 John, John)
  C589, CG507, G729, N454, P372 (PD), SH621, UM402
    H-3 Chr-130
"Christ Is Alive" (Acts, 1 John) (C)
  CG205, E182, EL389, G246, P108, SA217, UM318, VU158
"A Place at the Table" (Acts, 1 John) (C)
  G769, WS3149

Additional Hymn Suggestions
"Swing Low, Sweet Chariot" (Acts)
  C643, G825, UM703
"Loving Spirit" (Acts)
  C244, EL397, G293, P323, S2123, VU387
"Deep in the Shadows of the Past" (Acts)
  G50, N320, P330, S2246
"Wonder of Wonders" (Acts, Baptism)
  C378, G489, N328, P499, S2247
"Baptized in Water" (Acts, Baptism)
  CG449, E294, EL456, G482, P492, S2248, SH666
"All Who Love and Serve Your City" (Acts, Pss)
  C670, E570/571, EL724, G351, P413, UM433
"Stand Up, and Bless the Lord" (Pss, 1 John)
  CG299, P491, SA391, UM662 (PD)
"For the Beauty of the Earth" (1 John)
  C56, CG341, E416, EL879, G14, P473, N28, SA14, SH21,
  UM92 (PD), VU226
"To God Be the Glory" (1 John)
  C72, CG349, G634, P485, SA279, SH545, UM98 (PD)
"There's a Wideness in God's Mercy" (1 John)
  C73, CG41, E470, EL587/88G435, N23, P298, SH526,
  UM121, VU271
"My Jesus, I Love Thee" (1 John)
  C349, CG361, SA878, SH303, UM172 (PD)
"Jesu, Thy Boundless Love to Me" (1 John)
  G703, P366, UM183, VU631
"Where Charity and Love Prevail" (1 John)
  CG264, E581, EL359, G316, N396, SH271, UM549
"O Perfect Love" (1 John)
  P533, SA780, UM645, VU491
"Healer of Our Every Ill" (1 John)
  C506, EL612, G795, S2213, SH339, VU619
"Source and Sovereign, Rock and Cloud" (1 John, John)
  C12, G11, UM113
"I Need Thee Every Hour" (John)
  C578, CG404, G735, N517, SA707, UM397, VU671
    H-3 Chr-107
"Like the Murmur of the Dove's Song" (John)
  C245, CG233, E513, EL403, G285, N270, P314, SH407,
  UM544, VU205

"Mothering God, You Gave Me Birth" (John)
  C83, N467, S2050, VU320
"God the Sculptor of the Mountains" (John)
  EL736, G5, S2060
"Canto de Esperanza" ("Song of Hope") (John) (C)
  G765, P432, S2186, SH721, VU424

Additional Contemporary and Modern Suggestions
"I've Just Come from the Fountain" (Acts, Baptism)
  S2250
"Taste and See" (Pss, Comm.)
  EL493, G520, S2267, SH691
"Ancient of Days" 798108 (Pss)
"Great Is the Lord" 1149 (1 John)
  CG325, G614, S2022, SH459
"Celebrate Love" 155246 (1 John)
"Ubi Caritas" ("Live in Charity") (1 John)
  C523, EL642, G205, S2179
"They'll Know We Are Christians" 26997 (1 John)
  AH4074, C494, CG272, G300, S2223, SH232
"Make Us One" 695737 (1 John)
"Bind Us Together" 1228 (1 John)
"You Are My King" ("Amazing Love") 2456623 (1 John)
"Love Moves You" ("Love Alone") 5775514 (1 John)
"No Greater Love" 930887 (1 John)
"I Could Sing of Your Love Forever" 1043199 (1 John)
"Foundation" 706151 (1 John, John)
"For Us" 7119349 (1 John, John)
"Love Moves You" ("Love Alone") 5775514 (1 John, John)
"Hosanna" 4785835 (John)
"Lord, Be Glorified" 26368 (John)
  EL744, G468, S2150, SA593, SH420
"Be Glorified" 429226 (John)
"Be Glorified" 2732646 (John)

Vocal Solos
"Wash, O God, Our Sons and Daughters" (Acts, Baptism)
  V-5 (1)   p. 64
"God So Loved" (Pss, 1 John)
  V-9   p. 28
"Wondrous Love" (1 John)
  V-6   p. 47
"I Am the Vine" (John)
  V-8   p. 280

Anthems
"Let Us Love One Another" (1 John)
Mark Sirett; Augsburg 978-1-5064-6361-2
SATB, organ (https://bit.ly/6361-2)

"Let Us Love One Another" (1 John)
Arnold Sherman; Lorenz S5781
Two-part, keyboard, opt. C-instrument (https://bit.ly/L-5781)

Other Suggestions
Visuals:
  Acts   Open scroll/Bible open to Isaiah, water (baptism)
  P   Poor being fed, globe, flags of nations, earth from
              space
  E   Cross, sacrificial love, Christ, 1 John 4:16b, 18a
  G   Grapevine, grapes, pruned branches, fire, John 15:5
Prayer: UM401. For Holiness of Heart (1 John)
Prayer: WSL28. "Eternal God" (John)
Baptism Prayer: WSL212. "Deep, flowing mystery" (Acts)
Theme Ideas: Baptism, Connection, God: Glory of God, God:
  Love of God, Growth, Jesus: Jesus our Savior, Love / Great
  Commandment

Acts 10:44-48

[44]While Peter was still speaking, the Holy Spirit fell upon all who heard the word. [45]The circumcised believers who had come with Peter were astounded that the gift of the Holy Spirit had been poured out even on the gentiles, [46]for they heard them speaking in tongues and extolling God. Then Peter said, [47]"Can anyone withhold the water for baptizing these people who have received the Holy Spirit just as we have?" [48]So he ordered them to be baptized in the name of Jesus Christ. Then they invited him to stay for several days.

Psalm 98 (G276, N686, P219, UM818)

O sing to the Lord a new song,
     for he has done marvelous things.
His right hand and his holy arm
     have gotten him victory.
[2]The Lord has made known his victory;
     he has revealed his vindication in the sight of the nations.
[3]He has remembered his steadfast love and faithfulness
     to the house of Israel.
All the ends of the earth have seen
     the victory of our God.
[4]Make a joyful noise to the Lord, all the earth;
     break forth into joyous song and sing praises.
[5]Sing praises to the Lord with the lyre,
     with the lyre and the sound of melody.
[6]With trumpets and the sound of the horn
     make a joyful noise before the King, the Lord.
[7]Let the sea roar and all that fills it,
     the world and those who live in it.
[8]Let the floods clap their hands;
     let the hills sing together for joy
[9]at the presence of the Lord, for he is coming
     to judge the earth.
He will judge the world with righteousness
     and the peoples with equity.

1 John 5:1-6

Everyone who believes that Jesus is the Christ has been born of God, and everyone who loves the parent loves the child. [2]By this we know that we love the children of God, when we love God and obey his commandments. [3]For the love of God is this, that we obey his commandments. And his commandments are not burdensome, [4]for whatever is born of God conquers the world. And this is the victory that conquers the world, our faith. [5]Who is it who conquers the world but the one who believes that Jesus is the Son of God?

[6]This is the one who came by water and blood, Jesus Christ, not with the water only but with the water and the blood. And the Spirit is the one that testifies, for the Spirit is the truth.

John 15:9-17

[9]As the Father has loved me, so I have loved you; abide in my love. [10]If you keep my commandments, you will abide in my love, just as I have kept my Father's commandments and abide in his love. [11]I have said these things to you so that my joy may be in you and that your joy may be complete.

[12]"This is my commandment, that you love one another as I have loved you. [13]No one has greater love than this, to lay down one's life for one's friends. [14]You are my friends if you do what I command you. [15]I do not call you servants any longer, because the servant does not know what the master is doing, but I have called you friends, because I have made known to you everything that I have heard from my Father. [16]You did not choose me, but I chose you. And I appointed you to go and bear fruit, fruit that will last, so that the Father will give you whatever you ask him in my name. [17]I am giving you these commands so that you may love one another."

Primary Hymns and Songs for the Day
"I Come with Joy" (Acts, 1 John, John, Comm.) (O)
    C420, CG456, E304, EL482, G515, N349, P507, SH682,
    UM617, VU477
        H-3   Hbl-70; Chr-105; Org-30
        S-2   #52. Choral and keyboard arrangement
"Come, Thou Fount of Every Blessing" (Acts)
    AH4086, C16, CG295/559, E686, EL807, G475, N459, P356,
    SA830, SH394, UM400 (PD), VU559
        H-3   Chr-57; Desc-79; Org-96
        S-1   #244. Descant
"Baptized in Water" (Acts, 1 John, Baptism)
    CG449, E294, EL456, G482, P492, S2248, SH666
"Lord, Make Us More Holy" (Acts, 1 John, John)
    G313, N75 (PD), P536
"There's a Wideness in God's Mercy" (Acts, John)
    C73, CG41, E470, EL587/88G435, N23, P298, SH526,
    UM121, VU271
        H-3   Chr-195; Desc-102; Org-179
"The Summons" (Acts John) (C)
    CG473, EL798, G726, S2130, SA695, SH598, VU567
        H-3   Chr-220
"Blest Be the Tie That Binds" (Acts, John) (C)
    C433, CG267, EL656, G306, N393, P438, SA812, SH701,
    UM557 (PD), VU602

Additional Hymn Suggestions
"Spirit of the Living God" 23488 (Acts)
    C259, CG234, G288, N283, P322, SA312/313, SH555,
    UM393, VU376, S-1 #212 Vocal desc. idea
"Like the Murmur of the Dove's Song" (Acts)
    C245, CG233, E513, EL403, G285, N270, P314, SH407,
    UM544, VU205
"Come Down, O Love Divine" (Acts, John)
    C582, E516, EL804, G282, N289, P313, SA295, UM475,
    VU367
"Filled with the Spirit's Power" (Acts, John)
    N266, UM537, VU194
"In Christ There Is No East or West" (Acts, John)
    C687, CG273, E529, EL650 (PD), G317/318, N394/395,
    P439/440, SA1006, SH226, UM548, VU606
"Here, O Lord, Your Servants Gather" (Acts, John)
    C278, EL530, G311, N72, P465, UM552, VU362
"Help Us Accept Each Other" (Acts, John)
    C487, G754, N388, P358, UM560
"New Songs of Celebration Render" (Pss)
    CG327, E413, G371, SH442, P218
"To God Be the Glory" (Pss, 1 John)
    C72, CG349, G634, P485, SA279, SH545, UM98 (PD)
"Blessed Assurance" (1 John)
    AH4083, C543, CG619, EL638, G839, N473, P341, SA455,
    SH320, UM369 (PD), VU337
"For the Healing of the Nations" (1 John)
    C668, CG698, G346, N576, SA1000, UM428, VU678
"Take Time to Be Holy" (John)
    C572, SA790, UM395 (PD), VU672
"What a Friend We Have in Jesus" (John)
    C585, CG409, EL742, G465, N506, P403, SA795, SH585/586,
    UM526 (PD), VU661
"Blessed Quietness" (John)
    C267, CG244, N284, S2142
"Healer of Our Every Ill" (John)
    C506, EL612, G795, S2213, SH339, VU619

Additional Contemporary and Modern Suggestions
"From Ashes to Beauty" 5288953 (Acts)
"Take Me to the Water" (Acts, Baptism)
    AH4045, C367, G480, N322, SH665, WS3165
"Clap Your Hands" 806674 (Pss)

"Shout to the Lord" 1406918 (Pss)
    CG348, EL821, S2074, SA264, SH426
"Someone Asked the Question" 1640279 (Pss)
    N523, S2144
"Sing unto the Lord a New Song" 571215 (Pss)
"I Will Celebrate" 21239 (Pss)
"My Tribute" 11218 (Pss, 1 John)
    AH4080, C39, CG574, N14, SH434, UM99; V-8 p. 5. Vocal Solo
"Jesus, Draw Me Close" 443680 (1 John)
"Light of the World" 73342 (1 John)
"Goodness Is Stronger than Evil" (1 John)
    EL721, G750, S2219
"Let It Be Said of Us" 1855882 (1 John, John)
"More Love, More Power" 60661 (1 John, John)
"They'll Know We Are Christians" 26997 (John)
    AH4074, C494, CG272, G300, S2223, SH232
"Bind Us Together" 1228 (John)
"Make Us One" 695737 (John)
"Ubi Caritas" ("Live in Charity") (John)
    C523, EL642, G205, S2179
"No Greater Love" 930887 (John)
"I Could Sing of Your Love Forever" 1043199 (John)
"Dwell" 4085652 (John)

Vocal Solos
"I've Just Come from the Fountain" (Acts, Baptism)
    V-7   p. 54/59
"Praise to the Lord, the Almighty" (Pss)
    V-6   p. 18
"Shout to the Lord" (with "All Creatures of Our God and King")
    (Pss)
    V-3 (2)   p. 32
"In Remembrance" (John, Comm.)
    V-5 (2)   p. 7
"This Is My Commandment" (John)
    V-8   p. 284

Anthems
"O For a Thousand Tongues to Sing" (Acts, Pss)
Arr. Eric Nelson; MorningStar 50-9510
SATB, organ, opt. brass and timp. (https://bit.ly/MS-9510)

"Ubi Caritas" (John)
Dan Forrest; Beckenhorst DF1016
SATB, piano, opt. instruments (https://bit.ly/DF-1016)

Other Suggestions
Visuals:
    Acts   Dove/ flames (Holy Spirit), water (baptism)
    P   Lyre, sheet music, trumpet, sea, floods, hills, scales of
            justice
    E   Water, wine, symbols of the Holy Spirit
    G   Sacrificial love, cross, friendship, fruit (love enacted),
            John 15:9c
Greeting: Psalm 98:1. Sing to the Lord.
Opening Prayer: UM335 or WSL52 (Acts)
Prayer: WSL62. "Wondrous God, our hearts" (Pss)
Prayer: WSL28. "Eternal God, rock and refuge" (John)
Prayer: UM481 (1 John, John)
Response: C30, CG316, EL846, G598, N760, S2067, SH596,
    VU431. *Amen Siakudumisa* ("Amen, We Praise Your Name,
    O God") (Acts, Pss)
Canticle: UM646. "Canticle of Love" (John). See S-1, p. 387.
Baptism Prayer: WSL212. "Deep, flowing mystery" (Acts)
Theme Ideas: Communion, Fruit of the Spirit, God: Love of
    God, Holy Spirit, Love / Great Commandment, Praise, Unity

Acts 1:1-11

In the first book, Theophilus, I wrote about all that Jesus began to do and teach [2]until the day when he was taken up to heaven, after giving instructions through the Holy Spirit to the apostles whom he had chosen. [3]After his suffering he presented himself alive to them by many convincing proofs, appearing to them during forty days and speaking about the kingdom of God. [4]While staying with them, he ordered them not to leave Jerusalem but to wait there for the promise of the Father. "This," he said, "is what you have heard from me; [5]for John baptized with water, but you will be baptized with the Holy Spirit not many days from now."

[6]So when they had come together, they asked him, "Lord, is this the time when you will restore the kingdom to Israel?" [7]He replied, "It is not for you to know the times or periods that the Father has set by his own authority. [8]But you will receive power when the Holy Spirit has come upon you, and you will be my witnesses in Jerusalem, in all Judea and Samaria, and to the ends of the earth." [9]When he had said this, as they were watching, he was lifted up, and a cloud took him out of their sight. [10]While he was going and they were gazing up toward heaven, suddenly two men in white robes stood by them. [11]They said, "Men of Galilee, why do you stand looking up toward heaven? This Jesus, who has been taken up from you into heaven, will come in the same way as you saw him go into heaven."

Psalm 47 (G261, N653, P194, UM781)

Clap your hands, all you peoples;
    shout to God with loud songs of joy.
[2]For the LORD, the Most High, is awesome,
    a great king over all the earth.
[3]He subdued peoples under us
    and nations under our feet.
[4]He chose our heritage for us,
    the pride of Jacob whom he loves. *Selah*
[5]God has gone up with a shout,
    the LORD with the sound of a trumpet.
[6]Sing praises to God, sing praises;
    sing praises to our King, sing praises.
[7]For God is the king of all the earth;
    sing praises with a psalm.
[8]God is king over the nations;
    God sits on his holy throne.
[9]The princes of the peoples gather
    as the people of the God of Abraham.
For the shields of the earth belong to God;
    he is highly exalted.

Ephesians 1:15-23

[15]I have heard of your faith in the Lord Jesus and your love toward all the saints, and for this reason [16]I do not cease to give thanks for you as I remember you in my prayers, [17]that the God of our Lord Jesus Christ, the Father of glory, may give you a spirit of wisdom and revelation as you come to know him, [18]so that, with the eyes of your heart enlightened, you may perceive what is the hope to which he has called you, what are the riches of his glorious inheritance among the saints, [19]and what is the immeasurable greatness of his power for us who believe, according to the working of his great power. [20]God put this power to work in Christ when he raised him from the dead and seated him at his right hand in the heavenly places, [21]far above all rule and authority and power and dominion and above every name that is named, not only in this age but also in the age to come. [22]And he has put all things under his feet and has made him the head over all things for the church, [23]which is his body, the fullness of him who fills all in all.

Luke 24:44-53

[44]Then he said to them, "These are my words that I spoke to you while I was still with you—that everything written about me in the law of Moses, the prophets, and the psalms must be fulfilled." [45]Then he opened their minds to understand the scriptures, [46]and he said to them, "Thus it is written, that the Messiah is to suffer and to rise from the dead on the third day [47]and that repentance and forgiveness of sins is to be proclaimed in his name to all nations, beginning from Jerusalem. [48]You are witnesses of these things. [49]And see, I am sending upon you what my Father promised, so stay here in the city until you have been clothed with power from on high."

[50]Then he led them out as far as Bethany, and, lifting up his hands, he blessed them. [51]While he was blessing them, he withdrew from them and was carried up into heaven. [52]And they worshiped him and returned to Jerusalem with great joy, [53]and they were continually in the temple blessing God.

Primary Hymns and Songs for the Day

"Hail the Day that Sees Him Rise" (Acts, Luke) (O)
  CG219, E214, SA221, SH203, UM312
      H-3   Hbl-72; Chr-50; Desc-69; Org-78
      S-1   #213. Descant
  N260, VU189
"Let the Whole Creation Cry" (Acts, Eph, Luke)
  C21, EL876, G679, P256 (PD)
"A Hymn of Glory Let Us Sing" (Acts, Luke)
  E218, G258, N259, P141
"Open the Eyes of My Heart" 2298355 (Acts, Eph, Luke)
  G452, SA270, SH378, WS3008
"Awesome God" 41099 (Acts, Eph, Luke)
  G616, S2040
"Shout to the Lord" 1406918 (Pss)
  CG348, EL821, S2074, SA264, SH426
"At the Name of Jesus" (Eph)
  CG424, E435, EL416, G264, SA74, SH657, UM168, VU335
      H-3   Chr-35; Org-65
      S-2   #99. Descant
"Crown Him with Many Crowns" (Acts, Pss, Eph, Luke) (C)
  C234, CG223. E494, EL855, G268, N301, P151, SA358,
  SH208, UM327 (PD), VU211
      H-3   Hbl-55; Chr-60; Desc-30; Org-27
      S-1   #86-88. Various treatments
"Jesus Shall Reign" (Pss, Eph) (C)
  C95, CG158, E544, EL434, G265, N300, P423, SA258, SH209,
  UM157 (PD), VU330
      C95   Descant
      H-3   Hbl-29; Chr-117; Desc-31; Org-31
      S-1   #100-103. Various treatments

Additional Hymn Suggestions

"Swing Low, Sweet Chariot" (Acts)
  C643, G825, UM703
"Ask Ye What Great Thing I Know" (Acts, Luke)
  CG443, N49, UM163 (PD), VU338
"Christ, Whose Glory Fills the Skies" (Acts, Luke)
  EL553, G662, P462/463, SA249, UM173, VU336
"Thine Be the Glory" (Acts, Luke) (C)
  C218, CG222, EL376, G238, N253, P122, SA276, SH192,
  UM308, VU173 (Fr.)
"He Lives" (Acts, Luke)
  C226, CG622, SA847, SH198, UM310
"Christ Is Alive" (Acts, Luke)
  CG205, E182, EL389, G246, P108, SA217, UM318, VU158
"Up from the Grave He Arose" (Acts, Luke)
  C224, CG207, SA228, SH185, UM322 (PD)
"Hail Thee, Festival Day" (Acts, Luke)
  E216, EL394, N262, P120, UM324, VU163
"Lo, He Comes with Clouds Descending" (Acts, Luke, Ascension)
  CG100, E57/58, EL435, G348, P6, SA260, UM718, VU25
"Jesus, the Very Thought of Thee" (Eph)
  C102, CG386, EL754, G629, N507, P310, SA85, UM175
"Hope of the World" (Eph)
  C538, E472, G734, N46, P360, UM178, VU215
"My Hope Is Built" (Eph)
  AH4105, C537, CG590, EL596/597, G353, N403, P379,
  SA662, SH324, UM368 (PD)
"Come, Share the Lord" (Eph, Comm.)
  C408, CG459, G510, S2269, VU469
"Alleluia, Alleluia" 32376 (Luke, Easter)
  CG196, E178, G240, P106, SA216, SH189, UM162, VU179
"Enviado Soy de Dios" ("Sent Out in Jesus' Name") 6290823
  (Luke) (C)
  EL538, G747, S2184, SH718
"As We Gather at Your Table" (Luke, Comm.)
  EL522, N332, S2268, SH411, VU457

"I'll Fly Away" (Luke, Ascension)
  N595, S2282
"Go to the World" (Luke)
  CG481, G295, SH720, VU420, WS3158

Additional Contemporary and Modern Suggestions

"Veni Sancte Spiritus" ("Holy Spirit, Come to Us") (Acts)
  EL406, G281, S2118
"Come, Holy Spirit" 26351 (Acts)
  S2125, (See also S2124,)
"Come, Holy Spirit" 3383953 (Acts)
  WS3092 (See also SH223, WS3091)
"Kum Ba Yah" 2749763 (Acts)
  C590, G472, P338, UM494
"Holy Spirit, Rain Down" 2405227 (Acts, Eph)
"He Is Exalted" 17827 (Pss, Ascension)
  AH4082, CG342, S2070, SH423
"Forever" 3148428 (Eph)
  CG53, SA363, WS3023
"Give Me Jesus" (Eph)
  CG546, EL770, N409, SH306, WS3140
"No Sweeter Name" 4447984 (Eph)
"What A Beautiful Name" 7068424 (Eph)
"Cornerstone" 6158927 (Eph)
"Lord, I Lift Your Name on High" 117947 (Ascension)
  AH4071, CG606, EL857, S2088, SA379, SH205
"See What a Morning" 4108797 (Luke, Ascension)
"I Will Rise" 5183450 (Luke Ascension)

Vocal Solos

"Give Me Jesus" (Eph)
  V-3 (1)   p. 53
  V-7   p. 24/28
  V-8   p. 256
"Jesus Christ is Risen Today" (Ascension)
  V-1   p. 50
"If God Be For Us" from Messiah (Ascension)
  V-2
"Great Things" (Ascension)
  V-9   p. 36

Anthems

"How Great Thou Art & Majesty" (Acts, Eph, Luke)
Arr. Joel Raney; Hope C-5108
SATB, piano, opt. piano 4-hand (https://bit.ly/C-5108)

"Hail the Day that Sees Him Rise" (Ascension)
Victor C. Johnson; Lorenz 10/4348L
SAB, organ, opt. brass (https://bit.ly/L-4348)

Other Suggestions

These ideas may be used on May 12 as Ascension Sunday.
Visuals:
  Acts   Water, dove, flames, shell (baptism)
  P   Clapping hands, feet, trumpet, singing, shield
  E   Witnessing, Ascension, risen Christ, saints
  G   Bible, risen Christ, map or globe, Ascension,
              Luke 24:48
Introit: EL529, G392, S2273, SH611. "Jesus, We Are Here" (Acts)
Call to Worship: WSL35. "Let us gather" (Luke)
Prayer: UM323. The Ascension (Acts, Luke, Eph)
Response:C30, CG316, EL846, G598, N760, S2067, SH596,
  VU431. *Amen Siakudumisa* ("Amen, We Praise Your Name,
  O God") (Acts, Pss)
Theme Ideas: Discipleship / Following God, Faith, God: Call of
  God / Listening, Holy Spirit, Hope, Praise, Resurrection

Acts 1:15-17, 21-26

[15]In those days Peter stood up among the brothers and sisters (together the crowd numbered about one hundred twenty persons) and said, [16]"Brothers and sisters, the scripture had to be fulfilled, which the Holy Spirit through David foretold concerning Judas, who became a guide for those who arrested Jesus, [17]for he was numbered among us and was allotted his share in this ministry." . . .

[21]"So one of the men who have accompanied us during all the time that the Lord Jesus went in and out among us, [22]beginning from the baptism of John until the day when he was taken up from us—one of these must become a witness with us to his resurrection." [23]So they proposed two, Joseph called Barsabbas, who was also known as Justus, and Matthias. [24]Then they prayed and said, "Lord, you know everyone's heart. Show us which one of these two you have chosen [25]to take the place in this ministry and apostleship from which Judas turned aside to go to his own place." [26]And they cast lots for them, and the lot fell on Matthias, and he was added to the eleven apostles.

Psalm 1 (G457, N621, UM738)

Happy are those
    who do not follow the advice of the wicked
or take the path that sinners tread
    or sit in the seat of scoffers,
[2]but their delight is in the law of the Lord,
    and on his law they meditate day and night.
[3]They are like trees
    planted by streams of water,
which yield their fruit in its season,
    and their leaves do not wither.
In all that they do, they prosper.
[4]The wicked are not so
    but are like chaff that the wind drives away.
[5]Therefore the wicked will not stand in the judgment
    nor sinners in the congregation of the righteous,
[6]for the Lord watches over the way of the righteous,
    but the way of the wicked will perish.

1 John 5:9-13

[9]If we receive human testimony, the testimony of God is greater, for this is the testimony of God that he has testified to his Son. [10]Those who believe in the Son of God have the testimony in their hearts. Those who do not believe in God have made him a liar by not believing in the testimony that God has given concerning his Son. [11]And this is the testimony: God gave us eternal life, and this life is in his Son. [12]Whoever has the Son has life; whoever does not have the Son of God does not have life.

[13]I write these things to you who believe in the name of the Son of God, so that you may know that you have eternal life.

John 17:6-19

[6]"I have made your name known to those whom you gave me from the world. They were yours, and you gave them to me, and they have kept your word. [7]Now they know that everything you have given me is from you, [8]for the words that you gave to me I have given to them, and they have received them and know in truth that I came from you, and they have believed that you sent me. [9]I am asking on their behalf; I am not asking on behalf of the world but on behalf of those whom you gave me, because they are yours. [10]All mine are yours, and yours are mine, and I have been glorified in them. [11]And now I am no longer in the world, but they are in the world, and I am coming to you. Holy Father, protect them in your name that you have given me, so that they may be one, as we are one. [12]While I was with them, I protected them in your name that you have given me. I guarded them, and not one of them was lost except the one destined to be lost, so that the scripture might be fulfilled. [13]But now I am coming to you, and I speak these things in the world so that they may have my joy made complete in themselves. [14]I have given them your word, and the world has hated them because they do not belong to the world, just as I do not belong to the world. [15]I am not asking you to take them out of the world, but I ask you to protect them from the evil one. [16]They do not belong to the world, just as I do not belong to the world. [17]Sanctify them in the truth; your word is truth. [18]As you have sent me into the world, so I have sent them into the world. [19]And for their sakes I sanctify myself, so that they also may be sanctified in truth."

Primary Hymns and Songs for the Day

"A Mighty Fortress Is Our God" (John) (O)
    C65, CG418, E687/688, EL503/504/505, G275, N439/440,
    P259/260, SA1, SH651, UM110 (PD), VU261/262/263
        H-3   Chr-19; Desc-35; Org-34
        S-1   #111-113. Various treatments
"Arise, Your Light Is Come" (Acts, 1 John, John)
    EL314, G744, N164, P411, VU79
"Kum Ba Yah" 2749763 (1 John)
    C590, G472, P338, UM494
"What a Friend We Have in Jesus" (1 John, John)
    C585, CG409, EL742, G465, N506, P403, SA795, SH585/586,
    UM526 (PD), VU661
"Lord, Make Us More Holy" (1 John, John)
    G313, N75 (PD), P536
"Thy Word Is a Lamp" (John)
    C326, CG38, G458, UM601
"Goodness Is Stronger than Evil" (John)
    EL721, G750, S2219
"We Praise You, O God, Our Redeemer" (John)
    CG356, EL870, G612, N420, VU218
        H-3   Chr-206; Desc-61; Org-68
        S-1   #192-194. Various treatments
"Be Still, My Soul" (John) (C)
    C566, CG57, G819, N488, SH330, UM534, VU652
        H-3   Chr-36

Additional Hymn Suggestions

"Blessed Assurance" (Acts)
    AH4083, C543, CG619, EL638, G839, N473, P341, SA455,
    SH320, UM369 (PD), VU337
"Open My Eyes, That I May See" (Acts)
    C586, CG395, G451, P324, SH583, UM454, VU371
"God the Spirit, Guide and Guardian" (Acts)
    C450, G303, N355, P523, UM648, VU514
"O Holy City, Seen of John" (Acts)
    E582/583, G374, N613, P453, UM726, VU709
"To God Be the Glory" (1 John, John)
    C72, CG349, G634, P485, SA279, SH545, UM98 (PD)
"Pues Si Vivimos" ("When We Are Living") (1 John)
    C536, CG265, EL639, G822, N499, P400, SH299, UM356, VU581
"I Know Whom I Have Believed" (1 John)
    CG588, SA843, SH529, UM714 (PD)
"O Holy Spirit, Root of Life" (1 John)
    C251, EL399, N57, S2121, VU379
"Living for Jesus" (1 John)
    C610, S2149
"There Are Some Things I May Not Know" ("Yes, God Is Real")
    (1 John)
    N405, S2147
"Come, Let Us with Our Lord Arise" (1 John, John)
    E49, S2084
"Hope of the World" (John)
    C538, E472, G734, N46, P360, UM178, VU215
"Take Time to Be Holy" (John)
    C572, SA790, UM395 (PD), VU672
"I Want Jesus to Walk with Me" (John)
    C627, CG635, EL325, G775, N490, P363, SH135, UM521
"What a Friend We Have in Jesus" (John)
    C585, CG409, EL742, G465, N506, P403, SA795, SH585/586,
    UM526 (PD), VU661
"Break Thou the Bread of Life" (John)
    C321, CG35, EL515, G460, N321, P329, SA802, SH552,
    UM599 (PD), VU501

Additional Contemporary and Modern Suggestions

"Oh, I Know the Lord's Laid His Hands on Me" (Acts)
    S2139
"There Is a Redeemer" 11483 (Acts)
    CG377, G443, SA204, SH495
"Nobody" 7121827 (Acts, John)
"My Life Is in You, Lord" 17315 (1 John)
"Santo, Santo, Santo" ("Holy, Holy, Holy") (1 John)
    C111, CG3, EL473, G595, N793, S2007, SH452
"Holy, Holy" 18792 (1 John)
    P140, S2039
"You Are My All in All" 825356 (1 John)
    CG571, G519, SH335, WS3040
"You Are My King" ("Amazing Love") 2456623 (1 John)
"I Believe In Jesus" 61282 (1 John)
"Love Moves You" ("Love Alone") 5775514 (1 John, John)
"O God in Whom We Live" (1 John, John)
    WS3153
"Lord, Be Glorified" 26368 (John)
    EL744, G468, S2150, SA593, SH420
"Make Us One" 695737 (John)
"Bind Us Together" 1228 (John)
"Be Glorified" 429226 (John)
"Be Glorified" 2732646 (John)
"I Could Sing of Your Love Forever" 1043199 (John)
"Jesus We Love You" 7030068 (John)
"Awaken" 5491647 (John)
"The Family Prayer Song" 1680466 (Christian Home)

Vocal Solos

"God So Loved" (1 John)
    V-9   p. 28
"That's Why We Are Beautiful" (John)
    V-8   p. 160

Anthems

"There Is a Savior" (Acts, John)
arr. Mary McDonald; Hope C6253
SATB, piano, opt. orchestra (https://bit.ly/C-6253)

"My Mother's Love" (Mother's Day)
Tom Shelton; Hinshaw HMC-2352
Unison Children and Women, piano (https://bit.ly/HMC-2352)

Other Suggestions

*Today may also be celebrated as Ascension Sunday using the ideas
    for May 9.*
Visuals:
Acts   Peter, open Bible, Judas, 2 men, casting lots
    P   Path, trees/water/fruit, chaff/wind, scales
    E   Open Bible, hearts/people, 5:1b, 12a
    G   Jesus praying, praying hands
For more prayers and litanies, see The Abingdon Worship Annual
    2024.
Introit: WS3150. "Father, We Have Heard You Calling" (Acts)
Responsive Invocation: WSL36 (Acts, Easter)
Prayer: WSL34 (Acts, Easter)
Resources for Mothers Day & Festival of Christian Home:
    Prayer: WSL62 (Mother's Day, Christian Home)
    Prayer: WSL201. "God our Creator" (Mother's Day)
    Prayer of Confession: N836 (Christian Home)
Resources for Graduation Sunday:
    Offering Prayer: WSL144 (Graduation, Children's Sunday)
    Litany of Guidance: WSL163 (Graduation)
    Blessing: WSL40. May the Spirit of God be in you.
Theme Ideas: Communion, God: Glory of God, God: Guidance,
    Jesus: Jesus our Savior, Unity

Acts 2:1-21

When the day of Pentecost had come, they were all together in one place. [2]And suddenly from heaven there came a sound like the rush of a violent wind, and it filled the entire house where they were sitting. [3]Divided tongues, as of fire, appeared among them, and a tongue rested on each of them. [4]All of them were filled with the Holy Spirit and began to speak in other languages, as the Spirit gave them ability.

[5]Now there were devout Jews from every people under heaven living in Jerusalem. [6]And at this sound the crowd gathered and was bewildered, because each one heard them speaking in the native language of each. [7]Amazed and astonished, they asked, "Are not all these who are speaking Galileans? [8]And how is it that we hear, each of us, in our own native language? [9]Parthians, Medes, Elamites, and residents of Mesopotamia, Judea and Cappadocia, Pontus and Asia, [10]Phrygia and Pamphylia, Egypt and the parts of Libya belonging to Cyrene, and visitors from Rome, both Jews and proselytes, [11]Cretans and Arabs—in our own languages we hear them speaking about God's deeds of power." [12]All were amazed and perplexed, saying to one another, "What does this mean?" [13]But others sneered and said, "They are filled with new wine."

[14]But Peter, standing with the eleven, raised his voice and addressed them, "Fellow Jews and all who live in Jerusalem, let this be known to you, and listen to what I say. [15]Indeed, these are not drunk, as you suppose, for it is only nine o'clock in the morning. [16]No, this is what was spoken through the prophet Joel:

[17]'In the last days it will be, God declares,
that I will pour out my Spirit upon all flesh,
and your sons and your daughters shall prophesy,
and your young men shall see visions,
and your old men shall dream dreams.
[18]Even upon my slaves, both men and women,
in those days I will pour out my Spirit,
and they shall prophesy.
[19]And I will show portents in the heaven above
and signs on the earth below,
blood, and fire, and smoky mist.
[20]The sun shall be turned to darkness
and the moon to blood,
before the coming of the Lord's great and glorious
day.
[21]Then everyone who calls on the name of the Lord shall be
saved.'"

Psalm 104:24-34, 35b (G34, N889/890, P224 SH219, UM826)

[24]O Lᴏʀᴅ, how manifold are your works!
In wisdom you have made them all;
the earth is full of your creatures.
[25]There is the sea, great and wide;
creeping things innumerable are there,
living things both small and great.
[26]There go the ships
and Leviathan that you formed to sport in it.
[27]These all look to you
to give them their food in due season;
[28]when you give to them, they gather it up;
when you open your hand, they are filled with good things.
[29]When you hide your face, they are dismayed;
when you take away their breath, they die
and return to their dust.
[30]When you send forth your spirit, they are created,
and you renew the face of the ground.
[31]May the glory of the Lᴏʀᴅ endure forever;
may the Lᴏʀᴅ rejoice in his works—
[32]who looks on the earth and it trembles,
who touches the mountains and they smoke.

[33]I will sing to the Lᴏʀᴅ as long as I live;
I will sing praise to my God while I have being.
[34]May my meditation be pleasing to him,
for I rejoice in the Lᴏʀᴅ.
. . . .
[35b]Bless the Lᴏʀᴅ, O my soul.
Praise the Lᴏʀᴅ!

Romans 8:22-27

[22]We know that the whole creation has been groaning together as it suffers together the pains of labor, [23]and not only the creation, but we ourselves, who have the first fruits of the Spirit, groan inwardly while we wait for adoption, the redemption of our bodies. [24]For in hope we were saved. Now hope that is seen is not hope, for who hopes for what one already sees? [25]But if we hope for what we do not see, we wait for it with patience.

[26]Likewise the Spirit helps us in our weakness, for we do not know how to pray as we ought, but that very Spirit intercedes with groanings too deep for words. [27]And God, who searches hearts, knows what is the mind of the Spirit, because the Spirit intercedes for the saints according to the will of God.

John 15:26-27; 16:4b-15

[26]"When the Advocate comes, whom I will send to you from the Father, the Spirit of truth who comes from the Father, he will testify on my behalf. [27]You also are to testify, because you have been with me from the beginning. . . .

16 [4b]"I did not say these things to you from the beginning, because I was with you. [5]But now I am going to him who sent me, yet none of you asks me, 'Where are you going?' [6]But because I have said these things to you, sorrow has filled your hearts. [7]Nevertheless, I tell you the truth: it is to your advantage that I go away, for if I do not go away, the Advocate will not come to you, but if I go, I will send him to you. [8]And when he comes, he will prove the world wrong about sin and righteousness and judgment: [9]about sin, because they do not believe in me; [10]about righteousness, because I am going to the Father, and you will see me no longer; [11]about judgment, because the ruler of this world has been condemned.

[12]"I still have many things to say to you, but you cannot bear them now. [13]When the Spirit of truth comes, he will guide you into all the truth, for he will not speak on his own but will speak whatever he hears, and he will declare to you the things that are to come. [14]He will glorify me because he will take what is mine and declare it to you. [15]All that the Father has is mine. For this reason I said that he will take what is mine and declare it to you."

Primary Hymns and Songs for the Day
"Love Divine, All Loves Excelling" (Acts, Rom, John) (C)
  C517, CG281, E657, EL631, G366, N43, P376, SA262,
  SH353/354, UM384 (PD), VU333
       H-3   Hbl-46; Chr-26, 134; Desc-53; Org-56
       S-1   #168-171. Various treatments
"O Splendor of God's Glory Bright" (Acts)
  E5, EL559, G666, N87, P474, UM679 (PD), VU413
       H-3   Chr-19
"Come, Holy Ghost, Our Souls Inspire" (Acts, Rom)
  E503/504, N268, G278, P125, UM651, VU201
       H-3   Hbl-14, 52
       S-2   #186. Handbell arrangement
"Lord, Listen to Your Children Praying" 22829 (Acts, Rom)
  C305, CG389, G469, S2193, SH577, VU400
"Spirit of the Living God" 23488 (Acts, John)
  C259, CG234, G288, N283, P322, SA312/313, SH555,
  UM393, VU376, S-1 #212 Vocal desc. idea
       H-3   Chr-176
       S-1   #212. Vocal descant idea
"Veni Sancte Spiritus" ("Holy Spirit, Come to Us") (Acts, Rom, John)
  EL406, G281, S2118
"Kum Ba Yah" 2749763 (Rom)
  C590, G472, P338, UM494
"Every Time I Feel the Spirit" (Acts, Rom) (C)
  C592, G66, N282, P315, UM404
"They'll Know We Are Christians" 26997 (Acts) (C)
  AH4074, C494, CG272, G300, S2223, SH232

Additional Hymn Suggestions
"Gather Us In" (Acts, Comm.) (O)
  C284, EL532, G401, S2236, SH393
"Sweet, Sweet Spirit" (Acts)
  C261, CG241, G408, N293, P398, SH410, UM334
"Breathe on Me, Breath of God" (Acts)
  C254, CG235, E508, G286, N292, P316, SA294, SH224/273,
  UM420 (PD), VU382 (Fr.)
"Wind Who Makes All Winds that Blow" (Acts)
  C236, CG226, N271, P131, UM538, VU196
"Like the Murmur of the Dove's Song" (Acts)
  C245, CG233, E513, EL403, G285, N270, P314, SH407,
  UM544, VU205
"Loving Spirit" (Acts, Pentecost)
  C244, EL397, G293, P323, S2123, VU387
"In the Midst of New Dimensions" (Acts, Pentecost)
  G315, N391, S2238
"Deep in the Shadows of the Past" (Acts)
  G50, N320, P330, S2246
"Come, Share the Lord" (Acts, Comm.)
  C408, CG459, G510, S2269, VU469
"Spirit, Spirit of Gentleness" (Acts, Rom)
  C249, EL396, G291, N286, P319, S2120, VU375
"My Hope Is Built" (Acts, Rom)
  AH4105, C537, CG590, EL596/597, G353, N403, P379,
  SA662, SH324, UM368 (PD)
"Spirit of God, Descend upon My Heart" (Acts, Rom)
  C265, CG243, EL800, G688, N290, P326, SA290, SH277,
  UM500 (PD), VU378
"Come Down, O Love Divine" (Acts, John)
  C582, E516, EL804, G282, N289, P313, SA295, UM475,
  VU367
"Healer of Our Every Ill" (Acts, John)
  C506, EL612, G795, S2213, SH339, VU619
"Santo" ("Holy") (Rom)
  EL762, G594, SH39, S2019
"Imploramos tu piedad" ("For the Troubles and the Suffering")
  (Rom)
  CG691, G764, SH579
"Open My Eyes, That I May See" (John)
  C586, CG395, G451, P324, SH583, UM454, VU371

Additional Contemporary and Modern Suggestions
"Here As In Heaven" 7051506 (Acts, Pentecost)
"Start a Fire" 7017142 (Acts, Pentecost)
"Set A Fire" 5911299 (Acts, Pentecost)
"I Will Call upon the Lord" 11263 (Acts)
  G621, S2002
"Holy, Holy" 18792 (Acts)
  P140, S2039
"Dios Está Aquí" ("God Is Here Today") 3170575 (Acts)
  G411, S2049, SH382
"Where the Spirit of the Lord Is" 27484 (Acts)
  C264, S2119
"Wa Wa Wa Emimimo" ("Come, O Holy Spirit, Come") (Acts,
  Pentecost)
  G283, S2124, VU383 (See also S2125)
"Holy Ground" 21198 (Acts)
  C112, G406, S2272, SA400
"As We Gather" 35469 (Acts)
"Open the Eyes of My Heart" 2298355 (Acts)
  G452, SA270, SH378, WS3008
"Shout to the North" 1562261 (Acts, Rom)
  G319, SA1009, WS3042
"Already Here" (Acts, Rom, Pentecost)
"From Ashes to Beauty" 5288953 (Acts, Rom)
"Cornerstone" 6158927 (Acts, Rom)
"Holy Spirit, Rain Down" 2405227 (Acts, John)
"Surely the Presence of the Lord" 7909 (Acts, John)
  C263, UM328; S-2 #200. Stanzas for soloist
"Come, Holy Spirit" 3383953 (Acts, John)
"Bless His Holy Name" 17566 (Pss)
"10,000 Reasons" ("Bless The Lord") 6016351 (Pss)
"Change My Heart, O God" 1565 (Rom)
  EL801, G695, S2152, SA409, SH507
"Cry of My Heart" 844980 (Rom)
"Dwell" 4085652 (Pentecost)

Vocal Solos
"I Feel the Spirit Moving" (Acts, Pentecost)
  V-3 (1)   p. 22
"Spirit of God" (Acts, Pentecost)
  V-8   p. 170
"A Covenant Prayer" (Rom)
  V-1   p. 6

Anthems
"Gracious Spirit, Dwell with Me" (Acts, Pentecost)
Arr. K. Lee Scott; Augsburg 9780800646134
2-part mixed, organ (https://bit.ly/AF-46134)

"Spirit of God, Descend upon My Heart" (Acts)
Arr. Heather Sorenson; Soundforth Music 10/5086SF
SATB, piano, opt. violin/cello (https://bit.ly/SF-5086)

Other Suggestions
Visuals:
  Acts Wind, tongues of fire, praising, all races of people
  P   Sea/ships, whales, dove, volcano, singing, Ps 104:35b
  E   Praying hands, Holy Spirit (flames, descending dove)
  G   Briefcase (Advocate), Trinity (triangle, trefoil, others)
Introit: G283, S2124/S2125, VU383, SH223, WS3091/WS2092.
  "Come, Holy Spirit" (Acts)
Prayer: WSL39, UM329, UM542, or UM574 (Acts, Pentecost)
Theme Ideas: Creation, Holy Spirit, Praise, Vision

Isaiah 6:1-8

In the year that King Uzziah died, I saw the Lord sitting on a throne, high and lofty, and the hem of his robe filled the temple. [2]Seraphs were in attendance above him; each had six wings: with two they covered their faces, and with two they covered their feet, and with two they flew. [3]And one called to another and said,

"Holy, holy, holy is the Lord of hosts;
the whole earth is full of his glory."

[4]The pivots on the thresholds shook at the voices of those who called, and the house filled with smoke. [5]And I said, "Woe is me! I am lost, for I am a man of unclean lips, and I live among a people of unclean lips, yet my eyes have seen the King, the Lord of hosts!"

[6]Then one of the seraphs flew to me, holding a live coal that had been taken from the altar with a pair of tongs. [7]The seraph touched my mouth with it and said, "Now that this has touched your lips, your guilt has departed and your sin is blotted out." [8]Then I heard the voice of the Lord saying, "Whom shall I send, and who will go for us?" And I said, "Here am I; send me!"

Psalm 29 (G259, N637, P180, UM761)

Ascribe to the Lord, O heavenly beings,
ascribe to the Lord glory and strength.
[2]Ascribe to the Lord the glory of his name;
worship the Lord in holy splendor.
[3]The voice of the Lord is over the waters;
the God of glory thunders,
the Lord, over mighty waters.
[4]The voice of the Lord is powerful;
the voice of the Lord is full of majesty.
[5]The voice of the Lord breaks the cedars;
the Lord breaks the cedars of Lebanon.
[6]He makes Lebanon skip like a calf
and Sirion like a young wild ox.
[7]The voice of the Lord flashes forth flames of fire.
[8]The voice of the Lord shakes the wilderness;
the Lord shakes the wilderness of Kadesh.
[9]The voice of the Lord causes the oaks to whirl
and strips the forest bare,
and in his temple all say, "Glory!"
[10]The Lord sits enthroned over the flood;
the Lord sits enthroned as king forever.
[11]May the Lord give strength to his people!
May the Lord bless his people with peace!

Romans 8:12-17

[12]So then, brothers and sisters, we are obligated, not to the flesh, to live according to the flesh—[13]for if you live according to the flesh, you will die, but if by the Spirit you put to death the deeds of the body, you will live. [14]For all who are led by the Spirit of God are children of God. [15]For you did not receive a spirit of slavery to fall back into fear, but you received a spirit of adoption. When we cry, "Abba! Father!" [16]it is that very Spirit bearing witness with our spirit that we are children of God, [17]and if children, then heirs: heirs of God and joint heirs with Christ, if we in fact suffer with him so that we may also be glorified with him.

John 3:1-17

Now there was a Pharisee named Nicodemus, a leader of the Jews. [2]He came to Jesus by night and said to him, "Rabbi, we know that you are a teacher who has come from God, for no one can do these signs that you do unless God is with that person." [3]Jesus answered him, "Very truly, I tell you, no one can see the kingdom of God without being born from above." [4]Nicodemus said to him, "How can anyone be born after having grown old? Can one enter a second time into the mother's womb and be born?" [5]Jesus answered, "Very truly, I tell you, no one can enter the kingdom of God without being born of water and Spirit. [6]What is born of the flesh is flesh, and what is born of the Spirit is spirit. [7]Do not be astonished that I said to you, 'You must be born from above.' [8]The wind blows where it chooses, and you hear the sound of it, but you do not know where it comes from or where it goes. So it is with everyone who is born of the Spirit." [9]Nicodemus said to him, "How can these things be?" [10]Jesus answered him, "Are you the teacher of Israel, and yet you do not understand these things?

[11]"Very truly, I tell you, we speak of what we know and testify to what we have seen, yet you do not receive our testimony. [12]If I have told you about earthly things and you do not believe, how can you believe if I tell you about heavenly things? [13]No one has ascended into heaven except the one who descended from heaven, the Son of Man. [14]And just as Moses lifted up the serpent in the wilderness, so must the Son of Man be lifted up, [15]that whoever believes in him may have eternal life.

[16]"For God so loved the world that he gave his only Son, so that everyone who believes in him may not perish but may have eternal life.

[17]"Indeed, God did not send the Son into the world to condemn the world but in order that the world might be saved through him."

Primary Hymns and Songs for the Day

"Holy, Holy, Holy! Lord God Almighty" (Isa, Trinity) (O)
C4, CG1, E362, EL413, G1, N277, P138, SA31, SH450,
UM64/65, VU315
- N277 Descant
- C4 Descant
- H-3 Hbl-68; Chr-99; Desc-80; Org-97
- S-1 #245-248. Various treatments.

"Send Me, Lord" (Isa)
C447, EL809, G746, N360, SH723, UM497, VU572
- S-2 #173. Percussion arrangement

"Let All Mortal Flesh Keep Silence" (Isa, Comm.)
C124, CG81, E324, EL490, G347, N345, P5, UM626 (PD),
VU473 (Fr.)
- H-3 Hbl-20, 74; Chr-124; Desc-87; Org-116
- S-1 #268-269. Handbell part and descant

"Santo" ("Holy") (Isa)
EL762, G594, SH39, S2019

"Holy God, We Praise Thy Name" (Isa, Rom)
CG9, E366, EL414 (PD), G4, N276, P460, SH431, UM79,
VU894 (Fr.)
- H-3 Chr-78, 98; Desc-48; Org-48
- S-1 #151-153. Harmonization and descants

"Wash, O God, Our Sons and Daughters" (Rom, John, Baptism)
C365, EL445, G490, SH669, UM605, VU442
- H-3 Hbl-14, 64; Chr-132, 203
- S-2 #22. Descant

"Womb of Life" (Rom, John, Trinity)
C14, G3, N274, S2046

"Here I Am, Lord" (Isa) (C)
C452, CG482, EL574, G69, SA1002, SH608, UM593, VU509
- H-3 Chr-97; Org-54

"To God Be the Glory" (John) (C)
C72, CG349, G634, P485, SA279, SH545, UM98 (PD)

Additional Hymn Suggestions

"Ye Watchers and Ye Holy Ones" (Isa, Trinity)
E618, EL424, P451, UM90

"Santo, Santo, Santo" ("Holy, Holy, Holy") (Isa, Comm.)
C111, CG3, EL473, G595, N793, S2007, SH452

"Mine Eyes Have Seen the Glory" (Isa, Pss)
C705, CG439, EL890, G354, N610, SA263, UM717

"Creating God, Your Fingers Trace" (Rom, Trinity)
C335, E394, EL684, N462, P134, UM109, VU265

"Pues Si Vivimos" ("When We Are Living") (Rom)
C536, CG265, EL639, G822, N499, P400, SH299, UM356,
VU581

"Every Time I Feel the Spirit" (Rom)
C592, G66, N282, P315, UM404

"Baptized in Water" (Rom, Baptism)
CG449, E294, EL456, G482, P492, S2248, SH666

"Mothering God, You Gave Me Birth" (Rom, John)
C83, N467, S2050, VU320

"Lift High the Cross" (John)
C108, CG415, E473, EL660, G826, N198, P371, SH162,
UM159, VU151

"O Love, How Deep" (John, Trinity)
E448/449, EL322, G618, N209, P83, SH115, UM267, VU348

"We Know That Christ Is Raised" (John, Baptism)
E296, EL449, G485, P495, UM610, VU448

"Womb of Life" (John, Trinity)
C14, G3, N274, S2046

"He Came Down" 4679219 (John)
EL253, G137, S2085, SH88

"Gather Us In" (John)
C284, EL532, G401, S2236, SH393

"O Breath of Life" (John)
C250, SA818, UM543, VU202, WS3146

"O Holy Spirit, Root of Life" (John, Trinity)
C251, EL399, N57, S2121, VU379

"Holy Spirit, Come, Confirm Us" (Trinity) (C)
N264, UM331

"Come, Join the Dance of Trinity" (Trinity)
EL412, WS3017

Additional Contemporary and Modern Suggestions

"Santo, Santo, Santo" ("Holy, Holy, Holy") (Isa)
C111, CG3, EL473, G595, N793, S2007, SH452

"You Are My All in All" 825356 (Isa, John)
CG571, G519, SH335, WS3040

"Holy, Holy" 18792 (Isa, Rom)
P140, S2039

"Spirit of the Living God" 23488 (Rom)
C259, CG234, G288, N283, P322, SA312/313, SH555,
UM393, VU376, S-1 #212 Vocal desc. idea

"You Are My King" ("Amazing Love") 2456623 (Rom, John)

"They'll Know We Are Christians" 26997 (Rom, Trinity)
AH4074, C494, CG272, G300, S2223, SH232

"O How He Loves You and Me" 15850 (John)
CG600, S2108, SH535

"Celebrate Love" 155246 (John)

"Love Moves You" ("Love Alone") 5775514 (John)

"For Us" 7119349 (John, Trinity)

"I Believe In Jesus" 61282 (John, Trinity)

"That's Why We Praise Him" 2668576 (John, Easter)

"There Is a Redeemer" 11483 (John, Trinity)
CG377, G443, SA204, SH495

"How Great Is Our God" 4348399 (Trinity)
CG322, SH458, WS3003

"Our God Saves" 4972837 (Trinity)

"We Believe" 6367165 (Trinity)

"Doxology" 5465879 (Trinity)

Vocal Solos

"Alleluia" (Isa, Trinity)
- V-8 p. 358

"The Gospel of Grace" (John)
- V-3 (1) p. 44

"Wash Me in Your Water" (John, Baptism)
- V-5 (2) p. 18

"It Won't Stop" (John, Trinity)
- V-8 p. 70

Anthems

"Here I Am, Lord" (Isa)
Arr. Mary McDonald; Alfred 42956
SATB, keyboard (https://bit.ly/A-42956)

"Is He Worthy?" (Isa, John)
Arr. Lloyd Larson; Hope C6378
SATB, piano, opt. rhythm (https://bit.ly/C-6378)

Other Suggestions

Visuals:
- O Seraphs, incense, glowing coals
- P Storm, flames, lightning, wind, skipping calf
- E Crown (heirs), open manacles (handcuffs)
- G Wind, white garment, water, flame/dove (Holy Spirit)

Litany: CG11. "God the Trinity" (Trinity)

Canticle: UM80. "Canticle of the Holy Trinity"

Affirmation of Faith: G34, N883, UM880. The Nicene Creed
(Trinity)

Theme Ideas: God: Glory of God, Holy Spirit, New Creation,
Resurrection

1 Samuel 3:1-20

Now the boy Samuel was ministering to the LORD under Eli. The word of the LORD was rare in those days; visions were not widespread.

²At that time Eli, whose eyesight had begun to grow dim so that he could not see, was lying down in his room; ³the lamp of God had not yet gone out, and Samuel was lying down in the temple of the LORD, where the ark of God was. ⁴Then the LORD called, "Samuel! Samuel!" and he said, "Here I am!" ⁵and ran to Eli and said, "Here I am, for you called me." But he said, "I did not call; lie down again." So he went and lay down. ⁶The LORD called again, "Samuel!" Samuel got up and went to Eli and said, "Here I am, for you called me." But he said, "I did not call, my son; lie down again." ⁷Now Samuel did not yet know the LORD, and the word of the LORD had not yet been revealed to him. ⁸The LORD called Samuel again, a third time. And he got up and went to Eli and said, "Here I am, for you called me." Then Eli perceived that the LORD was calling the boy. ⁹Therefore Eli said to Samuel, "Go, lie down, and if he calls you, you shall say, 'Speak, LORD, for your servant is listening.'" So Samuel went and lay down in his place.

¹⁰Now the LORD came and stood there, calling as before, "Samuel! Samuel!" And Samuel said, "Speak, for your servant is listening." ¹¹Then the LORD said to Samuel, "See, I am about to do something in Israel that will make both ears of anyone who hears of it tingle. ¹²On that day I will fulfill against Eli all that I have spoken concerning his house, from beginning to end. ¹³For I have told him that I am about to punish his house forever for the iniquity that he knew, because his sons were blaspheming God, and he did not restrain them. ¹⁴Therefore I swear to the house of Eli that the iniquity of Eli's house shall not be expiated by sacrifice or offering forever."

¹⁵Samuel lay there until morning; then he opened the doors of the house of the LORD. Samuel was afraid to tell the vision to Eli. ¹⁶But Eli called Samuel and said, "Samuel, my son." He said, "Here I am." ¹⁷Eli said, "What was it that he told you? Do not hide it from me. May God do so to you and more also, if you hide anything from me of all that he told you." ¹⁸So Samuel told him everything and hid nothing from him. Then he said, "It is the LORD; let him do what seems good to him."

¹⁹As Samuel grew up, the LORD was with him and let none of his words fall to the ground. ²⁰And all Israel from Dan to Beer-sheba knew that Samuel was a trustworthy prophet of the LORD.

Psalm 139:1-6, 13-18 (G28/29/426, UM854)

O LORD, you have searched me and known me.
²You know when I sit down and when I rise up;
    you discern my thoughts from far away.
³You search out my path and my lying down
    and are acquainted with all my ways.
⁴Even before a word is on my tongue,
    O LORD, you know it completely.
⁵You hem me in, behind and before,
    and lay your hand upon me.
⁶Such knowledge is too wonderful for me;
    it is so high that I cannot attain it.
. . . .
¹³For it was you who formed my inward parts;
    you knit me together in my mother's womb.
¹⁴I praise you, for I am fearfully and wonderfully made.
    Wonderful are your works;
that I know very well.
    ¹⁵My frame was not hidden from you,

when I was being made in secret,
    intricately woven in the depths of the earth.
¹⁶Your eyes beheld my unformed substance.
    In your book were written
all the days that were formed for me,
    when none of them as yet existed.
¹⁷How weighty to me are your thoughts, O God!
    How vast is the sum of them!
¹⁸I try to count them—they are more than the sand;
    I come to the end—I am still with you.

2 Corinthians 4:5-12

⁵For we do not proclaim ourselves; we proclaim Jesus Christ as Lord and ourselves as your slaves for Jesus's sake. ⁶For it is the God who said, "Light will shine out of darkness," who has shone in our hearts to give the light of the knowledge of the glory of God in the face of Christ.

⁷But we have this treasure in clay jars, so that it may be made clear that this extraordinary power belongs to God and does not come from us. ⁸We are afflicted in every way but not crushed, perplexed but not driven to despair, ⁹persecuted but not forsaken, struck down but not destroyed, ¹⁰always carrying around in the body the death of Jesus, so that the life of Jesus may also be made visible in our bodies. ¹¹For we who are living are always being handed over to death for Jesus's sake, so that the life of Jesus may also be made visible in our mortal flesh. ¹²So death is at work in us but life in you.

Mark 2:23–3:6

²³One Sabbath he was going through the grain fields, and as they made their way his disciples began to pluck heads of grain. ²⁴The Pharisees said to him, "Look, why are they doing what is not lawful on the Sabbath?" ²⁵And he said to them, "Have you never read what David did when he and his companions were hungry and in need of food, ²⁶how he entered the house of God when Abiathar was high priest and ate the bread of the Presence, which it is not lawful for any but the priests to eat, and he gave some to his companions?" ²⁷Then he said to them, "The Sabbath was made for humankind and not humankind for the Sabbath, ²⁸so the Son of Man is lord even of the Sabbath."

3 Again he entered the synagogue, and a man was there who had a withered hand. ²They were watching him to see whether he would cure him on the Sabbath, so that they might accuse him. ³And he said to the man who had the withered hand, "Come forward." ⁴Then he said to them, "Is it lawful to do good or to do harm on the Sabbath, to save life or to kill?" But they were silent. ⁵He looked around at them with anger; he was grieved at their hardness of heart and said to the man, "Stretch out your hand." He stretched it out, and his hand was restored. ⁶The Pharisees went out and immediately conspired with the Herodians against him, how to destroy him.

Primary Hymns and Songs for the Day

"Open My Eyes, that I May See" (1 Sam, 2 Cor) (O)
  C586, CG395, G451, P324, SH583, UM454, VU371
    H-3   Chr-157; Org-108
"Be Thou My Vision" (1 Sam, 2 Cor)
  C595, CG71, E488, EL793, G450, N451, P339, SA573, SH640,
  UM451, VU642
    H-3   Hbl-15, 48; Chr-36; Org-153
    S-1   #319. Arr. for organ and voices in canon
"Send Me, Lord" (1 Sam)
  C447, EL809, G746, N360, SH723, UM497, VU572
    S-2   #173. Percussion arrangement
"Here I Am, Lord" (1 Sam)
  C452, CG482, EL574, G69, SA1002, SH608, UM593, VU509
    H-3   Chr-97; Org-54
"The Lone, Wild Bird" (Pss)
  P320, S2052, VU384
"Lord of the Dance" (Mark)
  G157, P302, SA141, UM261, VU352
    H-3   Chr-106; Org-81
"God Is Here" (2 Cor)
  C280, CG298, EL526, G409, N70, P461, UM660
    H-3   Hbl-61; Chr-132; Org-2
    S-1   #4-5. Instrumental and vocal descants
"Come, Labor On" (Mark)
  E541, G719, N532, P415
    H-3   Org-109
    H-5   #91. Harmonization
"We Cannot Measure How You Heal" (Mark)
  CG540, G797, SH341, VU613, WS3139
    S-2   #33-37. Various treatments
"Lord, Speak to Me" (1 Sam) (C)
  CG503, EL676, G722, N531, SA773, SH557, UM463, VU589
    H-3   Hbl-75; Chr-131; Desc-22; Org-18
    S-1   #52. Descant

Additional Hymn Suggestions

"I Am Thine, O Lord" (1 Sam)
  AH4087, C601, CG504, N455, SA586, UM419 (PD)
"Lord, You Give the Great Commission" (1 Sam)
  C459, CG651, S2176, EL579, G298, P429, UM584, VU512
"Lord, Whose Love Through Humble Service" (1 Sam, Mark)
  C461, CG650, E610, EL712, P427, SH239, UM581
"O Master, Let Me Walk with Thee" (Pss, Mark)
  C602, CG660, E659/E660, EL818, G738, N503, P357, SA667,
  SH612, UM430 (PD), VU560
"I Want to Walk as a Child of the Light" (2 Cor)
  CG96, E490, EL815, G377, SH352, UM206
"Pues Si Vivimos" ("When We Are Living") (2 Cor)
  C536, CG265, EL639, G822, N499, P400, SH299, UM356, VU581
"This Little Light of Mine" (2 Cor)
  N525, SH257, UM585 (See also AH4150, EL677, N524)
"Christ Beside Me" (2 Cor)
  G702, S2166
"O Christ, the Healer" (Mark)
  C503. EL610, G793, N175, P380, UM265
"We Come to You for Healing, Lord" (Mark)
  EL617, G796
"Where Cross the Crowded Ways of Life" (Mark)
  C665, CG657, E609, EL719, G343, N543, UM427, VU681
"What Does the Lord Require" (Mark)
  C659, E605, P405, UM441
"You Satisfy the Hungry Heart" (Mark, Comm.)
  C429, CG468, EL484, G523, P521, SH672, UM629, VU478
"Una Espiga" ("Sheaves of Summer") (Mark, Comm.)
  C396, G532, N338, UM637
"In the Midst of New Dimensions" (Mark)
  G315, N391, S2238

Additional Contemporary and Modern Suggestions

"Oh, I Know the Lord's Laid His Hands on Me" (1 Sam, Pss)
  S2139
"All of Me" 6290160 (1 Sam)
"Let My Words Be Few" 3040980 (1 Sam)
"Lead Me, Lord" 1609045 (1 Sam)
"Nobody" 7121827 (1 Sam, Pss)
"He Knows My Name" 2151368 (1 Sam, Pss)
"In the Secret" 1810119 (Pss)
"The Potter's Hand" 2449771 (Pss)
"These Hands" 3251827 (Pss)
"Wonderfully Made" 5768239 (Pss)
"Great Are You Lord" 6460220 (2 Cor)
"My Life Is in You, Lord" 17315 (2 Cor)
"Shine, Jesus, Shine" 30426 (2 Cor)
  CG156, EL671, G192, S2173, SA261, SH102
"Light of the World" 73342 (2 Cor)
"Siyahamba" ("We Are Marching") 1321512 (2 Cor)
  C442, CG155, EL866, G853, N526, S2235, SA903, SH717,
  VU646
"Mighty to Save" 4591782 (2 Cor)
"Walking in the Light of God" (2 Cor)
"Marvelous Light" 4491002 (2 Cor, Mark)
"Life-Giving Bread" (2 Cor, Mark, Comm.)
  S2261
"What Does the Lord Require of You" 456859 (Mark)
  C661, CG690, G70, S2174, VU701

Vocal Solos

"Come, Thou Fount of Every Blessing" (1 Sam)
  V-3 (3)   p. 22
"Be Thou My Vision" (1 Sam)
  V-6   p. 13
"Borning Cry" (1 Sam, Pss)
  V-5 (1)   p. 10
"Here's One" (2 Cor, Mark)
  V-7   p. 32/36

Anthems

"Here I Am, Lord" (1 Sam)
Arr. Arnold B. Sherman; Hope C5311
SAB, piano or handbells (https://bit.ly/C-5311)

"We Cannot Measure How You Heal" (Mark)
Arr. John L. Bell; GIA Publications G-8016
SATB, keyboard, opt. flute/cello (https://bit.ly/G-8016)

Other Suggestions

Visuals:
  O   Listening, lamp, boy, old man, service to others, 3:4b,
         5b, 9b
  P   Hand, pregnant woman, newborn child, baby examin-
         ing fingers, hourglass
  E   Light/darkness, Christ, treasure chest, clay pots or
         urns (various sizes, some cracked), service to others
  G   Wheat/bread, outstretched hands
Prayer: UM403. For True Life (1 Sam)
Prayer: WSL51. "O Mysterious God" (1 Sam, Pss)
Prayer: UM489 (1 Sam, 2 Cor)
Alternate Lessons: Deut 5:12-15; Ps 81:1-10 (See p. 3.)
Theme Ideas: Faithfulness, God: Call of God / Listening,
  Healing, Light, Vision

1 Samuel 8:4-20 (11:14-15)

⁴Then all the elders of Israel gathered together and came to Samuel at Ramah ⁵and said to him, "You are old, and your sons do not follow in your ways; appoint for us, then, a king to govern us, like other nations." ⁶But the thing displeased Samuel when they said, "Give us a king to govern us." Samuel prayed to the LORD, ⁷and the LORD said to Samuel, "Listen to the voice of the people in all that they say to you, for they have not rejected you, but they have rejected me from being king over them. ⁸Just as they have done to me from the day I brought them up out of Egypt to this day, forsaking me and serving other gods, so also they are doing to you. ⁹Now then, listen to their voice; only, you shall solemnly warn them and show them the ways of the king who shall reign over them."

¹⁰So Samuel reported all the words of the LORD to the people who were asking him for a king. ¹¹He said, "These will be the ways of the king who will reign over you: he will take your sons and appoint them to his chariots and to be his horsemen, and to run before his chariots, ¹²and he will appoint for himself commanders of thousands and commanders of fifties and some to plow his ground and to reap his harvest and to make his implements of war and the equipment of his chariots. ¹³He will take your daughters to be perfumers and cooks and bakers. ¹⁴He will take the best of your fields and vineyards and olive orchards and give them to his courtiers. ¹⁵He will take one-tenth of your grain and of your vineyards and give it to his officers and his courtiers. ¹⁶He will take your male and female slaves and the best of your cattle and donkeys and put them to his work. ¹⁷He will take one-tenth of your flocks, and you shall be his slaves. ¹⁸And on that day you will cry out because of your king, whom you have chosen for yourselves, but the LORD will not answer you on that day."

¹⁹But the people refused to listen to the voice of Samuel; they said, "No! We are determined to have a king over us, ²⁰so that we also may be like other nations and that our king may govern us and go out before us and fight our battles." . . .

(11 ¹⁴Samuel said to the people, "Come, let us go to Gilgal and there renew the kingship." ¹⁵So all the people went to Gilgal, and there they made Saul king before the LORD in Gilgal. There they sacrificed offerings of well-being before the LORD, and there Saul and all the Israelites rejoiced greatly.)

Psalm 138 (G334, N138, P247, SH497, UM853)

I give you thanks, O LORD, with my whole heart;
    before the gods I sing your praise;
²I bow down toward your holy temple
    and give thanks to your name for your steadfast love and
        your faithfulness,
    for you have exalted your name and your word
    above everything.
³On the day I called, you answered me;
    you increased my strength of soul.
⁴All the kings of the earth shall praise you, O LORD,
    for they have heard the words of your mouth.
⁵They shall sing of the ways of the LORD,
    for great is the glory of the LORD.
⁶For though the LORD is high, he regards the lowly,
    but the haughty he perceives from far away.
⁷Though I walk in the midst of trouble,
    you preserve me against the wrath of my enemies;
you stretch out your hand,
    and your right hand delivers me.
⁸The LORD will fulfill his purpose for me;
    your steadfast love, O LORD, endures forever.
    Do not forsake the work of your hands.

2 Corinthians 4:13–5:1

¹³But just as we have the same spirit of faith that is in accordance with scripture—"I believed, and so I spoke"—we also believe, and therefore we also speak, ¹⁴because we know that the one who raised Jesus will also raise us with Jesus and will present us with you in his presence. ¹⁵Indeed, everything is for your sake, so that grace, when it has extended to more and more people, may increase thanksgiving, to the glory of God.

¹⁶So we do not lose heart. Even though our outer nature is wasting away, our inner nature is being renewed day by day. ¹⁷For our slight, momentary affliction is producing for us an eternal weight of glory beyond all measure, ¹⁸because we look not at what can be seen but at what cannot be seen, for what can be seen is temporary, but what cannot be seen is eternal.

5 For we know that, if the earthly tent we live in is destroyed, we have a building from God, a house not made with hands, eternal in the heavens.

Mark 3:20-35

²⁰Then he went home, and the crowd came together again, so that they could not even eat. ²¹When his family heard it, they went out to restrain him, for people were saying, "He has gone out of his mind." ²²And the scribes who came down from Jerusalem said, "He has Beelzebul, and by the ruler of the demons he casts out demons." ²³And he called them to him and spoke to them in parables, "How can Satan cast out Satan? ²⁴If a kingdom is divided against itself, that kingdom cannot stand. ²⁵And if a house is divided against itself, that house will not be able to stand. ²⁶And if Satan has risen up against himself and is divided, he cannot stand, but his end has come. ²⁷But no one can enter a strong man's house and plunder his property without first tying up the strong man; then indeed the house can be plundered.

²⁸"Truly I tell you, people will be forgiven for their sins and whatever blasphemies they utter, ²⁹but whoever blasphemes against the Holy Spirit can never have forgiveness but is guilty of an eternal sin"—³⁰for they had said, "He has an unclean spirit."

³¹Then his mother and his brothers came, and standing outside they sent to him and called him. ³²A crowd was sitting around him, and they said to him, "Your mother and your brothers are outside asking for you." ³³And he replied, "Who are my mother and my brothers?" ³⁴And looking at those who sat around him, he said, "Here are my mother and my brothers! ³⁵Whoever does the will of God is my brother and sister and mother."

Primary Hymns and Songs for the Day
"Sing Praise to God Who Reigns Above" (1 Sam, 2 Cor, Mark) (O)
C6, CG315, E408, EL871, G645, N6, P483, UM126 (PD),
VU216
H-3   Hbl-92; Chr-173; Desc-76; Org-91
S-1   #237. Descant
"If Thou But Suffer God to Guide Thee" (1 Sam, Pss, 2 Cor) (O)
C565, CG76, E635, EL769, G816, N410, P282, SA40, SH326,
UM142 (PD), VU285 (Fr.) and VU286
H-3   Chr-108; Desc-103; Org-179
"My Faith Looks Up to Thee" (2 Cor)
C576, CG407, E691, EL759, G829, P383, SA726, UM452,
VU663
H-3   Hbl-77; Chr-138; Org-108
S-2   #142. Flute/violin descant
"In the Lord I'll Be Ever Thankful" (2 Cor, Comm.)
G654, S2195, SH316
"I'm Gonna Live So God Can Use Me" (2 Cor, Mark)
C614, G700, P369, S2153, SH632, VU575
"This Is My Father's World" (Mark)
C59, E651, CG17, EL824 (PD), G370, P293, SA66, SH17,
UM144, VU296
H-3   Hbl-31, 99; Chr-87, 102, 197; Org-159
S-1   #326. Transposition in D major
"Who Is My Mother, Who Is My Brother?" (Mark, Comm.)
C486, CG275, S2225
"Lead On, O Cloud of Presence" (1 Sam, Mark) (C)
C633, S2234, VU421
H-3   Hbl-74; Chr-123; Desc-64; Org-71
S-1   #9-197. Various treatments

Additional Hymn Suggestions
"O God of Every Nation" (1 Sam)
C680, CG46, E607, EL713, G756, P289, UM435, VU677
"Open My Eyes, That I May See" (1 Sam, 2 Cor)
C586, CG395, G451, P324, SH583, UM454, VU371
"Pues Si Vivimos" ("When We Are Living") (1 Sam, 2 Cor, Mark)
C536, CG265, EL639, G822, N499, P400, SH299, UM356,
VU581
"Lead On, O King Eternal" (1 Sam, Mark)
C632, CG63, E555, EL805, G269, N573, P447/ P448, SA964,
UM580
"Jesus, Lover of My Soul" (2 Cor)
C542, CG406, E699, G440, N546, P303, SA257, SH542/543,
UM479, VU669
"By Gracious Powers" (2 Cor)
E695/696, G818, N413, P342, UM517
"We Shall Overcome" (2 Cor)
AH4047/4048, C630, G379, N570, UM533
"Be Still, My Soul" (2 Cor)
C566, G891, N488, SH330, UM534, VU652
"We Know That Christ Is Raised" (2 Cor)
E296, EL449, G485, P495, UM610, VU448
"Here, O My Lord, I See Thee" (2 Cor, Comm.)
C416, CG460, E318, G517, N336, P520, UM623, VU459
"We Walk by Faith and Not by Sight" (2 Cor)
CG634, E209, EL635, G817, N256, P399, S2196, SH660
"My Hope Is Built" (2 Cor, Mark)
AH4105, C537, CG590, EL596/597, G353, N403, P379,
SA662, SH324, UM368 (PD)
"In Christ There Is No East or West" (2 Cor, Mark)
C687, CG273, E529, EL650 (PD), G317/318, N394/395,
P439/440, SA1006, SH226, UM548, VU606
"Jesús Es Mi Rey Soberano" ("O Jesus, My King") (Mark)
C109, P157, SH211, UM180
"Lord of the Dance" (Mark)
G157, P302, SA141, UM261, VU352

"O Love, How Deep" (Mark)
E448/449, EL322, G618, N209, P83, SH115, UM267, VU348
"They'll Know We Are Christians" 26997 (Mark)
AH4074, C494, CG272, G300, S2223, SH232
"Gather Us In" (Mark)
C284, EL532, G401, S2236, SH393

Additional Contemporary and Modern Suggestions
"The Family Prayer Song" 1680466 (1 Sam, Mark)
"Glorify Thy Name" 1383 (Pss)
CG8, S2016, SA582, SH427
"Give Thanks" (Pss)
C528, CG373, G647, S2036, SA364, SH489
"He Is Exalted" 17827 (Pss)
AH4082, CG342, S2070, SH423
"I Exalt You" 17803 (Pss)
"Be Exalted, O God" ("I Will Give Thanks") 21112 (Pss)
"We Bow Down" 20003 (Pss)
"Hallelujah" ("Your Love Is Amazing") 3091812 (Pss)
"You Are Good" 3383788 (Pss)
"You Are My All in All" 825356 (Pss)
"Your Love, Oh Lord" 1894255 (Pss)
"Came to My Rescue" 4705190 (Pss)
"Here As In Heaven" 7051506 (1 Cor)
"My Redeemer Lives" 2397964 (1 Cor)
"Open the Eyes of My Heart" 2298355 (1 Cor)
G452, SA270, SH378, WS3008
"Able" 1256560 (1 Cor, Mark)
"Jesus, Lover of My Soul" 1198817 (1 Cor, Mark)
"Cornerstone" 6158927 (1 Cor, Mark)
"Grace Alone" 2335524 (1 Cor, Mark)
CG43, S2162, SA699.
"I'm So Glad Jesus Lifted Me" (Mark)
C529, EL860 (PD), N474, S2151
"Sing the Praise of God Our Maker" (Mark)
"The Dark Is Not Your Time" 7132934 (Mark)

Vocal Solos
"I Couldn't Hear Nobody Pray" (1 Sam)
V-7   p. 40/43
"The Body of the Lord" (Mark, Comm.)
V-8   p. 344
"Man of Your Word" (Mark)
V-9   p. 71

Anthems
"We Shall Overcome" (2 Cor)
Arr. Tom Trenney; Augsburg 9781506414010
SATB with djembe (https://bit.ly/AF-14010)

"Lord, for Thy Tender Mercy's Sake" (Mark)
Richard Farrant; Oxford 9780193852976
SATB *a cappella* (https://bit.ly/5-2976)

Other Suggestions
Visuals:
O   Crown, purple, Samuel, symbols of political power
P   Crown, rejoicing, victory
E   Bible, new growth coming out of decay, heavenly home
G   Crowns, kingdoms/house divided, chains, strength, family
Call to Worship: C486, CG275, S2225, stanza 1. "Who Is My Mother, Who Is My Brother?" (Mark, Comm.)
Alternate Lessons: Gen 3:8-15; Ps 130
See The Abingdon Worship Annual 2024 *for more ideas.*
Theme Ideas: Children / Family of God, Faith, Faithfulness, God: Kingdom of God, Healing

1 Samuel 15:34–16:13

[34]Then Samuel went to Ramah, and Saul went up to his house in Gibeah of Saul. [35]Samuel did not see Saul again until the day of his death, but Samuel grieved over Saul. And the LORD was sorry that he had made Saul king over Israel.

16 The LORD said to Samuel, "How long will you grieve over Saul? I have rejected him from being king over Israel. Fill your horn with oil and set out; I will send you to Jesse the Bethlehemite, for I have provided for myself a king among his sons." [2]Samuel said, "How can I go? If Saul hears of it, he will kill me." And the LORD said, "Take a heifer with you and say, 'I have come to sacrifice to the LORD.' [3]Invite Jesse to the sacrifice, and I will show you what you shall do, and you shall anoint for me the one whom I name to you." [4]Samuel did what the LORD commanded and came to Bethlehem. The elders of the city came to meet him trembling and said, "Do you come peaceably?" [5]He said, "Peaceably. I have come to sacrifice to the LORD; sanctify yourselves and come with me to the sacrifice." And he sanctified Jesse and his sons and invited them to the sacrifice.

[6]When they came, he looked on Eliab and thought, "Surely his anointed is now before the LORD." [7]But the LORD said to Samuel, "Do not look on his appearance or on the height of his stature, because I have rejected him, for the LORD does not see as mortals see; they look on the outward appearance, but the LORD looks on the heart." [8]Then Jesse called Abinadab and made him pass before Samuel. He said, "Neither has the LORD chosen this one." [9]Then Jesse made Shammah pass by. And he said, "Neither has the LORD chosen this one." [10]Jesse made seven of his sons pass before Samuel, and Samuel said to Jesse, "The LORD has not chosen any of these." [11]Samuel said to Jesse, "Are all your sons here?" And he said, "There remains yet the youngest, but he is keeping the sheep." And Samuel said to Jesse, "Send and bring him, for we will not sit down until he comes here." [12]He sent and brought him in. Now he was ruddy and had beautiful eyes and was handsome. The LORD said, "Rise and anoint him, for this is the one." [13]Then Samuel took the horn of oil and anointed him in the presence of his brothers, and the spirit of the LORD came mightily upon David from that day forward. Samuel then set out and went to Ramah.

Psalm 20 (G548, N631, P169)

The LORD answer you in the day of trouble!
    The name of the God of Jacob protect you!
[2]May he send you help from the sanctuary
    and give you support from Zion.
[3]May he remember all your offerings
    and regard with favor your burnt sacrifices.   *Selah*
[4]May he grant you your heart's desire
    and fulfill all your plans.
[5]May we shout for joy over your victory
    and in the name of our God set up our banners.
    May the LORD fulfill all your petitions.
[6]Now I know that the LORD will help his anointed;
    he will answer him from his holy heaven
    with mighty victories by his right hand.
[7]Some take pride in chariots and some in horses,
    but our pride is in the name of the LORD our God.
[8]They will collapse and fall,
    but we shall rise and stand upright.
[9]Give victory to the king, O LORD;
    answer us when we call.

2 Corinthians 5:6-10 (11-13), 14-17

[6]So we are always confident, even though we know that while we are at home in the body we are away from the Lord—[7]for we walk by faith, not by sight. [8]Yes, we do have confidence, and we would rather be away from the body and at home with the Lord. [9]So whether we are at home or away, we make it our aim to be pleasing to him. [10]For all of us must appear before the judgment seat of Christ, so that each may receive due recompense for actions done in the body, whether good or evil.

([11]Therefore, knowing the fear of the Lord, we try to persuade people, but we ourselves are well known to God, and I hope that we are also well known to your consciences. [12]We are not commending ourselves to you again but giving you an opportunity to boast about us, so that you may be able to answer those who boast in outward appearance and not in the heart. [13]For if we are beside ourselves, it is for God; if we are in our right mind, it is for you.) [14]For the love of Christ urges us on, because we are convinced that one has died for all; therefore all have died. [15]And he died for all, so that those who live might live no longer for themselves but for the one who for their sake died and was raised.

[16]From now on, therefore, we regard no one from a human point of view; even though we once knew Christ from a human point of view, we no longer know him in that way. [17]So if anyone is in Christ, there is a new creation: everything old has passed away; look, new things have come into being!

Mark 4:26-34

[26]He also said, "The kingdom of God is as if someone would scatter seed on the ground [27]and would sleep and rise night and day, and the seed would sprout and grow, he does not know how. [28]The earth produces of itself first the stalk, then the head, then the full grain in the head. [29]But when the grain is ripe, at once he goes in with his sickle because the harvest has come."

[30]He also said, "With what can we compare the kingdom of God, or what parable will we use for it? [31]It is like a mustard seed, which, when sown upon the ground, is the smallest of all the seeds on earth, [32]yet when it is sown it grows up and becomes the greatest of all shrubs and puts forth large branches, so that the birds of the air can make nests in its shade."

[33]With many such parables he spoke the word to them as they were able to hear it; [34]he did not speak to them except in parables, but he explained everything in private to his disciples.

Primary Hymns and Songs for the Day

"All Hail the Power of Jesus' Name" (2 Cor) (O)
  C91, CG339, E450, EL634, G263, N304, P142, SA73, SH207,
  UM154 (PD)
    H-3   Hbl-45; Chr-22; Desc-24; Org-20
    S-1   #66-70. Various treatments
  C92, CG340, P143, UM155 (PD)
    H-3   Desc-29; Org-27
    S-2   #50-51. Descant and interlude
  E451, VU334

"Loving Spirit" (1 Sam, Mark)
  C244, EL397, G293, P323, S2123, VU387

"We Walk by Faith" (2 Cor, Mark)
  CG634, E209, EL635, G817, N256, P399, S2196, SH660
    H-3   Chr-21

"For the Fruits of This Creation" (Mark)
  C714, E424, CG376, EL679, G36, N425, P553, SA15, UM97,
  VU227
    H-3   Chr-60, 67, 73, 79; Org-6
    S-2   #14. Descant

"God of the Fertile Fields" (Mark)
  C695, CG668, G714
    H-3   Hbl-28, 53; Chr-56; Desc-57; Org-63
    S-1   #185-186. Descant and harmonization

Pues Si Vivimos ("When We Are Living") (2 Cor, Mark,
  Comm.) (C)
  C536, CG265, EL639, G822, N499, P400, SH299, UM356, VU581
    S-1   #320. Orff instrument arrangement
    H-3   Chr-218; Org-155

Additional Hymn Suggestions

"Open My Eyes, That I May See" (1 Sam)
  C586, CG395, G451, P324, SH583, UM454, VU371

"Send Me, Lord" (1 Sam)
  C447, EL809, G746, N360, SH723, UM497, VU572

"Here I Am, Lord" (1 Sam)
  C452, CG482, EL574, G69, SA1002, SH608, UM593, VU509

"In the Midst of New Dimensions" (1 Sam)
  G315, N391, S2238

"Gather Us In" (1 Sam, Mark)
  C284, EL532, G401, S2236, SH393

"What Wondrous Love Is This" (2 Cor)
  C200, CG171, E439, EL666, G215, N223, P85, SA207, SH177,
  UM292, VU147 (Fr.)

"Love Divine, All Loves Excelling" (2 Cor)
  C517, CG281, E657, EL631, G366, N43, P376, SA262,
  SH353/354, UM384 (PD), VU333

"Womb of Life" (2 Cor)
  C14, G3, N274, S2046

"My Song Is Love Unknown" (2 Cor)
  E458, EL343, G209, N222, P76, S2083, SA149, VU143

"Just a Closer Walk with Thee" (2 Cor)
  C557, EL697, G835, S2158, SH584

"I'll Fly Away" (2 Cor)
  N595, S2282

"Mothering God, You Gave Me Birth" (2 Cor, Mark)
  C83, N467, S2050, VU320

"The Care the Eagle Gives Her Young" (Mark)
  C76, N468, UVU269

Sois la Semilla ("You Are the Seed") (Mark)
  C478, N528, UM583

"Come, Ye Thankful People, Come" (Mark)
  C718, CG372, E290, EL693, G367, N422, P551, SA9, SH355,
  UM694 (PD), VU516

"Hymn of Promise" (Mark)
  C638, CG545, G250, N433, UM707, VU703

"God the Sculptor of the Mountains" (Mark)
  EL736, G5, S2060

"Bring Forth the Kingdom" (Mark)
  N181, S2190, SH130

Additional Contemporary and Modern Suggestions

"Spirit of the Living God" 23488 (1 Sam)
  C259, CG234, G288, N283, P322, SA312/313, SH555,
  UM393, VU376, S-1 #212 Vocal desc. idea

"Sanctuary" 24140 (1 Sam)
  G701, S2164, SH265

"Awesome in This Place" 847554 (1 Sam)

"From Ashes to Beauty" 5288953 (1 Sam)

"Nobody" 7121827 (1 Sam)

"Refresh My Heart" 917518 (1 Sam, 2 Cor)

"Shout to the Lord" 1406918 (Pss)
  CG348, EL821, S2074, SA264, SH426

"Desert Song" 5060793 (Pss)

"Promises" 6454250 (Pss, 2 Cor)

"We Want to See Jesus Lifted High" 1033408 (2 Cor)

"Oceans" ("Where Feet May Fail") 6428767 (2 Cor)

"We Believe" 6367165 (2 Cor)

"You Have Saved Us" 5548514 (2 Cor)

"Jesus, Draw Me Close" 443680 (2 Cor)

"You Are My King" ("Amazing Love") 2456623 (2 Cor)

"One Way" 4222082 (2 Cor, Mark)

"I Will Not Forget You" 2694306 (Mark)

"This Kingdom" 1650898 (Mark)

"Dream Small" 7112606 (Mark)

"The Family Prayer Song" 1680466 (Father's Day)

Vocal Solos

"My Heart Is Steadfast" (1 Sam, 2 Cor)
  V-5 (2)   p. 40
"Just a Closer Walk with Thee" (2 Cor)
  V-8   p. 323
"The Blessing" (1 Sam, 2 Cor)
  V-9   p. 10

Anthems

"Just a Closer Walk with Thee" (2 Cor)
Arr. Joel Raney, Hope C6371
SATB, piano, opt. orchestra (https://bit.ly/C-6371)

"Thanks Be To God" (Mark)
Allen Pote; Hope C-5881
SATB, keyboard, opt. oboe (https://bit.ly/C-5881)

Other Suggestions

Visuals:
  O   Several vials of oil, anointing
  P   Vials of oil, rejoicing, victory
  E   Cross wrapped with white cloth, resurrection, recon-
       ciliation
  G   Bag of seeds, several small plants, one larger plant,
       stalks of wheat

Call to Worship: G283, S2124, VU383. "Come, O Holy Spirit,
  Come" (1 Sam)

Call to Prayer: UM388, stanza 1. "O Come and Dwell in Me"
  (2 Cor)

Offering Prayer: WSL111. "Holy God, we give you" (2 Cor)

Benediction: CG520, EL551, S2241. "The Spirit Sends Us Forth
  to Serve" (1 Sam)

Alternate Lessons: Eze 17:22-24; Ps 92:1-4, 12-15

Theme Ideas: Faith, God: Call of God / Listening, God:
  Kingdom of God, Growth, New Creation, Vision

1 Samuel 17:(1a, 4-11, 19-23), 32-49

(Now the Philistines gathered their armies for battle. . . . [4]And there came out from the camp of the Philistines a champion named Goliath, of Gath, whose height was four cubits and a span. [5]He had a helmet of bronze on his head, and he was armed with a coat of mail; the weight of the coat was five thousand shekels of bronze. [6]He had greaves of bronze on his legs and a javelin of bronze slung between his shoulders. [7]The shaft of his spear was like a weaver's beam, and his spear's head weighed six hundred shekels of iron, and his shield-bearer went before him. [8]He stood and shouted to the ranks of Israel, "Why have you come out to draw up for battle? Am I not a Philistine, and are you not servants of Saul? Choose a man for yourselves, and let him come down to me. [9]If he is able to fight with me and kill me, then we will be your servants, but if I prevail against him and kill him, then you shall be our servants and serve us." [10]And the Philistine said, "Today I defy the ranks of Israel! Give me a man, that we may fight together." [11]When Saul and all Israel heard these words of the Philistine, they were dismayed and greatly afraid. . . .

[19]Now Saul, and they, and all the men of Israel were in the valley of Elah fighting with the Philistines. [20]David rose early in the morning, left the sheep with a keeper, took the provisions, and went as Jesse had commanded him. He came to the encampment as the army was going forth to the battle line, shouting the war cry. [21]Israel and the Philistines drew up for battle, army against army. [22]David left the things in charge of the keeper of the baggage, ran to the ranks, and went and greeted his brothers. [23]As he talked with them, the champion, the Philistine of Gath, Goliath by name, came up out of the ranks of the Philistines and spoke the same words as before. And David heard him. . . .)

[32]David said to Saul, "Let no one's heart fail because of him; your servant will go and fight with this Philistine." [33]Saul said to David, "You are not able to go against this Philistine to fight with him, for you are just a boy, and he has been a warrior from his youth." [34]But David said to Saul, "Your servant used to keep sheep for his father, and whenever a lion or a bear came and took a lamb from the flock, [35]I went after it and struck it down, rescuing the lamb from its mouth, and if it turned against me, I would catch it by the jaw, strike it down, and kill it. [36]Your servant has killed both lions and bears, and this uncircumcised Philistine shall be like one of them, since he has defied the armies of the living God." [37]David said, "The Lord, who saved me from the paw of the lion and from the paw of the bear, will save me from the hand of this Philistine." So Saul said to David, "Go, and may the Lord be with you!"

[38]Saul clothed David with his armor; he put a bronze helmet on his head and clothed him with a coat of mail. [39]David strapped Saul's sword over the armor, and he tried in vain to walk, for he was not used to them. Then David said to Saul, "I cannot walk with these, for I am not used to them." So David removed them. [40]Then he took his staff in his hand and chose five smooth stones from the wadi and put them in his shepherd's bag, in the pouch; his sling was in his hand, and he drew near to the Philistine.

[41]The Philistine came on and drew near to David, with his shield-bearer in front of him. [42]When the Philistine looked and saw David, he disdained him, for he was only a youth, ruddy and handsome in appearance. [43]The Philistine said to David, "Am I a dog, that you come to me with sticks?" And the Philistine cursed David by his gods. [44]The Philistine said to David, "Come to me, and I will give your flesh to the birds of the air and to the wild animals of the field." [45]But David said to the Philistine, "You come to me with sword and spear and javelin, but I come to you in the name of the Lord of hosts, the God of the armies of Israel, whom you have defied. [46]This very day the Lord will deliver you into my hand, and I will strike you down and cut off your head, and I will give the dead bodies of the Philistine army this very day to the birds of the air and to the wild animals of the earth, so that all the earth may know that there is a God in Israel [47]and that all this assembly may know that the Lord does not save by sword and spear, for the battle is the Lord's, and he will give you into our hand."

[48]When the Philistine drew nearer to meet David, David ran quickly toward the battle line to meet the Philistine. [49]David put his hand in his bag, took out a stone, slung it, and struck the Philistine on his forehead; the stone sank into his forehead, and he fell face down on the ground.

Psalm 9:9-20 (G356, N625, SH253, UM744)

[9]The Lord is a stronghold for the oppressed,
  a stronghold in times of trouble.
[10]And those who know your name put their trust in you,
  for you, O Lord, have not forsaken those who seek you.
[11]Sing praises to the Lord, who dwells in Zion.
  Declare his deeds among the peoples.
[12]For he who avenges blood is mindful of them;
  he does not forget the cry of the afflicted.
[13]Be gracious to me, O Lord.
  See what I suffer from those who hate me;
  you are the one who lifts me up from the gates of death,
[14]so that I may recount all your praises
  and, in the gates of daughter Zion,
  rejoice in your deliverance.
[15]The nations have sunk in the pit that they made;
  in the net that they hid has their own foot been caught.
[16]The Lord has made himself known; he has executed judgment;
  the wicked are snared in the work of their own hands.
          Higgaion. Selah
[17]The wicked shall depart to Sheol,
  all the nations that forget God.
[18]For the needy shall not always be forgotten,
  nor the hope of the poor perish forever.
[19]Rise up, O Lord! Do not let mortals prevail;
  let the nations be judged before you.
[20]Put them in fear, O Lord;
  let the nations know that they are only human. *Selah*

2 Corinthians 6:1-13

As we work together with him, we entreat you also not to accept the grace of God in vain. [2]For he says,
  "At an acceptable time I have listened to you,
    and on a day of salvation I have helped you."
Look, now is the acceptable time; look, now is the day of salvation! [3]We are putting no obstacle in anyone's way, so that no fault may be found with our ministry, [4]but as servants of God we have commended ourselves in every way: in great endurance, afflictions, hardships, calamities, [5]beatings, imprisonments, riots, labors, sleepless nights, hunger; [6]in purity, knowledge, patience, kindness, holiness of spirit, genuine love, [7]truthful speech, and the power of God; with the weapons of righteousness for the right hand and for the left; [8]in honor and dishonor, in ill repute and good repute. We are treated as impostors and yet are true, [9]as unknown and yet are well known, as dying and look—we are alive, as punished and yet not killed, [10]as sorrowful yet always rejoicing, as poor yet making many rich, as having nothing and yet possessing everything.

[11]We have spoken frankly to you Corinthians; our heart is wide open to you. [12]There is no restriction in our affections but only in yours. [13]In return—I speak as to children—open wide your hearts also.

Mark 4:35-41

[35]On that day, when evening had come, he said to them, "Let us go across to the other side." [36]And leaving the crowd behind, they took him with them in the boat, just as he was. Other boats were with him. [37]A great windstorm arose, and the waves beat into the boat, so that the boat was already being swamped. [38]But he was in the stern, asleep on the cushion, and they woke him up and said to him, "Teacher, do you not care that we are perishing?" [39]And waking up, he rebuked the wind and said to the sea, "Be silent! Be still!" Then the wind ceased, and there was a dead calm. [40]He said to them, "Why are you afraid? Have you still no faith?" [41]And they were filled with great fear and said to one another, "Who then is this, that even the wind and the sea obey him?"

Primary Hymns and Songs for the Day

"How Firm a Foundation" (Mark) (O)
C618, CG425, E636/637, EL796, G463, N407, P361, SA804,
SH291, UM529 (PD), VU660
- H-3   Hbl-27, 69; Chr-102; Desc-41; Org-41
- S-1   #133. Harmonization
         #134. Performance note

"Fight the Good Fight" (1 Sam)
E552, G846, P307 (PD), SA952, VU674
- H-3   Hbl-29, 57; Chr-117; Desc-31; Org-31
- S-1   #100-103. Various treatments.

"I Greet Thee, Who My Sure Redeemer Art" (2 Cor, Mark)
G624, N251, P457, VU393
- H-3   Chr-78, 106; Desc-101; Org-165

"Give to the Winds Thy Fears" (2 Cor, Mark)
CG55, G815, N404, P286, SA643, UM129 (PD), VU636
- H-3   Chr-71; Desc-39; Org-39
- S-1   #129. Descant

"Be Still, My Soul" (2 Cor, Mark)
C566, CG57, G819, N488, SH330, UM534, VU652
- H-3   Chr-36

"Lonely the Boat" (Mark)
G185, P373, UM476

"Eternal Father, Strong to Save" (Mark)
C85, CG14, E608, EL756, G8, P562 (PD), S2191, SA11,
VU659
- H-3   Chr-63; Desc-74; Org-89

"It Is Well with My Soul" (2 Cor, Mark) (C)
C561, CG573, EL785, G840, N438, SA741, SH305, UM377
- H-3   Chr-113

Additional Hymn Suggestions

"Lead Me, Lord" (1 Sam)
C593, N774, UM473 (PD), VU662

"Saranam, Saranam" ("Refuge") (1 Sam)
G789, UM523

"By Gracious Powers" (1 Sam, Pss)
E695/696, G818, N413, P342, UM517

"We Shall Overcome" (1 Sam, Pss)
AH4047/4048, C630, G379, N570, UM533

"A Mighty Fortress Is Our God" (1 Sam, Pss, Mark)
C65, CG418, E687/688, EL503/504/505, N439/440,
P259/260, SA1, SH651, UM110 (PD), VU261/262/263

"God of Grace and God of Glory" (1 Sam, Pss, Mark) (C)
C464, CG285, E594/595, EL705, G307, N436, P420, SA814,
SH250, UM577, VU686

"O Day of God, Draw Nigh" (2 Cor)
C700, E601, N611, P452, UM730 (PD), VU688/689

"In the Singing" (2 Cor, Comm.)
EL466, G533, S2255

"God of the Sparrow, God of the Whale" (Mark)
C70, EL740, G22, N32, P272, UM122, VU229

"My Hope Is Built" (Mark)
AH4105, C537, CG590, EL596/597, G353, N403, P379,
SA662, SH324, UM368 (PD)

"Be Still, My Soul" (Mark)
C566, G891, N488, SH330, UM534, VU652

"Jesus, Lover of My Soul" (Mark)
C542, CG406, E699, G440, N546, P303, SA257, SH542/543,
UM479, VU669

"Blessed Quietness" (Mark)
C267, CG244, N284, S2142

"His Eye Is on the Sparrow" (Mark)
C82, G661, N475, S2146, SH322

"My Life Flows On" ("How Can I Keep from Singing") (Mark)
C619, CG592, EL763, G821, N476, S2212, SA663, VU716

Additional Contemporary and Modern Suggestions

"Oh, I Know the Lord's Laid His Hands on Me" (1 Sam)
S2139

"Nada Te Turbe" ("Nothing Can Trouble") (1 Sam, Pss)
CG73, G820, N772, S2054, SH292, VU290

"My Savior Lives" 4882965 (Pss)

"Ah, Lord God" 17896 (1 Sam, Pss)

"What a Mighty God We Serve" 2245023 (1 Sam, Pss)

"Great and Mighty Is He" 66665 (1 Sam, Pss)

"Awesome God" 41099 (1 Sam, Mark)
G616, S2040

"The Battle Belongs to the Lord" 21583 (1 Sam, 2 Cor)

"Foundation" 706151 (1 Sam, 2 Cor, Mark)

"Promises" 6454250 (1 Sam, 2 Cor, Mark)

"We Want to See Jesus Lifted High" 1033408 (2 Cor)

"Counting on God" 5064366 (2 Cor)

"I Will Boast" 4662350 (2 Cor)

"Through It All" 18211 (2 Cor)
C555, UM507

"Be Still and Know That I Am God" (Mark)
G414, N743, S2057, SH55

"Be Still and Know" 2758912 (2 Cor, Mark)

"Oh Lord, You're Beautiful" 14514 (Mark)

"Healer of Our Every Ill" (Mark)
C506, EL612, G795, S2213, SH339, VU619

"Across the Lands" 3709898 (Mark)

"How Can I Keep from Singing" 4822372 (Mark)

"Jesus, Lover of My Soul" 1198817 (Mark)

"You Never Let Go" 4674166 (Mark)

"Oceans" ("Where Feet May Fail") 6428767 (Mark)

"Cornerstone" 6158927 (Mark)

"My Hope Is In You" 6070957 (Mark)

Vocal Solos

"Joshua Fit the Battle of Jericho" (1 Sam, 2 Cor)
- V-3 (1)   p. 57

"What God Hath Promised" (2 Cor)
- V-8   p. 297

"It Is Well with My Soul" (Mark)
- V-5 (2)   p. 35

"Peace Be Still" (Mark)
- V-9   p. 64

Anthems

"If You But Trust in God to Guide You" (1 Sam)
Arr. David M. Cherwien; MorningStar MSM-60-9027
SATB, organ, opt. flute, cello (https://bit.ly/MS-9027)

"Be Still and Know That I Am God" (Mark)
Allen Pote; Hinshaw HMC-2548
SATB, piano (https://bit.ly/HMC-2548)

Other Suggestions

Visuals:
- **O**   Armor, sword/spear, slingshot, stones, bag
- **P**   Globe, scales of justice, rejoicing
- **E**   Clock set for worship hour, all ages enduring hardship, poor smiling
- **G**   Boat, storm at sea, fear, peace, calm, sleeping, Jesus in command

Call to Worship: C593, N774, UM473 (PD), VU662. "Lead Me, Lord" (1 Sam)

Scripture Response: C566, G891, N488, SH330, UM534, VU652, stanza 2. "Be Still, My Soul" (Mark)

Alternate Lessons: Job 38:1-11; Ps 107:1-3, 23-32

Theme Ideas: Comfort, Courage, Faith, Faithfulness, God: Providence / God our Help

2 Samuel 1:1, 17-27

After the death of Saul, when David had returned from defeating the Amalekites, David remained two days in Ziklag. . . .

[17]David intoned this lamentation over Saul and his son Jonathan. [18](He ordered that The Song of the Bow be taught to the people of Judah; it is written in the Book of Jashar.) He said,

[19]"Your glory, O Israel, lies slain upon your high places!
How the mighty have fallen!
[20]Tell it not in Gath;
proclaim it not in the streets of Ashkelon,
or the daughters of the Philistines will rejoice;
the daughters of the uncircumcised will exult.
[21]You mountains of Gilboa,
let there be no dew or rain upon you
nor bounteous fields!
For there the shield of the mighty was defiled,
the shield of Saul, anointed with oil no more.
[22]From the blood of the slain,
from the fat of the mighty,
the bow of Jonathan did not turn back,
nor the sword of Saul return empty.
[23]Saul and Jonathan, beloved and lovely!
In life and in death they were not divided;
they were swifter than eagles;
they were stronger than lions.
[24]O daughters of Israel, weep over Saul,
who clothed you with crimson, in luxury,
who put ornaments of gold on your apparel.
[25]How the mighty have fallen
in the midst of the battle!
Jonathan lies slain upon your high places.
[26]I am distressed for you, my brother Jonathan;
greatly beloved were you to me;
your love to me was wonderful,
passing the love of women.
[27]How the mighty have fallen,
and the weapons of war perished!"

Psalm 130 (G424, N709, P240, UM848)

Out of the depths I cry to you, O LORD.
[2]Lord, hear my voice!
Let your ears be attentive
to the voice of my supplications!
[3]If you, O LORD, should mark iniquities,
Lord, who could stand?
[4]But there is forgiveness with you,
so that you may be revered.
[5]I wait for the LORD; my soul waits,
and in his word I hope;
[6]my soul waits for the Lord
more than those who watch for the morning,
more than those who watch for the morning.
[7]O Israel, hope in the LORD!
For with the LORD there is steadfast love,
and with him is great power to redeem.
[8]It is he who will redeem Israel
from all its iniquities.

2 Corinthians 8:7-15

[7]Now as you excel in everything—in faith, in speech, in knowledge, in utmost eagerness, and in our love for you—so we want you to excel also in this generous undertaking. [8]I do not say this as a command, but I am, by mentioning the eagerness of others, testing the genuineness of your love. [9]For you know the generous act of our Lord Jesus Christ, that though he was rich, yet for your sakes he became poor, so that by his poverty you might become rich. [10]And in this matter I am giving my opinion: it is beneficial for you who began last year not only to do something but even to desire to do something. [11]Now finish doing it, so that your eagerness may be matched by completing it according to your means. [12]For if the eagerness is there, the gift is acceptable according to what one has, not according to what one does not have. [13]For I do not mean that there should be relief for others and hardship for you, but it is a question of equality between [14]your present abundance and their need, so that their abundance may also supply your need, in order that there may be equality. [15]As it is written,

"The one who had much did not have too much,
and the one who had little did not have too little."

Mark 5:21-43

[21]When Jesus had crossed again in the boat to the other side, a great crowd gathered around him, and he was by the sea. [22]Then one of the leaders of the synagogue, named Jairus, came and, when he saw him, fell at his feet [23]and pleaded with him repeatedly, "My little daughter is at the point of death. Come and lay your hands on her, so that she may be made well and live." [24]So he went with him.

And a large crowd followed him and pressed in on him. [25]Now there was a woman who had been suffering from a flow of blood for twelve years. [26]She had endured much under many physicians and had spent all that she had, and she was no better but rather grew worse. [27]She had heard about Jesus and came up behind him in the crowd and touched his cloak, [28]for she said, "If I but touch his cloak, I will be made well." [29]Immediately her flow of blood stopped, and she felt in her body that she was healed of her disease. [30]Immediately aware that power had gone forth from him, Jesus turned about in the crowd and said, "Who touched my cloak?" [31]And his disciples said to him, "You see the crowd pressing in on you; how can you say, 'Who touched me?'" [32]He looked all around to see who had done it. [33]But the woman, knowing what had happened to her, came in fear and trembling, fell down before him, and told him the whole truth. [34]He said to her, "Daughter, your faith has made you well; go in peace, and be healed of your disease."

[35]While he was still speaking, some people came from the synagogue leader's house to say, "Your daughter is dead. Why trouble the teacher any further?" [36]But overhearing what they said, Jesus said to the synagogue leader, "Do not be afraid; only believe." [37]He allowed no one to follow him except Peter, James, and John, the brother of James. [38]When they came to the synagogue leader's house, he saw a commotion, people weeping and wailing loudly. [39]When he had entered, he said to them, "Why do you make a commotion and weep? The child is not dead but sleeping." [40]And they laughed at him. Then he put them all outside and took the child's father and mother and those who were with him and went in where the child was. [41]Taking her by the hand, he said to her, "Talitha koum," which means, "Little girl, get up!" [42]And immediately the girl stood up and began to walk about (she was twelve years of age). At this they were overcome with amazement. [43]He strictly ordered them that no one should know this and told them to give her something to eat.

Primary Hymns and Songs for the Day
"O God, Our Help in Ages Past" (2 Sam) (O)
　　C67, CG566, E680, EL632, G687, N25, P210, SA47, SH41,
　　UM117 (PD), VU806
　　　　　H-3　Hbl-87; Chr-60, 143; Desc-93; Org-132
　　　　　S-1　#293-296. Various treatments
"Out of the Depths I Cry to You" (2 Sam, Pss, Mark)
　　EL600, G424, N483, P240, SH513, UM515
"Come, Ye Sinners, Poor and Needy" (Mark) (O)
　　CG471, G415, UM340
"Healer of Our Every Ill" (2 Sam, Mark)
　　C506, EL612, G795, S2213, SH339, VU619
"God, Whose Giving Knows No Ending" (2 Cor)
　　C606, CG671, G716, N565, P422
　　　　　H-3　Hbl-14, 64; Chr-132, 203
　　　　　S-2　#22. Descant
"Where Cross the Crowded Ways of Life" (2 Cor, Mark)
　　C665, CG657, E609, EL719, G343, N543, UM427, VU681
　　　　　H-3　Chr-178, 180; Org-44
　　　　　S-1　#141-143 Various treatments
"Cuando el Pobre" ("When the Poor Ones") (2 Cor, Mark)
　　C662, EL725, G762, P407, SH240, UM434, VU702
"The Church of Christ in Every Age" (2 Cor, Mark) (C)
　　C475, EL729, G320, N306, P421, UM589, VU601
　　　　　H-3　Hbl-93; Chr-60, 84; Desc-102; Org-175
　　　　　S-2　#191. Harmonization
"Draw Us in the Spirit's Tether" (Mark, Comm.)
　　C392, EL470, G529, N337, P504, UM632, VU479

Additional Hymn Suggestions
"Abide with Me" (2 Sam, Pss)
　　C636, CG543, E662, EL629, G836, N99, P543, SA529, SH475,
　　UM700 (PD), VU436
"Out of the Depths" (2 Sam, Pss)
　　C510, N554, S2136, VU611
"Hear My Prayer, O God" (2 Sam, Pss, Mark)
　　G782, WS3131
"I'm Gonna Live So God Can Use Me" (2 Cor)
　　C614, G700, P369, S2153, SH632, VU575
"Gather Us In" (2 Cor, Comm.)
　　C284, EL532, G401, S2236, SH393
"O Christ, the Healer" (Mark)
　　C503, EL610, G793, N175, P380, UM265
"Woman in the Night" (Stanza 2) (Mark)
　　C188, G161, UM274
"Pass Me Not, O Gentle Savior" (Mark)
　　AH4107, N551, SA782, UM351 (PD), VU665
"Just As I Am, Without One Plea" (Mark, Comm.)
　　C339, CG500, E693, EL592, G442, N207, P370, SA503,
　　SH500, UM357 (PD), VU508
"An Outcast among Outcasts" (Mark)
　　N201, S2104
"This Is My Song" (Independence Day)
　　C722, CG697, EL887, G340, N591, UM437

Additional Contemporary and Modern Suggestions
"Cares Chorus" 25974 (2 Sam, Pss)
"Be Still and Know That I Am God" (2 Sam, Pss, Mark)
　　G414, N743, S2057, SH55
"Be Still and Know" 2758912 (2 Sam, Pss, Mark)
"Wait for the Lord" (Pss)
　　CG644, EL262, G90, SH580, VU22, WS3049
"People Need the Lord" 18084 (Pss, Mark)
"Give Thanks" (2 Cor)
　　C528, CG373, G647, S2036, SA364, SH489
"He Who Began a Good Work in You" 15238 (2 Cor)
"Make Me a Servant" 33131 (2 Cor)
　　CG651, S2176

"In the Lord I'll Be Ever Thankful" (2 Cor)
　　G654, S2195, SH316
"Here I Am to Worship" 3266032 (2 Cor)
　　CG297, SA114, SH395, WS3177
"Take This Life" 2563365 (2 Cor)
"These Hands" 3251827 (2 Cor)
"Oh Lord, You're Beautiful" 14514 (Mark)
"Open Our Eyes, Lord" 1572 (Mark)
　　CG392, S2086, SA386, SH562
"El-Shaddai" 26856 (Mark)
　　UM123, S-2 #54 Verses for Vocal Solo
"Surely the Presence of the Lord" 7909 (Mark)
　　C263, UM328; S-2 #200. Stanzas for soloist
"Spirit Song" 27824 (Mark)
　　C352, SH409, UM347
"Turn Your Eyes upon Jesus" 15960 (Mark)
　　CG472, SA445, UM349
"Something Beautiful" 18060 (Mark)
"Awesome God" 41099 (Mark)
　　G616, S2040
"I'm So Glad Jesus Lifted Me" (Mark)
　　C529, EL860 (PD), N474, S2151
"Change My Heart, O God" 1565 (Mark)
　　EL801, G695, S2152, SA409, SH507
"How Can I Keep from Singing" 4822372 (Mark)
"You Never Let Go" 4674166 (Mark)
"Awaken" 5491647 (Mark)
"Restored" 5894615 (Mark)
"The Dark Is Not Your Time" 7132934 (Mark)

Vocal Solos
"Like a Child" (2 Sam, Pss)
　　V-8　　　　p. 356
"Into the Sea" ("It's Gonna Be OK") (2 Sam, Pss)
　　V-9　　　　p. 48
"Nobody Knows the Trouble I've Seen" (Pss, Mark)
　　V-7　　　　p. 64/68
"Rise Up" ("Lazarus") (Mark)
　　V-9　　　　p. 97

Anthems
"I Will Wait for You" (Pss)
Arr. Victor Johnson; Choristers Guild CGA1607
SATB, piano (https://bit.ly/CG-1607)

"Out of the Depths I Cry to Thee" (Pss)
Arr. K. Lee Scott; Augsburg 9780800647322
2-part mixed, keyboard (https://bit.ly/AF-47322)

Other Suggestions
Visuals:
　　O　　Bow/sword, mourning, dead soldiers
　　P　　Darkness, prayer, patient waiting, early dawn,
　　　　　Ps 130:5, 6a
　　E　　Kindness, Jesus, poverty/wealth, full offering plate
　　G　　Boat, child dead/woman reaching, child well/woman
　　　　　rejoicing, Jesus healing
Prayer: UM461. For Those Who Mourn (2 Sam)
Prayer: UM446. Serving the Poor (2 Cor)
Prayer Response: CG399, EL751, G471, S2200, SH311/517/
　　"O Lord, Hear My Prayer" (Pss)
Benediction: C437, SH722, UM665, VU964. "Go Now in Peace"
　　(Mark)
Alternate Lessons: Wis 1:13-15; 2:23-24; Lam 3:23-33 or Ps 30
Theme Ideas: Grief, Healing, Lament, Stewardship

2 Samuel 5:1-5, 9-10

Then all the tribes of Israel came to David at Hebron and said, "Look, we are your bone and flesh. ²For some time, while Saul was king over us, it was you who led out Israel and brought it in. The LORD said to you, 'It is you who shall be shepherd of my people Israel, you who shall be ruler over Israel.'" ³So all the elders of Israel came to the king at Hebron, and King David made a covenant with them at Hebron before the LORD, and they anointed David king over Israel. ⁴David was thirty years old when he began to reign, and he reigned forty years. ⁵At Hebron he reigned over Judah seven years and six months, and at Jerusalem he reigned over all Israel and Judah thirty-three years. . . .

⁹David occupied the stronghold and named it the city of David. David built the city all around from the Millo inward. ¹⁰And David became greater and greater, for the LORD of hosts was with him.

Psalm 48 (N654, UM782)

Great is the LORD and greatly to be praised
    in the city of our God.
His holy mountain, ²beautiful in elevation,
    is the joy of all the earth,
Mount Zion, in the far north,
    the city of the great King.
³Within its citadels God
    has shown himself a sure defense.
⁴Then the kings assembled;
    they came on together.
⁵As soon as they saw it, they were astounded;
    they were in panic; they took to flight;
⁶trembling took hold of them there,
    pains as of a woman in labor,
⁷as when an east wind shatters
    the ships of Tarshish.
⁸As we have heard, so have we seen
    in the city of the LORD of hosts,
in the city of our God,
    which God establishes forever.   *Selah*
⁹We ponder your steadfast love, O God,
    in the midst of your temple.
¹⁰Your name, O God, like your praise,
    reaches to the ends of the earth.
Your right hand is filled with victory.
    ¹¹Let Mount Zion be glad;
let the towns of Judah rejoice
    because of your judgments.
¹²Walk about Zion; go all around it;
    count its towers;
¹³consider well its ramparts;
    go through its citadels,
that you may tell the next generation
    ¹⁴that this is God,
our God forever and ever.
    He will be our guide forever.

2 Corinthians 12:2-10

²I know a person in Christ who fourteen years ago was caught up to the third heaven—whether in the body or out of the body I do not know; God knows. ³And I know that such a person—whether in the body or out of the body I do not know; God knows—⁴was caught up into paradise and heard things that are not to be told, that no mortal is permitted to repeat. ⁵On behalf of such a one I will boast, but on my own behalf I will not boast, except of my weaknesses. ⁶But if I wish to boast, I will not be a fool, for I will be speaking the truth. But I refrain from it, so that no one may think better of me than what is seen in me or heard from me, ⁷even considering the exceptional character of the revelations. Therefore, to keep me from being too elated, a thorn was given me in the flesh, a messenger of Satan to torment me, to keep me from being too elated. ⁸Three times I appealed to the Lord about this, that it would leave me, ⁹but he said to me, "My grace is sufficient for you, for power is made perfect in weakness." So I will boast all the more gladly of my weaknesses, so that the power of Christ may dwell in me. ¹⁰Therefore I am content with weaknesses, insults, hardships, persecutions, and calamities for the sake of Christ, for whenever I am weak, then I am strong.

Mark 6:1-13

He left that place and came to his hometown, and his disciples followed him. ²On the Sabbath he began to teach in the synagogue, and many who heard him were astounded. They said, "Where did this man get all this? What is this wisdom that has been given to him? What deeds of power are being done by his hands! ³Is not this the carpenter, the son of Mary and brother of James and Joses and Judas and Simon, and are not his sisters here with us?" And they took offense at him. ⁴Then Jesus said to them, "Prophets are not without honor, except in their hometown and among their own kin and in their own house." ⁵And he could do no deed of power there, except that he laid his hands on a few sick people and cured them. ⁶And he was amazed at their unbelief.

Then he went about among the villages teaching. ⁷He called the twelve and began to send them out two by two and gave them authority over the unclean spirits. ⁸He ordered them to take nothing for their journey except a staff: no bread, no bag, no money in their belts, ⁹but to wear sandals and not to put on two tunics. ¹⁰He said to them, "Wherever you enter a house, stay there until you leave the place. ¹¹If any place will not welcome you and they refuse to hear you, as you leave, shake off the dust that is on your feet as a testimony against them." ¹²So they went out and proclaimed that all should repent. ¹³They cast out many demons and anointed with oil many who were sick and cured them.

Primary Hymns and Songs for the Day

"Guide Me, O Thou Great Jehovah" (2 Sam, Mark) (O)
  C622, CG33, E690, EL618, G65, N18/19, P281, SA27, SH51,
  UM127 (PD), VU651 (Fr.)
    H-3   Hbl-25, 51; Chr-89; Desc-26; Org-23
    S-1   #76-77. Descant and harmonization
"Savior, Like a Shepherd Lead Us" (2 Sam, Mark)
  C558, CG405, E708, EL789, G187, N252, P387, SH538, UM381
    H-3   Chr-167; Org-15
    S-2   #29. Harmonization
"Spirit of God, Descend upon My Heart" (2 Cor)
  C265, CG243, EL800, G688, N290, P326, SA290, SH277,
  UM500 (PD), VU378
    H-3   Chr-175; Desc-77; Org-94
    S-2   #125-128. Various treatments
"You Are My All in All" 825356 (2 Cor)
  CG571, G519, SH335, WS3040
"Just a Closer Walk with Thee" (2 Cor, Mark)
  C557, EL697, G835, S2158, SH584
"Send Me, Lord" (Mark)
  C447, EL809, G746, N360, SH723, UM497, VU572
    S-2   #173. Percussion arrangement
"The Summons" (Mark)
  CG473, EL798, G726, S2130, SA695, SH598, VU567
    H-3   Chr-220
"Lead Me, Guide Me" (2 Cor, Mark)
  C583, CG403, EL768, G740, S2214, SH582
"Spirit of the Living God" 23488 (Mark, Comm.)
  C259, CG234, G288, N283, P322, SA312/313, SH555,
  UM393, VU376, S-1 #212 Vocal desc. idea
    H-3   Chr-176
    S-1   #212. Vocal descant idea
"Enviado Soy de Dios" ("Sent Out in Jesus' Name") 6290823
(Mark) (C)
  EL538, G747, S2184, SH718

Additional Hymn Suggestions

"Lead Me, Lord" (2 Sam)
  C593, N774, UM473 (PD), VU662
"Come, We That Love the Lord" (2 Sam, Pss)
  CG549, E392, N379, SA831, UM732, VU715
"Marching to Zion" (2 Sam, Pss)
  C707, CG550, EL625, N382, SA831, UM733, VU714
"Guide My Feet" (Pss, 2 Cor, Mark)
  CG637, G741, N497, P354, S2208, SH54
"Come, Ye Sinners, Poor and Needy" (2 Cor)
  CG471, G415, UM340
"Amazing Grace" (2 Cor)
  AH4091, C546, CG587, E671, EL779, G649, N547/548, P280,
  SA453, SH523, UM378 (PD), VU266 (Fr.)
"Come, Thou Fount of Every Blessing" (2 Cor)
  AH4086, C16, CG295/559, E686, EL807, G475, N459, P356,
  SA830, SH394, UM400 (PD), VU559
"O Love That Wilt Not Let Me Go" (2 Cor)
  C540, CG631, G833, N485, SA616, SH314, UM480, VU658
"Lord, Whose Love Through Humble Service" (2 Cor, Mark)
  C461, CG650, E610, EL712, P427, SH239, UM581
"We've a Story to Tell to the Nations" (Mark) (C)
  C484, C427, SA943, UM569 (PD)
"O Zion, Haste" (Mark)
  C482, CG479, E539, EL668, UM573 (PD)
"Lord, You Give the Great Commission" (Mark)
  C459, CG651, S2176, EL579, G298, P429, UM584, VU512
"The Church of Christ in Every Age" (Mark)
  C475, EL729, G320, N306, P421, UM589, VU601
"Sent Forth by God's Blessing" (Mark) (C)
  CG519, EL547, N76, SH715, UM664, VU481
"Lord of All Hopefulness" (Mark)
  CG678, E482, EL765, G683, S2197, SA772, SH464
"We All Are One in Mission" (Mark)
  CG269, EL576, G733, P435, S2243

Additional Contemporary and Modern Suggestions

"Great Is the Lord" 1149 (Pss)
  CG325, G614, S2022, SH459
"How Great Are You, Lord" 2888576 (Pss)
"Great Are You Lord" 6460220 (Pss)
"God Will Make a Way" 458620 (Pss)
"Awesome Is the Lord Most High" 4674159 (Pss)
"My Savior Lives" 4882965 (Pss, 2 Cor)
"Beautiful Savior" 2492216 (Pss, 2 Cor)
"Give Thanks" (2 Cor)
  C528, CG373, G647, S2036, SA364, SH489
"Grace Alone" 2335524 (2 Cor)
  CG43, S2162, SA699.
"You Are My Hiding Place" 21442 (2 Cor)
  C554, S2055, SH46
"Shout to the North" 1562261 (2 Cor)
  G319, SA1009, WS3042
"Amazing Grace" ("My Chains Are Gone") 4768151 (2 Cor)
"The Power of Your Love" 917491 (2 Cor)
"All Things Are Possible" 2245140 (2 Cor)
"Good to Me" 313480 (2 Cor)
"Guide My Feet" (Mark, 2 Cor)
  CG637, G741, N497, P354, S2208, SH54
"Awesome God" 41099 (Mark)
  G616, S2040
"Step by Step" 696994 (Mark)
  CG495, G743, WS3004
"Canto de Esperanza" ("Song of Hope") (Mark)
  G765, P432, S2186, SH721, VU424
"Every Move I Make" 1595726 (Mark)
"Song for the Nations" 20340 (Mark) (C)
"Carry the Light" 126402 (Mark) (C)

Vocal Solos

"O Thou That Tellest Good Tidings to Zion" (2 Sam, Pss)
"Rejoice Greatly, O Daughter of Zion" (2 Sam, Pss)
  V-2
"Who You Are to Me" (2 Cor, Mark)
  V-9   p. 124

Anthems

"The Lord Now Sends Us Forth" (Mark)
Arr. Michael Burkhardt; MorningStar MSM-50-5412
Two-part, piano, opt. percussion (https://bit.ly/MS-5412)

"Will You Come and Follow Me" (Mark)
Tom Trenney; MorningStar 50-8751
SATB, piano (https://bit.ly/MS-8751)

Other Suggestions

Visuals:
  O   Shepherd, crown, oil
  P   People at worship, fear, globe, right hand
  E   Clay vessels of varying sizes/conditions, handicap sign
  G   Teams of two, staff, sandals, tunic, oil
Response to Scripture: CG96, E490, EL815, G377, SH352,
  UM206, refrain. "I Want to Walk as a Child of the Light"
  (2 Sam)
Response: AH4015, C33, CG323, EL856, G625, N35, P467, SA49,
  SH14, UM77, VU238, stanza 1. "How Great Thou Art" (Pss)
Benediction: WS3183. "As We Go" (Pss, Mark)
Alternate Lessons: Eze 2:1-5; Ps 123
Theme Ideas: Discipleship / Following God, God: Call of God /
  Listening, God: Shepherd, Grace

2 Samuel 6:1-5, 12b-19

David again gathered all the chosen men of Israel, thirty thousand. [2]David and all the people with him set out and went from Baale-judah to bring up from there the ark of God, which is called by the name of the Lord of hosts who is enthroned on the cherubim. [3]They carried the ark of God on a new cart and brought it out of the house of Abinadab, which was on the hill. Uzzah and Ahio, the sons of Abinadab, were driving the new cart [4]with the ark of God, and Ahio went in front of the ark. [5]David and all the house of Israel were dancing before the Lord with all their might, with songs and lyres and harps and tambourines and castanets and cymbals. . . .

[12b]So David went and brought up the ark of God from the house of Obed-edom to the city of David with rejoicing, [13]and when those who bore the ark of the Lord had gone six paces, he sacrificed an ox and a fatted calf. [14]David danced before the Lord with all his might; David was girded with a linen ephod. [15]So David and all the house of Israel brought up the ark of the Lord with shouting and with the sound of the trumpet.

[16]As the ark of the Lord came into the city of David, Michal daughter of Saul looked out of the window and saw King David leaping and dancing before the Lord, and she despised him in her heart.

[17]They brought in the ark of the Lord and set it in its place, inside the tent that David had pitched for it, and David offered burnt offerings and offerings of well-being before the Lord. [18]When David had finished offering the burnt offerings and the offerings of well-being, he blessed the people in the name of the Lord of hosts [19]and distributed food among all the people, the whole multitude of Israel, both men and women, to each a cake of bread, a portion of meat, and a cake of raisins. Then all the people went back to their homes.

Psalm 24 (G364, N634, P177, SH150, UM755)

The earth is the Lord's and all that is in it,
   the world, and those who live in it,
[2]for he has founded it on the seas
   and established it on the rivers.
[3]Who shall ascend the hill of the Lord?
   And who shall stand in his holy place?
[4]Those who have clean hands and pure hearts,
   who do not lift up their souls to what is false
   and do not swear deceitfully.
[5]They will receive blessing from the Lord
   and vindication from the God of their salvation.
[6]Such is the company of those who seek him,
   who seek the face of the God of Jacob.   *Selah*
[7]Lift up your heads, O gates!
   and be lifted up, O ancient doors,
   that the King of glory may come in!
[8]Who is the King of glory?
   The Lord, strong and mighty,
   the Lord, mighty in battle.
[9]Lift up your heads, O gates!
   and be lifted up, O ancient doors,
   that the King of glory may come in!
[10]Who is this King of glory?
   The Lord of hosts,
   he is the King of glory.   *Selah*

Ephesians 1:3-14

[3]Blessed be the God and Father of our Lord Jesus Christ, who has blessed us in Christ with every spiritual blessing in the heavenly places, [4]just as he chose us in Christ before the foundation of the world to be holy and blameless before him in love. [5]He destined us for adoption as his children through Jesus Christ, according to the good pleasure of his will, [6]to the praise of his glorious grace that he freely bestowed on us in the Beloved. [7]In him we have redemption through his blood, the forgiveness of our trespasses, according to the riches of his grace [8]that he lavished on us. With all wisdom and insight [9]he has made known to us the mystery of his will, according to his good pleasure that he set forth in Christ, [10]as a plan for the fullness of time, to gather up all things in him, things in heaven and things on earth. [11]In Christ we have also obtained an inheritance, having been destined according to the purpose of him who accomplishes all things according to his counsel and will, [12]so that we, who were the first to set our hope on Christ, might live for the praise of his glory. [13]In him you also, when you had heard the word of truth, the gospel of your salvation, and had believed in him, were marked with the seal of the promised Holy Spirit; [14]this is the pledge of our inheritance toward redemption as God's own people, to the praise of his glory.

Mark 6:14-29

[14]King Herod heard of it, for Jesus's name had become known. Some were saying, "John the baptizer has been raised from the dead, and for this reason these powers are at work in him." [15]But others said, "It is Elijah." And others said, "It is a prophet, like one of the prophets of old." [16]But when Herod heard of it, he said, "John, whom I beheaded, has been raised."

[17]For Herod himself had sent men who arrested John, bound him, and put him in prison on account of Herodias, his brother Philip's wife, because Herod had married her. [18]For John had been telling Herod, "It is not lawful for you to have your brother's wife." [19]And Herodias had a grudge against him and wanted to kill him. But she could not, [20]for Herod feared John, knowing that he was a righteous and holy man, and he protected him. When he heard him, he was greatly perplexed, and yet he liked to listen to him. [21]But an opportunity came when Herod on his birthday gave a banquet for his courtiers and officers and for the leaders of Galilee. [22]When his daughter Herodias came in and danced, she pleased Herod and his guests, and the king said to the girl, "Ask me for whatever you wish, and I will give it." [23]And he swore to her, "Whatever you ask me, I will give you, even half of my kingdom." [24]She went out and said to her mother, "What should I ask for?" She replied, "The head of John the baptizer." [25]Immediately she rushed back to the king and requested, "I want you to give me at once the head of John the Baptist on a platter." [26]The king was deeply grieved, yet out of regard for his oaths and for the guests, he did not want to refuse her. [27]Immediately the king sent a soldier of the guard with orders to bring John's head. He went and beheaded him in the prison, [28]brought his head on a platter, and gave it to the girl. Then the girl gave it to her mother. [29]When his disciples heard about it, they came and took his body and laid it in a tomb.

Primary Hymns and Songs for the Day

"Praise to the Lord, the Almighty" (2 Sam) (O)
    C25, CG319, E390, EL858 (PD) and 859, G35, N22, P482,
    SA56, SH453, UM139, VU220 (Fr.) and VU221
        H-3   Hbl-89; Chr-163; Desc-69; Org-79
        S-1   #218-222. Various treatments
"God of Grace and God of Glory" (Eph, Mark) (O)
    C464, CG285, E594/595, EL705, G307, N436, P420, SA814,
    SH250, UM577, VU686
        H-3   Hbl-25, 51; Chr-89; Desc-26; Org-23
        S-1   #76-77. Descant and harmonization
Cantad al Señor ("O Sing to the Lord") (2 Sam, Eph)
    CG328, EL822, G637, P472, SH429, VU241
        H-3   Hbl-72; Chr-151; Org-18
"Blessed Assurance" (Eph)
    AH4083, C543, CG619, EL638, G839, N473, SA455,
    SH320, UM369 (PD), VU337
        H-3   Chr-39
        S-1   #24. Harmonization
"Wild and Lone the Prophet's Voice" (Mark)
    G163, P409, S2089
"It Is Well with My Soul" (Eph, Mark (C)
    C561, CG573, EL785, G840, N438, SA741, SH305, UM377
        H-3   Chr-113
"Amazing Grace" (Eph, Mark) (C)
    AH4091, C546, CG587, E671, EL779, G649, N547/548, P280,
    SA453, SH523, UM378 (PD), VU266 (Fr.)
        H-3   Hbl-14, 46; Chr-27; Desc-14; Org-4
        S-2   #5-7. Various treatments

Additional Hymn Suggestions

"Praise the Lord with the Sound of Trumpet" (2 Sam)
    S2020, VU245
"When in Our Music God Is Glorified" (2 Sam)
    C7, CG309, E420, EL850/851, G641, N561, P264, UVU533
"Let All the World in Every Corner Sing" (2 Sam, Pss)
    CG314, E402/403, G636, P468, S41, UM93
"From All That Dwell Below the Skies" (2 Sam, Pss)
    C49, CG330, E380, G327, N27, P229, UM101 (PD)
Cantemos al Señor ("Let's Sing unto the Lord") (2 Sam, Pss)
    C60, EL555, G669, N39, SH432, UM149
"My Tribute" 11218 (Eph)
    AH4080, C39, CG574, N14, SH434, UM99; V-8 p. 5. Vocal Solo
"There's a Wideness in God's Mercy" (Eph)
    C73, CG41, E470, EL587/88G435, N23, SH526, UM121,
    VU271
"Children of the Heavenly Father" (Eph)
    CG69, EL781, N487, SH42, UM141
"Blessed Assurance" (Eph)
    AH4083, C543, CG619, EL638, G839, N473, P341, SA455,
    SH320, UM369 (PD), VU337
"Gather Us In" (Eph, Comm.)
    C284, EL532, G401, S2236, SH393
"Baptized in Water" (Eph, Baptism)
    CG449, E294, EL456, G482, P492, S2248, SH666
"How Firm a Foundation" (Mark)
    C618, CG425, E636/637, EL796, G463, N407, P361, SA804,
    SH291, UM529 (PD), VU660
"Be Still, My Soul" (Mark)
    C566, G891, N488, SH330, UM534, VU652
"Rejoice in God's Saints" (Mark)
    C476, EL418, G732, UM708

Additional Contemporary and Modern Suggestions

"Clap Your Hands" 806674 (2 Sam)
"El-Shaddai" 26856 (2 Sam)
"I Could Sing of Your Love Forever" 1043199 (2 Sam)
"We Will Dance" 1034438 (2 Sam)

"Be Glorified" 2732646 (2 Sam)
"Awesome in This Place" 847554 (2 Sam, Pss)
"Holy Ground" 21198 (2 Sam, Pss)
    C112, G406, S2272, SA400
"Hosanna" 4785835 (Pss)
"Just Let Me Say" 1406413 (Pss)
"Awaken" 5491647 (Pss, Eph)
"Holy, Holy" 18792 (Eph)
    P140, S2039
"Lord, I Lift Your Name on High" 117947 (Eph)
    AH4071, CG606, EL857, S2088, SA379, SH205
"Grace Alone" 2335524 (Eph)
    CG43, S2162, SA699.
"He Who Began a Good Work in You" 15238 (Eph)
"Hallelujah" ("Your Love Is Amazing") 3091812 (Eph)
"We Fall Down" 2437367 (Eph)
    G368, WS3187
"You Are My King" ("Amazing Love") 2456623 (Eph)
"Amazing Grace" ("My Chains Are Gone") 4768151 (Eph)
"Take, O Take Me as I Am" 4562041 (Eph)
    EL814, G698, SH620, WS3119
"Healer of Our Every Ill" (Mark)
    C506, EL612, G795, S2213, SH339, VU619
"Through It All" 18211 (Mark)
    C555, UM507
"We Shall Overcome" (Mark)
    AH4047/4048, C630, G379, N570, UM533
"Be Still and Know That I Am God" (Mark)
    G414, N743, S2057, SH55
"Be Still and Know" 2758912 (Mark)
"I Believe In Jesus" 61282 (Mark)

Vocal Solos

"I Will Sing of Thy Great Mercies" (2 Sam, Eph)
    V-4   p. 43
"My Cup Overflows" (Pss)
    V-8   p. 302
"Lift Up Your Heads" (Pss)
    V-10   p. 38
"Amazing Grace" (Eph)
    V-8   p. 56
"Famous For" ("I Believe") (Eph, Mark)
    V-9   p. 22

Anthems

"In His Hands" (Eph)
Arr. Tim Osiek; Beckenhorst BP2274
SATB, piano (https://bit.ly/BP-2274)

"In Christ an Inheritance Is Ours" (Eph)
Michael D. Costello; MorningStar 60-6010
SATB with flute, oboe, organ, opt. cello (https://bit.ly/MS-6010)

Other Suggestions

Visuals:
    O   Ark of Covenant, man dancing (video "David")
    P   Earth/sea/river, bowl/water/towel, hand with heart, gates
    E   Adoption papers, Christus Rex, last will and testament, rejoicing
    G   Feasting, dancing, dinner platter
Scripture Response: G157, P302, SA141, UM261, VU352, refrain.
    "Lord of the Dance" (2 Sam)
Scripture Response: E293, G730, N295, P364, UM712, stanza 1.
    "I Sing a Song of the Saints of God" (Mark)
Alternate Lessons: Amos 7:7-15; Ps 85:8-13
Theme Ideas: Assurance, Faithfulness, God: Glory of God, Grace, Praise

2 Samuel 7:1-14a

Now when the king was settled in his house and the Lord had given him rest from all his enemies around him, [2]the king said to the prophet Nathan, "See now, I am living in a house of cedar, but the ark of God stays in a tent." [3]Nathan said to the king, "Go, do all that you have in mind, for the Lord is with you."

[4]But that same night the word of the Lord came to Nathan, [5]"Go and tell my servant David: Thus says the Lord: Are you the one to build me a house to live in? [6]I have not lived in a house since the day I brought up the people of Israel from Egypt to this day, but I have been moving about in a tent and a tabernacle. [7]Wherever I have moved about among all the people of Israel, did I ever speak a word with any of the tribal leaders of Israel, whom I commanded to shepherd my people Israel, saying, 'Why have you not built me a house of cedar?' [8]Now therefore thus you shall say to my servant David: Thus says the Lord of hosts: I took you from the pasture, from following the sheep to be prince over my people Israel, [9]and I have been with you wherever you went and have cut off all your enemies from before you, and I will make for you a great name, like the name of the great ones of the earth. [10]And I will appoint a place for my people Israel and will plant them, so that they may live in their own place and be disturbed no more, and evildoers shall afflict them no more, as formerly, [11]from the time that I appointed judges over my people Israel, and I will give you rest from all your enemies. Moreover, the Lord declares to you that the Lord will make you a house. [12]When your days are fulfilled and you lie down with your ancestors, I will raise up your offspring after you, who shall come forth from your body, and I will establish his kingdom. [13]He shall build a house for my name, and I will establish the throne of his kingdom forever. [14]I will be a father to him, and he shall be a son to me."

Psalm 89:20-37 (G67, N678, P209, UM807)

[20]I have found my servant David;
  with my holy oil I have anointed him;
[21]my hand shall always remain with him;
  my arm also shall strengthen him.
[22]The enemy shall not outwit him;
  the wicked shall not humble him.
[23]I will crush his foes before him
  and strike down those who hate him.
[24]My faithfulness and steadfast love shall be with him,
  and in my name his horn shall be exalted.
[25]I will set his hand on the sea
  and his right hand on the rivers.
[26]He shall cry to me, 'You are my Father,
  my God, and the Rock of my salvation!'
[27]I will make him the firstborn,
  the highest of the kings of the earth.
[28]Forever I will keep my steadfast love for him,
  and my covenant with him will stand firm.
[29]I will establish his line forever
  and his throne as long as the heavens endure.
[30]If his children forsake my law
  and do not walk according to my ordinances,
[31]if they violate my statutes
  and do not keep my commandments,
[32]then I will punish their transgression with the rod
  and their iniquity with scourges,
[33]but I will not remove from him my steadfast love
  or be false to my faithfulness.
[34]I will not violate my covenant
  or alter the word that went forth from my lips.
[35]Once and for all I have sworn by my holiness;
  I will not lie to David.
[36]His line shall continue forever,
  and his throne endure before me like the sun.
[37]It shall be established forever like the moon,
  an enduring witness in the skies." *Selah*

Ephesians 2:11-22

[11]So then, remember that at one time you gentiles by birth, called "the uncircumcision" by those who are called "the circumcision"—a circumcision made in the flesh by human hands—[12]remember that you were at that time without Christ, being aliens from the commonwealth of Israel and strangers to the covenants of promise, having no hope and without God in the world. [13]But now in Christ Jesus you who once were far off have been brought near by the blood of Christ. [14]For he is our peace; in his flesh he has made both into one and has broken down the dividing wall, that is, the hostility between us, [15]abolishing the law with its commandments and ordinances, that he might create in himself one new humanity in place of the two, thus making peace, [16]and might reconcile both to God in one body through the cross, thus putting to death that hostility through it. [17]So he came and proclaimed peace to you who were far off and peace to those who were near, [18]for through him both of us have access in one Spirit to the Father. [19]So then, you are no longer strangers and aliens, but you are fellow citizens with the saints and also members of the household of God, [20]built upon the foundation of the apostles and prophets, with Christ Jesus himself as the cornerstone; [21]in him the whole structure is joined together and grows into a holy temple in the Lord, [22]in whom you also are built together spiritually into a dwelling place for God.

Mark 6:30-34, 53-56

[30]The apostles gathered around Jesus and told him all that they had done and taught. [31]He said to them, "Come away to a deserted place all by yourselves and rest a while." For many were coming and going, and they had no leisure even to eat. [32]And they went away in the boat to a deserted place by themselves. [33]Now many saw them going and recognized them, and they hurried there on foot from all the towns and arrived ahead of them. [34]As he went ashore, he saw a great crowd, and he had compassion for them, because they were like sheep without a shepherd, and he began to teach them many things. . . .

[53]When they had crossed over, they came to land at Gennesaret and moored the boat. [54]When they got out of the boat, people at once recognized him [55]and rushed about that whole region and began to bring the sick on mats to wherever they heard he was. [56]And wherever he went, into villages or cities or farms, they laid the sick in the marketplaces and begged him that they might touch even the fringe of his cloak, and all who touched it were healed.

Primary Hymns and Songs for the Day
"Hail to the Lord's Anointed" (2 Sam)
　　C140, CG98, EL311, G149, N104, P205, SH112, UM203, VU30
"I Love Thy Kingdom, Lord" (2 Sam, Eph)
　　C274, CG262, E524, G310, N312, P441, UM540
　　　　H-3　Hbl-16; Chr-106, 167; Desc-97; Org-147
　　　　S-1　#311. Descant and harmonization
"O-So-So" ("Come Now, O Prince of Peace") (Eph)
　　EL247, G103, S2232, SH235
"In God Alone" (Eph, Mark)
　　G814, WS3135
"I Heard the Voice of Jesus Say" (Mark)
　　CG577, E692, EL611, G182, N489, SA424, SH127, VU626
　　　　H-3　Hbl-15, 20, 34, 84; Chr-150; Org-67
　　　　S-2　#100-103. Various treatments
"Near to the Heart of God" (Mark)
　　C581, CG383, G824, P527, UM472 (PD)
"Shepherd Me, O God" (Mark)
　　EL780, G473, S2058, SH365
"The Church's One Foundation" (2 Sam, Eph) (C)
　　C272, CG246, E525, EL654, G321, N386, P442, SH233, UM545/546, VU332 (Fr.)
　　　　H-3　Hbl-94; Chr-180; Desc-16; Org-9
　　　　S-1　#25-26. Descant and harmonization
"God the Spirit, Guide and Guardian" (Mark) (C)
　　C450, G303, N355, P523, UM648, VU514

Additional Hymn Suggestions
"The God of Abraham Praise" (2 Sam) (O)
　　C24, CG45, E401, EL831, G49, N24, P488, SH50, UM116 (PD), VU255
"Lead On, O King Eternal" (2 Sam) (O)
　　C632, CG63, E555, EL805, G269, N573, P447/ P448, SA964, UM580
"Lord, Speak to Me" (2 Sam, Pss)
　　CG503, EL676, G722, N531, SA773, SH557, UM463, VU589
"How Firm a Foundation" (Pss, Eph)
　　C618, CG425, E636/637, EL796, G463, N407, P361, SA804, SH291, UM529 (PD), VU660
"It Is Well with My Soul" (Eph)
　　C561, CG573, EL785, G840, N438, SA741, SH305, UM377
"Here, O Lord, Your Servants Gather" (Eph)
　　C278, EL530, G311, N72, P465, UM552, VU362
"Christ Is Made the Sure Foundation" (Eph) (C)
　　C275, CG248, E518, EL645, G394, N400, P416/417, SA246, SH225, UM559 (PD), VU325
"Just a Closer Walk with Thee" (Eph)
　　C557, EL697, G835, S2158, SH584
"Built on a Rock" (Eph)
　　C273, CG247, EL652, WS3147
"Hope of the World" (Eph, Mark)
　　C538, E472, G734, N46, P360, UM178, VU215
"Lord of the Dance" (Mark)
　　G157, P302, SA141, UM261, VU352
"Tell Me the Stories of Jesus" (Mark)
　　C190, SA151, UM277 (PD), VU357
"Dear Lord and Father of Mankind" (Mark)
　　(Alternate Text: "Dear God, Creator good and kind.")
　　C594, CG413, E652/563, G169, N502, P345, SA456, UM358 (PD), VU608
"Savior, Like a Shepherd Lead Us" (Mark)
　　C558, CG405, E708, EL789, G187, N252, P387, SH538, UM381
"Where Cross the Crowded Ways of Life" (Mark)
　　C665, CG657, E609, EL719, G343, N543, UM427, VU681
"Kum Ba Yah" 2749763 (Mark)
　　C590, G472, P338, UM494
"You, Lord, are Both Lamb and Shepherd" (Mark)
　　G274, SH210, VU210, WS3043

Additional Contemporary and Modern Suggestions
"On Eagle's Wings" (2 Sam, Pss)
　　C77, CG51, EL787, G43, N775, SH318, UM143, VU807/808, S-2 #143. Stanzas for soloist
"Everlasting God" 4556538 (2 Sam, Pss)
"I Will Call upon the Lord" 11263 (Pss)
　　G621, S2002
"Hallelujah" ("Your Love Is Amazing") 3091812 (Pss)
"God of Wonders" 3118757 (Pss)
"Who Can Satisfy My Soul Like You?" 208492 (Pss)
"Psalm 62" ("My Soul Finds Rest") 5040902 (Pss)
"Jesus, Draw Me Close" 443680 (Eph)
"Sanctuary" 24140 (Eph)
　　G701, S2164, SH265
"Make Us One" 695737 (Eph)
"Bind Us Together" 1228 (Eph)
"Cornerstone" 6158927 (Eph)
"O Come To The Altar" 7051511 (Eph)
"We Believe" 6367165 (Eph)
"Firm Foundation" 1355753 (Eph)
"Foundation" 706151 (Eph)
"There Is None Like You" 674545 (Mark)
"Oh Lord, You're Beautiful" 14514 (Mark)
"People Need the Lord" 18084 (Mark)
"Here Is Bread, Here Is Wine" 983717 (Mark, Comm.)
　　EL483, S2266
"Across the Lands" 3709898 (Mark)
"Fill My Cup, Lord" 15946 (Mark, Comm.)
　　C351, UM641 (refrain only), WS3093

Vocal Solos
"Just a Closer Walk with Thee" (Eph)
　　V-8　　　p. 323
　　V-5 (2)　p. 31
"Serenity" (Mark)
　　UM499

Anthems
"I Heard the Voice of Jesus Say" (Mark)
Sondra K. Tucker; MorningStar 50-3521
SATB, oboe, organ (https://bit.ly/MS-3521)

"Savior, Like a Shepherd Lead Us" (Mark)
Patricia Mock; Shawnee Press HL-35027663
SATB, piano, opt. C-instrument (https://bit.ly/SP-7663)

Other Suggestions
Visuals:
　　O　Cedar, churches under construction
　　P　Rock, star of David, oil, geneological chart, father/son
　　E　Walls crumbling, family, Christian unity, cornerstone
　　G　Resting, boat, sheep, healing, cloak with fringe
Introit: E487, EL816, N331, UM164 (PD), VU628. "Come, My Way, My Truth, My Life" (Mark)
Introit: G414, N743, S2057, SH55. "Be Still and Know That I Am God" (Eph, Mark)
Call to Worship or Communion: WSL65. "Jesus said" (Mark)
Scripture Response: UM541, stanza 1. "See How Great a Flame Aspires" (2 Sam, Eph)
Response: UM93, stanza 1. "Let All the World" (2 Sam)
Benediction: G753, S2171, SA608, SH616 VU684. "Make Me a Channel of Your Peace" (Eph)
Alternate Lessons: Jer 23:1-6; Ps 23
Theme Ideas: Children / Family of God, Discipleship / Following God, God: Shepherd, Healing, Jesus: Cornerstone, Prayer, Unity

2 Samuel 11:1-15

In the spring of the year, the time when kings go out to battle, David sent Joab with his officers and all Israel with him; they ravaged the Ammonites and besieged Rabbah. But David remained at Jerusalem.

[2]It happened, late one afternoon when David rose from his couch and was walking about on the roof of the king's house, that he saw from the roof a woman bathing; the woman was very beautiful. [3]David sent someone to inquire about the woman. It was reported, "This is Bathsheba daughter of Eliam, the wife of Uriah the Hittite." [4]So David sent messengers to get her, and she came to him, and he lay with her. (Now she was purifying herself after her period.) Then she returned to her house. [5]The woman conceived, and she sent and told David, "I am pregnant."

[6]So David sent word to Joab, "Send me Uriah the Hittite." And Joab sent Uriah to David. [7]When Uriah came to him, David asked how Joab and the people fared and how the war was going. [8]Then David said to Uriah, "Go down to your house and wash your feet." Uriah went out of the king's house, and there followed him a present from the king. [9]But Uriah slept at the entrance of the king's house with all the servants of his lord and did not go down to his house. [10]When they told David, "Uriah did not go down to his house," David said to Uriah, "You have just come from a journey. Why did you not go down to your house?" [11]Uriah said to David, "The ark and Israel and Judah remain in booths, and my lord Joab and the servants of my lord are camping in the open field; shall I then go to my house to eat and to drink and to lie with my wife? As you live and as your soul lives, I will not do such a thing." [12]Then David said to Uriah, "Remain here today also, and tomorrow I will send you back." So Uriah remained in Jerusalem that day. On the next day, [13]David invited him to eat and drink in his presence and made him drunk, and in the evening he went out to lie on his couch with the servants of his lord, but he did not go down to his house.

[14]In the morning David wrote a letter to Joab and sent it by the hand of Uriah. [15]In the letter he wrote, "Set Uriah in the forefront of the hardest fighting, and then draw back from him, so that he may be struck down and die."

Psalm 14 (G335, N626, SH26, UM746)

Fools say in their hearts, "There is no God."
   They are corrupt; they do abominable deeds;
     there is no one who does good.
[2]The Lord looks down from heaven on humankind
   to see if there are any who are wise,
     who seek after God.
[3]They have all gone astray; they are all alike perverse;
   there is no one who does good,
     no, not one.
[4]Have they no knowledge, all the evildoers
   who eat up my people as they eat bread
     and do not call upon the Lord?
[5]There they shall be in great terror,
   for God is with the company of the righteous.
[6]You would confound the plans of the poor,
   but the Lord is their refuge.
[7]O that deliverance for Israel would come from Zion!
   When the Lord restores the fortunes of his people,
     Jacob will rejoice; Israel will be glad.

Ephesians 3:14-21

[14]For this reason I bow my knees before the Father, [15]from whom every family in heaven and on earth takes its name. [16]I pray that, according to the riches of his glory, he may grant that you may be strengthened in your inner being with power through his Spirit [17]and that Christ may dwell in your hearts through faith, as you are being rooted and grounded in love. [18]I pray that you may have the power to comprehend, with all the saints, what is the breadth and length and height and depth [19]and to know the love of Christ that surpasses knowledge, so that you may be filled with all the fullness of God.

[20]Now to him who by the power at work within us is able to accomplish abundantly far more than all we can ask or imagine, [21]to him be glory in the church and in Christ Jesus to all generations, forever and ever. Amen.

John 6:1-21

After this Jesus went to the other side of the Sea of Galilee, also called the Sea of Tiberias. [2]A large crowd kept following him because they saw the signs that he was doing for the sick. [3]Jesus went up the mountain and sat down there with his disciples. [4]Now the Passover, the festival of the Jews, was near. [5]When he looked up and saw a large crowd coming toward him, Jesus said to Philip, "Where are we to buy bread for these people to eat?" [6]He said this to test him, for he himself knew what he was going to do. [7]Philip answered him, "Two hundred denarii would not buy enough bread for each of them to get a little." [8]One of his disciples, Andrew, Simon Peter's brother, said to him, [9]"There is a boy here who has five barley loaves and two fish. But what are they among so many people?" [10]Jesus said, "Make the people sit down." Now there was a great deal of grass in the place, so they sat down, about five thousand in all. [11]Then Jesus took the loaves, and when he had given thanks he distributed them to those who were seated; so also the fish, as much as they wanted. [12]When they were satisfied, he told his disciples, "Gather up the fragments left over, so that nothing may be lost." [13]So they gathered them up, and from the fragments of the five barley loaves, left by those who had eaten, they filled twelve baskets. [14]When the people saw the sign that he had done, they began to say, "This is indeed the prophet who is to come into the world."

[15]When Jesus realized that they were about to come and take him by force to make him king, he withdrew again to the mountain by himself.

[16]When evening came, his disciples went down to the sea, [17]got into a boat, and started across the sea to Capernaum. It was now dark, and Jesus had not yet come to them. [18]The sea became rough because a strong wind was blowing. [19]When they had rowed about three or four miles, they saw Jesus walking on the sea and coming near the boat, and they were terrified. [20]But he said to them, "It is I; do not be afraid." [21]Then they wanted to take him into the boat, and immediately the boat reached the land toward which they were going.

Primary Hymns and Songs for the Day
"Holy God, We Praise Thy Name" (Eph) (O)
    CG9, E366, EL414 (PD), G4, N276, P460, SH431, UM79,
    VU894 (Fr.)
        H-3   Chr-78, 98; Desc-48; Org-48
        S-1   #151-153. Harmonization and descants
"What Does the Lord Require of You" 456859 (2 Sam)
    C661, CG690, G70, S2174, VU701
"Lord Jesus, Think on Me" (2 Sam)
    E641, EL599 (PD), G417, P301, VU607
        H-3   Chr-96, 131; Desc-98; Org-156
"O Love, How Deep" (Eph)
    E448/449, EL322, G618, N209, P83, SH115, UM267, VU348
        H-3   Org-145
        S-1   #82-84. Various treatments
"Jesus, Priceless Treasure" (Eph, John)
    E701, EL775, G830, N480 P365, UM532 (PD), VU667/668
        H-3   Chr-117; Org-64
"All Who Hunger" (John, Comm.)
    C419, CG303, EL461, G509, S2126, VU460
        H-3   Chr-80; Desc-52
        S-1   #160-162. Various treatments
        S-2   #87-88. Brass and timpani
"Let Us Talents and Tongues Employ" (John) (C)
    C422, CG458, EL674, G526, N347, P514, VU468
        H-3   Hbl-75; Chr-127
"Break Thou the Bread of Life" (John, Comm.) (C)
    C321, CG35, EL515, G460, N321, P329, SA802, SH552,
    UM599 (PD), VU501
        H-3   Chr-44; Org-15

Additional Hymn Suggestions
"What Does the Lord Require" (2 Sam)
    C659, E605, P405, UM441
"To God Be the Glory" (Eph)
    C72, CG349, G634, P485, SA279, SH545, UM98 (PD)
"Jesus, the Very Thought of Thee" (Eph)
    C102, CG386, E642, EL754, G629, N507, P310, SA85, UM175
Pues Si Vivimos ("When We Are Living") (Eph)
    C536, CG265, EL639, G822, N499, P400, SH299, UM356,
    VU581
"Jesus Loves Me" (Eph, John)
    C113, CG603, EL595 (PD), G188, N327, P304, SA807,
    SH570, UM191, VU365
"Give to the Winds Thy Fears" (John)
    CG55, G815, N404, P286, SA643, UM129 (PD), VU636
"My Hope Is Built" (John)
    AH4105, C537, CG590, EL596/597, G353, N403, P379,
    SA662, SH324, UM368 (PD)
"Where Cross the Crowded Ways of Life" (John)
    C665, CG657, E609, EL719, G343, N543, UM427, VU681
"Jesus, Lover of My Soul" (John)
    C542, CG406, E699, G440, N546, P303, SA257, SH542/543,
    UM479, VU669
"Come, Ye Disconsolate" (John)
    C502, EL607, SH342, UM510 (PD)
"How Firm a Foundation" (John)
    C618, CG425, E636/637, EL796, G463, N407, P361, SA804,
    SH291, UM529 (PD), VU660
"Be Still, My Soul" (John)
    C566, G891, N488, SH330, UM534, VU652
"Break Thou the Bread of Life" (John, Comm.)
    C321, CG35, EL515, G460, N321, P329, SA802, SH552,
    UM599 (PD), VU501
"I Come with Joy" (John, Comm.)
    C420, CG456, E304, EL482, G515, N349, UM617, VU477
"You Satisfy the Hungry Heart" (John, Comm.)
    C429, CG468, EL484, G523, P521, SH672, UM629, VU478
"Gather Us In" (John, Comm.)
    C284, EL532, G401, S2236, SH393

Additional Contemporary and Modern Suggestions
"What Does the Lord Require of You" 456859 (1 Sam)
"If It Had Not Been for the Lord" 167076 (Pss)
"Humble Thyself in the Sight of the Lord" 26564 (Pss)
"Spirit Song" 27824 (Eph)
    C352, SH409, UM347
"Celebrate Love" 155246 (Eph)
"There's a Song" 2041825 (Eph)
"O Lord, Your Tenderness" 38136 (Eph)
"Lord, Be Glorified" 26368 (Eph)
    EL744, G468, S2150, SA593, SH420
"Give Me Jesus" (Eph)
    CG546, EL770, N409, SH306, WS3140
"Be Glorified" 2732646 (Eph)
"No Greater Love" 930887 (Eph)
"He Is Able" 115420 (Eph)
"I Could Sing of Your Love Forever" 1043199 (Eph)
"Think about His Love" 16299 (Eph)
"Jesus, Lover of My Soul" 1198817 (John)
"Cornerstone" 6158927 (John)
"Be Still and Know" 2758912 (John)
"There Will Be Bread" 4512352 (John)
"Eat This Bread" (John, Comm.)
    C414, EL472, G527, N788, SH671, UM628, VU466
"Be Still and Know That I Am God" (John)
    G414, N743, S2057, SH55
"Across the Lands" 3709898 (John)

Vocal Solos
"Wondrous Love" (Eph)
    V-6   p. 47
"Christ Living Within You"
    V-8   p. 177
"Peace Be Still" (John)
    V-9   p. 64

Anthems
"Christ Has Broken Down the Wall" (Eph)
Mark Miller; Choristers Guild CGA1224
SATB, piano (https://bit.ly/CGA-1224)

"O Love, How Deep" (Eph)
Arr. Vicki Tucker Courtney; Alfred 00-39155
SATB, keyboard (https://bit.ly/A-39155)

Other Suggestions
Visuals:
    O   Bath towel, sword
    P   Broken bread, fear, rescue, rejoicing
    E   Kneeling in prayer, globe, flags of nations, missions,
              love
    G   Dried fish, 5 loaves, 12 baskets, boat, storm, Jesus
              walking
Call to Prayer: EL752, S2207. "Lord, Listen to Your Children"
Prayer: WSL55, UM446 (John, Comm.)
Scripture Response: C659, E605, P405, UM441, stanza 2. "What
    Does the Lord Require?" (2 Sam)
Scripture Response: C200, CG171, E439, EL666, G215, N223,
    P85, SA207, SH177, UM292, VU147, stanza 2. "What
    Wondrous Love Is This" (Eph)
Alternate Lessons: 2 Kgs 4:42-44; Ps 145:10-18
Theme Ideas: Bread of Life, Communion, God: Love of God,
    Grace, Justice, Sin and Forgiveness

2 Samuel 11:26–12:13a

[26]When the wife of Uriah heard that her husband was dead, she made lamentation for him. [27]When the mourning was over, David sent and brought her to his house, and she became his wife and bore him a son.

But the thing that David had done displeased the LORD,

12 and the LORD sent Nathan to David. He came to him and said to him, "There were two men in a certain city, the one rich and the other poor. [2]The rich man had very many flocks and herds, [3]but the poor man had nothing but one little ewe lamb that he had bought. He brought it up, and it grew up with him and with his children; it used to eat of his meager fare and drink from his cup and lie in his bosom, and it was like a daughter to him. [4]Now there came a traveler to the rich man, and he was loath to take one of his own flock or herd to prepare for the wayfarer who had come to him, but he took the poor man's lamb and prepared that for the guest who had come to him." [5]Then David's anger was greatly kindled against the man. He said to Nathan, "As the LORD lives, the man who has done this deserves to die; [6]he shall restore the lamb fourfold because he did this thing and because he had no pity."

[7]Nathan said to David, "You are the man! Thus says the LORD, the God of Israel: I anointed you king over Israel, and I rescued you from the hand of Saul; [8]I gave you your master's house and your master's wives into your bosom and gave you the house of Israel and of Judah, and if that had been too little, I would have added as much more. [9]Why have you despised the word of the LORD, to do what is evil in his sight? You have struck down Uriah the Hittite with the sword and have taken his wife to be your wife and have killed him with the sword of the Ammonites. [10]Now, therefore, the sword shall never depart from your house, for you have despised me and have taken the wife of Uriah the Hittite to be your wife. [11]Thus says the LORD: I will raise up trouble against you from within your own house, and I will take your wives before your eyes and give them to your neighbor, and he shall lie with your wives in broad daylight. [12]For you did it secretly, but I will do this thing before all Israel and in broad daylight." [13]David said to Nathan, "I have sinned against the LORD."

Psalm 51:1-12 (G421, N657, P195/196, UM785)

Have mercy on me, O God,
    according to your steadfast love;
according to your abundant mercy,
    blot out my transgressions.
[2]Wash me thoroughly from my iniquity,
    and cleanse me from my sin.
[3]For I know my transgressions,
    and my sin is ever before me.
[4]Against you, you alone, have I sinned
    and done what is evil in your sight,
so that you are justified in your sentence
    and blameless when you pass judgment.
[5]Indeed, I was born guilty,
    a sinner when my mother conceived me.
[6]You desire truth in the inward being;
    therefore teach me wisdom in my secret heart.
[7]Purge me with hyssop, and I shall be clean;
    wash me, and I shall be whiter than snow.
[8]Let me hear joy and gladness;
    let the bones that you have crushed rejoice.
[9]Hide your face from my sins,
    and blot out all my iniquities.
[10]Create in me a clean heart, O God,
    and put a new and right spirit within me.
[11]Do not cast me away from your presence,
    and do not take your holy spirit from me.
[12]Restore to me the joy of your salvation,
    and sustain in me a willing spirit.

Ephesians 4:1-16

I, therefore, the prisoner in the Lord, beg you to walk in a manner worthy of the calling to which you have been called, [2]with all humility and gentleness, with patience, bearing with one another in love, [3]making every effort to maintain the unity of the Spirit in the bond of peace: [4]there is one body and one Spirit, just as you were called to the one hope of your calling, [5]one Lord, one faith, one baptism, [6]one God and Father of all, who is above all and through all and in all.

[7]But each of us was given grace according to the measure of Christ's gift. [8]Therefore it is said,
    "When he ascended on high, he made captivity itself a
        captive;
    he gave gifts to his people."
[9](When it says, "He ascended," what does it mean but that he had also descended into the lower parts of the earth? [10]He who descended is the same one who ascended far above all the heavens, so that he might fill all things.) [11]He himself granted that some are apostles, prophets, evangelists, pastors and teachers [12]to equip the saints for the work of ministry, for building up the body of Christ, [13]until all of us come to the unity of the faith and of the knowledge of the Son of God, to maturity, to the measure of the full stature of Christ. [14]We must no longer be children, tossed to and fro and blown about by every wind of doctrine by people's trickery, by their craftiness in deceitful scheming; [15]but speaking the truth in love, we must grow up in every way into him who is the head, into Christ, [16]from whom the whole body, joined and knit together by every ligament with which it is equipped, as each part is working properly, promotes the body's growth in building itself up in love.

John 6:24-35

[24]So when the crowd saw that neither Jesus nor his disciples were there, they themselves got into the boats and went to Capernaum looking for Jesus.

[25]When they found him on the other side of the sea, they said to him, "Rabbi, when did you come here?" [26]Jesus answered them, "Very truly, I tell you, you are looking for me not because you saw signs but because you ate your fill of the loaves. [27]Do not work for the food that perishes but for the food that endures for eternal life, which the Son of Man will give you. For it is on him that God the Father has set his seal." [28]Then they said to him, "What must we do to perform the works of God?" [29]Jesus answered them, "This is the work of God, that you believe in him whom he has sent." [30]So they said to him, "What sign are you going to give us, then, so that we may see it and believe you? What work are you performing? [31]Our ancestors ate the manna in the wilderness, as it is written, 'He gave them bread from heaven to eat.' " [32]Then Jesus said to them, "Very truly, I tell you, it was not Moses who gave you the bread from heaven, but it is my Father who gives you the true bread from heaven. [33]For the bread of God is that which comes down from heaven and gives life to the world." [34]They said to him, "Sir, give us this bread always."

[35]Jesus said to them, "I am the bread of life. Whoever comes to me will never be hungry, and whoever believes in me will never be thirsty."

Primary Hymns and Songs for the Day

"Glorious Things of Thee Are Spoken" (John) (O)
    C709, CG282, E522/523, EL647, G81, N307, P446, SA535,
    UM731 (PD)
        H-3   Hbl-61; Chr-72; Desc-17; Org-11
        S-1   #27. Descant
               #28. Harmonization in F major
"You Are My All in All" 825356 (2 Sam, Eph)
    CG571, G519, SH335, WS3040
"Hope of the World" (2 Sam, Eph, John)
    C538, E472, G734, N46, P360, UM178, VU215
        H-3   Chr-100
        S-1   #343. Descant
        S-2   #189. Introduction
"Lamb of God" 16787 (2 Sam, John)
    EL336, G518, S2113
"Somos Uno en Cristo" ("We Are One in Christ Jesus") 6368975 (Eph)
    C493, EL643, G322, S2229, SH227
        H-3   Chr-208
"One Bread, One Body" (Eph, John, Comm.) (C)
    C393, EL496, G530, SH678, UM620, VU467
        H-3   Chr-156
"Eat This Bread" (John, Comm.)
    C414, EL472, G527, N788, SH671, UM628, VU466
        S-1   #144. Four-part setting of refrain
"In Christ There Is No East or West" (Eph) (C)
    CG273, E529, EL650 (PD), G317, N394, P440, UM548,
    VU606
        H-3   Chr-111; Desc-74; Org-88
        S-1   #231-233. Various treatments
    C687, G318, N395, P439, SA1006
        H-3   Hbl-104; Chr-219; Desc-95; Org-143
        S-2   #162. Harmonization
    SH226

Additional Hymn Suggestions

"Just as I Am, Without One Plea" (2 Sam, Pss)
    C339, CG500, E693, EL592, G442, N207, P370, SA503,
    SH500, UM357 (PD), VU508
"Give Me Jesus" (Pss, Eph)
    CG546, EL770, N409, SH306, WS3140
"I Sing a Song of the Saints of God" (Eph)
    E293, G730, N295, P364, UM712 (PD)
"Come, Share the Lord" (Eph, Comm.)
    C408, CG459, G510, S2269, VU469
"Guide Me, O Thou Great Jehovah" (John)
    C622, CG33, E690, EL618, G65, N18/19, P281, SA27, SH51,
    UM127 (PD), VU651 (Fr.)
"Bread of the World" (John, Comm.)
    C387, E301, G499, N346, P502, UM624, VU461
"You Satisfy the Hungry Heart" (John, Comm.)
    C429, CG468, EL484, G523, P521, SH672, UM629, VU478
"All Who Hunger" (John, Comm.)
    C419, CG303, EL461, G509, S2126, VU460
"Gather Us In" (John, Comm.)
    C284, EL532, G401, S2236, SH393
"Fill My Cup, Lord" 15946 (John, Comm.) (C)
    C351, UM641 (refrain only), WS3093

Additional Contemporary and Modern Suggestions

"What Does the Lord Require of You" 456859 (2 Sam)
    C661, CG690, G70, S2174, VU701
"Change My Heart, O God" 1565 (2 Sam, Pss)
    EL801, G695, S2152, SA409, SH507
"Give Me a Clean Heart" 314764 (2 Sam, Pss)
    AH4125, C515, N188, S2133
"The Dark Is Not Your Time" 7132934 (2 Sam, Pss)
"Restored" 5894615 (2 Sam, Pss)

"Confitemini Domino" ("Come and Fill Our Hearts") (Pss)
    EL538, G466, S2157
"Purify My Heart" 1314323 (Pss)
"Hosanna" 4785835 (Pss)
"Refiner's Fire" 426298 (Pss)
"Set A Fire" 5911299 (Pss)
"The Power of Your Love" 917491 (Pss)
"Give Us Clean Hands" 2060208 (Pss)
"Because of Your Love" 4662501 (Pss)
"Grace Like Rain" 3689877 (Pss, Eph)
"Forever" 3148428 (Eph)
    CG53, SA363, WS3023
"Grace Alone" 2335524 (Eph)
    CG43, S2162, SA699.
"The Servant Song" 72673 (Eph)
    C490, CG289, EL659, G727, N539, S2222, SA1005, SH264,
    VU595
"They'll Know We Are Christians" 26997 (Eph)
    AH4074, C494, CG272, G300, S2223, SH232
"Make Us One" 695737 (Eph)
"We Are the Body of Christ" (Eph)
    S2227
"Bind Us Together" 1228 (Eph)
"We Believe" 6367165 (Eph)
"Halle, Halle, Halleluja" 2659190 (John)
    C41, CG433, EL172, G591, N236, S2026, SH694, VU958
"Jesus, Name above All Names" 21291 (John)
"You Who Are Thirsty" 814453 (John, Comm.)
"Come to the Table" 675056 (John, Comm.)
    EL481, S2264
"Fill My Cup, Lord" 15946 15946 (John, Comm.)
    C351, UM641 (refrain only), WS3093
"Hungry" ("Falling on My Knees") 2650364 (John)
"All Who Are Thirsty" 2489542 (John)
"O Come To The Altar" 7051511 (John)
"Holy and Anointed One" 164361 (John)

Vocal Solos

"Hold on to Me" (2 Sam, Pss)
    V-9   p. 53
"One Bread, One Body" (Eph, John, Comm.)
    V-3 (2)   p. 40

Anthems

"Kyrie Eleison" (2 Sam, Pss)
Schubert/ed. Pfautsch; Hope LP-3711
SATB, keyboard (https://bit.ly/LP-3711)

"Lord Jesus Christ, Life-Giving Bread" (John)
Timothy Shaw; MorningStar 50-6128
SATB, piano (https://bit.ly/MS-6128)

Other Suggestions

Visuals:
    O   Lamb, sword
    P   Water, hyssop, snow, rejoicing, heart, baptism
    E   Unity, no. 1, baptism, gifts, building, Christ, ministry,
         binding
    G   Boat, seal, bread, feeding, pitcher of water, flowing
         water
Call to Prayer: EL538, G466, S2157. "Come and Fill Our Hearts"
    (Pss)
Response: SH519, UM483, UM484 or S2275. *"Kyrie"* (Pss)
Response: C299, S2277. "Lord, Have Mercy" (Pss)
Alternate Lessons: Exod 16:2-4, 9-15; Ps 78:23-29
Theme Ideas: Bread of Life, Communion, Justice, Sin and
    Forgiveness, Unity

2 Samuel 18:5-9, 15, 31-33

⁵The king ordered Joab and Abishai and Ittai, saying, "Deal gently for my sake with the young man Absalom." And all the people heard when the king gave orders to all the commanders concerning Absalom.

⁶So the army went out into the field against Israel, and the battle was fought in the forest of Ephraim. ⁷The men of Israel were defeated there by the servants of David, and the slaughter there was great on that day, twenty thousand men. ⁸The battle spread over the face of all the country, and the forest claimed more victims that day than the sword.

⁹Absalom happened to meet the servants of David. Absalom was riding on his mule, and the mule went under the thick branches of a great oak. His head caught fast in the oak, and he was left hanging between heaven and earth, while the mule that was under him went on. . . .

¹⁵And ten young men, Joab's armor-bearers, surrounded Absalom and struck him and killed him. . . .

³¹Then the Cushite came, and the Cushite said, "Good tidings for my lord the king! For the Lord has vindicated you this day, delivering you from the power of all who rose up against you." ³²The king said to the Cushite, "Is it well with the young man Absalom?" The Cushite answered, "May the enemies of my lord the king and all who rise up to do you harm be like that young man."

³³The king was deeply moved and went up to the chamber over the gate and wept, and as he went he said, "O my son Absalom, my son, my son Absalom! Would I had died instead of you, O Absalom, my son, my son!"

Psalm 130 (G424, N709, P240, SH573, UM848)

Out of the depths I cry to you, O Lord.
  ²Lord, hear my voice!
Let your ears be attentive
  to the voice of my supplications!
³If you, O Lord, should mark iniquities,
  Lord, who could stand?
⁴But there is forgiveness with you,
  so that you may be revered.
⁵I wait for the Lord; my soul waits,
  and in his word I hope;
⁶my soul waits for the Lord
  more than those who watch for the morning,
  more than those who watch for the morning.
⁷O Israel, hope in the Lord!
  For with the Lord there is steadfast love,
  and with him is great power to redeem.
⁸It is he who will redeem Israel
  from all its iniquities.

Ephesians 4:25–5:2

²⁵So then, putting away falsehood, let each of you speak the truth with your neighbor, for we are members of one another. ²⁶Be angry but do not sin; do not let the sun go down on your anger, ²⁷and do not make room for the devil. ²⁸Those who steal must give up stealing; rather, let them labor, doing good work with their own hands, so as to have something to share with the needy. ²⁹Let no evil talk come out of your mouths but only what is good for building up, as there is need, so that your words may give grace to those who hear. ³⁰And do not grieve the Holy Spirit of God, with which you were marked with a seal for the day of redemption. ³¹Put away from you all bitterness and wrath and anger and wrangling and slander, together with all malice. ³²Be kind to one another, tenderhearted, forgiving one another, as God in Christ has forgiven you.

5 Therefore be imitators of God, as beloved children, ²and walk in love, as Christ loved us and gave himself up for us, a fragrant offering and sacrifice to God.

John 6:35, 41-51

³⁵Jesus said to them, "I am the bread of life. Whoever comes to me will never be hungry, and whoever believes in me will never be thirsty." . . .

⁴¹Then the Jews began to complain about him because he said, "I am the bread that came down from heaven." ⁴²They were saying, "Is not this Jesus, the son of Joseph, whose father and mother we know? How can he now say, 'I have come down from heaven'?" ⁴³Jesus answered them, "Do not complain among yourselves. ⁴⁴No one can come to me unless drawn by the Father who sent me, and I will raise that person up on the last day. ⁴⁵It is written in the prophets, 'And they shall all be taught by God.' Everyone who has heard and learned from the Father comes to me. ⁴⁶Not that anyone has seen the Father except the one who is from God; he has seen the Father. ⁴⁷Very truly, I tell you, whoever believes has eternal life. ⁴⁸I am the bread of life. ⁴⁹Your ancestors ate the manna in the wilderness, and they died. ⁵⁰This is the bread that comes down from heaven, so that one may eat of it and not die. ⁵¹I am the living bread that came down from heaven. Whoever eats of this bread will live forever, and the bread that I will give for the life of the world is my flesh."

Primary Hymns and Songs for the Day

"There's a Wideness in God's Mercy" (2 Sam, Eph)
　C73, CG41, E470, EL587/88G435, N23, P298, SH526,
　UM121, VU271
　　　　　H-3　　Chr-195; Desc-102; Org-179
"Lord, I Want to Be a Christian" (Eph)
　C589, CG507, G729, N454, P372 (PD), SH621, UM402
　　　　　H-3　　Chr-130
"Help Us Accept Each Other" (Acts, John)
　C487, G754, N388, P358, UM560
"Make Me a Channel of Your Peace" (Eph)
　G753, S2171, SA608, SH616 VU684
"Make Me a Channel of Your Peace" 6399315 (Eph)
"There Is a Redeemer" 11483 (Eph, John)
　CG377, G443, SA204, SH495
"Jesus, Thou Joy of Loving Hearts" (John)
　C101, CG394, E649, G494, N329, SA340, SH6688, VU472
　　　　　H-3　　Hbl-73; Chr-208; Desc-89; Org-119
"Gather Us In" (John)
　C284, EL532, G401, S2236, SH393
"Precious Lord, Take My Hand" (2 Sam, Pss) (C)
　C628, CG400, EL773, G834, N472, SH336, UM474, VU670
　　　　　H-3　　Chr-164; Org-116
"God Be with You Till We Meet Again" (John) (C)
　C434, CG523, EL536, G541/542, N81, P540, SA1027,
　UM672/673, VU422/423

Additional Hymn Suggestions

"Out of the Depths I Cry to You" (2 Sam, Pss)
　EL600, G424, N483, P240, SH513, UM515
"Be Still, My Soul" (2 Sam, Pss)
　C566, G891, N488, SH330, UM534, VU652
"Abide with Me" (2 Sam, Pss)
　C636, CG543, E662, EL629, G836, N99, P543, SA529, SH475,
　UM700 (PD), VU436
"Out of the Depths" (2 Sam, Pss)
　C510, N554, S2136, VU611
"Take My Life, and Let It Be" (Eph)
　C609, CG490, E707, EL583/EL685, G697, P391, N448,
　SA623, SH627/628, UM399 (PD), VU506
"O Master, Let Me Walk with Thee" (Eph)
　C602, CG660, E659/E660, EL818, G738, N503, P357, SA667,
　SH612, UM430 (PD), VU560
"Woke Up This Morning" (Eph)
　C623, N85, S2082
"Healer of Our Every Ill" (Eph)
　C506, EL612, G795, S2213, SH339, VU619
"Hope of the World" (Eph, John) (O)
　C538, E472, G734, N46, P360, UM178, VU215
"Bread of the World" (John, Comm.)
　C387, E301, G499, N346, P502, UM624, VU461
"You Satisfy the Hungry Heart" (John, Comm.)
　C429, CG468, EL484, G523, P521, SH672, UM629, VU478
"God the Sculptor of the Mountains" (John)
　EL736, G5, S2060
"All Who Hunger" (John, Comm.)
　C419, CG303, EL461, G509, S2126, VU460
"Come to the Table of Grace" 7034746 (John, Comm.)
　G507, WS3168
"God Be with You Till We Meet Again" (2 Sam, John) (C)
　G542, P540, UM673 (PD), VU423

Additional Contemporary and Modern Suggestions

"Be Still and Know That I Am God" (2 Sam, Pss)
　G414, N743, S2057, SH55
"Be Still and Know" 2758912 (2 Sam, Pss)
"I Love the Lord" 1168957 (Pss)
　CG613, G799, P362, N511, SH343, VU617, WS3142

"Santo, Santo, Santo" ("Holy, Holy, Holy") (Eph)
　C111, CG3, EL473, G595, N793, S2007, SH452
"Holy, Holy" 18792 (Eph)
　P140, S2039
"Celebrate Love" 155246 (Eph)
"O How He Loves You and Me" 15850 (Eph)
　CG600, S2108, SH535
"I've Got Peace Like a River" (Eph)
　C530, G623, N478, P368, S2145, SH276, VU577
"To Know You More" 1767420 (Eph)
"Purify My Heart" 1314323 (Eph)
"Glory To God Forever" 5384338 (Eph)
"Love Moves You" ("Love Alone") 5775514 (Eph)
"Jesus We Love You" 7030068 (Eph, John)
"There Will Be Bread" 4512352 (Eph, John)
"Halle, Halle, Halleluja" 2659190 (John)
　C41, CG433, EL172, G591, N236, S2026, SH694, VU958
"Father, I Adore You" 26557 (John)
　CG4, S2038, SH587
"Jesus, Name above All Names" 21291 (John)
"Light of the World" 73342 (John)
"Come to the Table" 675056 (John, Comm.)
　EL481, S2264
"Eat This Bread" (John, Comm.)
　C414, EL472, G527, N788, SH671, UM628, VU466
"Take Our Bread" (John, Comm.)
　C413, UM640
"Fill My Cup, Lord" 15946 (John, Comm.)
　C351, UM641 (refrain only), WS3093
"Feed Us, Lord" 4636207 (John, Comm.)
　G501, WS3167
"O Come To The Altar" 7051511 (John, Comm.)
"Oceans" ("Where Feet May Fail") 6428767 (John)
"Holy and Anointed One" 164361 (John)
"All Who Are Thirsty" 2489542 (John)
"Enough" 3599479 (John)
"Song of Hope" ("Heaven Come Down") 5111477 (John)

Vocal Solos

"Nobody Knows the Trouble I've Seen" (2 Sam, Pss)
　V-7　　　　　p. 64/68
"Take My Life, and Let It Be" (Eph)
　V-3 (3)　　　p. 17
　V-8　　　　　p. 262

Anthems

"Peace" (Eph)
Mock/Nichols; Hope C6288
SAB, piano (https://bit.ly/C-6288)

"Shepherd of Souls" (John)
Arr. Scott Attwood; Augsburg 9781506445731
SAB, piano (https://bit.ly/AF-45731)

Other Suggestions

Visuals:
　O　　Tree limb, man weeping
　P　　Waiting for dawn, forgiveness, praying hands, weeping
　E　　Setting sun, children, sacrificial offering, portrait of
　　　　Christ
　G　　Bread, love feast, communion, anointing with oil,
　　　　baptism
Canticle: UM516. "Canticle of Redemption" (Pss)
Prayer: UM481. The Prayer of Saint Francis (Eph)
Alternate Lessons: 1 Kgs 10:4-8; Ps 34:1-8
Theme Ideas: Bread of Life, Communion, Faithfulness, Grief,
　Jesus: Mind of Christ, Lament, Peace

1 Kings 2:10-12; 3:3-14

[10]Then David slept with his ancestors and was buried in the city of David. [11]The time that David reigned over Israel was forty years; he reigned seven years in Hebron and thirty-three years in Jerusalem. [12]So Solomon sat on the throne of his father David, and his kingdom was firmly established. . . .

3 [3]Solomon loved the Lord, walking in the statutes of his father David, except that he sacrificed and offered incense at the high places. [4]The king went to Gibeon to sacrifice there, for that was the principal high place; Solomon used to offer a thousand burnt offerings on that altar. [5]At Gibeon the Lord appeared to Solomon in a dream by night, and God said, "Ask what I should give you." [6]And Solomon said, "You have shown great and steadfast love to your servant my father David because he walked before you in faithfulness, in righteousness, and in upright-ness of heart toward you, and you have kept for him this great and steadfast love and have given him a son to sit on his throne today. [7]And now, O Lord my God, you have made your servant king in place of my father David, although I am only a little child; I do not know how to go out or come in. [8]And your ser-vant is in the midst of the people whom you have chosen, a great people so numerous they cannot be numbered or counted. [9]Give your servant, therefore, an understanding mind to govern your people, able to discern between good and evil, for who can govern this great people of yours?"

[10]It pleased the Lord that Solomon had asked this. [11]God said to him, "Because you have asked this and have not asked for yourself long life or riches or for the life of your enemies but have asked for yourself understanding to discern what is right, [12]I now do according to your word. Indeed, I give you a wise and discerning mind; no one like you has been before you, and no one like you shall arise after you. [13]I give you also what you have not asked, both riches and honor all your life; no other king shall compare with you. [14]If you will walk in my ways, keeping my statutes and my commandments, as your father David walked, then I will lengthen your life."

Psalm 111 (G652, N696, UM832)

Praise the Lord!
I will give thanks to the Lord with my whole heart,
    in the company of the upright, in the congregation.
[2]Great are the works of the Lord,
    studied by all who delight in them.
[3]Full of honor and majesty is his work,
    and his righteousness endures forever.
[4]He has gained renown by his wonderful deeds;
    the Lord is gracious and merciful.
[5]He provides food for those who fear him;
    he is ever mindful of his covenant.
[6]He has shown his people the power of his works,
    in giving them the heritage of the nations.
[7]The works of his hands are faithful and just;
    all his precepts are trustworthy.
[8]They are established forever and ever,
    to be performed with faithfulness and uprightness.
[9]He sent redemption to his people;
    he has commanded his covenant forever.
    Holy and awesome is his name.
[10]The fear of the Lord is the beginning of wisdom;
    all those who practice it have a good understanding.
    His praise endures forever.

Ephesians 5:15-20

[15]Be careful, then, how you live, not as unwise people but as wise, [16]making the most of the time, because the days are evil. [17]So do not be foolish, but understand what the will of the Lord is. [18]Do not get drunk with wine, for that is debauchery, but be filled with the Spirit, [19]as you sing psalms and hymns and spiritual songs to one another, singing and making melody to the Lord in your hearts, [20]giving thanks to God the Father at all times and for everything in the name of our Lord Jesus Christ.

John 6:51-58

[51]I am the living bread that came down from heaven. Whoever eats of this bread will live forever, and the bread that I will give for the life of the world is my flesh."

[52]The Jews then disputed among themselves, saying, "How can this man give us his flesh to eat?" [53]So Jesus said to them, "Very truly, I tell you, unless you eat the flesh of the Son of Man and drink his blood, you have no life in you. [54]Those who eat my flesh and drink my blood have eternal life, and I will raise them up on the last day, [55]for my flesh is true food, and my blood is true drink. [56]Those who eat my flesh and drink my blood abide in me and I in them. [57]Just as the living Father sent me and I live because of the Father, so whoever eats me will live because of me. [58]This is the bread that came down from heaven, not like that which the ancestors ate, and they died. But the one who eats this bread will live forever."

Primary Hymns and Songs for the Day

"Guide Me, O Thou Great Jehovah" (1 Kgs, John) (O)
    C622, CG33, E690, EL618, G65, N18/19, P281, SA27, SH51,
    UM127 (PD), VU651 (Fr.)
    H-3   Hbl-25, 51; Chr-89; Desc-26; Org-23
        S-1   #76-77. Descant and harmonization

"Step by Step" 696994 (1 Kgs)
    CG495, G743, WS3004

"Be Thou My Vision" (1 Kgs, Eph, John)
    C595, CG71, E488, EL793, G450, N451, P339, SA573, SH640,
    UM451, VU642
        H-3   Hbl-15, 48; Chr-36; Org-153
        S-1   #319. Arr. for organ and voices

"O Word of God Incarnate" (1 Kgs, John)
    C322, E632, EL514, G459, N315, P327, UM598 (PD), VU499
    H-3   Hbl-86; Chr-153; Org-95
    S-1   #243. Harmonization

"Give Thanks" (Eph)
    C528, CG373, G647, S2036, SA364, SH489

"In the Singing" (Eph, John, Comm.)
    EL466, G533, S2255

"Bread of the World" (John, Comm.) (C)
    C387, E301, G499, N346, P502, UM624, VU461

"Now Thank We All Our God" (Pss, Eph, John) (C)
    C715, CG371, E396/397, EL839/840, G643, N419, P555,
    SA45, SH485, UM102 (PD), VU236 (Fr.)
    H-3   Hbl-78; Chr-140; Desc-81; Org-98
    S-1   #252-254. Various treatments

Additional Hymn Suggestions

"What Does the Lord Require" (1 Kgs)
    C659, E605, P405, UM441

"Great Is Thy Faithfulness" (1 Kgs, Pss)
    AH4011, C86, CG48, EL733, G39, N423, P276, SA26, SH48,
    UM140, VU288

"O Master, Let Me Walk with Thee" (1 Kgs, Pss)
    C602, CG660, E659/E660, EL818, G738, N503, P357, SA667,
    SH612, UM430 (PD), VU560

"O Worship the King" (Pss, Eph) (O)
    C17, CG52, E388, EL842, G41, N26, P476, SA52, SH2, UM73
    (PD), VU235

"Praise the Source of Faith and Learning" (Pss, Eph)
    N411, S2004

"O Holy Spirit, Root of Life" (Pss, Eph)
    C251, EL399, N57, S2121, VU379

"In the Lord I'll Be Ever Thankful" (Pss, Eph)
    G654, S2195, SH316

"When in Our Music God Is Glorified" (Eph)
    C7, CG309, E420, EL850/851, G641, N561, P264, UVU533

"Take Time to Be Holy" (Eph)
    C572, SA790, UM395 (PD), VU672

"Spirit of God, Descend upon My Heart" (Eph)
    C265, CG243, EL800, G688, N290, P326, SA290, SH277,
    UM500 (PD), VU378

"O Spirit of the Living God" (Eph)
    N263, SH222, UM539

"Come, My Way, My Truth, My Life" (John)
    E487, EL816, N331, UM164 (PD), VU628

"Become to Us the Living Bread" (John)
    C423, P500, UM630

"God the Sculptor of the Mountains" (John)
    EL736, G5, S2060

"In Remembrance of Me" 25156 (John, Comm.)
    C403, CG462, G521, S2254, SH667

Additional Contemporary and Modern Suggestions

"What Does the Lord Require of You" 456859 (1 Kgs)
    C661, CG690, G70, S2174, VU701

"Jesus, Lover of My Soul" ("It's All about You") 1545484 (1 Kgs)
"There Is None Like You" 674545 (1 Kgs)

"Awesome God" 41099 (Pss)
    G616, S2040

"Great Is the Lord" 1149 (Pss)
    CG325, G614, S2022, SH459

"Ah, Lord God" 17896 (Pss)

"How Great Are You, Lord" 2888576 (Pss)

"Famous One" 3599431 (Pss)

"Because of Your Love" 4662501 (Pss)

"Grateful" 7023348 (Pss, Eph)

"I Will Give Thanks" 6266091 (Eph)

"Shine, Jesus, Shine" 30426 (Eph)
    CG156, EL671, G192, S2173, SA261, SH102

"Father, I Adore You" 26557 (John)
    CG4, S2038, SH587

"Here Is Bread, Here Is Wine" 983717 (John, Comm.)
    EL483, S2266

"Hungry" ("Falling on My Knees") 2650364 (John)

"Holy and Anointed One" 164361 (John)

"Oceans" ("Where Feet May Fail") 6428767 (John)

"Enough" 3599479 (John)

"Song of Hope" ("Heaven Come Down") 5111477 (John)

"Jesus Messiah" 5183443 (John, Comm.)

"O Come To The Altar" 7051511 (John, Comm.)

"All Who Are Thirsty" 2489542 (John, Comm.)

"There Will Be Bread" 4512352 (John, Comm.)

Vocal Solos

"Be Thou My Vision" (1 Kgs)
    V-6   p. 13

"My Tribute" ("To God Be the Glory") (Pss, Eph)
    V-8   p. 5

"Now Thank We All Our God" (Pss, Eph, John)
    V-6   p. 8

"Alive and Breathing" (Eph)
    V-9   p. 4

"Bread of the World in Mercy Broken" (John, Comm.)
    V-8   p. 82

Anthems

"Step by Step" 696994 (1 Kgs)
Arr. Ruth Elaine Schram; Lorenz 10/4222L
SATB, piano, opt. cello/digital strings (https://bit.ly/L-4222)

"The Bread That I Will Give" (John)
James Biery; GIA Publications G-5935
SATB a cappella (https://bit.ly/G-5935)

Other Suggestions

Visuals:
    O   Crown, scepter, royal robe, people exhibiting wisdom
    P   Images of creation, feasting, heart, humble praise
    E   Singing, musical instruments, hymnal, worship/
        revelry
    G   Communion broken bread, chalice, crucifix

Call to Worship or Call to Prayer: WS3025. "God Is Speaking"
    (1 Kgs)

Call to Worship: S2265. "Time Now to Gather" (John, Comm.)

Canticle: UM112. "Canticle of Wisdom" (1 Kgs) See S-1, p. 377.

Prayer of Confession: UM586 (1 Kgs, Eph)

Offering Prayer: WSL109. "O great and holy God" (Eph)

Response: AH4081, C531, SH496, UM84. "Thank You, Lord"
    (Pss)

Alternate Lessons: Prov 9:1-6; Ps 34:9-14

Theme Ideas: Bread of Life, Communion, Holy Spirit, Praise,
    Thanksgiving / Gratitude, Vision, Wisdom

1 Kings 8:(1, 6, 10-11), 22-30, 41-43

(Then Solomon assembled the elders of Israel and all the heads of the tribes, the leaders of the ancestral houses of the Israelites, before King Solomon in Jerusalem, to bring up the ark of the covenant of the LORD out of the city of David, which is Zion. . . . [6]Then the priests brought the ark of the covenant of the LORD to its place, in the inner sanctuary of the house, the most holy place, underneath the wings of the cherubim. . . . [10]And when the priests came out of the holy place, a cloud filled the house of the LORD, [11]so that the priests could not stand to minister because of the cloud, for the glory of the LORD filled the house of the LORD. . . .)

[22]Then Solomon stood before the altar of the LORD in the presence of the whole assembly of Israel and spread out his hands to heaven. [23]He said, "O LORD, God of Israel, there is no God like you in heaven above or on earth beneath, keeping covenant and steadfast love with your servants who walk before you with all their heart, [24]the covenant that you kept for your servant my father David as you declared to him; you promised with your mouth and have this day fulfilled with your hand. [25]Therefore, O LORD, God of Israel, keep for your servant my father David that which you promised him, saying, 'There shall never fail you a successor before me to sit on the throne of Israel, if only your children look to their way, to walk before me as you have walked before me.' [26]Therefore, O God of Israel, let your word be confirmed that you promised to your servant my father David.

[27]"But will God indeed dwell on the earth? Even heaven and the highest heaven cannot contain you, much less this house that I have built! [28]Regard your servant's prayer and his plea, O LORD my God, heeding the cry and the prayer that your servant prays to you today, [29]that your eyes may be open night and day toward this house, the place of which you said, 'My name shall be there,' that you may heed the prayer that your servant prays toward this place. [30]Hear the plea of your servant and of your people Israel when they pray toward this place; O hear in heaven your dwelling place; hear and forgive. . . .

[41]"Likewise when foreigners, who are not of your people Israel, come from a distant land because of your name [42]—for they shall hear of your great name, your mighty hand, and your outstretched arm—when foreigners come and pray toward this house, [43]then hear in heaven your dwelling place and do whatever the foreigners ask of you, so that all the peoples of the earth may know your name and fear you, as do your people Israel, and so they may know that your name has been invoked on this house that I have built.

Psalm 84 (CG50, G402, N675, P208, UM804)

How lovely is your dwelling place,
    O LORD of hosts!
[2]My soul longs, indeed it faints,
    for the courts of the LORD;
my heart and my flesh sing for joy
    to the living God.
[3]Even the sparrow finds a home
    and the swallow a nest for herself,
    where she may lay her young,
at your altars, O LORD of hosts,
    my King and my God.
[4]Happy are those who live in your house,
    ever singing your praise.   Selah
[5]Happy are those whose strength is in you,
    in whose heart are the highways to Zion.
[6]As they go through the valley of Baca,
    they make it a place of springs;
    the early rain also covers it with pools.
[7]They go from strength to strength;
    the God of gods will be seen in Zion.

[8]O LORD God of hosts, hear my prayer;
    give ear, O God of Jacob!   Selah
[9]Behold our shield, O God;
    look on the face of your anointed.
[10]For a day in your courts is better
    than a thousand elsewhere.
I would rather be a doorkeeper in the house of my God
    than live in the tents of wickedness.
[11]For the LORD God is a sun and shield;
    he bestows favor and honor.
No good thing does the LORD withhold
    from those who walk uprightly.
[12]O LORD of hosts,
    happy is everyone who trusts in you.

Ephesians 6:10-20

[10]Finally, be strong in the Lord and in the strength of his power; [11]put on the whole armor of God, so that you may be able to stand against the wiles of the devil, [12]for our struggle is not against blood and flesh but against the rulers, against the authorities, against the cosmic powers of this present darkness, against the spiritual forces of evil in the heavenly places. [13]Therefore take up the whole armor of God, so that you may be able to withstand on the evil day and, having prevailed against everything, to stand firm. [14]Stand, therefore, and belt your waist with truth and put on the breastplate of righteousness [15]and lace up your sandals in preparation for the gospel of peace. [16]With all of these, take the shield of faith, with which you will be able to quench all the flaming arrows of the evil one. [17]Take the helmet of salvation and the sword of the Spirit, which is the word of God. [18]Pray in the Spirit at all times in every prayer and supplication. To that end, keep alert and always persevere in supplication for all the saints. [19]Pray also for me, so that when I speak a message may be given to me to make known with boldness the mystery of the gospel, [20]for which I am an ambassador in chains. Pray that I may declare it boldly, as I must speak.

John 6:56-69

[56]Those who eat my flesh and drink my blood abide in me and I in them. [57]Just as the living Father sent me and I live because of the Father, so whoever eats me will live because of me. [58]This is the bread that came down from heaven, not like that which the ancestors ate, and they died. But the one who eats this bread will live forever." [59]He said these things while he was teaching in a synagogue at Capernaum.

[60]When many of his disciples heard it, they said, "This teaching is difficult; who can accept it?" [61]But Jesus, being aware that his disciples were complaining about it, said to them, "Does this offend you? [62]Then what if you were to see the Son of Man ascending to where he was before? [63]It is the spirit that gives life; the flesh is useless. The words that I have spoken to you are spirit and life. [64]But among you there are some who do not believe." For Jesus knew from the beginning who were the ones who did not believe and who was the one who would betray him. [65]And he said, "For this reason I have told you that no one can come to me unless it is granted by the Father."

[66]Because of this many of his disciples turned back and no longer went about with him. [67]So Jesus asked the twelve, "Do you also wish to go away?" [68]Simon Peter answered him, "Lord, to whom can we go? You have the words of eternal life. [69]We have come to believe and know that you are the Holy One of God."

Primary Hymns and Songs for the Day

"Come, Thou Almighty King" (1 Kgs, Eph) (O)
- C27, CG2, E365, EL408, G2, N275, P139, SA283, SH388, UM61 (PD), VU314
  - H-3   Hbl-28, 49, 53; Chr-56; Desc-57; Org-63
  - S-1   #185-186. Descant and harmonization

"Christ Is Made the Sure Foundation" (1 Kgs, Eph)
- C275, CG248, E518, EL645, G394, P416, SA246, SH225, UM559, VU325
  - H-3   Chr-49; Desc-103; Org-180
  - S-1   #346. Descant

"Great Is the Lord" 1149 (1 Kgs, Eph)
- CG325, G614, S2022, SH459

"Fight the Good Fight" (Eph)
- E552, G846, P307 (PD), SA952, VU674
  - H-3   Hbl-29, 57; Chr-117; Desc-31; Org-31
  - S-1   #100-103. Various treatments.

"Standing on the Promises" (Eph, John)
- AH4057, C552, CG625, G838, SA522, SH45, UM374 (PD)

"Break Thou the Bread of Life" (John, Comm.) (C)
- C321, CG35, EL515, G460, N321, P329, SA802, SH552, UM599 (PD), VU501
  - H-3   Chr-44; Org-15

"Let Us Build a House Where Love Can Dwell" (1 Kgs, Pss, John) (C)
- EL641, G301, SH228 (See also WS3152)

"Hope of the World" (Eph, John) (C)
- C538, E472, G734, N46, P360, UM178, VU215
  - H-3   Chr-100
  - S-1   #343. Descant
  - S-2   #189. Introduction

Additional Hymn Suggestions

"Let All the World in Every Corner Sing" (1 Kgs)
- CG314, E402/403, G636, P468, S41, UM93

"Immortal, Invisible, God Only Wise" (1 Kgs)
- C66, CG58, E423, EL834, G12, N1, SA37, UM103 (PD), VU264

"O God in Heaven" (1 Kgs)
- EL748, N279, UM119

"Praise God for This Holy Ground" (1 Kgs)
- G405, WS3009

"Blessed Quietness" (Pss)
- C267, CG244, N284, S2142

"Standing in the Need of Prayer" (Eph)
- C579, N519, UM352

"O God of Every Nation" (Eph)
- C680, CG46, E607, EL713, G756, P289, UM435, VU677

"Lead On, O King Eternal" (Eph)
- C632, CG63, E555, EL805, G269, N573, SA964, UM580

"Blessed Assurance" (John)
- AH4083, C543, CG619, EL638, G839, N473, P341, SA455, SH320, UM369 (PD), VU337

"Blessed Jesus, at Thy Word" (John)
- E440, EL520, G395, N74, P454, UM596 (PD), VU500

"In Remembrance of Me" 25156 (John, Comm.)
- C403, CG462, G521, S2254, SH667

Additional Contemporary and Modern Suggestions

"Holy Ground" 21198 (1 Kgs)
- C112, G406, S2272, SA400

"Ah, Lord God" 17896 (1 Kgs)

"Awesome in This Place" 847554 (1 Kgs)

"Here As In Heaven" 7051506 (1 Kgs)

"Song of Hope" ("God of Heaven, Come Down") 5111477 (1 Kgs, John)

"Let Us Offer to the Father" ("*Te Ofrecemos Padre Nuestro*") (1 Kgs, Pss)

"All I Need Is You" 488384 (Pss)

"As the Deer" 1431 (Pss)
- CG49, G626/778, S2025, SA571, VU766

"Who Can Satisfy My Soul Like You?" 208492 (Pss)

"Better Is One Day" 1097451 (Pss)

"Psalm 62" ("My Soul Finds Rest") 5040902 (Pss)

"Breathe" 1874117 (Pss, John)

"You Are My All in All" 825356 (Pss, Eph)
- CG571, G519, SH335, WS3040

"Shout to the North" 1562261 (Eph)
- G319, SA1009, WS3042

"You Are My Hiding Place" 21442 (Eph)
- C554, S2055, SH46

"The Battle Belongs to the Lord" 21583 (Eph)

"We Want to See Jesus Lifted High" 1033408 (Eph)

"All Things Are Possible" 2245140 (Eph)

"Good to Me" (Eph)

"Jesus We Love You" 7030068 (Eph, John)

"Hungry" ("Falling on My Knees") 2650364 (John)

"Father, I Adore You" 26557 (John)
- CG4, S2038, SH587

"Here Is Bread, Here Is Wine" 983717 (John, Comm.)
- EL483, S2266

"Eat This Bread" (John, Comm.)
- C414, EL472, G527, N788, SH671, UM628, VU466

"O Come To The Altar" 7051511 (John, Comm.)

"I Believe In Jesus" 61282 (John)

"Holy and Anointed One" 164361 (John)

"All Who Are Thirsty" 2489542 (John)

"Jesus, Lover of My Soul" ("It's All about You") 1545484 (John)

Vocal Solos

"Lord, Listen to Your Children" (1 Kgs, Eph)
- V-8   p. 168

"See a Victory" (Eph)
- V-9   p. 88

Anthems

"The Morning Trumpet" (Eph)
Arr. Mark Hayes; Lorenz 10/5190L
SATB, piano, opt. trumpet (https://bit.ly/L-5190)

"Come, Christians, Join to Sing!" (John)
Randall Kempton; Beckenhorst BP2273
SATB, piano 4-hands, opt. instruments (https://bit.ly/BP-2273)

Other Suggestions

Visuals:
- **O**   Praying hands, temple (church), hand, outstretched arm
- **P**   Churches, sparrows and nest, rain, water pooling, door
- **E**   Armor, praying hands, people in prayer
- **G**   Bread/wine/communion, line drawn, question mark, Christ

Call to Worship: EL529, G392, S2273, SH611. "Jesus, We Are Here" (Eph)

Prayer: UM423. Finding Rest in God (Pss)

Response: C305, CG389, G469, S2193, SH577, VU400. "Lord, Listen to Your Children Praying" (Pss, Eph)

Scripture Response: C323, CG163, N319, SA434, SH549, UM600, stanza 1. "Wonderful Words of Life" (John)

Benediction: S2281. "May You Run and Not Be Weary" 807099 (Eph)

Alternate Lessons: Josh 24:1-2a, 14-18; Ps 34:15-22

Theme Ideas: Assurance, Communion, Courage, Faithfulness, God: Glory of God, God: Word of God

THEME INDEX

Assurance: 7/14/24, 8/25/24
Baptism: 1/7/24, 2/18/24, 4/7/24, 4/28/24
Beatitudes / Blessings: 11/1/23
Bread of Life: 7/28/24, 8/4/24, 8/11/24, 8/18/24
Children / Family of God: 12/31/23, 12/31/23, 6/9/24, 7/21/24
Comfort: 6/23/24
Communion: 10/1/23, 3/24/24, 3/28/24, 4/14/24, 5/5/24, 5/12/24, 7/28/24, 8/4/24, 8/11/24, 8/18/24, 8/25/24
Compassion: 9/3/23, 9/17/23, 10/29/23
Connection: 4/28/24
Courage: 6/23/24, 8/25/24
Covenant: 10/8/23, 11/12/23, 12/31/23, 2/18/24, 2/25/24, 3/3/24, 3/17/24, 3/29/24
Creation: 10/8/23, 11/23/23, 1/7/24, 3/3/24, 5/19/24
Cross: 9/3/23, 2/25/24, 3/3/24, 3/29/24
Discipleship / Following God: 9/3/23, 10/8/23, 11/5/23, 1/14/24, 1/21/24, 1/28/24, 2/18/24, 2/25/24, 5/9/24, 7/7/24, 7/21/24
Doubt: 4/7/24
Faith: 4/7/24, 5/9/24, 6/9/24, 6/16/24, 6/23/24
Faithfulness: 9/24/23, 10/1/23, 10/8/23, 10/22/23, 11/12/23, 11/26/23, 12/3/23, 2/4/24, 2/4/24, 3/28/24, 6/2/24, 6/9/24, 6/23/24, 7/14/24, 8/11/24, 8/25/24
Fruit of the Spirit: 5/5/24
God
    Call of God / Listening: 9/3/23, 1/14/24, 1/21/24, 1/28/24, 5/9/24, 6/2/24, 6/16/24, 7/7/24
    God: Faithfulness: 10/8/23, 2/4/24
    God: Glory of God: 10/22/23, 10/29/23, 11/1/23, 11/23/23, 11/26/23, 12/31/23, 1/7/24, 2/4/24, 2/11/24, 4/28/24, 5/12/24, 5/26/24, 7/14/24, 8/25/24
    God: God's Time: 12/31/23
    Guidance: 4/14/24, 5/12/24
    Kingdom of God: 9/24/23, 10/8/23, 10/15/23, 11/19/23, 11/26/23, 12/3/23, 6/9/24, 6/16/24
    Love of God: 11/1/23, 12/24/23, 1/7/24, 3/10/24, 4/7/24, 4/14/24, 4/24/24, 4/28/24, 5/5/24, 7/28/24
    Mystery of God: 2/11/24
    Peace of God: 10/15/23
    Power of God: 11/26/23, 1/28/24
    Presence: 10/22/23
    Promises: 12/24/23, 12/24/23, 12/31/23, 1/6/24, 2/18/24, 2/25/24, 3/17/24
    Providence / God our Help: 9/17/23, 9/24/23, 10/1/23, 10/29/23, 11/5/23, 1/14/24, 1/21/24, 2/4/24, 3/10/24, 6/23/24
    Shepherd: 11/26/23, 12/10/23, 4/24/24, 7/7/24, 7/21/24
    Word of God: 10/8/23, 11/5/23, 11/19/23, 3/3/24, 8/25/24
Grace: 3/10/24, 3/29/24, 3/31/24, 4/14/24, 7/7/24, 7/14/24, 7/28/24
Grief: 6/30/24, 8/11/24
Growth: 4/28/24, 6/16/24
Healing: 1/28/24, 2/4/24, 6/2/24, 6/9/24, 6/30/24, 7/21/24

Holy Spirit: 12/17/23, 12/24/23, 1/7/24, 2/11/24, 2/18/24, 3/3/24, 4/7/24, 4/14/24, 5/5/24, 5/9/24, 5/19/24, 5/26/24, 8/18/24
Hope: 5/9/24
Humility: 11/19/23, 3/24/24
Inclusion: 9/17/23, 1/6/24, 3/31/24
Jesus:
    Body of Christ: 1/28/24
    Cornerstone: 10/8/23, 4/24/24, 7/21/24
    Crucifixion: 3/24/24, 3/29/24
    Jesus our Savior: 3/17/24, 3/29/24, 3/31/24, 4/14/24, 4/24/24, 4/28/24, 5/12/24
    Mind of Christ: 9/17/23, 10/1/23, 10/15/23, 3/24/24, 8/11/24
    Prophet: 3/3/24
    Return and Reign: 11/12/23, 11/19/23
Journey: 9/17/23, 9/24/23, 10/1/23, 10/29/23, 11/5/23, 12/10/23, 1/6/24, 1/7/24, 2/18/24, 3/10/24
Joy: 12/17/23, 12/31/23
Justice: 12/17/23, 12/24/23, 12/31/23, 7/28/24, 8/4/24
Lament: 9/24/23, 10/1/23, 3/24/24, 3/29/24, 6/30/24, 8/11/24
Light: 9/10/23, 12/17/23, 12/24/23, 12/31/23, 1/6/24, 2/11/24, 2/14/24, 4/7/24, 6/2/24
Love / Great Commandment: 9/3/23, 9/10/23, 10/29/23, 4/24/24, 4/28/24, 5/5/24
New Creation: 12/31/23, 5/26/24, 6/16/24
Passover: 9/10/23, 9/17/23, 3/28/24
Patience: 11/12/23, 11/19/23, 12/10/23, 12/31/23
Peace: 8/11/24
Praise: 10/8/23, 11/1/23, 11/23/23, 11/26/23, 12/24/23, 12/24/23, 12/31/23, 1/28/24, 2/4/24, 3/24/24, 3/31/24, 5/5/24, 5/9/24, 5/19/24, 7/14/24, 8/18/24
Prayer: 2/14/24, 7/21/24
Preparation: 10/15/23, 12/3/23, 12/10/23, 12/17/23, 1/21/24
Priorities: 10/15/23, 10/22/23, 11/12/23, 11/26/23, 2/14/24, 3/3/24
Reconciliation: 9/10/23, 9/17/23, 2/14/24
Redemption / Salvation: 12/3/23
Remembrance: 9/10/23, 3/28/24
Repentance: 9/10/23, 2/14/24, 4/14/24
Resurrection: 3/17/24, 3/31/24, 4/7/24, 4/14/24, 5/9/24, 5/26/24
Righteousness: 1/6/24
Service / Servanthood: 9/24/23, 11/5/23, 11/26/23, 12/31/23, 1/14/24, 3/17/24, 3/28/24
Sin and Forgiveness: 10/8/23, 10/15/23, 1/21/24, 1/28/24, 2/14/24, 2/18/24, 3/10/24, 3/17/24, 4/7/24, 7/28/24, 8/4/24
Stewardship: 10/22/23, 11/19/23, 11/23/23, 1/6/24, 6/30/24
Thanksgiving / Gratitude: 9/24/23, 10/15/23, 11/5/23, 11/23/23, 11/26/23, 3/10/24, 3/24/24, 3/31/24, 8/18/24
Unity: 10/1/23, 10/1/23, 1/6/24, 4/7/24, 5/5/24, 5/12/24, 7/21/24, 8/4/24
Vision: 5/19/24, 6/2/24, 6/16/24, 8/18/24
Waiting: 11/12/23, 11/19/23, 12/3/23, 12/10/23
Wisdom: 11/19/23, 11/26/23, 1/14/24, 3/3/24, 8/18/24
Worship: 3/3/24

SCRIPTURE INDEX

WORSHIP PLANNING SHEET 1

Date: _____ Color:_____

Preacher: _____

Liturgist: _____

Selected Scripture: _____

Selected Hymns	No.	Placement

Psalter #_____

Keyboard Selections

Title	Composer	Placement

Anthems

Title	Choir	Composer	Placement

Vocal Solos

Title	Singer	Composer	Placement

Other Ideas:

Acolytes: _____

Head Usher: _____

Altar Guild Contact: _____

Other Participants: _____

_____

WORSHIP PLANNING SHEET 2

Date: _____ Sunday: _____ Color: _____

Preacher: _____

Liturgist: _____

Opening Voluntary   Composer

_____

_____

Hymn   Tune Name   No.

_____

Opening Prayer: _____

Prayer for Illumination: _____

First Lesson: _____

Psalter: _____

Second Lesson: _____

Gospel Lesson: _____

Hymn   Tune Name   No.

_____

Response to the Word: _____

Prayers of the People: _____

Offertory   Composer

_____

Communion Setting: _____

Communion Hymns   Tune Name   No.

_____

_____

Closing Hymn   Tune Name   No.

_____

Benediction: _____

Closing Voluntary   Composer

_____

CONTEMPORARY WORSHIP PLANNING SHEET

Because of the diversity in orders of worship, you will want to adjust this planning sheet to meet the needs of your worship planning team. A common order used would consist of three to four opening praise choruses and lively hymns, a time of informal prayers of the congregation along with songs of prayer, reading of the primary scripture for the day, a drama or video to illustrate the day's theme, a message from the preacher, a testimony on the theme for the day (if a drama or video was not presented earlier), followed by closing songs appropriate to the mood of the service and the message. Any offering would usually be taken early in the service, and Holy Communion would normally take place following the message. Special music (solos, duets, instrumental music) can be used wherever it best expresses the theme of the service.

Date: _____ Sunday: _____

Thematic Emphasis or Topic: _____

Color: _____ Visual Focus: _____

Opening Songs:

_____

_____

Prayer Songs:

_____

Scripture Selection(s):

_____

Drama or Video:

_____

Message Title:

_____

Testimony: _____

Special Music:

_____

Closing Songs:

_____

Preacher: _____ Music Leader: _____

Worship Facilitator: _____ Prayer Leader: _____

NOTES

2023–2024 Lectionary Calendar

Lectionary verses and worship suggestions in this edition of *Prepare!* relate to the unshaded dates in the calendar below. Lectionary Year A: September 3, 2023–November 26, 2023; Lectionary Year B: December 3, 2023–August 25, 2024

2023

JANUARY								FEBRUARY								MARCH								APRIL						
S	M	T	W	T	F	S		S	M	T	W	T	F	S		S	M	T	W	T	F	S		S	M	T	W	T	F	S
1	2	3	4	5	6	7					1	2	3	4					1	2	3	4								1
8	9	10	11	12	13	14		5	6	7	8	9	10	11		5	6	7	8	9	10	11		2	3	4	5	6	7	8
15	16	17	18	19	20	21		12	13	14	15	16	17	18		12	13	14	15	16	17	18		9	10	11	12	13	14	15
22	23	24	25	26	27	28		19	20	21	22	23	24	25		19	20	21	22	23	24	25		16	17	18	19	20	21	22
29	30	31						26	27	28						26	27	28	29	30	31			23	24	25	26	27	28	29
																								30						

MAY								JUNE								JULY								AUGUST						
S	M	T	W	T	F	S		S	M	T	W	T	F	S		S	M	T	W	T	F	S		S	M	T	W	T	F	S
	1	2	3	4	5	6						1	2	3								1				1	2	3	4	5
7	8	9	10	11	12	13		4	5	6	7	8	9	10		2	3	4	5	6	7	8		6	7	8	9	10	11	12
14	15	16	17	18	19	20		11	12	13	14	15	16	17		9	10	11	12	13	14	15		13	14	15	16	17	18	19
21	22	23	24	25	26	27		18	19	20	21	22	23	24		16	17	18	19	20	21	22		20	21	22	23	24	25	26
28	29	30	31					25	26	27	28	29	30			23	24	25	26	27	28	29		27	28	29	30	31		
																30	31													

SEPTEMBER								OCTOBER								NOVEMBER								DECEMBER						
S	M	T	W	T	F	S		S	M	T	W	T	F	S		S	M	T	W	T	F	S		S	M	T	W	T	F	S
					1	2		1	2	3	4	5	6	7					1	2	3	4							1	2
3	4	5	6	7	8	9		8	9	10	11	12	13	14		5	6	7	8	9	10	11		3	4	5	6	7	8	9
10	11	12	13	14	15	16		15	16	17	18	19	20	21		12	13	14	15	16	17	18		10	11	12	13	14	15	16
17	18	19	20	21	22	23		22	23	24	25	26	27	28		19	20	21	22	23	24	25		17	18	19	20	21	22	23
24	25	26	27	28	29	30		29	30	31						26	27	28	29	30				24	25	26	27	28	29	30
																								31						

2024

JANUARY								FEBRUARY								MARCH								APRIL						
S	M	T	W	T	F	S		S	M	T	W	T	F	S		S	M	T	W	T	F	S		S	M	T	W	T	F	S
	1	2	3	4	5	6						1	2	3						1	2			1	2	3	4	5	6
7	8	9	10	11	12	13		4	5	6	7	8	9	10		3	4	5	6	7	8	9		7	8	9	10	11	12	13
14	15	16	17	18	19	20		11	12	13	14	15	16	17		10	11	12	13	14	15	16		14	15	16	17	18	19	20
21	22	23	24	25	26	27		18	19	20	21	22	23	24		17	18	19	20	21	22	23		21	22	23	24	25	26	27
28	29	30	31					25	26	27	28	29				24	25	26	27	28	29	30		28	29	30				
																31														

MAY								JUNE								JULY								AUGUST						
S	M	T	W	T	F	S		S	M	T	W	T	F	S		S	M	T	W	T	F	S		S	M	T	W	T	F	S
			1	2	3	4								1			1	2	3	4	5	6						1	2	3
5	6	7	8	9	10	11		2	3	4	5	6	7	8		7	8	9	10	11	12	13		4	5	6	7	8	9	10
12	13	14	15	16	17	18		9	10	11	12	13	14	15		14	15	16	17	18	19	20		11	12	13	14	15	16	1
19	20	21	22	23	24	25		16	17	18	19	20	21	22		21	22	23	24	25	26	27		18	19	20	21	22	23	24
26	27	28	29	30	31			23	24	25	26	27	28	29		28	29	30	31					25	26	27	28	29	30	31
								30																						

SEPTEMBER								OCTOBER								NOVEMBER								DECEMBER						
S	M	T	W	T	F	S		S	M	T	W	T	F	S		S	M	T	W	T	F	S		S	M	T	W	T	F	S
1	2	3	4	5	6	7				1	2	3	4	5						1	2		1	2	3	4	5	6	7
8	9	10	11	12	13	14		6	7	8	9	10	11	12		3	4	5	6	7	8	9		8	9	10	11	12	13	14
15	16	17	18	19	20	21		13	14	15	16	17	18	19		10	11	12	13	14	15	16		15	16	17	18	19	20	21
22	23	24	25	26	27	28		20	21	22	23	24	25	26		17	18	19	20	21	22	23		22	23	24	25	26	27	28
29	30							27	28	29	30	31				24	25	26	27	28	29	30		29	30	31				